John Evans

The Coins of the Ancient Britons

John Evans

The Coins of the Ancient Britons

ISBN/EAN: 9783741178139

Manufactured in Europe, USA, Canada, Australia, Japa

Cover: Foto ©Lupo / pixelio.de

Manufactured and distributed by brebook publishing software (www.brebook.com)

John Evans

The Coins of the Ancient Britons

THE COINS

OF

THE ANCIENT BRITONS.

ARRANGED AND DESCRIBED

BY

JOHN EVANS, F.S.A., F.G.S.,

HONORARY SECRETARY OF THE NUMISMATIC SOCIETY OF LONDON;

AND ENGRAVED

BY F. W. FAIRHOLT,

LONDON:
J. RUSSELL SMITH, 36, SOHO SQUARE.
864.

PREFACE.

The want of some systematic arrangement of the coinage of the Ancient Britons has long been felt, not only by collectors of coins, but by students of British history. It was with the view of supplying this want that the following work was commenced, and though at the outset my intention was only to give a list of such coins of this class as had already been published, with references to the passages in the various works in which they had been described or engraved, yet I found that a mere index, such as I had proposed, would be of comparatively little use, and I therefore resolved to proceed on a more comprehensive plan. I found that the notices and engravings of the various ancient British coins were scattered through a considerable number of different volumes; and, moreover, that many—indeed, I might say most—of the engravings that had been published of them were deficient in that scrupulous accuracy which is so necessary in a study of this kind; and having secured the invaluable assistance of my friend Mr. Fairholt, I determined that I would have the whole series re-engraved, wherever possible, either from the originals or from casts.

To carry out this scheme involved no little labour on my part, as the different coins which I wished to engrave are, many of them, of such rarity, that frequently there are only single specimens known of a given type, and those in various collections throughout the kingdom. The uniform courtesy with which my requests for impressions of coins have been met by the owners of cabinets of coins, and by those in charge of our public collections, has, however, been such, that I have been enabled, in a great measure, to surmount this difficulty. I am almost at a loss to say to which of all these gentlemen I am most indebted; but I take this opportunity of returning my thanks to each and all of them. To Professor William Ramsay, of Glasgow, my especial thanks are due, for the kind manner in which he has supplied me with impressions of such coins in the magnificent collection in the Hunterian Museum as I required. To Mr. Vaux and Mr. Madden, of the British Museum, I am also under great obligations; but, perhaps, above all, to Mr. C. Roach Smith, who not only furnished me with a large number of casts of British coins, and with notes as to the places where they were found, but also presented me with several scarce coins, and aided me in procuring others. To Mr. Akerman I am much indebted for the unvarying kindness with which he has assisted my labours in a field in which he has himself worked so long and so well. Mr. Webster, of Russell Street, Covent Garden, has also afforded me much aid, both in procuring coins for me, and in furnishing me with notes as to the places of discovery of various specimens which came under his notice.

With such varied assistance, extended now over a period of more than fourteen years, I have been enabled to obtain casts of nearly all the known types of British coins of which I had not specimens in my own collection; so that the whole of the engravings may be considered as from the originals, except in the few instances which I have specified in the text. Having for many years been in the habit of communicating to the Numismatic Society notices and drawings of such new types of ancient British coins as came under my notice, there are not so many coins in the present work, now published for the first time, as there otherwise would have been; there are, however, some twenty or more. My object, indeed, has been throughout, not so much to adduce new facts or new theories, as to reduce into a systematic and comprehensive form that which was already known; and, in doing this, to give such references as might enable those who wished to go farther into the subject, readily to find what other authors have written on any disputed point, and thus to judge how far my views are likely to be correct.

The student of history who, without taking any especial interest in numismatic pursuits, wishes to see what light is thrown by the native coinage on the early annals of this country, will find an abstract of the medallic history of each chieftain and district, as far as I am able to interpret it, in the introductory chapters, and in the notices prefixed to each of the various classes of coins. There are, however, various minor points suggested by the types or legends of different coins, which are, of necessity, commented upon only in the descriptions of the coins. A cursory glance will show whether any of these descriptions contain more than mere numismatic details.

I will only add, that the communication of any types possessing features of novelty, or of any fresh discoveries of British coins, will be most thankfully received and acknowledged.

JOHN EVANS.

NASH MILLS, HEMEL HEMPSTED.
January, 1864.

CONTENTS.

CHAPTER I.
Bibliography 1

CHAPTER II.
Date and Origin 17

CHAPTER III.
Arrangement 33

CHAPTER IV.
Uninscribed Gold Coins 46

CHAPTER V.
Uninscribed Silver Coins 90

CHAPTER VI.
Uninscribed Copper and Brass Coins 116

CHAPTER VII.
Tin Coinage 123

CHAPTER VIII.
Coins of the Channel Islands 127

CHAPTER IX.
Inscribed Coins 130

CHAPTER X.
Coins of the Western District 133
    Bodvoc 134
    Catti 139
    Comux 141
    Vocorio-ad (?) 143
    Antedrigus 144
    Seri 149

CHAPTER XI.

	Page
Coins of the South-Eastern District	151
Commius (?)	157
Tinc[ommius]	158
Verica, or Virica	170

CHAPTER XII.

Coins of the Kentish District	187
Eppillus	189
Dubnovellaunos	193
Vose[nos]	205
Amminus	209
Cear	211

CHAPTER XIII.

Coins of the Central District	215
Andoco[mius] (?)	216
Tasciovanus	220
Coins struck at Verulamium	246
Coins inscribed Tascio-Ricon, &c.	267
Coins of Tasciovanus inscribed Sego	273
Epaticcus	276
Cunobelinus	284
Gold Coins of Cunobelinus	295
Silver Coins of Cunobelinus	305
Copper Coins of Cunobelinus	321

CHAPTER XIV

Uncertain Coins	349

CHAPTER XV.

Coins of the Eastern District	357
Addedomarus	363
Gold Coins attributed to the Iceni	375
Silver Coins attributed to the Iceni	379

CHAPTER XVI

Coins of the Yorkshire District, or of the Brigantes	404

PRINCIPAL AUTHORS AND BOOKS REFERRED TO.

AKERMAN, JOHN YONGE.—Ancient Coins of Cities and Princes Geographically Arranged and Described: Hispania, Gallia, Britannia. 8vo., London, 1846.

Archæologia, or Miscellaneous Tracts Relating to Antiquity.—Published by the Society of Antiquaries of London. 4to., London, V. Y.

Archæological Journal, The.—Published under the direction of the Central Committee of the Archæological Institute of Great Britain and Ireland. 8vo., London, V. Y.

Archæological Association, The Journal of the British. 8vo., London, V. Y.

BATTELY, JOHN, S.T.P.—Antiquitates Rutupinæ. 2nd ed., 4to., Oxford, 1745.

CAMDEN, WILLIAM.—Britain, or a Chorographicall Description of the most Flourishing Kingdomes, England, Scotland, and Ireland. Translated into English by Philemon Holland. Fol., London, 1637.

CAMDEN, WILLIAM.—Britannia; with Large Additions and Improvements, by Edmund Gibson. Fol., London, 1695.

CAMDEN, WILLIAM.—Britannia &c.; enlarged by the Latest Discoveries, by Richard Gough. 2nd ed., 4 vols., fol., London, 1806.

COMBE, TAYLOR.—Veterum Populorum et Regum Numi qui in Musæo Britannico adservantur. 4to., London, 1814.

CROMWELL, THOMAS.—History and Description of the Ancient Town and Borough of Colchester, in Essex. 8vo., London, 1825.

DIXON, FREDERICK, F.G.S.—The Geology and Fossils of the Tertiary and Cretaceous Formations of Sussex. 4to., London, 1850.

Gentleman's Magazine, The, and Historical Review. By Sylvanus Urban, Gent. 8vo., London, V. Y.

HAWKINS, EDWARD, F.R.S., F.A.S., &c.—The Silver Coins of England, Arranged and Described, &c. 8vo., London, 1841.

ANCIENT BRITISH COINS.

CHAPTER I.

BIBLIOGRAPHY.

BEFORE offering any introductory remarks as to the general character, age, and distribution of the coins of the Ancient Britons, it will be well to notice in a succinct manner the principal authors who have already written upon the subject, and the various opinions which they have held.

The study of our native antiquities may be said to date from the days of Leland, who, however, relates that in all his travels through England he could never meet with one British coin. He attributed this absence of any indigenous coins to the fact (as stated by Gildas at the commencement of his history) that the Romans would not allow any metal to be struck in this country, except with the image of Cæsar. But not long after Leland's time, when the coins and other relics of antiquity with which our soil abounds began to receive greater and more enlightened attention, it was found that such coins did exist; and in the "Britannia" of the illustrious Camden, first published in 1586, woodcuts of some coins are given, one of Verulam, and others of Cunobeline. Plates of several other varieties of British coins, collected "with curious and chargeable search" by his friend and fellow-labourer, Sir Robert Cotton, were, however, inserted in the edition of 1600. These plates, three in number, comprised eighteen coins, and appeared in many subsequent editions, and it was not until Gough's edition of the "Britannia" that they were supplanted, although Nicolas Fabri de Peiresc, in writing to Camden in 1608, had made serious complaint of the inaccuracy of the engraver, whom he accuses "parum nimis felicitatis adhibuisse, adeo ut longè alia quam quæ in nominis continentur expresserit."

Of the eighteen coins originally engraved by Camden, fourteen are undoubtedly British, all of them with one exception inscribed; the other four are Gaulish; and it is a remarkable circumstance that of these fourteen British coins there are two, Nos. 9 and 13, which, until within the last few years, were not known to exist in any collection, but both of which I have here engraved from actual examples—in one case for the first time since the days of Camden. Although that judicious antiquary professed, so far as related to British coins, "to walke in a mirke and mistie night of iguorance," yet his attribution of some of the coins to Cunobeline, his reading of the names of the towns of Camulodunum and Verulamium upon them, and his interpretation of COM. as Commius, have stood the test of time, and ought alone to have sufficed to place the study of British coins on a firm and sure foundation. His interpretation of the legend TASCIA, as signifying Tribute-money, and his attribution of coins to Caractacus, are less happy; but had all his subsequent editors contributed in the same degree to the general stock of knowledge, and shown the same amount of care and judgment in making use of the materials at their command, it is possible that the present work would have been superfluous.

Next to Camden comes his friend and contemporary, Speed, whose principal work, "The History of Great Britain," appeared in 1614. He also had free access to the collections of that "worthy storer of antiquities," Sir Robert Cotton, of Cunington, of whose ancient British coins he gives numerous woodcuts.

Although, like Camden, he followed the unhappy custom of the time in giving perfectly circular representations of the coins, and of one uniform size, regardless of that of the originals, yet his illustrations are far more accurate than Camden's. He engraves also three types of the coins of Cunobeline which were not given by Camden, and one of Tasciovanus, which he assigns to Cassivellaunus. Like Camden, he inserts a few Gaulish coins, which he erroneously attributes to British princes, and in other respects the opinions of these two fathers of British archæology appear to agree pretty closely.

Passing by Sir Thomas Browne, who, in his " Hydriotaphia" (1658), incidentally mentions the silver coins of the Iceni, and Dr. Plot, who, in his " Natural History of Oxfordshire" (1677), published one or two uninscribed coins as British, the next author who added notably to the number of ancient British types is Gibson, the editor of Camden's " Britannia," and subsequently Bishop of London. His edition appeared in 1695, with two plates of *Nummi Britannici*, comprising upwards of thirty British coins, as well as a large number of Saxon and Gaulish. He still retained all that had originally been published by Camden, and added the other types which had been engraved by Speed, as well as several which were then published for the first time, and in engraving some of these latter, he most meritoriously introduced the plan of representing them of the size and shape of the originals. To these additions there are affixed initials or distinctive marks, to show the sources whence they were derived, and the R.T. which appears against many of them show that they were contributed by Ralph Thoresby, of Leeds. It does not argue well for the honesty of the collectors of those days that in Thoresby's diary is the following entry under June 6, 1694—" Received a kind visit from Mr. Dright Dixon (the Duke of Leeds his chaplain), who brought my coins from the Editors of Camden's ' Britannia,' the examining of which, and concern for the *loss and exchange of several*, took up forenoon." Unfortunately, the description of the plates was entrusted to Mr. Obadiah Walker, a gentleman whose incapacity to deal with this subject was only too well calculated at once to mislead the less intelligent among subsequent inquirers in the same field, and to disgust the more learned. When we read that the coin, Plate VI., No. 14, with "an Octogone, seems to have been of a Christian Prince; for by it the Christians anciently figured the Font for baptism;" that the head of Apollo on a Gaulish coin is "that of some British Prince in esteem for a holy man, as I collect from the pearls about his head, set in the ancient form of a glory; as also by the hand under the horse for the reverse," and that another coin bears "the head of Camalodunum when Christian," we can see some excuse for those who were subsequently driven to doubt the existence of any British coins at all. It would have been well had no subsequent antiquaries followed closely in Walker's footsteps, but unluckily it has been the exception and not the rule for any one to confine himself to the facts before him when treating of British antiquities of any kind.

Bishop Nicolson, the first portion of whose "English Historical Library" appeared in 1696, regarded these coins not as having been in any way intended for money, but simply as amulets, an opinion in which Thoresby seems to have concurred; and Dr. Salmon supposed "the coins, commonly called British, to have belonged to the Gauls and others that sacked Rome." Some correspondence between Dr. Salmon and Mr. Beaupré Bell, on the question, "Whether the Britons had impressed money," took place in 1720, and is preserved in Nichols' "Reliquiæ Galeanæ," in vol. iii. of the "Bibliotheca Topographica Britannica," p. 140. Bishop Nicolson concludes his argument by saying, "If any man dislikes my conjecture, I am willing* Sir John Pettus should umpire the matter between us; and his supposition (that Coin is an abstract of Coynobeline, who first coin'd money at Malden) will for ever decide the controversy."

The next engravings of coins of this series which made their appearance are those published by the Earl of Pem-

---

* Gloss. ad Fict. Min., voce Coin.

broke about 1746; but the representations, though comprising various types, are so vilely drawn and engraved as to render them utterly valueless.

Some three or four new types of British coins are engraved in Battely's "Antiquitates Rutupinae," second edition, published posthumously in 1745, though they are barely mentioned in the text.

Another antiquary who, about this time, contributed several new varieties to the list of British coins then known, was the Rev. Philip Morant, who, in his "History of Colchester," published in 1748, engraved several coins of Cunobeline, found principally in the neighbourhood of Colchester, to which he added a few more types in his "History of Essex," published in 1768.

The next author whom it is necessary to mention—the Rev. Francis Wise—exhibits, in combination with certain personal eccentricities of opinion on the subject of British coins, the natural revulsion from the credulity of one age to the scepticism of another. In his "Nummorum Antiquorum Scriniis Bodleianis reconditorum Catalogus" (1750), the sixteenth plate is of *Nummi Britannici* and contains eighteen British coins, inscribed and uninscribed, and for the most part different from those before engraved, together with six Gaulish coins. They are fairly engraved, and of the actual size, but justice is not done to the inscriptions upon them. When, however, Wise comes to describe the coins, he considers them as struck indifferently in Britain, Gaul, and Spain. Those reading TASC, for instance, he inclines to attribute to the Tascoduni or Tascodunitari, of Gallia Narbonensis; those with CVN or CVNO only, to the Cunei, a people of Spain, instead of to Cunobeline; while the CAMV on the same coin he refers, not to the town of Camulodunum, but to some unknown prince bearing a name partially similar!

The Rev. William Borlase, the author of "Observations on the Antiquities of Cornwall," published in 1754, apparently belongs to much the same school as Mr. Obadiah Walker.

The twelfth chapter of his third book is devoted to an account of "the Gold Coins found at Karn-Brê, in Cornwall, and what Nation they are to be ascrib'd unto," which is illustrated by a plate of twenty-five uninscribed coins, in most instances correctly drawn, and of the right size. But though Borlase, in his description of the coins, is in some instances extremely fanciful, yet his arguments to prove them of British origin, and to show that the inscribed coins are later than the uninscribed, and that the Karn-Brê coins are "elder than the Roman invasion," are sound, or, at all events, his propositions are correct. Edward Lhuyd* had been of the same opinion—that the Britons had gold coins before the coming of the Romans; for "if the Britons had learned the art from them, they would (though never so inartificially) have endeavoured to imitate their manner of coins," instead of which, "there have been found thick pieces of gold hollowed on one side, with variety of unintelligible marks upon them."

In 1763 the Rev. Dr. Pettingal communicated to the Society of Antiquaries a dissertation upon the TASCIA or legend upon the British coins of Cunobeline and others, which was ordered to be printed. It is illustrated by a plate of five coins of Cunobeline, from the collection of Matthew Duane, and admirably engraved. Dr. Pettingal does not travel beyond the bounds laid down in the title of his dissertation, but attempts to show that *tay*, or some similar word in the language of various nations, signified a prince or general, from whence *Tascia* had its name, as it was inscribed on the tribute money paid by the *tay* of each province or district to the Roman conquerors; that from *Tascia*, *task* is derived, and this again has been corrupted into *tax*. The dissertation shows a considerable amount of learning, but an insufficient acquaintance with facts and the usual course of events. The word under discussion is not TASCIA, but TASCIOVANVS, and in no country known to history has an extensive and complicated currency been struck simply

---

* Nicolson's "English History," lib. i. p. 30.

and expressly for the purpose of paying taxes to a foreign conqueror.

Dr. Pettingal's dissertation was quickly followed by Samuel Pegge's "Essay on the Coins of Cunobelin," which was published in 1766. He divides the coins of Cunobeline into six classes, and by this means places the coins now ascribed to Tasciovanus in a class by themselves, while his division of the coins which really belong to Cunobeline appears to me so judicious, that I have in part adopted it. Pegge, however, makes out that TASCIO was the name of the mint master of Cunobeline, and many of his descriptions of the types of the coins and of their probable meaning are supremely ridiculous. This essay is illustrated by two plates, comprising about thirty types, derived principally from Camden, the Pembroke Plates, Pettingal, Battely, and Wise, but including four coins from the collection of Mr. John White, then engraved for the first time, one of which was an altered coin, and another a cast in gold from an original in copper. These plates of Pegge's were subsequently copied in Henry's "History of Great Britain."

Contemporary with Pegge and Pettingal was Dr. Stukeley, who, prior to his death in 1765, had prepared twenty-three plates of the coins of the ancient British kings, which were published by his executor, Richard Fleming. They are not accompanied by any letter-press description, but on the first fifteen plates, which appear to have been engraved from Dr. Stukeley's own sketches, many of the coins have inscriptions beneath them, giving the names of the princes to whom he attributed them. The coins themselves are most inaccurately drawn, and in many instances are merely bad copies of the engravings in Camden and elsewhere. Among them are many Gaulish, Pannonian, and Spanish coins, and the attributions are generally fanciful in the extreme. Coins of the Iceni are attributed to Eli Maur Rex; others of Spain, with Celtiberian inscriptions, to Inmanuence and Androge Mandubras; and Gaulish coins figure as of Tinmee Rex, Curnticus, Marius, &c. &c.; while uninscribed coins do duty as those of Dunwallo, Minocan, and Arvirngus. But though these plates are disfigured by so many defects, they have the redeeming feature of occasionally presenting, side by side with the coins of Cunobeline, Roman coins, from which Dr. Stukeley thought, and occasionally with much show of reason, the types to have been derived. The remaining eight plates are much more accurately drawn, and are principally of coins in the collection of Joseph Tolson Lockyer, F.S.A., and M.P. for Ilchester; and in that of Mr. Ebenezer Mussel, F.S.A., of Bethnal Green. In these no attempt is made to attribute any of the coins, but a considerable number of Gaulish coins and some few Saxon are interspersed. Scattered through the twenty-three plates are several which I have now re-engraved from the originals, for the first time; and one at least (Stukeley, pl. iv, 7), which, though not at present known, may, I hope, ere long be re-discovered.

The plate of "British coins in Gold, Electrum, Silver, and Copper, in the Possession of John White, 1773," contains the best representations of British coins which, up to that time, had been published. Though comprising a considerable number of Gaulish and some few forgeries of British coins, a faithful idea of the general character of the ancient British coinage is conveyed. The plate is accompanied by two pages of description, but without any pretence to originality, except as far as regards a table of weights of the coins by which Mr. White attempts to show that the larger pieces were multiples of the smaller. His remarks on this part of the subject would have been of more value had not the heavier pieces been all Gaulish or Pannonian, and the lighter ones British.

The figures of British coins given by Whitaker in his "History of Manchester," 1773, are so bad, and his remarks upon them so absurd, that no further mention of him is needed.

In 1780 appeared a new edition of Camden's "Britannia," much enlarged, by Richard Gough. In this edition several of the types, originally engraved by Camden, are omitted, and their places supplied by others derived principally from White and Borlase. As might be expected, there are many of the Gaulish coins and forgeries of the former inserted, but the notes upon the various types and legends, by Gough, are, on the whole, judicious. He is, however, inclined to derive the British coinage from the Phœnician, and points out the resemblance in type between the coins of Sicily and those of Britain, and thinks that "we may safely venture to refer the coins of both people to the fifth century before Christ, when Sicily flourished under its own princes, and the Phœnicians drove a considerable trade with Britain." From such a heterogeneous mixture of coins as that on the plate before him, we cannot wonder at an antiquary not well versed in numismatics coming to conclusions as devoid of probability as this. It is rather singular that the coin of Verulamium, engraved as of that city, by Charles Combe, in his catalogue of Dr. William Hunter's coins, 1782, was not included in his plate by Gough.

The second edition of Pinkerton's "Essay on Medals" appeared in 1789. He gives engravings of two coins of Cunobeline, and thinks that the coins of Cunobeline are the only ones probably British. He says *probably*, "for the portraits, sizes, and seeming age of these coins vary so much, that some incline to think the name is that of some Gallic deity or hero. The CAMV and VER may be names of places or persons in Gaul. As for the TASCIA, it is common upon coins certainly Gallic, but its interpretation is dubious. In old German, *tasg* is a purse." In his third edition, published in 1808, he makes the remark, however, "that there are certainly British coins prior to Julius Cæsar, but they cannot be strictly appropriated, far less ascribed, to particular monarchs."

Between 1792 and 1798 the immortal Eckhel published his great work, the "Doctrina Numorum Veterum," but that distinguished numismatist, apparently from not being acquainted with what had already appeared upon the subject, does not allow any indigenous coinage to Britain. As instances of coins that had been attributed to this country, he cites coins from Pellerin and Haym, which he justly repudiates, but he also cites the coin ascribed to Verulamium by Charles Combe, which he dismisses with the remark, "Habebit vir eruditus, ipse Britannus, ejus sententiæ aptus causas, *sed quas ignoro*." In the Addenda, however, to his first volume, he shows that he had subsequently made himself acquainted with what Pinkerton, Walker, Wise, and Camden had written, and though he gives a list of coins of Cunobeline, yet fortified by the dictum of Sestini, that all the coins called British were really Gaulish, and irritated by the absurdities he found in our English authors, he leaves them as doomed to hopeless obscurity.

The catalogue of the coins of cities and princes preserved in the British Museum was published by Taylor Combe in 1814, but the only coins he admits as British are those of Cunobeline and Verulam, and those inscribed SEGO and BODVO, which he doubtfully assigns to Segonax and another king named Boduo. The coins of Eppillus, Verica, Epaticcus, Dubnovellaunus, and the Iceni, some of all of which he describes, and a few of which he engraves, are most unpatriotically referred to *Reguli* of Gaul. It is, however, but right to add that it is to Taylor Combe that we are indebted for the series of plates of British coins which illustrates Ruding's "Annals of the Coinage," first published in 1817, as they were engraved under his inspection. Though the coins are not quite faithfully drawn, these plates will always be of great value for reference. They contain, however, a large number of Gaulish coins, which I have tabulated below,* and, following the plan adopted by Taylor Combe, they

---

* Gaulish Coins in Ruding's Plates :—
   Plate I. None, though some are possibly common to Gaul and Britain.
   Plate II. Nos. 22 to 34.
   Plate III. Nos. 43, 45, 46 to 51 (Channel Islands), 53, 55 to 64, 66.
   Plate IV. Nos. 67 to 72.
   Plate V. None.
   Plate XXVI. Appendix No. 1.

exclude all the inscribed coins except those of Cunobeline and the others previously mentioned. The publication of these plates, containing, as they do, so large a number of uninscribed British coins, as well as of those of Cunobeline, with the weights of all accurately given, served to place the study of that series on a much firmer footing than that on which it ever before rested. In the introductory notice prefixed by Mr. Ruding to the explanation of the plates, he enters into and refutes some of the wild speculations in which the Rev. Edward Davies, the author of "Celtic Researches" and the "Mythology and Rites of the British Druids," had indulged, in some thirty-six pages of remarks upon British coins with which he concludes the latter work, published in 1809. It is hardly worth while to refer to this *farrago libelli*, but if any of my readers wish to become acquainted with the Helio-Arkite superstition, as manifested on coins, let them study Mr. Davies, and learn that these pieces were not intended for the common medium of trade, but were struck in honour of the gods of the Britons, in commemoration of the solemnities of their great festivals, and upon other sacred occasions. In the third edition of Ruding, 1840, there are notes to the explanation of the plates, usually containing just and sensible remarks, and there is also a supplementary plate of British coins (pl. A) principally compiled from those in the early volumes of the Numismatic Journal.

Before noticing this last-mentioned publication a word must be said about the "Essai sur les Médailles Antiques de Cunobelinus," published by the Marquis de Lagoy in 1820. Its main object is to prove the existence of an ancient British coinage, which had been ignored by men of such undoubted authority as Eckhel, Sestini, and Mionnet, and this is satisfactorily done by showing that the coins of Cunobeline are principally if not wholly found in England, and are only known in France through English authors, so that they cannot by any possibility be Gaulish. The pamphlet of only twenty pages is illustrated by a plate of nine coins principally taken from the Pembroke plates, but with one remarkably fine coin, of the type No. 10 of my Plate XII., added from the Marquis de Lagoy's own collection.

In the summer of 1836 that indefatigable antiquary, Mr. J. Y. Akerman, brought out the first number of the Numismatic Journal, a quarterly periodical, of which eight numbers forming two volumes appeared. In 1838 the title was changed for that of the Numismatic Chronicle, and the work was published under the auspices of the Numismatic Society, and completed its twentieth volume while still under the editorship of Mr. Akerman. In 1861 a new series of the Numismatic Chronicle was commenced, which has already completed its second volume. Scattered through these four and twenty volumes are a large number of papers on the subject of the ancient British coinage, by Messrs. Akerman, Birch, Burgon, Fairholt, Haigh, Hawkins, Loscombe, Oldfield, Beale Poste, C. Roach Smith, Martin F. Tupper, and myself. These are illustrated by twenty-four plates in addition to numerous woodcuts, so that the Numismatic Chronicle affords a mine of information on the subject of this series of coins, from which I have largely drawn, and as some seventeen of the papers and ten of the plates were communicated by myself, it will, I hope, be pardoned if I have sometimes repeated portions of these papers in the following pages.

But besides having the merit of starting the earliest numismatic periodical in England, devoted in a great measure to our own coinage, Mr. Akerman has published several independent numismatic works, more or less relating to the ancient British coinage. The principal of these, in this respect, is his "Ancient Coins of Cities and Princes—Hispania, Gallia, Britannia" (1846), which contains four well-executed plates of inscribed British coins, exhibiting seventy-seven specimens. In this work a much more comprehensive system of classification is adopted than in Ruding or any other earlier author. The coins of the sons of Comius—Eppillus, Verica, and Tinc[ommius]—are separately arranged, and the probable territories of each pointed out. The coins of

Tasciovanus also are now, for the first time, ranked by themselves, and a great deal is done towards reducing the whole of the inscribed series into an orderly arrangement.* No illustrations are given of the coins of the uninscribed series, which Mr. Akerman was inclined to regard as barbarous imitations of the better executed inscribed coins; and one of the conclusions at which he arrived was, "that if the Britons had a coinage of their own previously to the arrival of Cæsar, the fact is not proved by existing examples."

In an earlier work, the "Numismatic Manual" (1840), he had expressed a different opinion, and referred to papers in the Numismatic Journal and Chronicle, "which would convince the most sceptical that the Britons struck money previous to the arrival of Cæsar." Such was Mr. Hawkins' opinion, who, in his "Silver Coins of England," published in 1841, says that, "it may be safely asserted that, previous to the invasion of Julius Cæsar, in the year 55 A.C., and before the Roman dominion was generally established throughout this island, the Britons had a metallic currency of struck coin formed upon a Grecian model." In this work Mr. Hawkins gives two plates, containing a selection of thirty-one coins, of most of which the places of finding are given. There are, however, two of them (Nos. 17 and 29), which are, in all probability, Gaulish. In the remarks upon the coins, he insists strongly upon a point which cannot be urged too strongly, or too often, as to the necessity of careful observation of the localities where different types are found. "If every person, who can positively authenticate the place where such, or similar coins were turned up would record the circumstances, there is very little doubt but that in a short space of time, such a series of facts would be established that a tolerable numismatist would, upon a bare inspection of a coin, be able to pronounce, with truth and decision, the

---

* A valuable paper "On the condition of Britain from the descent of Cæsar to the coming of Claudius; accompanied by a Map of a portion of Britain in its ancient state, showing the finding of Indigenous Coins," from the pen of Mr. Akerman, is printed in The Archæologia, vol. xxxiii. p. 177.

district in which it originally circulated." The present volume will, I hope, in some measure prove the truth of Mr. Hawkins' remark, but still much remains to be done, which can only be effected in the manner he proposes; and I venture to take this opportunity of suggesting to all collectors of coins, that a communication to the Numismatic Society, of the type and place of discovery of any British coin, affords the best means of placing the facts in connection with it on record.

Various discoveries of the kind have been published in the pages of the Gentleman's Magazine and the Journals of the Archæological Institute and Archæological Association. Besides this there are in the earlier volumes of the Journal of the latter a number of papers on the coins of Cunobeline and of the ancient Britons, by the Rev. Beale Poste, which were, with some few subsequent additions, collected into a volume and published in 1853. Partly owing to the manner in which this work appeared, and partly owing to the uniformed nature of the author's views at the time the first part of the book was written, there is great confusion in its arrangement, and some passages seem to contradict each other. The principal conclusions at which Mr. Poste has arrived, judging also from a still later work of his, "Celtic Inscriptions on Gaulish and British Coins, &c." (1861), are, that the inscriptions on the latter are purely titular, and that some British princes (as, for instance, Caractacus, who had eight) had many distinct and different names, under several of which they appear upon the coins. The amount of reading and research of Mr. Poste is beyond all doubt most extensive and praiseworthy, but it is rendered valueless by his constant adherence to preconceived opinions, and by a want of practical acquaintance with coins. It would be needless and invidious to give instances of these defects, but it has of course been necessary to point out in the following pages many of the cases where the legends of coins have been misread and misinterpreted by Mr. Poste.

The "Collectanea Antiqua" of Mr. C. Roach Smith, the first

volume of which was commenced in 1843, though bearing on the title-page the date of 1848, is the next work that requires to be noticed. It will give some idea of the value of this book as a storehouse of facts relating to ancient British numismatics, when it is mentioned that nearly sixty British coins are engraved in the first volume, and the places are recorded where each was found. From the constant references I have made to this book it will be seen how much I am indebted to it. Its later volumes contain but few coins of this class, but this is accounted for by Mr. C. Roach Smith having communicated all discoveries of these coins which came under his notice to the Numismatic Society, or to me, and his having therefore probably not thought it necessary to repeat them in his "Collectanea Antiqua."

Only one other book remains to be cited, the "Monumenta Historica Britannica," published at great expense by the government in 1848. In this great national work the whole of the uninscribed British coins, as far as any representations of them are concerned, are entirely ignored, as are also all the inscribed coins, with the exception of those of Tasciovanus and Cunobeline. As so many coins of the other classes had already been published by Mr. Hawkins and Mr. Akerman, there was no excuse for their omission by Mr. Doubleday, to whom, instead of to some more competent person, this part of the work was delegated. The plate of British coins is, however, well engraved, though, in some instances, coins of the same type are given us belonging to two different classes; and one coin, No. 48, has been misread, and another, No. 50, is undoubtedly *false*.

Such are the principal works which treat of these coins. A few more will be found, included in the list of books referred to, placed at the end of the volume. Besides these, there are a few works on the Gaulish coinage, such as those of Lambert, Lelewel, and Duchalais, in which engravings of British coins are to be found, or mention is made of them, but it is needless to cite the particular opinions of each author. Some French numismatists have been prone to claim all British coins as of Gallic origin; but Duchalais, with needless liberality, assigns to Britain some few coins which certainly do not belong to this side of the Channel. I allude to Nos. 714 to 716 of his catalogue, and merely mention the fact that foreign numismatists may not think that I have overlooked these types. In the forthcoming work of M. F. de Saulcy on the Gaulic coinage, I make no doubt that these, and many other types of uncertain attribution, will be satisfactorily assigned. I believe also that some of the uninscribed types, which I have here engraved as British, will by him also be engraved as Gaulish, as they appear to have been current in both countries. Under such circumstances their true parentage can only be ascertained by the relative abundance of specimens in each country, which at present there are no means of determining. There is, however, so magnificent and extensive a series of the Gaulish coinage that that of Britain sinks into comparative insignificance by its side, and I am sure that M. de Saulcy, to whose kindness and courtesy I have already been often indebted, will pardon me for claiming as of British origin such coins as I know to have been frequently found in Britain, and such as, though scarce in Britain, I cannot find engraved in any work on the Gaulish coinage.

CHAPTER II.

DATE AND ORIGIN.

It will have been seen from the preceding chapter that there has been a considerable difference of opinion among those who have treated of this subject, as to the date at which a knowledge of the art of coining was introduced into Britain; and that some writers have even gone the length of denying the existence of any ancient British coinage at all. As it would be superfluous to insist on the fact, now universally admitted by Numismatists, that a British coinage did once exist, I shall confine myself in the present chapter to an attempt to determine the epoch of its commencement.

In the total absence of any contemporary historic records, the only two sources from which we can derive information on this interesting and important question are—first, the notices of historians as to the condition of Britain when first brought into contact with Roman civilisation; and, second, the testimony afforded by the coins themselves. From a careful examination of these two classes of witnesses, as I have elsewhere[*] endeavoured to show, the date of the earliest known British coinage may be deduced, if not with exact chronological accuracy, at all events with a tolerably close approximation to the truth.

Unfortunately, while Druidic speculations appear to have possessed a fatal attraction for archæologists, the valuable though fragmentary evidence of Roman historians would

---

[*] Num. Chron., vol. xii. p. 127.

seem to have been only partially examined, while that of the coins themselves has been almost entirely neglected. Of the many misapprehensions in which such a system of investigation was certain to result, none perhaps has been more prolific than the exaggerated importance which has been attached to a well-known passage in Cæsar's Commentaries, in spite of its notorious corruptness, and the refutation afforded by a comparison of passages in other authors, and even in Cæsar himself. It occurs in the description of Britain given in the Commentaries on the Gallic war (v. 12), where, according to the common text, we read—" *Utuntur aut ære aut annulis (taleis) ferreis ad certum pondus examinatis pro nummis*"—and on these words, the opinion that the coinage of the ancient Britons dates subsequently to the invasion of Julius Cæsar, mainly rests. Not only, however, is the passage corrupt,[*] but Mr. Hawkins[†] has shown that in a great number of MSS. the words "*aut nummo aureo*" occur after "*ære*," so that it would, after all, appear probable that, so far from Cæsar affirming that there were no coins in Britain at the time of his invasion, he expressly mentions a British currency of gold coins. The contrary opinion has, however, been supposed to derive additional support from two passages in the Letters of Cicero, whose brother accompanied Cæsar in his second expedition against Britain. In writing to Trebatius he makes use of the expression—" *In Britanniâ nihil esse audio neque auri neque argenti ;*"[‡] and again he writes to Atticus— " *Neque auri scrupulum esse ullum in illâ insulâ.*"[§] But both the letters in which these passages occur are written in a jocose style, and the expressions must be regarded as hyperbolical, and significant of the disappointment felt at Rome on account of the small amount of booty resulting

---

[*] The accepted reading is to some extent supported by the Greek version; but the date of the translation is too uncertain to afford any trustworthy evidence as to the integrity of the passage.
[†] Num. Chron., vol. i. p. 13—Silver Coins of England, p. 6.
[‡] Ep. ad Fam., vii. 7.
[§] Ep. ad Att., iv. 16.

from the British expedition, as compared with what was obtained in Gaul (though Strabo says it was considerable), rather than as authorising the belief that not only was there no coinage in Britain at the time, but that there was a total absence of the precious metals.

So far, indeed, was Cicero himself from believing this to have been the case, that he qualifies the remark with an "*id si ita est*," and in his very next letter to Atticus he writes that he had heard from Cæsar of the submission of Britain—"*nullâ predâ, imperatâ tamen pecuniâ.*"[*] And Cæsar himself, referring to the same subject, records that before leaving Britain—"*obsides imperat et quid in annos singulos vectigalis populo Romano Britannia penderet, constituit.*"[†] Dion Cassius[‡] calls this yearly tribute φόρον ἐτήσιον; and Eutropius[§] records that Julius "*Britannos, stipendiarios fecit.*" Suetonius[∥] also distinctly affirms "*pecunias et obsides imperavit.*"

Now, apart from this distinct mention of money, we can hardly imagine Cæsar imposing a yearly tax or tribute upon a people who were unacquainted with the precious metals or the use of money: and though some antiquaries have brought themselves to believe that the Britons first coined money for the purpose of paying this tribute, they have not attempted to assign reasons why they should have incurred the expense and trouble of doing this, instead of sending the gold and silver for the tribute in the form of bullion. That the tribute was for a time actually paid may be gathered from Diodorus;[¶] but from Strabo[**] we learn that it had, in the days of Augustus, been commuted for light export and import duties on the articles of commerce with Gaul. Judging from the expressions used by the different writers, I think it must be conceded that the tribute imposed by Julius must have been a money payment, or at all events a

---

[*] Ep. ad Att., iv. 17. [‖] Brev., vi. 17.
[†] De Bell. Gall., v. 22. [§] Vit. Jul. Cæs., xxv.
[‡] Lib. xl. sect. 3. [¶] Lib. v. cap. 21.
[**] Strabo, lib. ii. p. 200, Oxford ed. 1807.

payment of a certain amount of gold or silver, and not a tribute levied in kind, which, indeed, from the very conditions of the case, would have been almost impossible; so that did history throw no other light upon the subject, we should be justified in concluding that the use of the precious metals was known in Britain at the time of the invasion of Julius.

But, beyond this, there is strong evidence to be derived from the direct assertions of some of the ancient historians. "*Fert Britannia aurum, et argentum et alia metalla, pretium victoriæ*" are the words of Tacitus.[*] Φέρει δὲ σῖτον καὶ βοσκήματα, καὶ χρυσὸν, καὶ ἀργυρον, καὶ σίδηρον, says Strabo;[†] and Solinus[‡] speaks of the "*metallorum largum variamque copiam, quibus Britanniæ solum undique generum pollet.*" It may indeed be urged that these writers are all of them later than Cæsar; but it is to be observed that the information upon which some of them wrote was derived from earlier sources, and that not one of them treats the presence of gold and silver in this country as of recent date, or appears to have had the remotest conception that in the time of Julius Cæsar it was destitute of them.

When, however, we come to consider the character of the early commerce of this country with other nations, and the connection which, long before the days of Julius, existed between the people of Britain and those of Gaul, the supposed unacquaintance of the former with the use of money, becomes perfectly incredible. The intimate relations between Gaul and Britain in the time of Julius Cæsar are evident from his Commentaries. Some time before his first descent upon this country we find, for instance, a league[§] of Gaulish tribes, principally maritime, with the Veneti at their head, sending over to Britain for assistance. The skill in navigation of the Veneti, who occupied the southern part of Brittany, and who were the chief of these maritime states, is also mentioned, and both Cæsar and

[*] Vit. Agric., cap. 12.
[†] Lib. iv. p. 279.
[‡] Cap. xxii. sec. alias xxiv.
[§] De Bell. Gall., iii. 9.

Strabo speak of their frequent voyages to Britain. And though, on Cæsar's[*] inquiry among the Gauls as to the means of access to Britain and the character of the inhabitants, they professed ignorance; yet it was acknowledged that traders were in the habit of passing over, though it was said that their acquaintance with the country was limited to the coast and the region opposite to Gaul. Directly, however, that he prepared to send over Volusenus to make a reconnaissance, the news of his intentions was carried over to Britain by these traders, and ambassadors from not one or two, but from numerous states were sent to him, proving that there were much more ready means of communication between the two countries than Cæsar's informants had been previously willing to acknowledge. Subsequently,[†] Cæsar appears to have obtained better information, and relates that the coasts of Britain were inhabited by colonies which had crossed over from Belgic Gaul, who, in many cases, retained the names of their parent tribes, and, in some instances, even, seem to have been under the same rulers. Divitiacus,[‡] for instance, is mentioned as having not long before held dominion over a considerable part of Britain as well as of Gaul, so that we may well infer that as far as regards that portion of Britain most easy of access from the continent, the state of civilisation in the time of Julius Cæsar could not have been materially different on the two sides of the Channel. Indeed, he makes the remark himself that the inhabitants of Kent,[§] a wholly maritime region, differ but little in manners from the Gauls.

Long, however, before the days of Julius there had been a native coinage in Gaul; and long, too, before that time had the commerce between Britain and the more civilised parts of the world been conducted through that country. It is needless to enter here into the question of the early Phœnician intercourse with Britain, as their commerce appears to have been

[*] De Bell. Gall., iv. 20. [‡] B. G., ii. 4.
[†] B. G., v. 12. [§] B. G., v. 14.

conducted exclusively by barter, and I am not aware of any
traces of their presence in this country having as yet been
discovered. But the commerce between the Greek colony of
Massilia and Britain also commenced at an early period,*
and it seems probable dates back some centuries B.C. So
early as the days of Herodotus† (B.C. 445) the name of the
Cassiterides was known as that of the islands from which
tin was brought; and Polybius‡ (B.C. 160) speaks of the
Britannic Isles, and the preparation of tin, as subjects of
which other writers had largely treated. It seems possible
that at first this intercourse of the Greeks was direct by sea,
and conducted in the same manner as that of the Phœnicians
or Carthaginians, as Pytheas of Massilia appears to have
navigated as far as Britain. But it is certain that eventually
it was carried on overland through Gaul. Diodorus Siculus,§
a contemporary of Julius Cæsar, but who compiled a great
deal of his narrative from earlier sources, informs us that
the tin having been fused into ingots was conveyed to a
certain island named Ictis, where it was purchased by the
merchants, who conveyed it across into Gaul, and thence on
the backs of horses, by a thirty days' journey overland, to
the mouths of the Rhone. At what date this overland route
commenced is uncertain, but it seems probable that at the
close of the second Punic war, and the consequent abandon-
ment of their colonies in Spain by the Carthaginians, their
intercourse with Britain ceased; and as, during the continu-
ance of that war, the commerce of the Massaliotes (who were
allies of the Romans) would have been exposed to great
danger at the hands of the Carthaginians had it been
carried on directly by sea, and as we have no record of the
supply of tin having ceased, it may be inferred that the
intercourse through Gaul had already commenced by B.C. 200,
if not before. It would appear moreover to have been all
along conducted by Gaulish traders.

* See Henry's Great Britain, book i. c. 6; and Sir G. C. Lewis's Astronomy
of the Ancients, c. viii. sec. 3, et seq.
† Lib. iii. s. 115.   ‡ Lib. iii. c. 57.   § Lib. v. c. 22.

But whether this commerce was so carried on or not, the contiguity of Britain to the Continent is such that but slight skill in navigation suffices to connect the two sides of the Channel. We have seen how, in the time of Julius, there were already a number of Belgic tribes who had immigrated into Britain and occupied the country bordering on the sea; but besides this, we also learn that Britain was regarded by the Gauls as the birthplace of their religion,* whither also their more learned Druids resorted for the completion of their education. This connection, as regards religion, points to a very early date for the commencement of the intercourse between the two countries; and the difference in language which there was at the time of Tacitus,† though slight, may also be regarded as a witness of the Belgic colonisation of Britain having been at that time, of long standing. The natural channel of this intercourse would be between the coast of Kent and the opposite coast of Gaul, as involving the smallest amount of sea-passage; and, accordingly, we find from Cæsar‡ that the inhabitants of Kent were the most civilised of the British tribes, and most closely resembled their continental neighbours. It may therefore be fairly inferred, that as soon as the inhabitants of that part of Gaul became acquainted with the use of money, the use of it would also spread into the neighbouring part of Britain.

Now, as I have already observed, there had been a native coinage in that part of Gaul long before the days of Julius Cæsar.

The Phocæan colony of Massilia (*Marseille*) appears to have formed the centre from which civilisation spread through Gaul, as well as to have been the emporium of its commerce. It was founded about B.C. 600, and from intercourse with its inhabitants the neighbouring Gauls§ first learned the usages of civilised life, and after a time became acquainted with the art of coining. The early silver coins of Massilia

---

* Cæs. de Bell. Gall., vi. 13.
† Agricola, c. 11.
‡ Cæs. de Bell. Gall., v. 14.
§ Justin, xliii. 4.

(and none in gold are known) were occasionally imitated in the surrounding country; but when, about the year B.C. 356, the gold mines of Crenides (or Philippi) were acquired by Philip II. of Macedon, and worked so as to produce about £250,000 worth of gold per annum, the general currency of gold coins, which had before been of very limited extent, became much more extensive, and the *stater* of Philip—the *regale numisma* of Horace—became everywhere diffused, and seems at once to have been seized on by the barbarians who came in contact with Greek civilisation, as an object of imitation.

In Gaul this was especially the case, and the whole of the gold coinage of that country may be said to consist of imitations, more or less rude and degenerate, of the Macedonian Philippus.

Another reason for the adoption of the Philippus as the model for imitation in the Gaulish coinage, has been found in the probability that when Brennus plundered Greece, B.C. 279,* he carried away a great treasure of these coins, which thus became the gold currency of Gaul. This would, however, have had more effect in Pannonia, from whence the army of Brennus came, than in the more western Gaul.

The types of the Philippus, as will be seen from the annexed woodcut, are, on the obverse, the laureate head of

Apollo (or, as some have supposed, of young Hercules), and on the reverse, a charioteer in a biga, with the name of Philip beneath. The earliest of the Gaulish imitations follow the prototype pretty closely, but eventually both the head and the biga became completely transformed.

* Dürch. in Arch. Journ., vol. xix. p. 259, et ff.

If, therefore, as has already been shown to be most probably the case, the Britons derived their knowledge of the art of coining from the Gauls, we shall find upon their coins an imitation more or less rude of the types of the Macedonian Philippus; and the greater or lesser resemblance of the coins to the prototype may afford some means of approximately estimating the date. If, on the contrary, the art of coining was unknown in Britain till the time of Cæsar, the coins must either have been struck on the Roman model or on that of the later Gaulish coinage, in which nearly all reminiscence of the original Macedonian types had been lost, and which showed also unmistakable signs of Roman influence. We should, too, have a coinage of the three metals then in use, gold, silver, and bronze, and not one of gold only, as it would have been had it originated at an early period in the Gaulish coinage. Now what evidence do the coins themselves give upon this point? There are coins of gold of a type never occurring on the inferior metals, which, though occasionally discovered in France, are of very much more frequent occurrence in England, and are therefore, in all probability, of British origin, and on which the laureate head and the charioteer, though both considerably modified, can at once be identified.

Coins of this type are engraved in Plate A, Nos. 1 and 2, and are, as will subsequently be seen, beyond all doubt the earliest of the British series. The question now for consideration is, what date is to be assigned to them, judging merely from their type and weight, and the position of Britain in relation to those countries in which the Macedonian Philippus circulated. The death of Philip II. took place B.C. 336, so that we may safely say that his coins began to be imitated in Gaul as early as about or before B.C. 300; but the imitations of that period would be merely servile, even to the retaining the name of Philip on the coins, while the British coins show various innovations in the type, such, for instance, as the addition of drapery or a gorget to the neck of the laureate head, and a bandlet around it, the giving wings to the charioteer, and the coalition of the two horses of the biga. Unfortunately, as in so many other instances, many of the links connecting one type and the other are at present missing, so that we cannot trace it through all the intermediate phases of its existence. The type must, however, have been derived through Gaul, and it seems probable that some considerable time must have elapsed between the period when first the Philippi were imitated in the south of France, and their modified descendants were in circulation on the northern coast. Certainly these coins could never have been in circulation with the Philippi themselves, as their weight is considerably less. I have never known that of these British coins to exceed 120 grains, while the proper weight of the Macedonian stater is about 133 grains. At the same time the British coins are heavier than the Gaulish coins on which the charioteer has become modified into an androcephalous horse (Ruding, pl. ii. 22 to 30), as these rarely attain the weight of 115 grains, while they are in type also more remote from the original. The British coins are, therefore, in all probability earlier, though some of these Gaulish types have been assigned by Lelewel (pl. viii. 20—28) to 150—100 B.C.

Taking, then, all these circumstances into consideration, we should not greatly err if on the evidence already before us we assign to these, the earliest of the British coins, a date somewhere between 150 to 200 B.C.

But besides the method here adopted of tracing the age of a coin downwards in time from a given date, by means of the analogy of type and weight, there is another method open to us—that of tracing it upwards in time by the same means, from a type of ascertained date, and it will be well to see whether this also leads to the same results. It is a well known fact that among all nations, civilised and uncivilised, there is a strong tendency, for the sake of some small temporary gain to the governing power, to reduce the weight of the coins, so that the earlier coins of any country are as a rule heavier than those of a later date, even though of the same denomination. Our silver penny, for instance, of the present day weighs but 7½ grains, though its original weight of 24 grains may still be traced in our "pennyweight;" and the Roman *solidus* of the fourth century, consisting of 70 grains of gold, has its modern representatives in the English shilling and the French sou. We have already seen that the original weight of the Philippus, 133 grains, had been reduced to 120 grains before its modified descendants were introduced into Britain, and the same diminution in weight gradually takes place in the subsequent coins, until they weigh no more than 84 grains. As this reduction is not sudden, but appears to have been effected by gradual and almost insensible alterations, it may, when taken in conjunction with the alterations of type, give some idea of the time requisite for so great a change to have been effected, and thus, by adding the time necessary for the transition, to the ascertained age of one of the later coins, we are enabled to assign a date for the commencement of the series.

Coincident with this diminution in weight there is a remarkable change in the types of the coins, each successive imitation getting more and more remote from the original prototype. Among barbarous nations the laws which regulate the types of a coinage of this kind, consisting of successive copies of copies of a given original, are much the same as those which, according to our best naturalists, govern the succession of types in the organic kingdoms. As with plants or animals of any group or family, there are two tendencies to be traced in these successive copies—the one to retain the character of their ancestors, the other to vary from it. The main principle is, no doubt, that of "atavism," or taking the character of the parent; but another principle of more importance, as far as results are concerned—that of the perpetuation of varieties when they are in any way advantageous—is equally at work in both cases. In nature those varieties appear to have become more or less persistent which, in the "struggle for existence," have presented advantages over the parent forms in their relation to external conditions. But in the succession of types of these British coins, the requirements which new types had to fulfil in order to become to a certain extent persistent were, firstly, to present facility of imitation, and, secondly, symmetry of form. The natural instincts of uncivilised man seem to lead to the adoption of simple yet symmetrical forms of ornament, while in all stages of culture the saving of trouble is an object of universal desire. The reduction of a complicated and artistic design into a symmetrical figure of easy execution was the object of each successive engraver of the dies for these coins, though probably they were themselves unaware of any undue saving of trouble on their part, or of the results which ensued from it.

Looking at the prototype from which they copied, Plate A, Nos. 1 and 2, or, still better, No. 4, which is the same type, only reversed (probably by copying a coin on the die without reflecting that the impression would be in the opposite direction), we find that, as compared with the Philippus, the alterations already mentioned are in accordance with the principles which I have here laid down. The face, it is true, has been preserved, but the rest of the head has become conventionalised, and as it were reduced into a system. The front hair has become converted into three open crescents; the hair at the back of the head, instead of being in graceful and natural waves, is represented by two parallel rows of nearly similar locks; the wreath is reduced into a double row of leaves, all of one size, extending across the coin, while the head is crossed at its centre by a straight band ending in a hook where once was the ear, and the neck has an ornamental covering of beaded and plain straight lines. On the reverse a great metamorphosis has also taken place, but at present it will be needless to trace this. I may, however, remark that the tradition that there was a horse on the reverse of these coins appears to have been constant among the engravers, and that occasionally recourse was had to nature for a fresh sketch of the animal; while the fact that a head was being represented on the obverse appears, as will shortly be seen, to have been at last entirely forgotten. One of the causes that assisted to produce this result was, in addition to those already mentioned, that the dies were considerably larger than the coins struck from them, so that in engraving a fresh die in imitation of one of the coins, only a portion of the original device was presented to the engraver.

I will now trace downwards from the prototype, Plate A, Nos. 1 and 2, the succession of types to some of the inscribed coins whose age is approximately known, noting at the same time the weights of the coins at each successive stage, and will then consider how much earlier the prototype must be than the descendants, for so great changes to have taken place. In the Numismatic Chronicle, vol. xii. p. 127, I have given a sort of family tree of the derivation of some of these types, to which also the reader is referred. In order to assist in identifying the derivation of the uninscribed types, it will be found that in nearly all cases I have placed the more modern representatives of the wreath at about the same angle which the original occupies on Plate A, Nos. 1 and 2.

Looking at these two coins, the principal parts of the design, and those most easy to copy, are the locks of back hair, the crescents of front hair, the wreath, the cross-band, and the clothing of the neck. All of these are preserved on No. 8, but only a portion of the face is visible, and the weight, instead of being 120 grains, is 100½ grains, though the reduction is partly owing to wear. On the remaining coins of this plate the face has entirely disappeared, and in some, as No. 13, only the central portion of the original design has survived. Their weight is from 95 to 91 grains. In Plate B the same general character of type prevails; but on some, as Nos. 5 and 6, there is a rounded projection where the face should be. Coins of the type of No. 6 are found ranging from 103 to 95 grains. In Plate C, No. 7, we find the head beginning to assume a cruciform appearance,

with a weight of from 90 to 92 grains; and on No. 9 the
head has been reduced to a regular cruciform pattern; but,
as if in recognition of its origin, we find in the angles of the
cross locks of the back hair, a crescent representing the
front hair and the ornamental covering of the neck. The
weight is about 86 grains. In Plate D, No. 7, the same
type may be observed, but with locks of hair in each of the
angles. Returning to Plate C, the affinity between Nos. 9, 10,
and 12 is at once apparent, but No. 12 is in fact a coin of
Tasciovanus, though not showing the legend. The coin of
Eppillus, Plate III., No. 13, may, in like manner, be traced
through Plate C, No. 14, back to the prototype. The coins
of Dubnovellaunus, Plate IV., Nos. 6 to 9, and of Tinc-
[ommius], Plate I., Nos. 11 and 12, are also evidently
descendants from the same original, though widely differing
in type. On other coins of the former prince, Plate IV.,
No. 10, the place of the wreath is marked by merely a
raised band across the field of the coin; the usual weight of
all these inscribed coins never exceeding 84 grains.

Now, we have some means of assigning a date for all these
four princes, which cannot be very far from the truth.
Tinc[ommius] and Eppillus appear to have been the sons of
Commius the Atrebatian mentioned by Cæsar in his Commentaries; Dubnovellaunus is most probably the Damno
Bellaunus of the inscription of Augustus at Ancyra; and
Tasciovanus was the father of Cunobeline, and therefore a
contemporary of Augustus. Speaking generally, the date of
their coins here cited may be taken as some ten or twenty
years before the Christian era. We have then to consider
what period would be necessary for so complete a transformation of type as there is between them and their prototype, accompanied as it is by a diminution of weight from
120 to 84 grains. It must at once be evident that such a
metamorphosis of type as that which we find to have taken
place, could not possibly have been effected in the lapse of a
few years, as, though some of the intermediate forms are
at present wanting, there is reason for supposing that each

successive coin was struck in imitation of one already in circulation. It is, moreover, probable that the art of die-sinking must have been confined to but few individuals, and that when once they were provided with the necessary puncheons for the preparation of the dies, they would for many years adhere to the same type, though possibly slightly modified in some of its details. It is indeed inconceivable that the same engraver, who in his youth engraved dies which would produce coins like Plate A, No. 1, should in his old age, have, by constantly attempting to reproduce the same design, resulted in engraving such a burlesque upon it as that in Plate C, No. 12; or D, No. 13. So that though new types originated in the manner already described, they were in some measure due to the dies being engraved by fresh artists (if they are worthy the name), and possibly in fresh districts. A gradual diminution in the weight of the coins to the extent of 30 per cent., accompanied as it is by a debasement of the metal to apparently about the same extent, could only have been effected by spreading it over a lengthened period of time. I think that from 100 to 150 years is but a reasonable allowance for so complete a change in type and weight; and taking this in conjunction with the conclusions which have been obtained by the other methods of investigation here employed, we may regard it as, to say the least of it, highly probable that there was a native coinage in some parts of Britain as early as 150 B.C., if not earlier.

Assuming the diminution in weight to have been constant, and that the Philippus of 133 grains was first imitated in B.C. 300, and that the weight had become reduced to 84 grains in B.C. 20, the date at which the weight of 120 grains (that of our British prototype) would have been reached, is B.C. 226, but it is possible that the ratio of diminution was rather less rapid at first than subsequently. Looking at all the coincident circumstances, we may, I think, fix on B.C. 150 as the approximate date for the commencement of the British coinage. Had more been known as to the condition of the different parts of southern Britain at that early period, and as to the geographical range of certain types, and the districts in which they were originally struck, we might possibly have the use of coins carried back to a still earlier date, for Gaulish coins, even more closely allied to the Philippus than what I may term our indigenous prototype, have occasionally been found in England.

CHAPTER III.

ARRANGEMENT.

It now remains for me to say a few words as to the manner in which I have arranged the coins of the Ancient Britons in the following work, and to notice some of their general characteristics, especially in relation to their geographical distribution. It will be seen that the plates of the coins form two distinct series: the one lettered A to E, and the other numbered I. to XVII. The former comprises the uninscribed coins, and the latter those which bear inscriptions, as well as a few anepigraphous coins which can safely be assigned to certain districts. In the uninscribed series the first five plates contain the principal types of the gold coins; the next two, those in silver and copper; the next, those in tin; and the last, those of the Channel Islands, which, however, more properly belong to the Gaulish series. The classification of the uninscribed coins in accordance with the metal of which they are composed may possibly be regarded as unscientific. It must, however, be borne in mind that the silver and tin coinages commenced at a much later period than the gold, and that generally speaking they follow different prototypes. It would of course have been much more satisfactory had I been able to arrange all the coins in accordance with the different districts of the country in which they were probably struck; but, as I have already observed, there are not at present sufficient facts on record to enable me to do so, though in the description of each particular coin I have, where there was any circumstance to guide me, pointed out its probable home. I have, moreover, in the last two plates of the gold coins, grouped together various types which appear to be peculiar to Surrey and Sussex. In the other three plates the types may be regarded as following generally, though by no means exactly, their chronological order. It must not be supposed that in these five plates I have given representations of all the varieties of type which the uninscribed gold coins present: the mere alteration of the position of the flan, with regard to the dies (which were always larger than the coins struck from them), causes a considerable difference in the appearance of coins even from the same dies; and besides this, there are numerous minor details which vary on different coins of much the same general type, some of which I have occasionally mentioned in the descriptions. In one or two instances, I have placed among the uninscribed coins some which in reality belong to the inscribed series, but which, from their not having been properly placed on the dies, do not show their legends; but when this has been done (as in Plate C, No. 12), it has been mainly with the view of showing the intimate connection between their types and those really uninscribed. Some remarks with regard to the uninscribed silver, brass, and tin coins, will be found prefixed to the descriptions of the plates in which they are engraved, so that I need say no more at present as to the arrangement adopted for the anepigraphous series. That of the inscribed series is described farther on, and an introductory account is prefixed to the descriptions of the coins of each particular prince or district.

I will now, therefore, attempt to trace, in a succinct manner, the rise and progress of the art of coining in the different districts of Britain in which it was practised, having reference more particularly to the uninscribed series.

Although we have assigned the date of about 150 B.C. for the commencement of the British coinage, it is hard to say, with any degree of certainty, in what part of the country it actually commenced. The study of this class of coins is to some extent like that of geology: we have no written history on which to fall back, and the annals of the past have to be reconstructed from the evidence of contemporary yet dumb witnesses disinterred from the soil. But the numismatist has none of those aids which the geologist derives from the order of superposition, and the mineral characters of the rocks in which his fossils are preserved; and in the case of uninscribed coins, has nothing but the type and its geographical range on which to found any conclusion, unless, as in some rare instances it happens, the coins are associated with others of more certain date. The mere fact of finding a single coin of a certain class in a certain locality proves nothing, but when a considerable number of coins of much the same type are found at different times, in places all within a certain district, the proof becomes almost conclusive that they were originally struck within that district. And this holds true even with gold coins, which from their greater value and relative portability, have, as a rule, a much wider range than those in silver and copper.

One of the difficulties which arise in attempting to fix the spot where the earliest British coins were struck, is the very wide range of what is evidently the prototype, for coins like Plate A, No. 4, have been found in numerous localities, all the way from Cornwall to Suffolk. In Cornwall, however, they were associated with coins of a much later date, so that after all it is possible that their more extensive range than that of other types may be due to their having been longer in circulation, though the system on which they were current among coins of less weight and baser metal is difficult of explanation. It is also possible that on the first introduction of the art of coining into this country, and for some time afterwards, there was a moderately close adherence to the forms of the prototype as originally introduced, and that no secondary types became specialised in any particular district.

But in whatever manner and under whatever circumstances the first modifications of the original prototype originated, one thing is certain, that the currency of the British coins was, for a time, limited to the southern and eastern parts of

Britain, though it afterwards extended as far northwards along the eastern coast as Yorkshire. That this should have been the case, is quite in accordance with what the statements of the early historians would lead us to expect. In Cæsar's time, as we have already seen, the coast of Britain opposite to Gaul had long been tenanted by Belgic tribes, and the tribes of the interior are described as far more barbarous, and unacquainted even with agriculture, though possessing flocks and herds. The Silures of South Wales are expressly cited by Solinus,* as refusing money and employing simply barter, and Mela† relates that the tribes, the farther they were from the continent, the more ignorant were they of other riches than flocks and territory. The immigrants from the continent, who had driven back the earlier inhabitants into the interior, were no doubt considerably in advance of them in civilization, but it seems impossible to affix the limits of the territory possessed by each of the contending races at any given time. There is, however, a strong probability that the boundary of the country possessed by the Belgic tribes was from time to time extended. In consequence of this difficulty of defining the territory occupied by the different tribes, I have in the case of the inscribed coins preferred referring them to different districts, rather than to particular tribes. In the case of the uninscribed coins the same rule must be adopted, and I think that what few remarks I have to make on the subject of the extension of the use of coins through Britain, will be better understood if in general I refer to our present counties rather than to any more ancient division of the country, though mentioning the instances where any series of types seem to have been peculiar to a certain district, and therefore to have been struck by some particular tribe.

Returning then to the prototype, Plate A, Nos. 1 to 5 (for the smaller pieces are the quarters of the larger, and belong to the same period), I am, notwithstanding its wide range, much inclined to the opinion that its original home

* Cap. xxii. or al. xxii. † Lib. iii. c. 6.

was Kent. At all events, that is the county in which, as far as we have at present any record of the places where these coins have been found, they seem to be most abundant. We have, too, seen in the preceding chapter, that that part of Britain must have been from an early period in close connection with Gaul, and where, therefore, we might well expect that the acquaintance with a metallic currency originated. In this county, also, various modifications of the prototype have been found, but there are not many which can be said to be peculiar to it. Among the gold coins, Plate D, Nos. 7 and 8 are both frequently discovered in Kent, the latter also in Sussex, and Plate F, No. 15, and G, No. 13, seem to belong to it among the silver and brass, though these are of comparatively late date, and may possibly prove to have been inscribed. Some of the tin coins engraved in Plate H have been found in Kent and Middlesex, but we do not know enough about them to be at all certain as to the extent of their range. Its inscribed coins are described under Eppillus, Dubnovellaunus, Vosenos, and Amminus.

From the south-eastern parts of Kent the use of coins appears to have extended westwards and northwards, but we have no means at present of judging of the exact course it followed, or of the time it took to reach the more distant parts of the country. Following it westward along the coast, the counties of Sussex and Hants (comprising the territory of the Regni, and part, at all events, of the Belgæ) are those which first claim our attention, and they have some types peculiar to themselves. Among the larger and heavier coins which approach in character more nearly to the prototype, there are none which I can assign with confidence to this district, though no doubt several types were there struck. It seems possible, however, that the curious coins, Plate D, Nos. 2, 3, 4, belong to it, and that they are of Gaulish parentage—originating possibly with some Gaulish tribe which traded with Britain—rather than descended from the common British prototype. The coins most nearly approaching this latter, and which can with certainty be assigned to this district, are Plate E, Nos. 1, 2, 3, which are most common in Sussex and Hants. Plate E, Nos. 6 to 10, belong to the same counties, but Nos. 9 and 10 are also not uncommon on the French coast. The remainder of the coins in Plate E may be assigned to these two counties, with the exception of Nos. 13 and 14, which possibly may belong to Kent and Middlesex. Plate D, Nos. 9 and 10, have occasionally been found in Sussex. These types also are most intimately allied with some of those found in France.

Judging from the great variety of types, and the strange metamorphoses which the laureate head of Apollo and the charioteer have undergone, the uninscribed coinage of Kent and this part of Britain must have been of considerable duration. There was, at all events, time for the head entirely to disappear, as in Plate D, Nos. 8 and 10, or to leave merely a trace of its wreath, as in Plate E, Nos. 13, 14, in the shape of a projecting ridge across the field; and for the horse and driver to have been still more strangely distorted, as on Plate E, Nos. 9, 10, and 11, on which not a trace of their original form can be recognised. And it was not until the coins had thus degenerated, that the earliest of the inscribed series began to be struck in this district, which, though dating but few years after Cæsar's invasion, were, as will be seen, founded on such types as Plate D, No. 5, and Plate E, No. 10. The silver coinage of Surrey and Sussex appears to have commenced long after the gold, and to have been formed upon a different model, though also probably of Gaulish origin. Nos. 10 to 12 in Plate F were probably struck here, but there are no types in copper or brass that can be assigned to these counties. The inscribed coins are those struck by Tinc[ommius] and Verica.

Proceeding westward we find that the prototype with the laureate head, after passing through various phases, and becoming considerably modified, especially as to its reverse, assumed the forms shown on Plate B, Nos. 5 and 6, under which it took root in Dorsetshire, Wilts, and part of Hants; but whether the coins were struck by the Belgæ or Durotriges, or by both, I will not pretend to determine, though I think it must have been by the tribe last mentioned. It seems to have been the case that the type, having arrived at this state of degradation, was so easy to copy, that it offered little or no inducement for variation, and accordingly became persistent. The head may still be readily recognised, but the horse on the reverse is so much altered, that its neck and body have, by many, been considered to be the golden knife said to have been used by the Druids for cutting the sacred misletoe, which also was found upon the coin in the bunch of pellets above, though these are, in fact, merely the decomposed remains of the winged charioteer. The large gold coins range in weight from 103 to 92 grains, and there are none of the smaller pieces.

It is remarkable that in this district both silver and brass coins (Plate F, Nos. 1, 2, 3; G, Nos. 5, 6) were struck of the same module and the same type as the gold; whereas, in all the other parts of Britain, the coins of the inferior metals were, as a rule, of smaller size and of different types. There is another peculiarity attaching to this district, viz., that it never had an inscribed coinage; though a little to the north, in Somersetshire, Gloucestershire, and part of Wilts, an inscribed currency was developed, but apparently at a late period, and derived from a different modification of the prototype, and comprising silver coins of a totally different module and character. This affords a good instance of the difficulties (already alluded to) that there are in reconciling the districts to which certain types of British coins are peculiar, and which must therefore, at the time when they were current, have been inhabited by some particular tribe, with the geographical limits assigned to the various tribes by Ptolemy. According to his account, the territory of the Belgæ comprised Ischalis, Aquæ Calidæ, and Venta—*Ilchester*, *Bath*, and *Winchester*—and must, therefore, have included nearly the whole of Somersetshire, Wilts, and Hants; and yet in each of those counties we find a coinage totally distinct from any of the others. The coins of ANTEDRIGUS, CATTI, COMVX, &c., Plate I., Nos. 4 to 9, are most abundant near Frome, or midway between Bath and Ilchester; the coins of Tinc[ommius], Plate L., No. 11, to Plate II., No. 8, and some of the uninscribed coins in Plate E, are most abundant in Hampshire, while the uninscribed coins of which I have just been speaking range through Dorsetshire and Southern Wilts, and occasionally as far east as Portsmouth. Allowing them, as is probably the case, to have been struck by the Durotriges, yet it must be evident that the territory of the Belgæ could not, at the time when the Somersetshire coins were struck, have been of anything like the extent described by Ptolemy. It seems far more probable that at that period the Belgæ may have occupied only the eastern part of Hants and the western part of Sussex, and that some of the coins there found were struck by them.

But to return from this digression. The evidence which we at present possess, as to the extension of the British coinage westward beyond the territory of the Durotriges, is but slight. It appears, indeed, doubtful whether the Damnonii, who occupied Devonshire and Cornwall, though not entirely unacquainted with the use of money, ever had a coinage of their own, though possibly the coin found at Mount Batten, near Plymouth (Plate C, No. 4), may belong to this tribe. It must, however, be observed that I have met with no record of any other purely British coins found in Devonshire. The only discovery of British coins in Cornwall with which I am acquainted is that of Karn Brê (described in Borlase's Antiquities of Cornwall, p. 242, and in his Natural History, p. 322); and this seems to have been an isolated hoard, composed of coins of three classes, which are more commonly found in the southern counties, to the east of Devonshire.

Turning, now, to the more inland counties, to the west of Kent, we find that in Surrey the same modification of the original prototype (Plate B, Nos. 5, 6) as was in use in Dorsetshire and Wilts occasionally occurs, and even extends as far as Oxfordshire and Bucks. There must, however, have been other forms, from which the comparatively late types (Plate D, Nos. 6, 7, 8), which have been found only in Surrey, were derived. Nos. 9, 10, and 11 seem also to be peculiar to that county. Still further westward, in and around Berkshire, in what is commonly considered to have been the territory of the Atrebatii, we find coins of the types Plate B, Nos. 9 and 10, though the latter has a wide range, and was present in great numbers in the large hoard found at Whaddon Chase, as well as occurring in Sussex and elsewhere. The silver coins Plate F, Nos. 4 to 6, probably also belong to this part of Britain, while Plate F, Nos. 7 and 8, show the form the type assumed still farther west, though struck at a later period, when inscriptions were in use on the coins. In fact, the introduction of the use of money into Gloucestershire and the north of Wilts and Somerset does not appear to have taken place until some time after the days of Julius Cæsar. The coins inscribed BODVOC, found chiefly in Gloucestershire and the western part of Oxfordshire, seem to have been struck among the Boduni, and though based on a very late modification of the prototype, on which the obverse had entirely lost its original device and become perfectly plain, they seem to be the earliest coins of the district.

In Buckinghamshire and Oxfordshire, the district occupied by the Catyeuchlani, various early types have been found, but those peculiar to these counties are Plate C, Nos. 5 to 8. Nos. 9, 10, and 14 in the same plate belong probably to Herts, Beds, and Essex—the country of the Trinobantes, where, however, various of the earlier types are also found. The copper coins Plate G, Nos. 7 to 10, belong to the same part of Britain. It is to the territory occupied by the two tribes just mentioned, that the inscribed coins of Anduco-[mius], Tasciovanus, and Cunobelinus are to be assigned. Those of Epaticcus, and some of Tasciovanus, with SEGO upon them, appear to have been struck among the Segontiaci, whose territory lay farther west, and must have abutted on that of the Atrebatii.

Journeying northwards, there are no types which can at present be certainly assigned to the midland counties, though, no doubt, some of the modifications of the original prototype were there struck, and formed links in the chain which connects it with its very barbarous descendants in Norfolk and Yorkshire (Plates XIV. and XVII.), which are more particularly described farther on, and were probably struck by the Iceni and the Brigantes. The inscribed coins of Addedomaros, some of which exhibit the cruciform phase of the prototype, appear to have been struck in the southern part of the territory usually assigned to the Iceni, and the silver coins Plate G, Nos. 2 to 4, and those in copper, Plate G, Nos. 11 and 12, belong probably to the same part of the country. It is, however, needless to enter into further details, especially as so much uncertainty as to their original home attaches to many of the types; and, moreover, what little can be said concerning each will be found in the description of the Plates.

It would, however, appear probable from the brief summary I have here given, that the knowledge of the art of coining having been first communicated to some part of the south-eastern coast, most probably Kent, gradually spread from thence as a centre, and was adopted in the different districts of Britain which I have mentioned, at different periods, varying in time somewhat in proportion to the distances of each from the centre; while the coinage of each district derived its character in a great degree from the peculiar modification of the prototype with which it was first made acquainted.

The influence of the intercourse with Rome upon the character of the coinage will be treated of when I come to the inscribed portion of the series; but I have little doubt that in nearly every part of Britain where an inscribed coinage was current, one that was uninscribed had preceded it, and that, in most instances, the use of this uninscribed currency preceded the Roman invasion.

The use of money at so early a period in this country will no doubt appear almost incredible to those who have been accustomed to regard the Ancient Britons as the merest barbarians; but I think that such persons will find that their impressions as to the character of the Britons, have been derived from the descriptions of the tribes of the interior, rather than of those along the seaboard, who were mainly of Belgic origin, and to whom, for at all events a considerable period, the use of money was confined.

With regard to the sources from which the gold was derived for the coins, it appears probable that some of it at least was of native production. As I have already observed, gold is mentioned by both Strabo and Tacitus as one of the products of this country; and there is no doubt that the alluvial deposits of many of the streams of south-western Britain may have at one time contained gold to a considerable extent. Up to the present day, gold is still found in small quantities in Cornwall; and Borlase (Nat. Hist., p. 214) mentions a nugget found in the parish of Creed, near Granpont, in 1756, which weighed 15 dwt. 10 grains.

As to the method by which the coins were struck, we have no certain means of judging; but it seems likely that the dies in use amongst the Ancient Britons were of much the same character as the very curious die lately discovered at Avenches, in Switzerland,* and communicated to the Archæological Institute by Dr. Ferdinand Keller, of Zurich. This die, which is intended for striking the obverse side of one of the Helvetian degenerate imitations of the Philippus, consists of a disc of bronze inlaid in a cylindrical block of iron, probably with a view of preventing the expansion of the bronze. This latter metal is one of the hard alloys of copper and tin, with probably more of tin in its composition than ordinary bronze. The surface of the die is concave, so as to produce the convexity of surface so common among the coins of this class; and one reason for this concavity of the die appears to have been that the coins were struck from nearly spherical pieces of metal which were heated, and prevented from rolling in their place, while being struck, by the concavity of the lower die, which in all cases was that for the head or obverse

* Arch. Journ., vol. xii. p. 253.

side. It is said that on the surface of the bronze of this Helvetian die, around the head, are slight striæ, indications of a scraping or shaving instrument, employed in producing the concavity of the die; but such striæ may, I think, arise also from the effects of the expansion of the bullet-shaped *flans* when struck. It is certain that a striation of the surface, probably arising from this cause, may be frequently observed on the British coins; and coins are also occasionally found which have evidently been struck from the same die, though in a different state of wear. The devices upon the dies appear to me to have usually been produced by punches, rather than with the graver, though probably both were used; and looking at the character of the only die of the kind which at present is known, and looking at the minuteness of the differences which we occasionally find in coins apparently from distinct dies, it appears to me probable that, one die having been prepared, others were cast from it in bronze, and slightly retouched with the graver afterwards, so that duplicate dies could be reproduced at small expense. Of course this is merely conjecture.

That the Britons were accomplished workers in metal is beyond all doubt; but that they should have understood the art, not only of coining, but of counterfeiting coins, may appear surprising, as the art of forgery is usually regarded as one of the accompaniments of a high degree of civilisation. We have, however, numerous examples of these ancient forgeries, and I may cite imitations of the gold coins of Addedomaros, Dubnovellaunus, and Cunobeline, and of silver coins of Tasciovanus, as instances. Of the uninscribed coins ancient forgeries are rare—but I have met with one or two. The false gold coins are of copper or bronze, covered all over with a thin plating of gold, but which has been strong enough not to shell off when struck by the dies; and the silver coins have been fabricated in the same way, the *flans* having in each case been plated with the more precious metal before being struck. It has only been in consequence of the oxidisation of the inner core of baser metal that the fact of the coins being plated has now become apparent.

But enough has now been said as to the general character and distribution of the ancient British coinage, and I will therefore enter upon a more particular description of each of the coins in the plates. In doing this it will be convenient to make use of some terms which are not, I think, generally recognised in numismatics, but which the peculiar character of the coinage under consideration renders convenient. One of these in most frequent use is the term "ring ornament," which I have used for a circle, inclosing a dot in the centre, like the astronomical sign ☉; an ornament which, from the facility with which it can be engraved, has always been in constant use among uncivilised nations. When a ring ornament of this kind is surrounded by an outer circle of dots or beads, I have termed it a "decorated ring ornament." When a central pellet is surrounded by a circle of smaller pellets or ovals, I have called it a "rosette," or "star of pellets;" and when a pellet or roundle has a smaller pellet standing up in relief upon it, I have termed it an "ornamented pellet." In other respects I have as far as possible confined myself to the usual numismatic terms; or, where convenient for the description of forms, to the terms used in heraldry.

CHAPTER IV.

UNINSCRIBED GOLD COINS.

PLATE A, No. 1.

Obv.—Beardless bust to the right, the face projecting far beyond the neck, which is covered with drapery, or possibly a gorget, ornamented with plain and beaded lines. The front hair is represented by solid crescents, and the hair of the back of the head is arranged in tiers of flowing locks; across the head is a wreath formed of solid crescents, their points downwards; and at right angles to this, there is a plain band round the back of the head, terminating in a hook over the ear.

Rev.—Horse to the right, the lower joint of each leg divided into two, so as to give, in fact, eight legs. There is also some appearance of a double body. Below, a rosette; and above, an attempt to represent a winged victory, with a number of pellets in front, for the most part arranged in groups of four. In front of the horse, a diamond. *N*. 111 grains.

This type is remarkable from the bust having a much larger face than that usually found on the coins of this class, and is of considerable rarity; the specimen engraved, from my own collection, being the only one with which I am acquainted. I am not able to say in what part of the country it was found. Though differing in execution, the type so closely resembles that of No. 2 that any remarks upon it will be more in place when describing the next coin. Like the two subsequent coins it is slightly dished—or convex on the obverse, and concave on the reverse—and, like them, it is of fine gold.

Plate A, No. 2.

Obs.—Laureate beardless bust in profile, similar to that on No. 1, but the face smaller, and the gorget or drapery of the neck brought more forward. The crescents forming the front hair are slightly open. The back hair is arranged in two tiers, that nearest the wreath being the smaller of the two, and the wreath is formed of distinct leaves, their points downwards.

Rev.—Horse to the right; the legs represented by double lines, and the joints of the hind legs forming trefoils. Above, a Victory and various pellets, as on No. 1; below, a rosette; in front, crescents and pellets; behind, an oval wheel, or ring ornament. There is an exergual line, with traces of a row of ornaments below it. *N.* 118½ grains.

This coin is in my own collection. I have another specimen more closely resembling No. 4, but with the types the reverse way, which weighs but barely 100 grains. The wreath upon the head is formed of solid crescents.

Coins of this type are engraved in Wise, pl. xvi. 1, Stukeley, pl. xv. 4, Gough's Camden, No. 8, and in the map of Thurstable Hundred, &c., in Morant's Essex. The coin in the latter instance is reported to have been found at Ardley, Essex. The coin engraved in Stukeley, pl. iii. 10, belongs to this class, and is attributed by that learned antiquary to "Immanuentius," the father of Mandubratius, on grounds which it is now impossible to ascertain, but which probably are about as good as those on which he assigns two Celtiberian coins engraved with it to the same prince.

There can be no doubt of the derivation of the types, both of the obverse and reverse, of these coins, from those of the stater of Philip II. of Macedon (p. 24), though much has still to be learned as to the process of the derivation, and the successive phases the types must have gone through before reappearing in these forms. The Gaulish series does not seem to supply the intermediate links in the chain; so that, possibly, this British type must be regarded more as an original type, founded on that of the Philippus, than as merely a debased copy of it—a nationalised adoption of the head of Apollo* and the biga, and not simply an imitation of them. There can be no doubt that the types of the Gaulish imitations of the Philippus were, in many instances, greatly modified, in accordance with the religious belief of the people, and the national mythology; so that it is probable that the same influences may have produced their effect on the coinage of the Ancient Britons. Certainly the drapery or gorget on the neck, and the band with pendent hooks around the head, are peculiarities only found on this and the subsequent modifications of the type of the Philippus, and not on the original coin. The regular arrangement of the hair in tiers may possibly have been made to suit the engraver's convenience, but more probably this carefully dressed hair is one of the attributes of the Apollo Belinus of Gaul and Britain, whose head it has been supposed is here represented. *Crinitus* and *Intonsus* are epithets given by the Roman poets to Apollo, who is usually represented with long flowing locks both on Greek and Roman coins. Among the Gauls, the length of their hair gave rise to the name of Gallia Comata for one of the divisions of their country; while among many northern nations, length of hair was one of the characteristics of royalty.

The type of the reverse is also rather a reminiscence than a direct imitation of that of the Philippus. The chariot of the biga has nearly disappeared, or is at most represented by an ill-formed wheel, while the charioteer has become merged in a winged figure, probably Victory,† leaning far forward and nearly touching the horse's head. The two horses of the biga are combined into one, but in remembrance

---

* Leake (*Numismata Hellenica*, p. 3), and some other writers, regard the head upon the staters as that of a young Hercules, rather than an Apollo. I have, however, following Eckhel and others, preferred to regard it as being Apollo.

† This Victory may possibly have been originally adopted from some of the gold coins of Sicily, on which it is of frequent occurrence.

of its former duality, the legs are bifid. Had the renowned Sleipnir, the eight-legged horse of the Edda, which excelled all horses ever possessed by gods or men, had its portrait drawn, it would have presented much the same appearance. The exergual line is still preserved, but the inscription beneath it is only represented by a line of unmeaning ornaments. Whether the pellets in front of the Victory, the rosette beneath the horse, or the various objects in the field of these and many of the succeeding coins, were intended to have any symbolical meaning or mythological reference I will not attempt to determine. It appears to me that in most cases the adjuncts found upon the numerous degraded imitations of this type are merely the result of the engraver's laziness or incompetence, where they are not attributable to his ignorance of what the objects he was copying were originally designed to represent. And though I am willing to recognise a mythological and national element in this adaptation of the Macedonian stater, which forms the prototype of the greater part of the ancient British series, it is but rarely that this element can be traced with certainty upon its numerous subsequent modifications.

I have placed these coins at the commencement of the series as undoubtedly the most ancient, though probably those with the head and chariot in the other direction, Nos. 4 and 5, are of much the same period. I am not aware of any coins of the type of Nos. 1 and 2 having been found on the continent, and they are of much greater rarity in England than those with the devices turned in the other direction.

Plate A, No. 3.

Obv. and Rev.—Similar to No. 2.

N. 25 grains. Others 22, 26¼, 26¾, 27 grains.

This coin is the fourth part of those last described, though the specimens I have met with do not, any of them, quite come up to one-fourth of the weight of the larger pieces. That engraved from my own collection weighs 25 grains. They

are, however, usually much worn. These small coins present
several minor variations, and are equally common with the
large. Examples will be found engraved in Ruding, pl. i.
21, and Borlase's Natural History of Cornwall, pl. xxix. 8.
This latter was probably found at Karn Brê. I have two
specimens which were found in Kent, one of them at Mount
Ephraim, near Ash. A somewhat similar type is engraved
in Wise, pl. xvi. 13, but it is probably a modification of
this, and of rather later date, being more like Plate E, No. 2.
Compare also Lambert, pl. ii. 2.

PLATE A, No. 4.

Obv.—Precisely similar bust to that on No. 2, but turned to the
left instead of to the right.

Rev.—Horse and Victory, similar to those on No. 2, but turned
to the left. In front of the horse, triangles, crescents,
&c.; beneath, a radiated rosette, the lower part cut
off by the exergual line.

 ʀ. 114 grains. Usual weight, 107 to 120 grains.

The coins of this type vary considerably in module, being
from seven-eighths of an inch, to an inch and one-eighth in
diameter, and giving more or less of the design in proportion
to their size; they are occasionally much dished, but sometimes almost flat. There are also many varieties in the
ornamentation on the neck of the bust, and in the accessories on the field of the reverse and beneath the horse.
On a coin in the British Museum (116 grains) there is a star
of five points immediately above the horse, and traces of the
head of the second horse of the biga.

As the type has been so frequently engraved, I have con-
tented myself with giving a single specimen from my own
collection, which was found at Leighton Buzzard in 1849,
and which, though weighing only 114 grains, is the best
spread coin of the type I have ever seen. I have entries of
the discovery of other coins at Barden, near Tonbridge
Wells; near Gravesend; near Godalming; near Leatherhead; at Wildhall, near Hatfield; and at Stoke, Suffolk.
Other specimens have also been found at Oxted, Surrey

(Hawkins, pl. i. 4); Swanscombe, near Gravesend; Northfleet, and Boxley, near Maidstone (Beale Poste, p. 138, No. 1); at Erith, Kent (116 grains) (Arch. Assoc. Journal, xiii. p. 334); at Sutton Valence, Kent (107 grains) (Coll. Ant., vol. i. pl. vi. 4); at Birchington, Thanet (109 grains) (Coll. Ant., vol. i. pl. iv. 1); at Layer de la Haye, near Colchester (Num. Soc. Procs., April 27th, 1843); and at Karn Brê (110 grains) (Borlase, Ant. pl. xix. 16).

Engravings of this type will be found in Ruding, pl. i. 17, 18, and 19; Wise, pl. xvi. 2; Stukeley, pl. iii. 7; Gough's Camden, Nos. 50 and 51; Lambert, pl. vi. 14; and Lelewel, pl. viii. 33.

It will be seen from the list of localities where these coins have been found, that they are most abundant in Kent, though occurring as far west as Cornwall, and ranging in the other direction into Suffolk. They are by no means rare in England, and though Lambert and Lelewel claim this type as Gaulish, and even attribute it to the Bellovaci, yet neither gives an instance of the coins having been discovered on the continent, and Lelewel refers to Ruding for the type, while Lambert cites a coin in the *Cabinet Royal de Paris*, which may possibly have been purchased originally in this country. M. de Saulcy, however, informs me that coins of this type, both large and small, have been found near Beauvais. I have also seen one at Ghent, presumably found near that town. But on the whole evidence there can be but little doubt of their being of British rather than Gaulish origin. There is one remarkable feature in the British series as connected with these coins, viz., that though the head and horse upon them are to the left, and though they are of far more common occurrence than Nos. 2 and 3, with the designs to the right, yet every derivative from the type of the widespread head (and this embraces nearly the whole of the British series in gold) may, with hardly an exception, be traced to the prototype with the head to the right, even if, as in the case in some coins, the horse on the reverse is turned to the left.

PLATE A, No. 5.

Obv.—Laureate bust to the left, as on No. 4.
Rev.—Horse and Victory to the left, as on No. 4.
 N. 23¼ grains. Usual weight, 20 to 28 grains.

There is considerable variation in the module of these quarter-staters, but more diversity in the expression and size of the face than in the details of the type. They are found over nearly the same district as the coins last described. Besides the one engraved, with whose place of finding I am not acquainted, I have one that was discovered at Wendover, Bucks (20 grains), and others from the collection of the late Mr. Rolfe, of Sandwich, discovered at Elham, Kent, weighing 27¼ grains, and in Thanet, 20 grains. Specimens have also been found at Harrietsham, Kent (Arch. Assoc. Journ., vol. v. p. 82); Walmer (27 grains) (Coll. Ant., vol. i. pl. iv. 9); and at Karn Brê, Cornwall (25 and 26 grains) (Borlase Ants., pl. xix. 14 and 15).

Engravings of the type are also given in Ruding, pl. i. 20; Wise, pl. xvi. 14; White, No. 9; Gough's Camden, Nos. 48 and 49; Borlase's Nat. Hist. of Cornwall, pl. xxix. 7; and Beale Poste, p. 139, No. 7. These coins must be of extremely rare occurrence on the continent, as Lelewel (pl. iv. 10) borrows his engraving from Ruding, and Lambert does not give the type.

PLATE A, No. 6.

Obv.—Wide-spread laureate bust, in profile, to the right. The hair arranged in flowing and contorted locks. The wreath crossed by the band terminating in a hook; the neck covered with an ornamental gorget, as on No. 1. Two spikes project from the centre of the band, so as partly to fill up the spaces between the coils of hair.

Rev.—Peculiarly-formed horse, with a beaded mane, having the last joints of his legs split into two, and his tail forming a sort of trident at the point of insertion. Above, a rude wingless figure, holding an S-shaped object in his right hand. In front of the horse, a rosette and small cross; below, a solid crescent reversed, and a bird-like object; a zigzag below the exergual line. *N*. 115 grains.

A coin of this type, weighing 114 grains, was found at Over, Cambridgeshire, in 1802, and is now in my own collection. The head on the obverse differs slightly from that here engraved (which is also in my own collection), but the reverse is precisely similar. Another is engraved by Lelewel, pl. viii. 23, which, being struck from a different part of the dies, supplies some details not given in my coin, and which I have incorporated in the description. Lelewel's coin is taken from De Basto, and the original is said to have been found in Belgic Gaul; but though it is attributed by Lelewel, by no means confidently, to the Bellovaci (the same tribe to whom he assigned Nos. 4 and 5), yet it seems to me to have much greater affinity with the British than with the Gaulish coinage, and the fact of one of the coins having been found in Cambridgeshire points to the same conclusion. It is true that the arrangement of the hair is different from what is usually found on coins of British origin, yet many of the coins found at Whaddon Chase (see Plate C, No. 5) appear to have been derived from a prototype with the hair arranged in some such manner as on these coins, and the bandlet across the wreath and the decoration on the neck are such as appear to be peculiar to Britain. The horse on the reverse is also British in its character, as are likewise the various accessories in the field, the most remarkable of which is the bird-like object, to which I shall presently refer. It is remarkable that the small cruciform object in front of the horse appears also on the coins of the West of England (see Plate I.), which there is reason to suppose belong to a much later period.

The coin I have engraved was probably found in England, as it formerly formed part of the Pembroke collection. It is engraved in Pt. ii. pl. 94, of the Pembroke Coins; a woodcut of it is also given in Wright's Celt, Roman, and

Saxon, p. 84, but it is there considered to be Gaulish. In my attribution of this type to Britain, I am happy to say that I am borne out by Mr. Beale Poste, who at p. 139 of his work on British coins has engraved the coin given by Lelewel, and has shown reasons for assigning it to this country.

An additional reason may be gathered from the place of finding of the following coin.

PLATE A, No. 7.

Obv.—Laureate bust to the right, closely allied to that on No. 6.

Rev.—The eight-legged horse to the right, with a wingless figure above, a bird-like object below, and an oval wheel, or ring ornament, behind. *N*.

There can be no doubt that this is the fourth part of the former coin, the types being almost identical, and the same bird-like object being beneath the horse on both. What may be the meaning of this symbol I cannot say, but these are the only coins, whether British or Gaulish, on which I have observed it, so that it places beyond all doubt the relationship of the smaller and larger pieces.

Now the smaller coin, No. 7, was found on a farm called Stone Heap, in the parish of Northbrook, north-west of Dover, and as no similar coin has been, so far as I am aware, found in Gaul, the attribution of this class of coins to Britain is much strengthened by this discovery. I am indebted to Mr. Albert Way for impressions of the coin, which is now, I believe, in the Dover Museum. An account of its discovery is given in the Archaeological Journal, vol. xii. p. 84.

PLATE A, No. 8.

Obv.—Laureate bust to the right, similar to that on No. 2, though a smaller portion of it is visible, as it has been struck on a smaller flan.

Rev.—Horse to the right, with Victory above and rosette beneath, like that on No. 2, except as to the legs.

N. 109½ grains.

The specimen from which the engraving is made is in my own collection, but its place of finding is not known. It is, unfortunately, considerably worn, but it is of interest as presenting the bust in the transition state before the face becomes no longer recognisable. It is also remarkable as representing the horse with simple and fairly formed legs, instead of with the bifid extremities as on the previous coins.

Plate A, No. 9.

Obv.—Portion of laureate bust to the right, showing the wreath, portions of the hair, the decoration of the neck, and the bandlet across the wreath.

Rev.—Horse to the right, formed after a disjointed manner, the body being separated at the shoulder from the neck, which is "bird's beaked" on to it. The head is formed with a square nose, joined by two lines to a pellet. Above the horse are various pellets, and the remains of one of the arms of Victory. Towards the back is an elliptical figure, which represents the wheel of the biga; beneath is a pellet and a double ornamented exergual line. *N.* 95 grains.

This coin is of pale gold, considerably dished, and of rather peculiar workmanship, every portion of the design being thin and hard—presenting the same relative character, when compared with the other British coins, as the so-called Wire-money of George III. when contrasted with the rest of his Maundy money. It is to be observed that the leaves of the wreath, which on all the previous coins are pointed downwards, are on this one turned upwards, and are more rectangular in shape. The crooked termination of the covering of the neck, and the form of the crescents representing the hair around the forehead, are worthy of notice. The coin is in my own collection, but I am not aware of the place where it was found. One somewhat similar in character, especially as to the reverse, will be found in Ruding, pl. i. 15, from the Hunter collection. Its obverse shows the face more distinctly, and approaches more nearly to that of No. 9. It may, indeed, be regarded as a link between Nos. 8 and 9; its weight, 103½ grains, being also intermediate between them.

Plate A, No. 10.

Obv.—Remains of a laureate bust, apparently, to the right. The principal features are the two crescent-shaped objects representing the front hair; the face has disappeared, and the space is filled with a small square between two solid crescents, having in front a line of open diamonds. A portion only of the wreath is visible.

Rev.—Disjointed horse to the left; his fore-legs formed by straight lines ending in pellets. Above, various pellets, and some traces of the Victory; below, a solid crescent and a rosette of pellets, with some attempt at a beaded circle. It is difficult to say whether the crescent below the horse, on this and succeeding coins, is not part of the fore-leg.

N. 93 grains.

This coin is in the British Museum, and is engraved in Ruding, pl. i. 12. The place of finding is not known, but coins of this class are reported by Mr. Akerman (Num. Journ., vol. i. p. 221) to have been found in the inland counties.

Plate A, No. 11.

Obv.—Portion of laureate head to the right. The wreath and bandlet more apparent than on the last coin, and having different objects in front; among them one L-shaped figure, and a straight bar. The leaves of the wreath, above and below the bandlet, are turned in opposite directions.

Rev.—Horse to the left, much resembling that on No. 10, with remains of the Victory, and two elliptical ring ornaments above, and a crescent and pellet below. There is a zigzag exergual line, ornamented below with a series of crescents enclosing pellets, placed alternately upwards and downwards. *N*.

The coin from which the engraving was made was found near Loughborough, Leicestershire, in 1844, and is in the collection of the late T. Bateman, Esq., of Youlgrave. I have a specimen of the same type, but varying slightly in some of the details, which was presented to me by the Rev. H. Christmas, F.R.S. Its weight is 94 grains.

Plate A, No. 12.

Obv.—Portion of laureate head to the right, with only a small part of the wreath visible. The ornamentation on the neck forms a conspicuous object, and is similar in character to that upon No. 9, though much enlarged.

Rev.—Disjointed horse to the left; above, pellets, and a solid crescent reversed; below, a pellet and solid crescent. The exergue ornamented with a zigzag, having pellets in the angles. The legs of the horse have globular joints and feet, and the neck is deeply indented where it joins the body. *N*. 95 grains.

The coin here engraved was in the late Mr. Huxtable's collection, and formed a portion of the great hoard discovered at Whaddon Chase, though differing materially in type from the majority of the coins with which it was associated. The coin engraved by Stukeley, pl. iii. 4, may possibly have been of a similar type; and Ruding, pl. i. 13, though showing a different portion of the obverse, has a nearly similar reverse. The latter weighs 80¾ grains.

This and the succeeding coin exhibit strong proofs of a great difference in size between the dies and the coins struck from them. Though but little less than No. 2, which shows the whole bust, there is not much more than a third of it visible on either of these coins. In fact, coins as large as No. 12 might in all probability have been struck from the same obverse die, without showing any trace of the gorget on the neck, so as at first sight to have appeared of a totally different type.

Plate A, No. 13.

Obv.—Central portion of a laureate head to the right. The leaves of the wreath, which are large, rectangular and set at some distance apart, are turned upwards or

downwards, according as they are above or below the
bandlet across the head.

Rev.—Horse to the left, similar to that on No. 10; a reversed
solid crescent, and various globules above, among
which may be traced the two arms of Victory; a
larger pellet below. *N.* 91 grains.

On a very similar coin in the British Museum, weighing 91¼ grains, there is a radiated globe in front of the horse, and the legs have another joint carried beyond a double exergual line.

I have seen a coin of this type which was found in the neighbourhood of Buckingham. It is indeed evident that it is closely allied in type with the coin from Whaddon Chase, No. 12; and the discovery of both coins in Buckinghamshire, and of No. 11 near Loughborough, tends to show that this class of coins (Plate A, Nos. 10 to 13) belongs to the south midland district of England. The widespread head, which, if complete upon the dies, must have occupied a space twice the diameter of the coins, the entire absence of any attempt at a face, the character of the wreath, and the horse in all cases to the left, are all points of union. The agreement in weight, which ranges from about 90 to 95 grains, is also to be noticed.

Plate B, No. 1.

Obv.—Portion of a laureate head, similar to that on Nos. 11 to
13 of the last Plate. The leaves of the wreath are
all turned upward. There are traces of ornaments
in front in lieu of a face.

Rev.—Disjointed, square-nosed horse to the right, with a horn-
like ear. It has more the appearance of standing
than galloping, and has feet instead of mere globules
to stand on. Beneath is a pellet and a crescent,
which apparently forms part of the off fore-leg;
above may be recognised a portion of the two arms of
Victory; and in the field are various crescents, pellets,
and elliptical ring ornaments. There is an exergual
line, with the space below, divided into triangular
compartments, with pellets in each, like that on Plate A,
No. 12. *N.* 93¼ grains.

The specimen here engraved is in the collection at the British Museum, but I am not aware of its place of finding. From the character of the coin I am inclined to assign it to the Eastern Counties.

Plate B, No. 2.

Obv.—Similar to that of Plate A, No. 13, except that the field between the wreath and the front hair is covered with small dots, in the same way that "Or" is represented in heraldic engraving.

Rev.—Disjointed horse to the right, with globular feet; below, a rosette, with a large central pellet; and above, the mutilated remains of Victory, a solid crescent, and a number of pellets. Beneath the neck of the horse is a cross or four-pointed star, with curved rays. In front of the horse, a blazing star. The exergue is ornamented in the same manner as that of No. 1. *N.* 90 grains.

This is the same coin that is engraved in Ruding, pl. i. 11, the original being in the British Museum. I have a specimen, weighing $89\frac{1}{2}$ grains, which enables me to complete the description of the lower part of the coin. It is said to have been found in Norfolk. The most noteworthy feature on this coin is the cross-like figure beneath the horse's head, which may have been derived from that on No. 6 of Plate A. See also Plate C, No. 4, and Plate I., Nos. 1, 2, 3, 4, and 7, though these latter are of much later date.

Plate B, No. 3.

Obv.—Portion of laureate bust to the right, without any face, but the field of the coin slightly raised where the face ought to be; the wreath composed of leaves, and not of mere rectangular lumps.

Rev.—Completely disjointed horse, going in an uncertain direction, having neither head nor tail, and with only three legs visible. Above, a solid crescent, numerous pellets, and a chain-like band; below, a ring ornament, pellet, and annulet. The exergue ornamented as on the previous coins. *N.* $95\frac{1}{10}$ grains.

This coin was found at Waldingfield, Suffolk, in 1855, and was communicated to me by Professor Henslow, into whose possession it came, and who placed it in the Ipswich Museum. It is a curious instance of extreme degradation from the type of the Philippus on the reverse, while at the same time the bust on the obverse still retains its principal feature, if not its face.

PLATE B, No. 4.

Obv.—Portion of the laureate bust to the right, with a convex projection where the face should have been, but with no attempt to represent any features, though some parts of the device are continued beyond the projection. The wreath, and indeed the whole treatment, similar to that of the last coin.

Rev.—Disintegrated horse to the left; several globules above and one below; an almost rectangular solid crescent immediately above the horse's back. The horse, like that on the previous coins of the same Plate, has a horn-like ear. Æ. 96½ grains.

The coin here engraved is in my own collection, but its place of finding is unknown, though, like the preceding coins, it probably belongs to the Eastern Counties.

PLATE B, No. 5.

Obv.—Laureate bust to the right, with a single row of the locks of the back hair; the landlet across the wreath strongly developed; the three open crescents representing the front hair arranged in nearly a straight line, the upper one much the most open of the three; the drapery on the neck terminating in a curved pear-shaped object, and the face a mere swelling.

Rev.—Disjointed horse to the left; the line forming the neck and body curved upwards, and ending in a sort of three-beaked head, which appears to be pecking the horse's shoulder; the legs formed by straight lines terminating in pellets. Above are numerous globules, and below an elongated solid crescent, and a globule with four crooked rays, in general appearance something like a crab. Behind are three nearly horizontal lines connected with an elliptical ring ornament, usually beaked and looking like a bird's head, but the break sometimes formed with braked lines. Under the nose of the horse is occasionally a cross with curved arms, like that on Plate B, No. 2. The exergue is generally ornamented with a zigzag pattern like that on Plate B, No. 1.

N. 95½ grains. Usual weight about 95 grains.

This coin is in my own collection. I have another specimen, which formed part of the great Whaddon Chase hoard, and weighs 94½ grains. Others have been found near Tarring (95 grains) (Dixon's Sussex, p. 36), and near Dorchester (Durrner's sale, 1853). Mr. Durden, of Blandford, possesses specimens found near that town (92 grains), at Tarrant Gunville (92 grains), and at Sturminster Newton (93½ grains). The type is engraved in Ruding, pl. i. 9, and copied by Lelewel, pl. viii. 25. There are several varieties intermediate between this and the following coin. One with the horse to the right instead of to the left is engraved (whether erroneously or not I cannot say) in Wright's Celt, Roman, and Saxon, p. 84. They are considered by Akerman (Num. Journ., vol. i. p. 221) to be principally discovered on the southern coast, but to range as far as Oxfordshire; and I think that this view is correct. I have a note of one found at Swanliffe in that county. In general character the type is so closely allied to that of the next coin, that any remarks upon it may be made under the head of No. 6.

PLATE B, No. 6.

Obv.—Nearly similar to that of No. 5.

Rev.—Disintegrated horse to the left, similar to that on the last coin, but without the head-like adjuncts, and with a simple globule beneath the horse. The exergue as on No. 5. *N*. 90½ grains.

The specimen here engraved was found near Oxford, and is in my own collection. Others in the Museum collection were found near Wareham (94 grains), and at Horne, Surrey. Mr. Durden, of Blandford, has one found near Poole, Dorset (95 grains). Mr. Whitbourn has a specimen found near Basingstoke, and Mr. C. Roach Smith has communi-

cated to me one nearly similar found near Goodwood,
Sussex, in 1850. The coins found at Karn Brê in 1749, and
engraved in Borlase's Antiquities of Cornwall, pl. xix. 8 to
11 (98 to 103 grains), also belong to this class. The type
is engraved in Ruding, pl. i. 10, and in Poste's British
Coins, p. 139, No. 5. See also Stukeley, pl. xiii. 9. As
before remarked, it is closely allied to that of No. 5, and
also to that of No. 4. Very similar coins occur both in
silver and copper (see Plate F, Nos. 1, 2, and 3, and G,
Nos. 5 and 6).

The geographical range of this type seems to be extensive,
but the coarser and wider spread coins appear to belong to
the south-western part of England.

It is impossible to say what may have been intended by
the crab-like figure beneath the horse on No. 5, or the
strangely beaked figures upon it, though probably they
were originally intended to convey a meaning. There can,
however, be no doubt that the type of these coins as a
whole is a degenerate representation of that of Plate A,
Nos. 1 and 2, and that the globules or pellets in the field
are the legitimate descendants of those on the earlier coins,
which have, as might have been expected, increased and
multiplied.

PLATE B, No. 7.

Obv.—Portion of a laureate bust to the right; the protuberance
which represents the face usually showing the contour
of the cheek, and occasionally presenting an approach
to a profile.

Rev.—Dismembered horse of the same character as that on
Plate A, No. 1, but galloping to the right. Above
a solid crescent reversed, the arms of Victory, pellets,
and other objects; below, a globule.

N. 97 grains.

Coins of this type have been frequently found in Kent,
as for example, near Maidstone (102 grains) (Coll. Ant.,
vol. i. pl. vi. 5), and near Ryarsh (with an approach to
features in the face) (Num. Soc. Procs., January 24, 1861).

On another found near Elham, Kent (102 grains), from the collection of the late Mr. Rolfe, there are some curious dotted lines (something like those so frequently seen on the Gaulish gold coins) above the remains of Victory. I have seen another that was found near Gravesend. These coins are not, however, confined to Kent, for a number were found, towards the close of last century, near Haverhill, on the borders of Essex and Suffolk. One of these, weighing 101 grains, is engraved in the Gentleman's Magazine for 1793, pl. iii. fig. 2, p. 29; and another in the Numismatic Chronicle, vol. i. pl. ii. 14. About fifty coins were found in all, but it does not appear whether there were any other types among them. Another coin, rather more spread than usual, was found at Wootton, near Bedford, and is in the collection of the Rev. E. R. Williamson, of Campton, Beds. A very similar coin is engraved in Lelewel, pl. iv. 12, and some of the same type are said to have been found at Renaix sur l'Escaut in 1830. M. de Saulcy has shown me some found at Montreuil sur Mer, Maubeuge, and Longineul Ste. Marie.

It is to be remarked that the coins of this class are thicker and consequently less spread than many of those of even less weight. The coin engraved is in the British Museum.

PLATE B, No. 8.

Obv.—Plain and convex.

Rev.—Disjointed, tailless horse to the right; a pellet below; above, the arms of Victory, pellets, &c. The exergue is ornamented in various ways, sometimes with a cable and chain pattern, as on the coin engraved, sometimes with semicircles and pellets, as in Plate A, No. 11. On other specimens there is a simple cable, or the zigzag pattern as in Plate B, No. 3. Frequently the whole device is surrounded by a beaded circle. See Ruding, pl. i. 3 and 4.

N. 93 grains. Usual weight, 86 to 96 grains.

The obverse of these coins has in all cases been struck from dies having a concave recess (occasionally flattened, or with a band across its centre), and with a flat rim round it.

This rim has frequently had some indentations on it, which have sometimes almost the appearance of a legend when they happen to appear upon the coins. On some, these objects assume the form of S-shaped ornaments, somewhat resembling the locks of hair at the back of the head of the early coins, and of which they are possibly imitations.

There can be but little doubt that the engraver of the dies for this class of coins must in the first instance have copied a coin which had, or ought to have had, the laureate bust upon its convex side (possibly like Plate B, No. 7), but on which the bust had from wear, either of the die or coin, become obliterated, while the horse had still remained uninjured, having been protected by the concavity of the reverse. The raised band which occasionally runs across the obverse is a faint reminiscence of the wreath that forms so conspicuous a feature on the generality of the coins.

The coins of this type may be subdivided into two classes one represented by Ruding, pl. i. 1, 3, and 4; and the other by that here engraved, and that in the Numismatic Chronicle, vol. i. pl. ii. 2. Of each of these there are several minor varieties. The horses on those of the first have frequently a sort of spurs, something like those on a game cock, projecting from their hind-legs; or hair-like lines about the fetlock joints, as if they were of the cart-horse breed.

In the collection of the late Mr. Rolfe, of Sandwich, were specimens of the first class, found at Elham, in Kent (93 and 94½ grains), and at Folkstone (89 grains). Mr. Whitbourn, has one found near Godalming, with the exergue like that of Plate A, No. 11. The Rev. Mr. Pollexfen has one from Colchester. Coins of both classes were found in a field called the Golden Piece, near Ryarsh, in Kent (Num. Soc. Proc., Jan. 24, 1861), with a coin similar to Plate B, No. 7. The coin in Hawkins, pl. i. 1, was also found in Kent. Coins of the second class have been found near Barnet (93 grains), here engraved; at Sandown, Isle of Wight (Num. Chron., vol. i. pl. ii. 2; Revue Num., vol. iv. pl. xiii. 1); at Alfriston,

Sussex (97 grains) (Coll. Ant., vol. i. pl. vii. 4; Num. Soc. Procs., Dec. 23, 1841; Num. Chron., vol. vii. pl. iv. 1); near Broadstairs, in the late Mr. Rolfe's collection (80 grains and 92½ grains); near Sleaford, Lincolnshire, in the collection of A. Trollope, Esq., Lincoln; at Wiston and Pagham, Sussex (92½ grains), in the British Museum. In the collection of the Rev. Trafford Leigh was a coin of this type found at Dorchester, Oxon. Other coins have been found at Hadstock, Essex (91 grains) (Arch. Journ., vol. iv. p. 145), and on the shore at Sherringham, near Cromer (Arch. Journ., vol. iv. p. 252).

The type is also engraved in Stukeley, pl. xviii. 1; Wise, pl. xvi. 4, 5, and 7; Pembroke Coins, pt. ii. pl. 95; Borlase, Ants. of Cornwall, pl. xix. 10; and Gough's Camden, pl. i. 54.

Similar coins are of not unfrequent occurrence on the continent, mostly, if not always, of the first class. They are said by Lelewel to be found in the Belgic territory (pl. iii. 30), and are engraved as Gaulish in the Revue Numismatique, vol. ii. p. 82, pl. iii. 1, though reference is made to Gough's Camden. Others are engraved by Lambert, pl. vi. 3 and 4; pl. xi. bis, 11; but the place of finding is not given.

PLATE B, No. 9.

Obv.—Portion of the laureate bust to the right, without any signs of a face; the most remarkable feature being that one of the open crescents representing the front hair is made to form a portion of a serpent-like figure, with its head and open mouth close to the wreath.

Rev.—Horse similar to that on the last coin, but having a triple tail, and a wheel, instead of a globule, beneath it. The exergual line zigzagged and curved.

N. Usual weight about 90 grains.

Coins of this type, found at Ruscombe, Berks (91·4 grains), and near Maidenhead, are in the British Museum; as are also some from the Whaddon Chase find (89·1 and 91·2 grains). Another coin in the same collection weighs only 82·9 grains.

Another was found at Wonersh, near Grantley, in Surrey, weighing 83 grains. (Coll. Aut., vol. i. pl. lvi. 5.)

The coin from the same neighbourhood, Plate D, No. 5, is very closely allied to this type. Another was found at Hampstead Norris, Berks (64 grains) (Num. Soc. Proc., Nov. 20, 1862). This shows three pellets in front of the open crescents, arranged like those in Plate E, 1 and 2. Mr. C. Roach Smith has given me impressions of another, found at Selsey, Sussex, 1847. Another was discovered many years ago at Little Milton, Oxfordshire, and is engraved in Plot's Natural History of that county, pl. xv. 21. On this coin Dr. Plot discerned two faces, which he thought to be those of Prasutagus and Boadicea! But Mr. Walker could "see no resemblance of one or more faces, but rather imagined it to be some fortification!!" See Gibson's Camden, p. xciii., and pl. i. 29.

The coins engraved in Ruding, pl. i. 14, and Borlase, Ants., pl. xix. 23, seem closely to resemble this type, though the snake-like head is wanting. Very similar coins occur on the continent. See Lambert, pl. vi. 5 and 6, one of which was found at Soissons.

The serpent-like figure on the obverse is well worthy of notice, and occurs upon some of the inscribed coins (see Plate I., Nos. 10, 11, 12), with which the lighter of these uninscribed coins would appear to be nearly contemporary. The same feeling which produced this figure on the obverse of this type may be traced in the termination of the body of the horse on the reverse of Plate B, No. 5.

PLATE B, No. 10.

Obv.—Plain and convex.
Rev.—Horse to the right, with wheel below, the same as on the last coin. The exergual line usually formed with a zigzag. *N.* 90 grains.

The same remarks apply to the obverse of this coin as to that of No. 8. The device of the reverse is identical with that of No. 9, showing that though the obverse of the one is plain, and that of the other has a considerable portion of the laureate bust upon it, they are both derived from a common source. There are, indeed, some coins on which the device on the obverse is so faintly rendered that they seem intermediate between the two classes. The plain type seems to belong mainly to the central part of England, a large number of the coins, including the one here engraved, having been found in the Whaddon Chase hoard, in company with a vast number of other coins, principally of the types of Plate C, Nos. 5 to 8, but a few like Plate A, No. 12, and B, No. 5. (See Numismatic Chronicle, vol. xii. p. 1, where two specimens of the type now under consideration are engraved.) Others in the British Museum collection have been found at Ruscombe, Berks (91·1 grains); Maidenhead (92 grains); and Chipping Norton, Oxon (90 grains).

Mr. Webster has shown me one found at Harlington, Middlesex, in 1854. I have seen another which was found at Cowley, near Oxford, in 1859 (90¼ grains). Another is engraved in the Coll. Ant., vol. i. pl. vi. 3 (83 grains), found at Hollingbourne, Kent. They have also been found in Sussex; and two specimens, found at Worthing and Tarring, weighing 89 and 79 grains respectively, are engraved in Dixon, p. 36. The type is engraved in Ruding, pl. i. 2.

PLATE B, No. 11.

Obv.—Cruciform ornament formed by wreaths, with two open crescents placed back to back in the centre. The wreaths consist of two parallel corded lines, similar to the wreath or torse in heraldry on which crests are usually placed. In the angles of the cross are traces of the drapery or gorget on the neck of the laureate bust, and of the objects which represent the hair.

Rev.—Horse to the right, with a ring ornament on his shoulder and hind quarters; above, a wheel; and below, the same and an annulet; in front, a ring ornament and two pellets. In place of the Victory there is above the horse a wavy line. *N.*

The clothing of the neck, and the portions of the hair of the laureate bust, which are found on this coin, and on others with a somewhat similar cruciform ornament upon them, such as Plate C, No. 9, and Plate D, Nos. 6, 7, and 8, prove the derivation of the cruciform device from the same prototype as that which gave rise to so many other and distinct varieties of configuration.

The reverse of this coin is remarkable as having the wheel not only below, but above the horse. The formation of the body of the horse, with ring ornaments before and behind, may also be seen upon several other types.

The coin here engraved is in the Bodleian collection, at Oxford, and has already been given by Wise, pl. xvi. 12. Strictly speaking, it belongs to the inscribed series, as a coin of the same type, which I have engraved in Plate XIII., No. 13, shows some traces of an inscription. I have, however, retained it in this place as exhibiting one of the links between the laureate bust and the simple cruciform ornament.

PLATE B, No. 12.

Obv.—Convex and plain, but with traces of a raised band across it.
Rev.—Horse galloping to the left; above, an S-shaped figure, with a pellet in the centre of each curve; below, a trellised compartment; pellets beneath the head and tail, and several small ring ornaments in the field.
N. 85¾ grains.

This coin, in my own collection, is of red gold, and was found near Maidstone in 1861. It has not before been published. It was probably struck in Kent or Sussex, as some other coins of that part of Britain have similar trellised compartments upon the reverse. On the small gold coin, Plate E, No. 8, and on the silver coin of Dubnovellaunus, Plate IV., No. 11, they are below the horse or Pegasus. On Plate D, No. 11, there are two combined with a number of other ornaments. What appear to be Kentish coins of Dubnovellaunus and Vosenos have also plain obverses. The S-shaped figure, composed of two ring ornaments united, occurs on coins of Addedomaros, Plate XIV., Nos. 1 and 3. It is not unlikely that this type may eventually prove to have been inscribed.

Plate B, No. 13.

Obv.—Convex and plain, with the exception of some faintly raised streaks or bands.

Rev.—Horse to the right, with a ring ornament on his shoulder; above, an open right hand; below, a wheel; annulets in the field. *N*. 83 grains.

This coin was found at Horley, near Reigate, and an account of its discovery is given in the Arch. Journal, vol. xii. p. 83. It is also mentioned in vol. xiv. p. 74. There is another specimen in the British Museum, weighing 84¾ grains. The hand is of frequent occurrence on Gaulish coins, and is seldom found on those of British origin. This is, indeed, the solitary instance; yet, from the coin having been found in England, and no specimen that I am aware of having been published in any work on Gaulish coins, I think it may with propriety be attributed to Britain.

I have another somewhat similar coin, of red gold, but not showing the hand, with a radiated pellet in front of the horse, and a sort of serpent with a horned, goat-like head beneath the wheel. Its weight is 85¾ grains. Its place of finding is not known.

Plate B, No. 14.

Obv.—Portions of the laureate bust to the right, the wreath terminating in a sort of flower; the two open crescents representing the front hair conjoined at one end, and at the other terminating in graceful curves. In front, between them, is an ornamented pellet, which is the sole representative of the face. The whole within a beaded circle.

Rev.—Three-tailed, maneless horse to the right; above, a star and ornamented pellet; below, a pierced star of eight points (or possibly a flower) and a ring ornament; annulets in the field. *N*. 20¾ grains.

This coin, though found in a garden in St. John's Wood, belongs to the class more usually found on the southern coast, of which specimens are engraved in Plate E, Nos. 1, 2, and 3. It is here introduced on account of its similarity to the next coin, No. 15, which, from its having the plain and convex obverse, it was thought best to insert in this place.

Plate B. No. 15.

Obv.—Plain and convex.

Rev.—Three-tailed, maneless horse to the right; above, a beaded circle enclosing a pellet with a cross upon it; on either side of the neck a ring ornament; below, an annulet, and an S-shaped figure. *N*. 18½ grains.

This coin, of red gold, is in my own collection, but I am not aware of its place of finding, though I am inclined to assign it to the Southern part of England. The type of the reverse is closely allied to that of No. 14, and the peculiar formation of the near hind-leg of the horse on both these coins is worthy of notice. Like the preceding coin, this piece was no doubt current as the fourth part of the larger coins.

Plate C, No. 1.

Obv.—Portions of the laureate bust similar to that on Plate A, No. 13.

Rev.—Rude disjointed horse to the left; above, a solid crescent and the arms of Victory among several pellets; below, a globule surrounded by a circle of small dots; in front a radiated pellet, and below the head a small tribrach. There is an ornamented exergual device extending up between the legs of the horse. *N*. 93 grains.

This coin and No. 2 were among those so liberally presented to the British Museum by J. F. W. de Salis, Esq. I have a specimen of the same type, weighing 89½ grains; but it is not known where either of these coins was found. I have, however, seen a coin from the Whaddon Chase hoard of very nearly the same type. On the reverse of mine there is a line extending upwards from the crescent between the "arms of Victory," in the same manner as it does so frequently on the coins of the Yorkshire types, Plate XVII, Nos. 9, 10, 11, 12. The general correspondence in type with the Yorkshire coins points this coin out as one of the connecting links between the Southern and Northern parts of Britain, and I am in consequence inclined to assign it to the Midland Counties.

PLATE C, No. 2.

Obv.—Portions of the usual bust to the right, the leaves of the wreath turned downwards. The part where the face ought to be, ornamented in much the same manner as Plate A, No. 10.

Rev.—Singularly formed animal, with a flowing tail and bristly mane, its head held down as if in the act of feeding on a crescent in front; above, a small crescent and various pellets; below, a pellet and crescent. The animal is standing on an exergual space defined by beaded lines, and enclosing semicircles placed alternately with a central dot in each, such as are seen on Plate A, No. 11. *N.* 94 grains.

This type is of rare occurrence, and has not been hitherto engraved. The original is in the British Museum. I have another specimen, weighing 93½ grains, showing an L-shaped figure, and an oval ring divided by a line in front of the animal. Beyond the fact of a coin of the next and allied type having been found in Norfolk, there is little to guide us in assigning these coins to any particular district. The animal on the reverse differs from that on any other of the gold coins, and justifies the description given of it in the Sale Catalogue of the late Mr. Huxtable's collection: "An animal of an extinct race, standing on an ornamented ground." Like the animal on the next coin, it has a mane along its back; and, looking at the ears and the formidable row of teeth in its mouth, I think it may have been intended for a wolf, an animal occasionally represented on Gaulish coins, and apparently on some of Cunobeline. (See Plate X., No. 4.)

PLATE C, No. 3.

Obv.—Similar to the last, but the leaves of the wreath running upwards; or else, as is probably the case, the bust is turned in the opposite direction.

Rev.—Very peculiar animal, standing to the left, with a flowing tail, and a bristly mane extending all along its back; above, a crescent, a globule, and a figure like a hand with a thumb and only three fingers; below, a globule and a triangle of pellets; two pellets beneath the tail. The whole has been surrounded by a beaded circle. *N.* 89 grains.

This coin, which is in the British Museum, has been engraved in the Numismatic Journal, vol. i. pl. i. 4, and in Ruding, pl. A, 77. Its place of finding is not known. Another was found in September, 1832, at Norwich, and has been obligingly communicated to me by Mr. Fitch. It shows a crescent among the pellets on the reverse, as on the preceding coin, and there is an oval ring ornament above the tail of the animal, which is the exact counterpart of that on No. 2, though turned in the opposite direction. The two coins are evidently contemporaneous, and belong to the same district, wherever that may have been. The weight seems to show that they could not have come very late in the series, but the wolf on the reverse does not appear to have left any descendants.

PLATE C, No. 4.

Obv.—Convex, a branch or wreath springing from an annulet, and having another small annulet near its point.

Rev.—Rude horse to the right; above, a figure derived from the arms of Victory; in front, a ring ornament; below, a wheel; below the horse's head, a small cross; the whole surrounded by a circle of pellets placed at some little distance apart. *N.* 85 grains.

This coin was found with four others at Mount Batten, near Plymouth, in 1832, and is engraved in the Numismatic Journal, vol. i. pl. i. 7; Hawkins, pl. i. 6; and Ruding, pl. A, 80. There is reason for supposing this type to have been peculiar to the West of England, and to have been of comparatively late date, probably even of the time of Tiberius.

The analogy of the leaf-like ornament on the obverse with that on the gold coins of Antedrigus, and others of the West of England which come down as late as the days of Claudius (see Plate L., Nos. 4 to 7), is apparent, and the small cross occurs also upon them in the same position with regard to the horse. Some remarks upon the derivation of this ornament from the wreath on the head of the earlier coins will be found in the Numismatic Chronicle, New Series, vol. i. p. 0.

The succeeding coins in this Plate belong to a class found principally in the central part of England—in Oxfordshire, Bucks, Herts, Beds, and Essex. Nos. 5, 6, 7 and 8 are all from the great hoard discovered at Whaddon Chase in February, 1849. Allusion has already been made to this discovery in the description of Plate A, No. 12; B, No. 5 and No. 10. An account of it is given in the Numismatic Chronicle, vol. xii. p. 1, accompanied by a plate of the coins. Mr. Akerman there assigns these coins to "the important period just previous to the annexation of Britain as a Roman province." I cannot, however, but regard them as belonging to a still earlier period. Their weight, which is usually about 90 grains, or even a little more, proves them to be earlier than those of Cunobeline, or even Tasciovanus, whose coins rarely, if ever, exceed 85 grains. At the same time, the type of the obverse does not show so complete an oblivion of the original prototype as the cruciform ornament on the coins of Tasciovanus (see Plate V., Nos. 7, 8, &c., and Plate C, No. 12), which, indeed, seems rather to be a derivative from the Whaddon Chase coins. The absence of any Roman coins from the hoard is another indication of an earlier date, as in many of the hoards of the later British coins, such as those of Nunney,[*] Weston,[†] Almondbury,[‡] and Lightcliffe,[§] Roman coins were found

[*] Num. Chron., N.S., vol. i. p. 1.
[†] Num. Chron., vol. xv. p. 194.
[‡] Num. Chron., vol. i. p. 82.
[§] Num. Chron., N.S., vol. i. p. 79.

with them in greater or less number. My own opinion is that these coins are to be assigned to about the period of Cæsar's invasion—certainly to no later date.

To avoid repetition, it will be best to describe Nos. 5, 6, and 7 together.

PLATE C, Nos. 5, 6, 7.

Obv.—Portions of the large laureate bust, which has, however, assumed more of the character of a cruciform ornament. The leaves of the wreath run in opposite directions from an ornamented pellet in the centre; at right angles to the wreath is a band, terminating behind the head in a flower-like ornament, visible on No. 5; the two open crescents representing the front hair are usually connected together, and occasionally, as on No. 6, enclosed within a square compartment. The back hair, instead of having numerous locks arranged in two tiers, is formed by two waving tresses, one on each side of the cross-band. The clothing of the neck is interspersed with beaded or twisted lines, giving it rather the character of a wreath, and there are usually beaded lines on each side of the wreath itself.

Rev.—Horse galloping to the right; above, a curved figure similar in form to the locks of the back hair, and a triangle of pellets; below, an ornamented pellet; in front there is frequently a zigzag line terminating in an oval ring ornament. The exergue has usually a sort of wreath between two plain lines, with occasionally an ornamented pellet at the ends and centre. The space beneath is sometimes ornamented with vertical lines, like those on No. 1. There are many minor varieties in the details of both obverse and reverse. *N*. Usually from 89 to 92 grains.

The metal is frequently very base—not more than 11 carats fine.

Coins of this type were formerly scarce; but the great find at Whaddon Chase has made them, and those like Plate B, No. 10, the most common of the British coins. As already mentioned, an account of this discovery is given in the Numismatic Chronicle, vol. xii. p. 1, where numerous specimens are also engraved (pl. i. 1, 2, 3, 4, 5, and 7).

There is, however, no doubt that the number of coins found far exceeded that given as probable by Mr. Akerman. It must have been nearly 2,000, as a vast quantity found their way into the hands of some bullion dealers in London, besides the 420 which were traced at the time. Other notices of this find occur in the Procs. Soc. Ant., vol. i. p. 328, and Arch. Assoc. Journ., vol. v. p. 155. Beale Poste (p. 170) gives woodcuts of two coins supposed to belong to this find; but on one of them the horse is to the left, and it appears doubtful whether it was not found in Warwickshire. If correctly engraved, it is a new variety. The coin engraved in Ruding, pl. ii. 39, from the Hunter collection, belongs to this class, as does also that in Gibson's Camden, pl. ii. 21. A specimen of this type was found at Standon, near Puckeridge, Herts (Arch. Assoc. Journ., vol. ii. p. 347).

PLATE C, No. 8.

Obv.—The same as that of the preceding coins.
Rev.—The same, but instead of the pellet below the horse, a flower-like ornament of eight leaves, alternately long and short. ℕ. 90½ grains.

Several coins of this type were among those found at Whaddon Chase, and one of them is engraved in the Numismatic Chronicle, vol. xii. pl. i. 0. It is difficult to say whether the introduction of this ornament upon the coins is a mere freak of the artist, or whether it was intended to represent some sacred flower. A very similar ornament occurs on some of the Sussex coins (see Plate E, No. 2, and B, No. 14), and a four-petaled flower occurs on the gold coins of Eppillus (Plate III., Nos. 10 and 12).

PLATE C, No. 9.

Obv.—Cruciform ornament of two wreaths, crossing each other, with two open crescents back to back in the centre. In the angles of the cross appear locks of hair, the open crescents representing the front hair, and the ornamentation on the neck of the wide-spread bust of the earlier coins. On some specimens the wreaths terminate in ornamental pellets.

Rev.—Moderately well-shaped horse to the right; in front, a radiated pellet, or a representation of the sun; below, a wheel; and above, a curved figure, like that on the preceding coins, placed among several pellets, a small ring ornament, &c. *N.* 85½ grains.

The type of the obverse of this coin is well worthy of notice, as proving the derivation of the cruciform ornament which occurs on the coins of Tasciovanus and Andoco[mius] from the laureate bust of the early coins. It is closely allied to that of the coins found at Wonersh, near Guildford (Plate D, Nos. 6, 7, and 8), while the type of the reverse is more nearly connected with the Whaddon Chase coins.

The specimen engraved was found at Manuden, near Bishop's Stortford, and is in my own collection. I have another, considerably worn, found at Farthinghoe, near Brackley, Northamptonshire (Procs. Soc. Ant., vol. ii. p. 43), weighing 82¼ grains; and I have also seen one which was found at Hallaton, Leicestershire (Archaeological Journal, vi. p. 403). A specimen is engraved in Stukeley, pl. xix. 3, from the collection of Mr. Joseph Tolson Lockyer, F.S.A., and is so faithfully represented as to cause regret that so little pains were taken in engraving the other coins in that curious medley. The type is also given in the Numismatic Chronicle, vol. xix. p. 64, No. 4. On a coin of this type, in the possession of the Rev. G. A. Goddard, of Clyffe Pypart, a wreath or ear of corn forms the exergual line on the reverse.

Plate C, No. 10.

Obv.—Cruciform ornament, somewhat like that on No. 9, but with the wreaths terminating in ring ornaments, and one of them curved. In two of the angles formed by the cross are V-shaped figures, consisting of two narrow crescents conjoined to a pellet, and in the other two annulets conjoined by an open crescent; in the field are a number of small annulets.

PLATE C, NO. 11.

Rev.—Horse to the right, his eye being the centre of a ring ornament; above, a solid crescent reversed and a small annulet; below, a large ring ornament; above the horse's head an elliptical ring ornament and pellets; and in front of him a peculiar Y-shaped figure.
N. 84½ grains.

This type is closely allied to the preceding, and much resembles it in point of workmanship. The necks of the horses on both are thinned out in front, so as to form a sort of dewlap, which, in a less degree, is the case with some of the Whaddon Chase coins; and the mane is quite detached. The ears are also largely developed. The object in front of the horse is somewhat analogous to that on the Sussex coins, Plate E, Nos. 1, 2, 3, and 4.

The type is engraved in Ruding, pl. ii. 38, of which a variety is said to have been found at Mark's Tey, Essex (Num. Soc. Proc., May 23, 1843). I have no authentic account of the discovery of any coins of this type, but they probably belong to the central part of England. There is a curious coin, which appears to be of a type intermediate between this and the following, engraved in Stukeley, pl. xix. 6. I have not met with any actual specimens of it.

PLATE C, No. 11.

Obv.—Cruciform ornament, analogous to that on No. 10, but having one of the wreaths composed of more distinct leaves, and the crescents in the centre solid instead of open; the figures in the angles are also different.

Rev.—Horse galloping to the right; above, a starlike figure with curved rays, and below a wheel and pellet; a portion of some curved object above the horse's tail.
N. 79½ grains.

This coin is in the British Museum collection, but it is not known where it was found. It is of rather peculiar fabric, and considerably dished. The star with curved rays on the reverse connects it with the coins found near Guildford, Plate D, Nos. 6, 7, and 8.

Plate C, No. 12.

Obv.—Cruciform ornament, allied to that on No. 10, but with solid crescents in the centre, and all the wreaths terminating in ring ornaments. The ornaments in the angles of the cross are also rather different, there being a bracket-shape figure ⌒ in front of the hollow crescent, instead of the two annulets.

Rev.—Horse galloping to the right; above, a bucranium and a decorated ring ornament; in the field, other ring ornaments; in front of the horse, the traces of what may have been the head of a second horse; and below, what looks like a spare pair of hind-legs.

N. About 84 grains.

This coin is in the British Museum. The type belongs more properly to the inscribed series, being that of the coins of Tasciovanus, Plate V., No. 8. The dies have, however, been so large in proportion to the size of the *flan*, that on many of the coins there is no trace of the legend, and they have been engraved as anepigraphous in many instances. (See Gough's Camden, No. 29; White's plate, No. 3; Stukeley, pl. xv. 8; Numismatic Journal, vol. i. pl. ii. 9; and Ruding, pl. A, 95.) I have inserted it here to show the derivation of the type. Specimens were among the find of coins at High Wycombe, in 1827 (Archæologia, vol. xxii. p. 207), and another was found near Colchester, in 1850. The remarkable feature of the type is that there appears to be some reminiscence of the second horse of the bigæ of the Macedonian staters in the objects in front of, and below, the horse on the reverse.

Plate C, No. 13.

Obv.—Wreath of two corded lines crossing another corded line at right angles; in two of the compartments thus formed are crescents and annulets conjoined, like those on No. 10, in another a lock of hair, and in the fourth a quatrefoil and other objects, possibly derived from the clothing of the neck of the bust on the earlier coins.

Rev.—Horse galloping to the right; above, a rosette; below, a ring ornament, and another in front. The body of

PLATE C, NO. 14.

the horse is formed with a pellet on the shoulder and hind-quarters, and its tail seems to be three-fold, something like many of those on Plate B. *N*. 18½ grains.

This coin is in the Museum collection, but its place of finding is not known. The type of the obverse connects it with Nos. 9, 10, and 11 of this Plate, and No. 11 in Plate B. The horse is also similar in general character to those on the coins just mentioned, but has the pellets on the shoulder and rump. It probably belongs to the central part of Britain, and represents the quarter of the pieces of the larger module, though, as usual, it is rather less than a quarter of their weight. I have already published it in the Numismatic Chronicle, vol. xix. p. 64, No. 5.

PLATE C, No. 14.

Obv.—Cruciform ornament with two thin crescents in the centre, and horse-shoe shaped figures in the angles. As usual, one of the wreaths forming the cross is curved.

Rev.—Horse standing to the left, his off fore-leg raised and having a pellet beneath it, another pellet above his back, and an uncertain object beneath, somewhat like that in front of the horse on the coins of Tasciovanus, Plate V., No. 9. On a specimen of this type in the Bodleian Library, at Oxford, this object has a stem to it, and looks much like a nut in its husk.

N. 20½ grains.

This coin, which is in my own collection, was found in the neighbourhood of Biggleswade, and was published in the Numismatic Chronicle, vol. xix. p. 64, No. 10. I have another coin of the same type, found at Earl's Barton, Northamptonshire. The type of the obverse is closely connected with that of the preceding coins, and also with the coins of Eppillus, Andoco[mius], and Tasciovanus, Plate III., No. 19; V., Nos. 5 and 13. The horse on the reverse is also very similar to that on the coin of Eppillus, but is even more closely connected with that on the copper coin, also from the neighbourhood of Biggleswade, Plate C, No. 7. From its place of finding, as well as its type, it belongs to the central district, and is probably of much the same date as the coins of Eppillus and Tasciovanus.

PLATE D, No. 1.

Obv.—Plain and convex.

Rev.—Horse galloping to the right; above, what appear to be the representatives of the arms of Victory; below, a wheel; behind, a pellet; and in front, a pellet, and a semicircle connecting two pellets. *N*. 74 grains.

This coin is of very base gold, and was found at Mark's Tey, Essex. It was formerly in the collection of Mr. Warren, of Ixworth, but is now in my own. I have seen another specimen, weighing 60 grains, which was found with silver coins of Epaticcus, and a coin of Tiberius, in Savernake Forest, near Marlborough. The fabric is peculiar, and the form of the horse and the adjuncts are not readily connected with those of any other coins, but the coin is certainly posterior in date to the uniface coins, Plate B, Nos. 8 and 10. The semicircular object in front of the horse may possibly be intended to represent a torc. It resembles that on Plate XIV., No. 13, but occupies a different position on the coin. The arrangement of the horse's legs is somewhat like that on the silver coins reading ANTED and SVEI, Plate I., Nos. 8 and 9, and the uninscribed silver coins, Plate F, Nos. 4 to 8, &c.

PLATE D, No. 2.

Obv.—Several raised bands crossing another in the centre of the coin, so as to look somewhat like the branches of a tree, and with numerous small spikes springing from them in various directions.

Rev.—Horse to the left, with a sort of pole coming forward at an angle from his haunches, on which a human figure is squatting and apparently holding reins attached to the horse's head; beneath the horse is another pole and a lyre-shaped object. *N*. 118 grains.

This coin is in the British Museum. Others of the same type have been found on Enfield Chase (Numismatic Chronicle, vol. i. pl. ii. 10), and near the Whitman Hills, Dorchester, Oxfordshire (Numismatic Chronicle, vol. ii. p. 191, No. 5). The engraving of the latter is repeated by Lelewel, pl. viii. 24. The type being so nearly the same as that of the smaller coins or quarter-staters, Nos. 3 and 4 of the Plate, may be considered under the same head.

Plate D, No. 3.

Obv.—A number of raised lines or spikes crossing the field in various directions.
Rev.—Horse to the left with the squatting figure holding a pole above, and the lyre-shaped object beneath.
N. 27 to 29 grains.

Plate D, No. 4.

Obv.—As last, but fewer lines.
Rev.—As that of No. 2. N. 23 to 29 grains.

These are also in the National collection. There can be but little doubt that the types of both obverse and reverse of these coins are, like nearly all those of British gold coins, in some way derived from those of the Macedonian stater; but the manner in which this has taken place is not so readily discerned as in other cases, and most of the connecting links have still to be found. The coin engraved by Lelewel, pl. ii. 15, is, however, one of the chain. From their weight, and from their having been found at Karn Brê associated with coins of the type Plate A, Nos. 4 and 5, and B, No. 6, they seem to belong to the earlier portion of the series.

The posture of the figure upon the horse, which is to be observed also on some of the Gaulish coins (see Lambert, pl. ii. 28, and pl. iv. 16; Lelewel, pl. ii. 15), is very remarkable, as is also the presence of the lyre-shaped object under the horse, which does not occur on any others of the gold British coins. This object is, however, of common occurrence on the billon coins of the Channel Islands (see

Plate I), and on Gaulish coins in gold (see Lelewel, pl. ii. 12, 20, &c.; Lambert, pl. ii. 5, 18, 20, 28, &c.). On some of the early gold coins of Germany it appears as the principal type, surrounded by a torc (see Streber's "Regenbogen-Schüsselchen,"* pl. vii. 68). It is probable that the lyre may have been originally one of the adjuncts on the original Macedonian staters, but adopted and perpetuated by the Gauls and Britons as one of the attributes of Apollo Belinus, whose head is supposed to have been at first represented on these coins.

The type of the obverse has given rise to a good deal of amusing speculation. Borlase, on one coin, saw it as "the stem of a tree, with its collateral branches very distinct," and his engraver has inserted the head and fore-part of a bird among the branches. "The riches of the country where these were coined consisted in woods (not in money), and therefore they took the tree for their symbol." On another it appeared to him to look like "the plan of a town, of which the streets cross nearly at right angles, and the whole cut by one straight and wider street than the rest." He goes on to observe that this "ichnography of a city was probably inserted in the coin by the founder to record the erection of some city." But Mr. Polwhele goes much farther than this, and "is surprised that Dr. Borlase should have thus remarked upon the ground-plot of this city without venturing to conjecture what city it was." "It represents a British city; and it was found in Damnonium. Is it not natural to suppose that this was a city of Damnonium,—and probably the metropolis? This plan of the Damnonium city must immediately suggest the idea of the original Exeter, even to those who have never seen the modern. But whoever has visited the modern Exeter must instantly recognise it in the Karn Brê coin!"

With regard to the part of England to which these coins belong, there is some reason for assigning them to the southern coast. I have already mentioned that there were

* Munich, 1860.

a number of them in the Karn Brê find. One was, however, found in the Thames, near Kingston (Arch. Assoc. Journ., vi. p. 447), and others in London, and near Reigate (Arch. Assoc. Journ., xiii. p. 236; and Arch. Journ., x. p. 248). Mr. Whitbourn, of Godalming, had also two specimens, found in that neighbourhood, one of which he has kindly added to my collection. Both are considerably worn, and one weighs only 18 grains. The type is engraved in Ruding, pl. i. 7; Gough's Camden, Nos. 40, 41, 42, 53, 55; and Beale Poste, p. 139, Nos. 3 and 4.

But the occurrence of these coins is not limited to England; they are also found in France, and several are engraved by Lelewel (pl. ii. 25 to 29, and ix. 35), who considers them to belong to the maritime Belgæ. Some of his specimens were found at Audenard and Ecloos, in Flanders, and at Arras, and I have seen one which was found near Ghent. Another specimen is engraved by Lambert (pl. vi. 11), which is in the Museum at Rouen. M. de Saulcy is inclined to refer them to the Atrebates. It would thus appear—from the coins of this type being found indifferently on this side of the Channel and the other, but in both cases usually within the territory occupied by the Belgic tribes—that we have in them numismatic evidence of the correctness of Cæsar's account of the colonisation of the southern coast of Britain by the Belgæ, and of the intercourse which was maintained between the cognate tribes of Britain and the continent.

Plate D, No. 5.

Obv.—Very similar to that of Plate B, No. 9.

Rev.—Similar to that of Plate B, No. 9, except that above the horse is a trefoil ornament. *N.* 82 grains.

This coin also resembles very closely the coin with the legend COMMIOS [?] (Plate I., No. 10), and may, in fact, be of the same class, though not showing the legend. It is remarkable for the trefoil ornament above the horse, which has very much the appearance of having been formed by using the puncheon for the nose and mouth of the horse three times over. Specimens have been found between Odiham and Basingstoke (Mr. Whitbourn), and also at Farley Heath, near Guildford; so that, geographically, the type is connected with that of the subsequent coins. A specimen is engraved, though imperfectly, in the Transactions of the Surrey Archaeological Society, vol. i. No. 3, and reproduced in the Archaeological Journal, vol. xiii. p. 304.

The three next specimens are all varieties of the same type, and, having been found together, need not be separated in their descriptions.

PLATE D, Nos. 6, 7, 8.

Obv.—Cruciform ornament, formed by sets of five wreathed and beaded or plain lines, at right angles to each other, with two open crescents back to back in the centre, and two ornamented pellets between them. In the angles are placed portions of the wide-spread bust, such as locks of the back hair, the open crescents representing the hair on the forehead, and parts of the ornamentation on the neck.

Rev.—Horse galloping to the right; above, a star with curved arms (usually seven or eight) terminating in pellets; below, a wheel; in front, a rosette; behind and in front of the horse's head, an elliptical ring ornament; in the field, various pellets, or sometimes annulets and small crescents, and occasionally beaded lines, which on some specimens are introduced between the rays of the star. *N.* 82 to 83 grains.

The type of the obverse is intimately connected with that of Plate B, No. 11, and C, No. 9, and is of great interest as showing how completely the cruciform type had superseded that of the wide-spread bust, even while portions of the latter were retained as accessories of the design. The type of the reverse, with the star of curved rays above the horse, is allied to that of Plate C, No. 11, while the ornamental pellets which are found upon the obverse, and occasionally on the reverse, point to a connection with the Sussex coins.

This type was unknown until a discovery of coins at Wonersh, near Guildford, in 1848, when a shepherd-boy picked up nineteen of these and a number of the small gold coins, Nos. 10 and 11, Plate D, on a newly-mended road, where in all probability a hollow flint, which had originally been their receptacle, had been broken by the traffic. It will be subsequently seen that the coins found at High Wycombe, which belong probably to a slightly later period, were also enclosed in a hollow stone. It was reported at the time that all except two of these larger coins were melted down, but I have reason to believe that this was not the case, and that most, if not all, of those found were preserved. An account of their discovery, with engravings, is given by Mr. Martin F. Tupper, in the Numismatic Chronicle, vol. xi. p. 92, and also in his Farley Heath (1850), p. 21. They are also engraved in Smith's Coll. Ant., vol. i. pl. lvi.; the Arch. Journal, vol. xiii. p. 304; and the Transactions of the Surrey Archæological Society, as before cited.

Plate D, No. 9.

Obv.—A wreath and some traces of the hair of the laureate bust.

Rev.—Horse galloping to the right; above and below, a wheel; behind, an ornamented pellet, and several pellets in the field. *N*. 10 grains.

This coin, which is hitherto unpublished, was likewise found at Farley Heath, in 1800, and is in the collection of Mr. Whitbourn, of Godalming. It is of extremely base metal, and less in weight than most of the coins of this size. It seems to be connected with the coin Plate E, 5, and the character of the mane of the horse is the same as on some of the small gold coins of Cunobeline. (See Plate IX., No. 14.)

Plate D, No. 10.

Obv.—Plain and convex, but with a slightly raised band across the field. There has been a circular recess in the die nearly the same size as the coin, which shows a portion of the outline of the recess.

" —Horse galloping to the right; below, two annulets connected by an open crescent, and above apparently the same. In the field, an annulet and various pellets. *N*. 21 grains.

Two or three coins of this type were in the hoard discovered near Wonersh, above mentioned. That here engraved is in my own collection. It is also given in Smith's Coll. Ant., vol. i. pl. lvi. 6. On the specimen engraved in the Numismatic Chronicle, vol. xi. p. 62, No. 4, and in Tupper's Farley Heath, there appears to be a beaded ring ornament below the horse, and no pellets in the field. The obverse, with the raised band across it, seems to retain a reminiscence of the wreath which crosses the earlier coins, and resembles that of several other varieties, both uninscribed and inscribed. The horse, which has no mane, resembles in that respect some of the Sussex coins (Plate E), while its S-shaped flowing tail is similar to that on the larger coins found with it (Nos. 6, 7, and 8). The coin engraved in Stukeley, pl. xiv. 3, possibly belongs to this class, though the amphisbæna, or two-headed snake, above the horse, is no doubt a creation of the author or engraver. I have another coin of this type; but it is an ancient forgery, of copper plated with gold. It was found at Westgate Bay, near Margate.

PLATE D, No. 11.

Obv.—Plain and convex, with occasionally a raised band across. The die has had a circular recess in it, the same as that for the previous coin.

Rev.—An object resembling a branch of six leaves close together, standing on the point of a triangle, the base of which is a corded line between two stars, and within which is an annulet; below, is a small solid crescent between two annulets, and on each side of the branch are circular and rectangular trellised compartments; above, is an ornament formed of two concentric circles, with, on some coins, a small annulet on either side. *N*. 19 to 20 grains.

Of this type it is stated that there were six specimens in the find at Wonersh, near Guildford, of which two are engraved in the Numismatic Chronicle, vol. xi. p. 62, Nos. 5 and 6, and in Tupper's Farley Heath, p. 22; and one in the Coll. Ant., vol. i. pl. lvi. 7; and Beale

Poste, p. 168. One is also given in the Trans. of the Surrey Arch. Soc., and the Arch. Journal, vol. xiii., as before cited.

Another specimen is given by Battely in his Antiquitates Rutupinæ, pl. vi., as having been found at Reculver. The type of the reverse has, however, been most curiously metamorphosed by the engraver into a standing figure in long robes, wearing a conical cap, with two stars attached by long pins to his shoulders. By looking at Battely's engraving from the top instead of from the bottom, and comparing it with that here given, it will at once be seen how such a mistake could have occurred; and this error is extremely instructive as showing the tendency of engravers, who at any period have had these unintelligible devices to copy, to modify or give a new character to the device, while still retaining its general characteristics.

There is little doubt that the type of the coins now under consideration owes its regularity of design and some of its details to this natural propensity of the artists who engraved the dies. The connection of the reverse with that of No. 12 may readily be traced, but its similarity to that of Plate E, No. 11, is obvious, while this in its turn is connected with Plate E, No. 10, and other types, as will hereafter be seen. A trellised compartment, like that on the present coin, appears beneath the horse on Plate B, No. 12, Plate E, No. 8, and on the silver coin of Dubnovellaunus, Plate IV., No. 11.

Plate D, No. 12.

Obv.—A raised circular boss with a neatly formed four-leaved flower upon it.

Rev.—A figure like the bud of a flower, attached to a crooked branch, and having two S-shaped lines coming out of it; above, an ornamented pellet between two small annulets; on either side a zigzag line terminating in an annulet, and with an ornamented pellet below it; below, annulets, crescents, &c. The whole within a beaded circle. *N.* 10½ grains.

I do not know where this curious little coin was found.

It was formerly in Mr. Huxtable's collection, and is now in my own. The type of the reverse connects it with the Sussex coins, Plate E, No. 11, &c., as well as with the preceding coin from the neighbourhood of Guildford. The obverse, however, more closely resembles that of the next coin.

PLATE D, No. 13.

Obv.—A flower formed of four pointed and serrated leaves radiating from a ring ornament in the centre, and alternating with rounded loops.

Rev.—A long-tailed horse prancing to the right, with a ring ornament on his shoulder and another below; in the field, various annulets and pellets. *N.* 21 grains.

This pretty little coin was found at Dorchester, Oxfordshire, and is engraved in the Numismatic Chronicle, vol. iii. p. 152, No. 2. It is now in the British Museum. The type of the obverse, which closely resembles that of the previous coin, is also evidently allied with other coins, such as Plate C, No. 14, and D, No. 14, on which the connection of the type with the original wide-spread bust can be traced; so that, strange as it may appear, this four-leaved flower is derived by successive steps from the head of Apollo on the Macedonian *stater!* The character of the head of the horse on the reverse is much like that on the coins of Addedomaros, Plate XIV., Nos. 5 to 9.

PLATE D, No. 14.

Obv.—A ring ornament, surrounded by a circle of pellets, on either side of which the wreath with a central line of pellets appears, crossed by two corded lines. In two of the spaces formed by this cross are the figures representing locks of back hair, and in the other two the open crescents representing the front hair of the wide-spread bust of the prototype.

Rev.—Horse to the left, with a ring ornament connected by a line to the neck in front, and another below; above, a star of oval pellets; annulets, &c., in the field. *N.* 15 grains.

This little coin of red gold was found at Bracklesham,

Sussex, and was formerly in the collection of the late Mr. Dixon, of Worthing, who has given a woodcut of it in his Geology of Sussex, p. 80, No. 3. It is also engraved in the Numismatic Chronicle, vol. xix. p. 84, No. 9. It is now in the British Museum. The type of the obverse, though showing a strong tendency to become cruciform in character, retains many of the details of the earlier bust, and is not unlike that of the Sussex coins, Plate E, No. 3; while the mane of the horse on the reverse, running up into a star above, and the ring ornament attached in front of the horse, are the same on both coins, though the horses are turned in different directions. Its character, therefore, as well as its place of finding, assigns it to the Sussex district.

Plate E, No. 1.

Obv.—Portions of the wide-spread bust, the open crescents representing the front hair conjoined, and in front of them three ornamented pellets in lieu of a face. The band crossing the wreath is also decorated with pellets of the same kind, and there is a wheel introduced instead of the ornamentation of the neck.

Rev.—A horse walking to the right; a pellet connected with his neck in front, and an ornamented pellet on the other side; above and below, a wheel, and various pellets in front. There is an exergual line which is beaded.

N. Usually 18 to 20 grains.

It will be observed that the horse on this coin has no mane, and that the upper portion of the near hind-leg is represented by two lines. The peculiar feature of the obverse is the wheel, which has by some means been transferred to it from the reverse. The coin, no doubt, belongs to the Sussex district, like the subsequent coins, with which it is closely connected in type. Mr. Durden, of Blandford, possesses a specimen found at Andover, Hants.

Plate E, No. 2.

Obv.—Nearly similar to that of the last coin, but with the ornamentation of the neck, like that of Plate B, No. 9, instead of a wheel.

Rev.—Horse with a triple tail prancing to the right; a ring ornament connected to his chest in front; above, a star of oval pellets; and below, a flower of eight leaves, its centre pierced, and another ring ornament. In the field, annulets, &c.

N. 20½ grains; usual weight, 17 to 21 grains.

The coin here engraved is in my own collection, and was found at Bognor, in 1841. It is engraved in Dixon's Geology of Sussex, p. 11, No. 2. No. 3 on the same page is a portion of another coin of the same type, found at Selsey. The cuts are reproduced in the Arch. Journ., vol. viii. p. 112. Another specimen, also from Bognor, is given in the Numismatic Chronicle, vol. vii. pl. iv. 10. (See also Num. Soc. Procs., Dec. 23, 1841, and Dec. 28, 1843.) Another specimen, also from Bognor, where a considerable number of small gold coins were found on the sea-shore, is engraved in Smith's Coll. Ant., vol. i. pl. vii. 14. Three others, from the neighbourhood of Chichester, are engraved in the Numismatic Chronicle, vol. i. pl. ii. 7, 8, and 9. Another, found on Farley Heath, is given in the first volume of the Transactions of the Surrey Archæological Association, and in the Archæological Journal, vol. xiii. p. 304, No. 2. There are several varieties in the details of these coins—the horse being sometimes without a mane, and sometimes with one; there being also occasionally a beaded exergual line instead of the ring ornament, &c. I have a specimen with a long zigzag line instead of the third ornamented pellet. In conjunction with the crescents and the two other pellets it forms a horribly grotesque grinning face, when viewed in the proper direction. The coin engraved in Gibson's Camden, pl. ii. 9, belongs to this class, though erroneously described as silver; and that in Stukeley, pl. xiv. 1, is also intended to represent one of these coins. It would appear as if they were occasionally found on the other side of the Channel, as a variety is engraved by Lambert, pl. xi. *bis*, 12, from the cabinet of the Comte de Kergariou, which is repeated in Lelewel, pl. iv. 11. That in the Revue Numismatique, vol. iv. pl. xiii. 2, is taken from the Numismatic Chronicle, vol. i.

Plate E, No. 3.

Obv.—Nearly the same as last.

Rev.—The same as last, but with a whorl below the horse, and a beaded exergual line. *N.* 20 to 21 grains.

The horses on these coins, like those on the preceding, are sometimes maneless, and the exergual line is occasionally absent. There is great variation in the module both of these and the two preceding coins. A good wide-spread specimen is given by Ruding, pl. i. 16. The curling up of the mane, so as to connect it with the star above the horse, may sometimes be observed on the coins of the preceding type as well as on this. They belong, of course, to the same district. The specimen here engraved is in the British Museum. I have one with a maneless horse, with a pellet beneath the star, and several ornamented pellets in the field.

Plate E, No. 4.

Obv.—A cruciform ornament with a pellet in the centre, each limb of the cross being curved, and two of them terminating in heads of eagles, with a mane or crest running down behind their necks. The other two limbs end in ring ornaments, but have a sort of fringe extending from them. Behind the eagles' necks are two ring ornaments, and a third beneath one of the heads.

Rev.—Horse prancing to the left; above, a star; and below, a decorated ring ornament; in front of the horse, an annulet connected to the horse's neck. *N.* 16¾ grains.

The coin here engraved is in the Museum collection, and is also published in the Numismatic Chronicle, vol. xix. p. 64, No. 8. I have another specimen (17¼ grains), which formerly belonged to the late Mr. Huxtable. Though the place of finding of neither of them is known, the character of the reverse connects them with the South-eastern district. The cruciform ornament on the obverse is singular in its details, the eagle-like heads not occurring on any other coins. The ornamentation of the field in front of the eagle, is no doubt a reminiscence of the decoration on the neck of the wide-spread bust. It bears a resemblance to that above the horse on the reverse of the Gaulish coin in Lelewel, pl. iii. 22.

PLATE E, No. 5.

Obv.—A triple beaded wreath between two open crescents back to back.

Rev.—Horse prancing to the right, his hind-quarters formed with a ring ornament; above, in front, and behind, ornamental pellets; and below, a decorated ring ornament. The near foreleg of the horse bifid at the shoulder; the mane similar to that on Plate D, No. 9.

N. 16 to 18 grains.

This type has been engraved erroneously as with annulets instead of crescents on the obverse, in the Numismatic Journal, vol. i. pl. i. 11; and Ruding, pl. A, 84. A specimen is engraved in the Numismatic Chronicle, vol. ii. p. 231, No. 1, on which there appears an object above the horse, similar to a Lombardic Œ. From a cast of this coin, given me by Mr. C. Roach Smith, I think it is a crescent, ornamented with a Vandyke pattern. It was found at Ashdown Forest, in Sussex, with about twenty others, of types of Plate E, No. 8, in gold, and Plate F, Nos. 11 and 12, in silver. The obverse is another curious instance of the utter degradation of the earlier type, and may be compared with that of Plate D, No. 9, which is also closely allied to this in the character of its reverse.

PLATE E, No. 6.

Obv.—A circular wreath with a roundel in the centre.

Rev.—An animal resembling a dog or wolf to the right. Possibly a star above. N. 16 grains.

PLATE E, No. 7.

Obv.—Plain and convex.

Rev.—A wolf (?) or horse to the left; above, a star. N. 17 grains.

Both these coins were found on the sea-shore, at Bognor, with other coins of the types of Plate E, No. 2, Plate H., No. 4, and Plate III., No. 1. They are engraved in the Numismatic Chronicle, vol. vii. pl. iv. 8 and 11 (see Num.

Soc. Procs., December 23, 1841), and in Dixon's Geology of Sussex, p. 32, Nos. 4 and 3. No. 7 is also given in Smith's Coll. Ant., vol. i. pl. vii. 8. I have never seen the originals, so that the engravings here given are copied from those in the Numismatic Chronicle. It is curious to find the wreath assume the circular form, as it does on the obverse of No. 7; but this peculiarity may also be noticed on some of the German and Gaulish derivatives of the Philippus. It is difficult to say what animal it was intended to represent on the reverse of these coins, but it is not unlike that on the silver coin of Cunobeline, Plate X., No. 4. The star above it is also found on coins of Tinc[ommius] and Verica, which belong to the same district.

PLATE E, No. 8.

Obv.—Plain, the central portion convex.
Rev.—Horse to the left, with a ring ornament on his shoulder; above, a V formed by two curled lines, and two ring ornaments; below, a trellised compartment.
N. 20 grains.

This coin was found, with several others, at Ashdown Forest, Sussex, as before mentioned (see No. 5). It is engraved in the Numismatic Chronicle, vol. ii. p. 231, No. 2. Another coin, of nearly the same type, is engraved as No. 3; but this is described as being of brass. It must, however, probably have been an ancient forgery, so that I have not inserted it among the brass coins.

The connection between the latticed compartment below the horse and those on the reverse of Plate B, No. 12, and Plate D, No. 11, has already been pointed out.

PLATE F, No. 9.

Obv.—Two vertical objects like rudely-shaped Es, placed back to back beneath a curved figure like a fish, with a fin running all along its back, and with an S-shaped figure beneath the tail; in the field, various pellets, &c.
Rev.—A thin vertical line, crossed by a peculiar crooked object, with two or three lines coming out from it at either

end; in the angles an object like the wings of a butterfly, an arc of a circle between three pellets, a V-shaped figure with its outer edge jagged, and parts of other circles. *N.* 19 to 21 grains.

The specimen engraved is in my own collection. There were some coins of this type among those found at Karn Brê, which are engraved in Borlase's Antiquities of Cornwall, pl. xix. 1, 2, 3, and Gough's Camden, Nos. 37, 38, and 39, though it is not easy to recognise them; and probably the reverses offered some of the intermediate phases, which are numerous between this and the next coin in the Plate. In two specimens, also from Karn Brê, engraved in Borlase's Nat. Hist. of Cornwall, pl. xxix. 5 and 6, the devices are more distinct. Another specimen is given in Stukeley, pl. xxii. 1. There were also some in the find at Bognor, before mentioned (see Smith's Coll. Ant., vol. i. pl. vii. 6); and one in silver (?), said to have been found at Portsmouth, is in the British Museum. Their finding, like that of the two subsequent types, is not, however, confined to England, as a variety found at Douai is engraved in Lelewel, pl. ix. 30. But the questions of their geographical distribution and of the derivation of the types will be best discussed after an examination of the two subsequent types, with which this is closely allied.

PLATE E, No. 10.

Obv.—Device very like that on the last coin, except that the fish-like object has a series of indentations in it, and the S-shaped figure is absent. Only the right hand portion of the device is shown on the coin here engraved; on some coins there appears to be an outer circle of Vs.

Rev.—The transverse crooked line as on the last coin; above, an object like a palm-tree, between two oval protuberances; below, a number of marks something like Hebrew characters.

N. 20 to 23 grains; but occasionally lighter.

This specimen is also from my own collection. On some there is very much the appearance of the marks beneath the crooked line having been intended for an inscription, which

is, however, undecipherable. Coins of this type were among
the Bognor find (see Coll. Ant., vol. i. pl. vii. 3). They have
also been found near Romsey, Hants (Arch. Assoc. Journ.,
vol. ii. p. 330), and I have a variety, found at Chittenden,
near Sandwich, from the Rolfe collection. Another is engraved by Lelewel, pl. iii. 35, who says that similar coins
have been found near Amiens, and in the north of Belgic
Gaul. M. de Saulcy refers them to the Morini. The type
is too closely allied to that of No. 11 to be separately
considered.

Plate E, No. 11.

Obv.—Plain and convex, though with usually some irregularity
of surface, and occasionally traces of some device,
possibly a degenerate laureate head. Sometimes
also there are traces of an ornamented border round
the convex projection.

Rev.—The crooked line and palm-tree as on the last coin, but the
latter more nearly approaching in shape to the tree
or branch on Plate D, No. 11; above, a rosette of
pellets between two oval loops; on either side bands
and lines terminating in crescents and ornamental
pellets; and below, a crescent and other objects.
Æ. 19 to 21 grains.

This coin was found at Bognor, and is in my own collection. Others of this type have been found at Pagham
and Bracklesham, Sussex (Dixon, p. 36, No. 1 [badly en-
graved], and p. 80, No. 2; see also Arch. Assoc. Journ.,
vol. iii. p. 61). There were also some among the Bognor
find (Coll. Ant., vol. i. pl. vii. 1 and 2). Others were found
at Eastbourne (Arch. Assoc. Journ., vol. ii. p. 300), and near
Maidstone (Coll. Ant., vol. i. pl. vi. 6). I have another,
found at Westgate station, near Margate, from the Rolfe
collection. Plot, in his Nat. Hist. of Oxfordshire (pl. xv.
20), gives one as having been found at Wood Eaton, in that
county, in 1676; and one is engraved among the Pembroke
Coins, Pl. ii. pl. 94, and in Gibson's Camden, pl. i. 30. They
are also found upon the continent, and specimens are engraved in Lelewel, pl. iv. 6, and in the Revue Numismatique, vol. iii. pl. viii. 4 and 5. There are several coins of

this class in the Museum at Boulogne, which were found in that neighbourhood.

As has already been observed, the types of this and the two preceding coins are closely connected, and there are many intermediate varieties between them, the whole of which it would have occupied too much space to engrave. Some of them may, however, be seen in the Coll. Ant., vol. i. pl. vii. The crooked object upon the reverse has, by some, been considered to represent the sacred knife of the Druids, with which they are said to have cut the mistletoe from the oaks, and the branch above has been taken for the mistletoe itself. But such a view cannot for a moment be entertained. Whatever the objects on No. 11, or its more finished descendant, Plate D, No. 11, may have been intended to represent, it is probable that on the early coins the whole device is merely a degenerate representation of the horse and its rider, such as appear on Plate D, No. 4. It must nevertheless be confessed that, at present, there are several links missing in the pedigree. The connection of Plate D, No. 11, with Plate E, No. 9, can, however, be traced with certainty, and offers another curious instance of the tendency of an unintelligible device to assume, under a process of repeated imitations, a regular symmetrical pattern. Though these coins are of not unfrequent occurrence on the opposite side of the Channel, they seem to be rather more abundant in England; and though possibly current in both Britain and Gaul, they appear to belong to the British rather than to the Gaulish series. The resemblance of the device on the reverse of No. 9 to a jovial full face is very strong, and an affinity may be traced in it, not only to Plate IL, No. 4, but to the copper coin of Cunobeline, Plate XI., No. 10. The device on the obverse of Nos. 9 and 11 is probably a derivative from the laureate bust, but in what precise manner it has assumed this form it is hard to say. The fish-like object bears, however, some resemblance to the helmeted head on the silver coins, Plate F, No. 11, which belong to same district. It seems possible that the two E-shaped or boot-like objects may be the representatives of the wreath; but a careful observation of more specimens than are at present available, is necessary before any valid conclusion as to the derivation of these types can be attained. The device has been regarded as a galley with sails; but this is out of the question.

Plate E, No. 12.

Obv.—The letter A (?) formed as it is on the coins of Addedomarus, but with the cross stroke downwards from the right instead of from the left limb of the letter.

Rev.—Horse to the left, the mane formed as on E, No. 5; above, a rosette; and in the field, several annulets.

N. 17 grains.

This curious little coin, which is now in my own collection, formed part of the Bognor find, so frequently mentioned. It is engraved, but not with sufficient accuracy, in the Coll. Ant., vol. i. pl. vii. 11. Though inserted among the uninscribed coins, I am very doubtful whether it ought not to be regarded as inscribed; but it is possible that the A-like object may after all be merely a relic of the ornamentation on the neck of the wide-spread bust. Unfortunately the coin is so little spread that it shows only a small portion of the die, so that it is impossible to say whether there may not have been a legend on the reverse. Whether or not, the type belongs to the South-eastern district, and the coin is little, if at all, anterior to those of Tinc[ommius], with one of which it was found.

Plate E, No. 13.

Obv.—Plain and convex, with a raised band across it.

Rev.—A horse prancing to the right; above its back a branch of three leaves; ring ornaments in the field.

N. 16½ grains and 20 grains.

A specimen of this type, found in soil from the bed of the Thames, is described in C. Roach Smith's Coll. of London Antiquities, p. 99, and is engraved in the Numismatic Chronicle, vol. i. pl. ii. 3. That here engraved is in my own collection, but I do not know where it was found. The leaves above the horse give it very much the appearance of being a Pegasus, and it is described as such in the Numismatic Chronicle. There is, beneath the horse, on the Thames coin, and on another specimen which I possess, a crooked object, possibly a snake, like that on the coins of Dubnovellaunus and Vose[nos], Plate IV., Nos. 10 and 13, with which this type seems to be allied. This type has also the raised hand across the obverse, which is similar to that on Plate D, Nos. 10 and 11. It is not impossible that it may eventually prove to have been inscribed.

Plate E, No. 14.

Obv.—Plain and convex, with the raised band across.

Rev.—A horse prancing to the right; above, a ring ornament and pellet; below, a pentalpha; and behind, a star; the whole within a beaded circle. *N.* 19¼ grains.

A coin of this type was found at Reculver, and is engraved in Battely's Antiquitates Rutupinæ, pl. vi. Another is engraved in Ruding, pl. i. 6, from the Hunter collection, which is here reproduced, and which appears to be the same coin as that in Borlase's Antiquities of Cornwall, pl. xix. 21, and Gough's Camden, No. 58, though the weight is stated as 20¼ grains. It is also in Lelewel, pl. viii. 29.

The most remarkable feature of this coin is the occurrence upon it of the pentalpha, or pentagon, formed by five interlacing lines. Though of frequent occurrence on Gaulish coins (see Lambert, pl. ix. 31; pl. x. 9. Lelewel, pl. iv. 5; pl. viii. 4, &c. &c.), it is not met with on any other British coin. There is little doubt that some mystic signification was attached to this figure, so that this coin might have been cited to support the opinions which some have held as to the connection between the doctrine of the Druids and that of Pythagoras, whose symbol of Salus, or 'ΥΓΕΙΑ, was this triple interlaced triangle. Some interesting remarks upon this subject will be found in Eckhel, Doct. Num., vol. i. p. 63; and in Pierii Hieroglyphica, p. 351.

CHAPTER V.

UNINSCRIBED SILVER COINS.

The uninscribed British coins in silver are far less numerous than those in gold, and present but comparatively few varieties of type. There are, however, among them five or six distinct series, each having apparently a different geographical range; and though probably all are not of precisely the same period, yet it is evident that the whole of them are posterior to the earliest of the gold coins. It is indeed probable that by far the greater part of them belong to quite the latter stage of the British coinage, and that many of them are but little anterior in date to the invasion of Claudius. The most extensive series of the silver coins is that of the Iceni, or of the Norfolk and Suffolk district, which have a sufficiently well-marked character to form a class by themselves, the principal types of which are engraved in Plate XVI., and will be treated of in conjunction with the inscribed coins of the same district, with which indeed they are contemporary. The other classes are:—

I. Coins of the South-western district, which are principally found in Dorsetshire and the adjoining counties. There is a considerable range in the weight and fineness of metal in different specimens, but the lightest of them are far heavier than any of the silver coins of the other districts, and are evidently struck under a different monetary system. The heavier and finer coins of this class are probably of earlier date than the lighter and more alloyed, and are, indeed, most likely the earliest of the British coins in silver. Characteristic specimens are given in Plate F, Nos. 1 to 3.

II. Coins of the Western district, from Somersetshire to Berks, of which specimens are given in Plate F, Nos. 4 to 9. They do not appear to have extended over nearly so long a period as the Dorsetshire coins, and the latest of them come down to the days of Claudius.

III. Coins of the South-eastern district, or of Surrey and Sussex. These are of two modules, the smaller being the least of all the British coins. They probably belong to the period of Commius and his sons. The principal varieties are engraved on Plate F, Nos. 10 to 13.

IV. Coins of Kent. Of these but one variety is at present known, that in Plate F, No. 15.

V. Coins of the class represented in Plate G, Nos. 2 to 4, which probably belong to the Eastern part of England, but whose home is at present uncertain. The coin, Plate G, No. 1, appears to be connected with this class, and Plate F, No. 14, is probably Icenian.

It is, of course, impossible to say what proportionate value these silver coins bore to those in gold or copper of the same districts and period, nor is this point ever likely to be determined. It will, however, be subsequently seen that the silver coins have been found associated with gold; so that, besides the assistance afforded by similarity of type, we have direct evidence of certain coins of each metal having been in circulation together. Other points in relation to each class will be mentioned in the descriptions of the various coins.

Plate F, No. 1.

Obv.—Portions of the laureate bust similar to Plate B, Nos. 5 and 6.

Rev.—Disjointed horse to the left, like that on Plate B, No. 6; above, a number of pellets; behind, an oval ring ornament, and three transverse lines issuing from the horse's hind-leg. The exergual space ornamented with a zigzag and pellets, as on Plate B, No. 1.
Æ. 72 grains.

PLATE F, No. 2.

Obv.—As No. 1.
Rev.—As No. 1, but showing the upper part of the device with four ring ornaments above the pellets, instead of the lower part with the exergual space. There is a difference in the lines behind the horse's leg, the spaces between which are beaded. Æ 79½ grains.

The specimens engraved are both in the British Museum. It will be perceived that they are of the same type, though showing different parts of the device, the die, as usual, having been much larger than the *flan*.

A number of these coins were found near Blandford, Dorset, of which three are engraved in the Coll. Ant., pl. lvi. 10, 11, and 12. Associated with these were others, in copper, of the same type (Arch. Assoc. Journ., vol. ii. p. 336). Several others were found near Portsmouth, of which one is engraved in Hawkins, pl. i. 5; in the Num. Journ., vol. i. pl. i. 9; Ruding, pl. A, 82; and the Revue Num., vol. iv. pl. xiii. 10. About twenty others were discovered at Tollard Royal, Wilts (Arch. Assoc. Journ., vol. ii. p. 336). Twenty-seven more were found at Farnham, near Thickthorne, Cranbourne Chase, Dorsetshire, in 1858, some of which, as well as one from Danebury Hill, Hants, are in the British Museum. Hutchins, in his History of Dorset, vol. ii. p. 400, mentions seventy or eighty British silver coins of this type as having been found at Ockford Fitzpaine Hill, near Blandford. Their average weight is said to have been 83 grains.

Many coins of this type are in the collection of Mr. Henry Durden, of Blandford, who has kindly furnished me with the following particulars of their finding:—

Blandford	2 specimens,	63, 81	grains.
Hod-Hill (very base metal)	2 ,,	49, 52	,,
Iwerne Minster	1 ,,	68	,,
Langton, near Blandford	2 ,,	76, 77	,,
Mere (Wilts)	1 ,,	63	,,
Moore Critchell	1 ,,	80	,,
Shapwick	1 ,,	80	,,
Shroton	1 ,,	62	,,
Tarrant Gunville	2 ,,	82	,,
Tisbury (Wilts)	1 ,,	77	,,
Tollard Royal	1 ,,	79	,,

Mr. Durden has known other specimens found at Tarrant Crawford and Bere Regis, near Blandford; at Jordan Hill, near Weymouth; and within a British earthwork at Worbarrow Bay, near Wareham. The latter weighs 52 grains. Two of them, weighing 72 and 78 grains, were found at Cann, near Shaftesbury, in 1849, with a human skeleton and a bronze Celt. The latter is of the socketed form, and like fig. 284 in Wilde's Catalogue of the Mus. Royal Irish Acad., but longer in proportion. It is now in Mr. Durden's collection. Another of these coins was found at Silchester (Arch. Journ., vol. xi. p. 57); and a plated specimen was discovered at South Petherton, Somersetshire.

The type is engraved in Ruding, pl. iii. 44, from a specimen in the Hunter collection weighing 76½ grains. The silver of some of these coins is considerably alloyed, and there is great diversity in the weight of different specimens, as well as in the extent to which they are spread; but on the point of weight I will speak farther after having described the next coin, No. 3, which belongs to the same class.

PLATE F, No. 3.

Obv.—Similar to the two last.
Rev.—Like that of No. 1, but much more coarsely executed.
Æ. 55 grains.

The coin here engraved is in my own collection, and shows a degree of coarseness of execution in the horse (!) on the reverse almost incredible. In fact, were it not for other coins, it would be utterly impossible to recognise any animal whatever in the assemblage of lumps and straight strokes with which the field is covered. I am not acquainted with the place of its discovery; but two coins of the same character are engraved in Borlase's Antiquities of Cornwall, pl. xix. 24 and 25, and Gough's Camden, Nos. 56 and 57, which were found in the parish of Swacliffe, near Madmarston Castle, Oxfordshire, in 1740. Mr. Durden has another from Hod Hill, weighing 52 grains. The coin in Stukeley, pl. xvii. 1, is of the same type, as is also one in

Lambert, pl. vi. 9. The latter, which is of copper plated with silver, was found among the ruins of the ancient station of Jort, near St. Pierre-sur-Dives (Calvados).

The close resemblance of these coins to those in gold, Plate B, Nos. 4 to 6, seems to prove that they must have been struck by the same people, and at the same time, though probably the type of the laureate bust, and the charioteer, having once attained this extreme of degradation, may have been persistent in this state for a lengthened period, as indeed the extreme diversity in the weight and fineness of the metal of the coins would suggest. Different specimens range from about 90 grains down to not more than 40 grains; and as they occur of all intermediate weights, the lighter coins cannot have been intended to represent half the value of the larger; and the inference is, that the type must have remained unchanged for a considerable period, while the weight was gradually reduced. As before observed, there are brass coins of the same class (see Plate G, Nos. 5 and 6).

Plate F, No. 4.

Obv.—A stolid looking head in profile to the right; the hair represented by a number of crescent-shaped bosses placed back to back, with usually three or more small pellets on each; between the hair and the face is usually a beaded band, forming the arc of a circle. The eye is represented by an annulet or ring ornament, and the chin by a circular boss. The mouth is formed by two projecting lines ending in pellets. The eyebrow or forehead is indented like the fish-like object on the gold Sussex coins, Plate E, 10. In front of the face are two curved S-shaped figures, and the lowest lock of hair is of the same form. In the field are various annulets, ring ornaments, and pellets.

Rev.—Three-tailed horse to the left, its head and shoulder formed with ring ornaments; above, a kind of triquetra, the limbs springing from a ring ornament or pellet in the centre; below, a rosette: in the field, ring ornaments, annulets, and pellets, sometimes ornamented. *B.* 14 to 18 grains.

There were eight or ten of these coins in the find at Nunney, near Frome, which is described in the Numismatic Chronicle, N.S., vol. i. p. 1, where also one of them is engraved, pl. i. 11. I possess another specimen, which was found near Cirencester. Another is given, though inaccurately in the Numismatic Chronicle, vol. i. pl. ii. 6, and others in Stukeley, pl. xxii. 3 and 8; and Wise, pl. xvi. 19. The type is so closely connected with that of the subsequent coins, that it will be best to consider them all together.

Plate F, No. 5.

Obv.—Rude head in profile to the left; in front, two curved objects, pellets, &c.

Rev.—Horse to the left, with various annulets and other objects in the field. Æ. 18½ grains.

This coin is copied from Ruding, Appendix, pl. xxix. 1; and from its analogy with the preceding coin—although the head is turned in the other direction—is probably British. The formation of the body of the horse with two ring ornaments, and other details, as far as can be judged from the engraving alone, seem to be of a British rather than a Gaulish character. It is, however, engraved in Lelewel, pl. viii. 34, and is there classed as "Gallo-Breton." The next coin in Ruding's plate is also probably British, but is apparently engraved without sufficient regard to accuracy. I have therefore omitted it from my Plate.

Plate F, No. 6.

Obv.—Rude head in profile, like that on No. 4, but a cross in place of the chin, and the crescents forming the hair converted into groups of three pellets each.

Rev.—Very like that of No. 4, but the ring ornament is the principal feature of what was a sort of triquetra. Æ. 13 to 19 grains.

There were five specimens of this type among the Nunney find, already mentioned. That here engraved was found near Tewkesbury, in 1858. I have also specimens found near Oxford, and near Letcombe Regis, Berks.

Plate F, No. 7.

Obv.—Rude head in profile to the right; the outlines of the face portrayed by a thick, crooked line, which bifurcates to form the mouth; the back of the head is defined by a beaded semicircle, while two ring ornaments seem to represent the eye and the ear, with a small cross by way of decoration between them. The hair is rendered by a beaded semicircle, with an inner series of crescents with pellets in the centre of each, like ring ornaments overlapping each other. In front of the face are several curved or dolphin-shaped figures, ring ornaments, and pellets, and the whole seems to have been surrounded on the die by a double ring of pellets placed alternately and some little distance apart.

Rev.—Three-tailed horse to the left, as on No. 6, with ring ornaments on the shoulder and haunch. There is usually the same quatrefoil or star below the horse, and above a ring ornament, with a straight projection from it to the left, and two thin solid crescents like ears to its right. Between the ring ornament and the horse a solid crescent. In the field are various pellets, occasionally ornamented like those on the gold coins, Plate D, 7; E, 1 and 2, &c. These coins are usually much dished. Æ. About 18 grains.

Plate F, No. 8.

Obv.—As No. 7.
Rev.—As No. 7, but a small cross above the horse, and with ring ornaments in the field. Æ. About 16 grains.

There were about 180 coins of these two types in the find at Nunney, near Frome, already mentioned, two of which are engraved in the Numismatic Chronicle, N.S., vol. i. pl. i. 13 and 14. They varied in weight from 13 to 21½ grains, but the average weight was 18¼ grains.

Previously to this discovery the type was nearly unknown; for though specimens belonging to this class are engraved in Hawkins, pl. i. 15; Ruding, pl. A, 66; Revue Numismatique, vol. iv. pl. xiii. 13; and the Numismatic Journal, vol. i. pl. i. 13; yet they did not convey the slightest impression of there being any attempt to represent a human face upon them. The coin in Hawkins and in the Numismatic Journal was found at Mount Batten, near Plymouth, in company with a number of coins of the class usually found in the Channel Islands.

It is of course evident that the devices upon the coins Nos. 4 to 8 may be regarded as the same, though progressively degenerating, in the same manner as the silver on which they were struck appears to have been gradually more and more alloyed, the metal of the coins like No. 4 being usually finer than that of those like No. 8. It is not, however, easy to determine from whence the type of the head in profile, with the curved objects in front, was derived. There are such curved or dolphin-shaped figures in front of the face on some of the coins of the Channel Islands (see Plate I, No. 4, &c.); and as such coins of both classes have been found together, they possibly have a common origin. This is possibly to be found in the gold coins of the Armorican coast, on some few of which these dolphin-shaped figures occur, and on most of which there are flowing beaded lines in front of the face. There are also among the Gaulish coins imitations of those of Rhoda, on which there are two dolphins in front of the head of Ceres.

There is a curious similarity in the arrangement of the hair on No. 4 to that on a Gaulish imitation of the Philippus (Lelewel, pl. ii. 14), and the degenerate portraits on Nos. 6 to 8 are well worth a comparison with the type of portrait No. 10, given in Lelewel, pl. x.

With regard to the date of these coins, there is no doubt that they are among the latest of the British series, as unworn specimens were found at Frome in company with coins of Claudius and of Antonia. There were also with them inscribed coins of the types Plate I., Nos. 4, 7, 8, and 9, thus proving the interesting fact that uninscribed and inscribed coins were current together in the West of England, in the same manner as had already been proved to have been the case in the Eastern district, by the finds of Icenian coins at Weston and elsewhere. It is to be remarked that in neither district have British copper coins been found in company with the silver coins, though at Frome there were some Roman copper coins present, as well as some British coins in gold. The proportion of the silver coins to the gold it is of course now impossible to determine; but taking into account the superior weight of the gold coins, as well as the greater intrinsic value of the metal, it would seem as if a large number of the silver coins—possibly forty or fifty—may have been the equivalent of one of those in gold.

Plate F, No. 9.

Obv.—Portions of a face in profile, much the same as on Nos. 4 and 6. There is however a star of pellets on the forehead and in front of the face, and a ring ornament and row of solid crescents in lieu of the dolphin-shaped objects.

Rev.—A horse galloping to the right; above, a solid crescent; below, a four-leaved flower, a crescent, and several pellets. Æ. 16½ grains.

The coin here engraved is in my own collection, but I do not know where it was found. Another specimen of the same type is in the collection of the Rev. J. H. Pollexfen, of Colchester, and was found at that place. It weighs 14⅞ grains. It will be observed that while the horses on Nos. 6, 7, and 8 closely resemble those on the coins inscribed SVEI and ANTED (Plate I., Nos. 8 and 9), the horse on the reverse of this coin is like that on the silver coin reading BODVOC (Plate I., No. 3), a fact which corroborates its attribution to the Western district, notwithstanding that one of the coins was found at Colchester. The succeeding coins belong to another part of the country.

Plate F, No. 10.

Obv.—Head in profile to the right, the hair turned back; a double line, the inner one braided and the other formed of S-shaped figures, carried round the back of the head, after the manner of the crest to a helmet. In front, a rosette and two ornamented pellets.

Rev.—Horse to the right; in front, a ring ornament (?); above, a beaded wheel; in the field, various annulets and pellets. Æ. 16½ grains.

The horse on this coin is represented in a different manner from that on any other British coins. The lengthened mouth, the small, detached, and oval ears, and the threaded edge given to the neck and body, are all peculiar. The specimen here engraved was formerly in the collection of the late Mr. Huxtable, but is now in mine. It is also engraved in the Numismatic Chronicle, vol. ii. p. 191, No. 4, and in Lelewel, pl. viii. 31. The same coin, apparently, is engraved in Stukeley, pl. xviii. 10, having been at that time in the collection of Mr. Joseph Tolson Lockyer, F.S.A. A second coin is engraved as No. 3 of the plate in the Numismatic Chronicle, above cited, but the place of discovery of neither is known. I have little hesitation in assigning them to the South-eastern, or Sussex district. There is an evident connection between the head on this and on the two next coins, and an analogy between many of the details of the reverse and those on the gold coins found near Guildford (Plate D, Nos. 6, 7, &c.).

PLATE F, No. 11.

Obv.—A helmeted head in profile to the right, the side of the helmet ribbed. Occasionally there is a circle of pellets and a rosette upon the neck.

Rev.—Horse to the right, with ring ornaments on the shoulder and rump; the eye formed by another ring ornament; the mane as wide as the neck, and formed by a strong outer line with cross strokes; above, an ornament like the astronomical sign ♈, the horns enclosing pellets on either side, something like a rude full face; below, a part of a large wheel, and in the field various small annulets. Æ. 17 to 19¾ grains.

Five coins of this type were found at Ashdown Forest, Sussex, together with two of the small silver coins, No. 12, and gold coins of the types Plate E, Nos. 5 and 8. They are engraved in the Numismatic Chronicle, vol. ii. p. 231, from whence I have copied. Another specimen, discovered at Farley Heath, near Guildford, which is now in the British

Museum, is engraved in the Arch. Assoc. Journ., vol. v. p. 157, and Poste's British Coins, p. 154; but the helmeted head has been mistaken for the "dubious representation of some animal," and is made to look very like a squirrel. A mistake of this kind illustrates the transitions which actually took place in the types of the British coins; as for instance, those of the Iceni (Plate XVI, Nos. 8, 11, and 12), where we find a human head converted, with but few intermediate stages, into a boar.

I have two others of these Sussex coins, said to have been found at Pevensey. One of these, which is much corroded, weighs only 13 grains, as was the case with one in the same condition from Ashdown Forest. Others weigh from 17 to 19½ grains, or as nearly as possible the same as the gold coins with which they were found associated. There must therefore, in all probability, have been some well-defined proportion in the value of silver and gold respectively, which may be assumed to have been either 12 or 10 to 1, the former proportion being the more likely.*

The original of the type of the galeated head on the obverse is probably to be sought for among the Gaulish coinage. It may, for instance, have been such a coin as that of COIOS ORCITIRIX (Revue Numismatique, N.S., vol. v. pl. v. 2), the head on which, though turned in the opposite direction, bears a great resemblance to that on these British coins. The horse on the reverse more nearly approaches that on the gold coins Plate E, No. 5, which were found with these in silver.

Plate F, No. 12.

Obv. & Rev.—Nearly the same as last, but much smaller.
Æ. 3½ and 4 grains.

These are probably the smallest of the British coins, and must have been intended for the quarters of the pieces last described. They were found associated with them at Ash-

---

* See Sabatier, "Production de l'or, &c., chez les Anciens," p. 50.

down Forest, and are engraved in the Numismatic Chronicle, vol. ii. p. 231. Mr. C. Roach Smith has communicated to me some others, found on the Downs near Lancing. The existence of such small coins would seem to imply a considerable degree of civilisation among those for whom they were struck, and the types and character of both the gold and silver coins from this hoard justify our assigning them to a late period among the uninscribed coins, probably subsequent to the invasion of Julius Cæsar, and but little, if at all, before the issue of the inscribed coins of the sons of Commius. In the find near Lancing they were indeed associated with coins of Verica and Tinc[ommius].

PLATE F, No. 13.

Obv.—Head in profile to the left, with what may have been intended for a helmet. The eye formed by a ring ornament, and two others in front of the face.

Rev.—Horse to the left; in front, a ring ornament; above, what may be the same device as on No. 11; below, an uncertain object. *Æ* 15 grains.

This coin, which is in the cabinet of Mr. Whitbourn, of Godalming, was found at Farley Heath. Another, from the same locality, is engraved in the Arch. Assoc. Journ., vol. v. p. 157, No. 1, and in Poste's British Coins, p. 154. It is there stated that it is also engraved in Stukeley, pl. xvii. 4; but this is probably an error, as Stukeley's coin comes much nearer to one of the Gaulish coins reading ΚΑΛΕΤΕΔΟΥ. It is not unlikely that a Gaulish quinarius, of that or some similar type, may have been the original from which these coins were imitated. The treatment of the face is, however, essentially British, and approximates to that of the earlier coins of the Western district (Nos. 4 and 6, &c., in the same Plate). The date of this type must be much the same as that of Nos. 11 and 12. They appear to have been found at Farley Heath, associated with silver coins of Verica (Plate II., Nos. 4 and 6). A number of copper or brass coins, of the type Plate G,

Nos. 2 and 3, have been found at the same place, if not in immediate association with the silver coins.

Plate F, No. 14.

Obv.—Horse standing to the right; above, a beaded circle with a pellet in the centre; below, a ring ornament.
Rev.—A boar standing to the right; ring ornaments above, below, and in front. Æ. 18½ grains.

I have taken this coin from the Numismatic Chronicle, vol. i. pl. ii. 1, where it is described as being in the cabinet of Mr. Lucas, but no place of finding is mentioned. From its being of larger size than the generality of the Icenian coins, and from my not having seen the original, I have placed the coin in this Plate rather than in Plate XVI., to which, from its general similarity to Nos. 12, 13, and 14, it would seem more properly to belong.

Plate F, No. 15.

Obv.—Griffin (?) to the right; above and behind a ring ornament.
Rev.—A horse to the left; ring ornaments above, below, and between his forelegs. Æ. 10½ grains.

This coin was kindly presented to me by Mr. C. Roach Smith, and is engraved in his Coll. Ant., vol. i. pl. vi. 1. It was found at a place called the Slade,* in the parish of Boughton Montchelsea, on the site of a Roman dwelling and burial place, with Roman coins ranging from Claudius to Gratianus. There were, however, found at the same place four British coins in copper of the types Plate XI., No. 12, and Plate XIII., Nos. 5 and 6. Another silver coin of the same type was found in the Isle of Thanet (Smith's Coll. Ant., vol. i. pl. lvi. 9), which is now in my own collection. It is barely possible that these coins may eventually prove to have been inscribed; but, under any circumstances, they seem to belong to Kent, and were probably struck but shortly before the days of Eppillus.

* See Archæologia, vol. xxix. p. 419.

PLATE G, No. 1.

Obv.—Rude head in profile to the right; the hair represented by four curved and twisted coils; the ear formed by an open crescent; a band across the forehead with indentations upon it, like the fish-shaped object on the gold coin, Plate E, 10. Behind the neck a ring ornament; in front a crooked figure. In the field various zigzags. The whole surrounded by a beaded circle.

Rev.—A two-tailed horse galloping to the right, its fore-legs formed with double lines at the shoulder, one of the hind-legs partly formed by a beaded line, and with the feet turned the wrong way; the mane as on Plate F, No. 11; above, a starlike figure, the rays ending in ornamented pellets; below, a boar standing on three legs to the right; in front, a flower (?), like that beneath the horse on Plate E, No. 2; behind, a zigzag. The whole within a beaded circle.

Æ. 18½ grains.

This coin, which was found at Richborough, was formerly in the collection of the late Mr. Rolfe, of Sandwich, and is now in my own. It has been engraved in Smith's Coll. Ant., vol. i. pl. lv. 12, but was at that time considered to bear more analogy to the Gaulish than the British series. It has, however, so many points in common with some of the British coins, especially those of the South-eastern district, that I have ventured to claim it as British, and I do so the more readily as I do not think that the type is known in France. It was probably struck from some Gaulish prototype with the boar beneath the horse, but the workmanship, as well as the character of the adjuncts, seem to me to fix its home on this side of the Channel.

PLATE G, No. 2.

Obv.—Beardless head in profile, to the left; the hair in long twisted coils, arranged so as to resemble a helmet, with a curved line ending in a ring ornament forming a crest; in front, several figures formed by annulets standing on two diverging crescents; behind, a figure like a written M; beneath the neck (which has a beaded edge), three small ring ornaments.

Rev.—A horse galloping to the right, its head formed with a ring ornament, its tail thick and bushy; above, a singular bird to the left, with large ears and no legs, the head and body formed with ring ornaments; in front of the bird a rosette, and below the horse a beaded ring ornament; in the field, various annulets and ring ornaments. Æ. 18½ grains.

This curious little coin, which has lost a small portion of its edge, was found near Bury St. Edmund's, and is now in my own cabinet. It is hitherto unpublished. From its place of finding, and from the assurance of MM. de Souley and de Longpérier that the type is unknown in France, I have no hesitation in claiming it as British; and though at present it is impossible to say to what part of Britain it is to be assigned, it is of great importance as corroborating the attribution of the two next coins in the Plate to Britain also. The workmanship of this coin is very neat, and the relief sharp and clear. The small adjuncts are of much the same character as those on some of the Sussex coins, but from the place of finding, this coin may probably have been struck further north. The bird is of an order unknown to naturalists of the present day, though allied to the heraldic martlets and the mediæval birds of Paradise. It may have been intended for a mythical cock. We learn from Cæsar that it was not lawful for the Britons to eat hares, poultry, or geese, though they kept them for pleasure:—"Leporem, et gallinam, et anserem gustare, fas non putant, hæc tamen alunt, animi voluptatisque causá."[*] The cock (gallus) appears as the principal type on a Gaulish coin (Lambert, pl. vii. 34), and curiously combined with a human head, for which it forms a helmet, on another (Lambert, pl. vii. 35). It seems possible that the head on the obverse of this coin, and of Nos. 1, 3, and 4, may be intended for that of Victory, who, under the name of Andate or Andraste, appears to have been highly venerated by the Britons.[†]

[*] De Bell. Gall., lib. v. cap. 12.
[†] Dion Cassius, lib. lxii. p. 1004. Ed. 1752.

PLATE G, No. 3.

Obv.—Head in profile to the left, very like that on the last coin.
Rev.—Horse walking to the left, a ring on its shoulder, its head formed with a ring ornament, others above and behind; beneath the horse another and three pellets. Æ. 15 grains.

This coin is in my own collection, but I do not know where it was found. Like the former, it is unpublished, and from its close connection with it, and from the type being apparently unknown in France, there is little doubt of its being of British origin. The workmanship is not quite so good as that of the last coin. The horse is British in character, and may be compared with that on Plate D, No. 13, though turned in the opposite direction.

PLATE G, No. 4.

Obv.—Head in profile to the left, of much the same character as that on the last coin, but larger; in front, a rosette of pellets.
Rev.—Long-horned goat with flowing mane, walking to the right, its shoulder formed with a ring, and its head with a ring ornament; others above, below, before, and behind; the whole surrounded by a circle of pellets. Æ. 14½ grains.

This is also an unpublished coin, in my own collection, but the place of finding is not known. I have, however, another specimen, an ancient forgery, of copper plated with silver, which was found in Kent, and was formerly in the Rolfe collection. The goat, for such it appears to be, is not unlike that on some of the Gaulish series (Lambert, pl. vii. 1 to 4), but the style of work is quite different, and the obverse of those coins has a laureate head. The goat appears on one of the copper coins of Verulam (Plate VIII., No. 2), but this is the only other coin on which it is found. It is curious to observe the perfect similarity of treatment of the horse on the preceding coin, and the goat on this. With the exception of the horns and mane, the animals are identical, and the adjuncts in the field are also precisely the same. The coins are therefore evidently almost, if not quite, contemporary, and future discoveries will probably enable us to decide with certainty the part of the country in which they were struck. Though the plated coin was found in Kent, I think their home will prove to be rather further north, in Essex or some adjacent county. Since this plate was engraved I have added another new type in silver to my collection, of which a woodcut is here given.

It may be thus described—

Obv.—Beardless head in profile to the left; a curved object in front like an S reversed.

Rev.—Horse galloping to the left; above, a rosette and an annulet; below, a ring ornament. The off fore-leg is split at the shoulder, and the tail is trifid at the end. There is a curved dotted line beneath the head, and there appears to be an exergual line. Æ. 18¾ grains.

This coin was found within a few miles of Bury St. Edmund's, and is hitherto unpublished. The face on the obverse is fairly rendered, and bears some resemblance to that of Plate G, No. 2, but the ear is peculiar. The hair is not shown on this coin. The curved object in front seems to be an exaggerated and possibly earlier form of that in the same position in Plate F, Nos. 4 and 5. The horse on the reverse is well drawn, but it has the fore-leg split in the manner in which it is shown on so many of the coins of the Iceni (Plates XV. and XVI.). From the general character of the coin, as well as the place of finding, it is probable that it was struck in Cambridgeshire or Suffolk, and that it is of earlier date than the more common coins of the Iceni.

CHAPTER VI.

UNINSCRIBED COPPER AND BRASS COINS.

The uninscribed copper and brass coins of the Ancient Britons present but few varieties of type. Not only are they much scarcer than those in gold, but when discovered they are frequently so much corroded by time, that it is with difficulty that any devices can be discerned upon them. It also occasionally happens that what have been regarded as mute pieces, are, by the discovery of better preserved specimens, shown to have been inscribed. It is probable that this will eventually be found to be the case with at least half of those engraved in Plate G. It is, indeed, a question whether any beside Nos. 5 and 6, and possibly 11 and 12, can be authoritatively quoted as specimens of the uninscribed coinage of the Britons. Such being the case, it is useless to attempt any particular classification of them beyond that implied in the remarks which will be made as to the places where the various types have been found, when each is described. The inferior metals appear to have been the last which were introduced into the British currency, and were not probably in general use, unless possibly in the South-western district, before the invasion of Cæsar. I may observe that, in describing these coins, I have used the words brass and copper in their widest sense, and not in their strict chemical meaning. It is probable that in most cases the coins are of bronze (copper and tin) rather than of brass (copper and zinc), and that very few indeed are of pure copper. Without sacrificing some coins for the sake of having them analysed, it is impossible to speak with confidence as to the exact nature of the metal of which they are composed.

PLATE G, Nos. 5, 6.

Obv.—Portions of the laureate bust to the right.

Rev.—Extremely barbarous horse, with numerous pellets in the field; behind, a circle crossed by a line. There is an exergual line, and the space beneath appears to have been ornamented. Æ. 52 grains.

These coins are usually but badly struck, and I have engraved two specimens, in order to complete the type, which is much the same as that of the gold coins, Plate B, No. 6, and of those in silver, Plate F, Nos. 1, 2, and 3. Others are engraved in Ruding, pl. iii. 52, and Stukeley, pl. i. 2.

Those here engraved were found with several others of the same type, as well as with other British coins, at Furley Heath, near Guildford, and were presented to the British Museum by the late Mr. Henry Drummond. Two others were found at Langton, near Blandford, Dorset, associated with silver coins of the same type (Arch. Assoc. Journ., vol. ii. p. 336). Several have been found by Mr. Durden, in the camp at Hod Hill, near Blandford; in one instance associated with a second brass coin of one of the early emperors, and two *terra-cotta* beads. I have a specimen found at Conygore Hill, near Dorchester, weighing 48½ grains. They appear to belong to the class of coins usually found in Dorsetshire and Wilts, but they must have been current at least as far to the east as Surrey. Their weight is usually considerably greater than that of the coins in the same metal of other districts, as has been already observed with regard to the coins in silver of corresponding type. The type of these coins, which is derived from that of the gold coins, assigns them a place among the latest of the uninscribed series; but they may have been struck over a considerable period, extending down to the time of the Roman occupation, as the device, having attained the extreme of degeneracy, may have remained nearly persistent, and the uninscribed coins do not appear to have been superseded by inscribed, in the part of Britain where these coins were struck.

Plate G, No. 7.

Obv.—Head in profile to the left, the hair turned back and represented by corded lines; in front, a star, and behind the ear a ring ornament.

Rev.—Horse to the left, its head formed with a ring ornament, and another on his shoulder; above, a ring ornament; and below, a rosette; pellets in the field; an S-shaped figure in front of the mouth. Æ. 25½ grains.

This coin was found in the neighbourhood of Biggleswade, and is engraved in the Num. Chron., vol. xix. p. 64, No. 11. I have seen two others from the same part of the country. The peculiar head on the obverse is, to some extent, connected with that of Plate XIII., No. 11. It also bears a general resemblance to that on some of the coins of Tasciovanus, in silver, Plates VI., Nos. 3 and 4. The horse on the reverse is identical in character with that of Plate C, No. 14, one coin of which type was found in the same neighbourhood, and another at Earl's Barton, in Northamptonshire. We cannot therefore err in ascribing these copper coins to the Central district. It is, however, probable that they will eventually prove to be inscribed, though the object in front of the horse's mouth is more probably a bridle, like that on some of the Icenian coins, than the letter S.

Plate G, No. 8.

Obv.—Portion of a head of much the same character as that on the last.

Rev.—Horse to the left; in the field annulets and pellets. Æ. 14 grains.

This coin, which is but badly preserved, is in the collection of Mr. Joseph Warren, of Ixworth, and was found at Icklingham, Suffolk. It is intimately connected with the last type, but the head of the horse and the symbols in the field are different. I have a nearly similar specimen found at

Verulam, with ring ornaments above and below the horse. It is much corroded, and weighs only 20 grains. Another from Bedfordshire, in still worse condition, weighs but 14½ grains. I have seen another found in the neighbourhood of Harlow, on the borders of Herts and Essex. These coins will probably eventually prove to be inscribed.

PLATE G, No. 9.

Obv.—Head in profile to the right, the hair turned back, a kind of wheel in the place of the ear, and a ring ornament below it, another in front of the mouth.

Rev.—Eagle to the right devouring a serpent; above a rosette of pellets; below, a ring ornament. Æ. 36¾ grains.

This coin, which is in my own collection, is engraved in the Num. Chron., vol. xix. p. 64, No. 12, and like No. 7, was found in the neighbourhood of Biggleswade. The head is very peculiar, almost Mexican or Peruvian in character, and unlike any other in the series, though allied to that on Plate XIII., No. 11. The type of the reverse is connected with that of the silver coins of Eppillus and Epaticcus (Plate IV., No. 1; Plate VIII., Nos. 13 and 14), and of the copper coins of Eppillus and Verulam (Plate IV. Nos. 2, 3, 5; Plate VIII., No. 1.) It is, however, differently treated; and the eagle is more like that on some of the Gaulish coins. Unfortunately this, the only specimen at present known, is considerably worn. Some future discovery will probably show that it belongs to the inscribed series. It is difficult to suggest the derivation of the types; but an eagle devouring a serpent is of common occurrence on coins of some of the towns of Italy and Sicily.

PLATE G, No. 10.

Obv.—Head in profile to the right, possibly laureate.

Rev.—Horse galloping to the left; above, a ring ornament and trefoil; in front, an annulet. Æ. 35 grains.

There is little doubt that this coin, which is in the British Museum, was struck at Verulam, and probably by Tasciovanus. The head is very similar to that of Plate VII. No. 8. The reverses are also of much the same character, though this has a horse instead of a Pegasus; and the ring ornament and trefoil combined are of common occurrence on the reverses of several of the coins of Verulam. It was probably originally inscribed.

Plate G, No. 11.

Obv.—Two boars back to back; beneath each an annulet; in the centre behind them, a wheel with a line carried on between their backs.

Rev.—A horse to the right; above and below, uncertain objects.
Æ.

I have taken this coin from the Num. Chron., vol i. pl. ii. 4. It is said to have been found at or near Liverpool with other British coins. In type, it is closely allied to the succeeding coin, which, it will be seen, there is some reason for assigning to the Icenian district. The symmetrical arrangement of the two boars, with annulets beneath them, and a wheel behind, and probably also in front, shows a tendency to a regular cruciform arrangement, such as is found on many of the gold coins, and suggests that this type is a derivative from some other and earlier form. The subsequent coin affords a sort of connecting link with some of the Gaulish series.

Plate G, No. 12.

Obv.—Two boars, placed alternately, the head of one to the tail of the other, with a wheel in the centre between their legs.

Rev.—Horse to the right, with large, clumsy feet; above, a curved figure like a horn. There is either a circle surrounding the whole, or a curved exergual line.
Æ. 22 grains.

This coin, in my own collection, is hitherto unpublished. It was found at Brettenham, Norfolk, where, I believe, other British coins have also been discovered. The horse on the reverse is very peculiar, and differs from those upon any of the Icenian coins; yet the place of finding, and the occurrence of the boars, so frequent upon the coins of the Iceni, will, I think, justify us in assigning this piece to that tribe.

The connection of the obverse type with that of the preceding coin has already been mentioned. In both cases we have the two boars and the wheel, but occupying different relative positions. What is very remarkable is the occurrence of the same animals and wheel upon some of the Gaulish coins in tin or brass (see Lelewel, pl. ix. 22). On other nearly similar coins one of the animals more nearly resembles a wolf (see Lelewel, pl. i. 17; Lambert, pl. i. 15; Revue Num., vol. v. pl. xviii. 9).

A Gaulish coin in tin, with the two boars, is engraved in Ruding, pl. iv. 70, as British. It will be observed that some of the Gaulish coins of the same class as those cited have, on the obverse, a regular cruciform ornament (Lelewel, pl. ix. 13), while others have locks of hair arranged in a pattern, divided by a central line (Lelewel, pl. iv. 61), and others again, a head in profile (Lelewel, pl. ix. 12). I mention this in order to show that the degeneration of the head of Apollo into two boars and a wheel, impossible as it may at first appear, is, in fact, but a comparatively easy transition when once the head has been reduced into a form of regular pattern. The boar, being held in such veneration among all the Celtic nations, is of frequent occurrence upon the Gaulish coins, as well as on those of the Channel Islands, and on many British coins, especially those of the Iceni. In the transmutations which the types so frequently underwent, the boar is often found usurping the place of some other adjunct. It occurs beneath the horse, or above his back; or even supplants the horse or bull, and becomes the principal type on Gaulish coins. On coins of Dubnorix we find it surmounting an ensign held by a warrior. It seems to have been the adopted badge of the Æduans and their allies. (See Lelewel, Type Gaulois, p. 152, et seqq.)

Some interesting remarks on the boar, or "*Sus Gallicus*," as the symbol of the Gaulish nation, have been published by M. de la Saussaye, in the Rev. Num., vol. v. p. 243.

Plate G, No. 13.

Obv.—Wolf standing to the left, in front of a tree; below, an annulet.
Rev.—Horse to the right; below, an annulet; above, a flower. Æ. 24 grains.

The coin here engraved was in the collection of the late Mr. Huxtable, and was found by him amongst gravel dredged from the bed of the Thames at London Bridge. It is now in my own collection. Two other specimens of this type were procured, with other British and many Roman coins, from the hill above Kits Coty House,* near Maidstone, by the late Mr. Charles. One of them is engraved in Smith's Collectanea Antiqua, vol. i. pl. v. 6; and the other in the Num. Chron., vol. i. p. 84. I am much inclined to think that the brass coin found near Canterbury, and described in the Num. Soc. Procs. for Feb. 23, 1843, as *obv.* convex, a rude figure of a horse; *rev.* concave, an elephant, was, in fact, another coin of this type. There seems every probability of these coins belonging to the Kentish district, as not only have they been found principally in Kent, but there is a flatness about the coins which, as well as the style of workmanship, connects them with the silver coins, Plate F, No. 16, which have been found exclusively in Kent. It is difficult to trace the derivation of the type of the wolf, if such the animal be, but it bears considerable resemblance to that of the reverse of the gold coins, Plate C, No. 2. Whether any superstitious reverence attached to the wolf among the Britons, as was apparently the case among some nations, I am not aware. The wolf occurs occasionally upon Gaulish coins.

Plate G, No. 14.

Obv.—Uncertain animal to the right.
Rev.—Horse standing to the left, within a beaded circle.

This coin is copied from the Coll. Ant., vol. i. pl. xli. 13, and was found with Roman remains at Springhead, near Southfleet, Kent. It appears to be but badly preserved, and will, I have no doubt, eventually be proved to belong to the inscribed series.

* An account of this discovery is given in the Archæologia, vol. xxx p. 335.

CHAPTER VII.

TIN COINAGE.

The materials for writing an account of the ancient British coinage of tin, or rather of an alloy in which that metal preponderates, are extremely scanty, there being no record of more than two or three discoveries of such coins having taken place in this country. It is true that a considerable number of coins of this metal are engraved in Ruding, 55 to 73 (pl. iii. and iv.), as being of British origin, but by far the greater number of these are undoubtedly Gaulish, and 65 and 73 are the only coins which can lay any valid claim to being regarded as British coins. Mr. W. Allen, of Winchmore Hill, has communicated a coin of the type of Ruding, pl. iv. 71, found at Lilly Hoo, near Luton, Beds; but it is, I think, beyond all doubt, of Gaulish origin.

We might, indeed, have expected to have found many of the earliest of the British coins composed of tin, as that metal was one of the first articles of commerce between Britain and more civilised nations, and thus possessed a certain intrinsic value which would have rendered it a fitting medium of exchange. As has been already observed, the Cassiterides were known as the islands from which the Greeks obtained their tin as early as the days of Herodotus; and Polybius, writing about B.C. 160, mentions the British Isles, and the method there in use of preparing this metal. Yet it does not appear that tin, in the shape of coins, was ever current in that part of Britain where tin was produced, inasmuch as the coins of this metal, so far as our present knowledge

extends, have nearly all been found in the Kentish district,
though one of them has occurred as far west as Dorsetshire.

It is needless to enter into any minute description of the
types of these coins, nine of which are portrayed in Plate G.
On the obverse of the first eight is a curiously rude representation of a head in profile, possibly helmeted, sometimes
to the right, and sometimes to the left. The eye in all
cases is represented by a simple circle or by a ring ornament,
and the outline of the face by two crescents, one above the
other. The device on the reverse is apparently intended
for a bull, which is turned indifferently to the right or left,
regardless of the direction of the head upon the obverse.
There is generally an exergual line, and sometimes, as on
No. 1, some flourishes beneath it.

All these coins have been cast, and not struck; and for
this purpose it would seem that wooden moulds were frequently used, as the impression of the grain of the wood,
and in some cases of the medullary rays, may be seen upon
the coins. Some years ago I called attention to this fact in
the Numismatic Chronicle, vol. xvii. p. 18. On a pig of lead
found in the neighbourhood of the lead mines of Shelve,
Shropshire, and inscribed IMP. HADRIANI AVG, similar
marks are observable, showing that either the model or
pattern from which the pig was cast was formed of oak, or
else that the pig itself had been cast in an oaken mould
(Arch. Assoc. Journ., vol. xvi. p. 350).

The usual weight of the coins Nos. 1 to 7 is from 19 to
25 grains, but from the fact of the coins being cast, there is
considerable variation in weight. The average weight of
sixteen specimens in my own collection is 22½ grains, but
individual coins range from 17 up to 35 grains. The coins
seem to have been cast in strings or chains, and afterwards
separated by cutting through the runlets which connected
them, portions of which are left projecting from the coins.
In nearly all cases these projections occur above and below
the head on the obverse, and in front of and behind the
bull on the reverse; but why it should have suited the

artists bent to engrave one of these objects vertically and the other horizontally, is not apparent. It is possible that the moulds may have been burnt into the wood by the use of a model in brass, or some less fusible metal than tin. The division of the runlets appears to have been effected by means of a chisel, and not with shears. The last coins of the chain had of course but one runlet: Nos. 5 and 6 in the plate appear to have been such.

Coins of these types have been found in St. James's Park (Numismatic Journal, vol. i. pl. i. 2), and at Lenham Heath, Kent, in 1781 (Ibid., No. 1), some of which are in the British Museum. In the latter case the metal is erroneously specified in the engraving as silver. They are copied from the Numismatic Journal into the Revue Numismatique, vol. iv. pl. xiii. 9, 14; and into Ruding, pl. A, 1 and 2. A number more were found at Quex Park, near Birchington, in the Isle of Thanet, in the year 1853 (Numismatic Chronicle, vol. xvi. p. 184). These came into the hands of the late Mr. Rolfe, of Sandwich, and are now in my own collection. Nos. 1, 2, 4, 6, and 7 are all from this hoard.

A specimen closely resembling No. 2 was found at Weycock, Berks, where it was associated with Roman remains. A woodcut of it is given in the Arch. Journ., vol. vi. p. 120. Others are engraved in Hawkins, pl. ii. 30 and 31, but it is not stated where they were found; No. 29 in the same plate is Gaulish. A coin in Mr. Durden's collection, found at Hod Hill, near Blandford, has three pellets in triangle, instead of the ring in the centre of the head. It is from the extremely rude Gaulish coins in brass, with the head in profile on the obverse, and the bull upon the reverse, that the types of these British coins are derived. These brass coins (Lelewel, pl. i. 18; iv. 24; Lambert, pl. i. 10, &c.) are of frequent occurrence through the north-west of France, and derived their type in turn from the brass coins of Massilia, of Greek fabric (Akerman, pl. xvi. 12, &c.). The degeneration of the head of Apollo is nearly as complete in the case of the tin coins as on those in gold.

No. 8 in the Plate is a coin of smaller module, but with the same types as the larger coins, with some of which it agrees in weight, being 19¼ grains. I am uncertain where it was found, or whether it is of really British origin. It is in my own collection.

No. 9 has on the obverse a boar to the right, and on the reverse an animal possibly intended for a goat. Its weight is 55⅗ grains. It is in the Hunter collection, at Glasgow, and is engraved in Ruding, pl. iv. 73, from whence I have copied it, as I have not met with the same types on any Gaulish coins, and it is therefore probably British.

With regard to the date to be assigned to these tin coins, not much can be said. To use the words of Mr. Hawkins (p. 15), their form and fabric are so unlike those of any other known coin, that little can be safely asserted respecting them, or the exact period when they were in circulation. I do not, however, think that they can belong to an early period of the British coinage, but should assign them a date nearly as late as that of the inscribed coins, though it may be supposed that such extremely barbarous pieces would hardly have formed part of the same currency as the neatly-executed coins of Vose[nos], Dubnovellaunus, and Eppillus, which seem to have been the earliest inscribed coins of the Kentish district, where, as before mentioned, the tin currency apparently originated. At the same time it must be remembered that their small intrinsic value points to a degree of civilisation requiring small change for ordinary commercial transactions, and that the degeneracy of their type is another argument against their being of any great antiquity in the series.

CHAPTER VIII.

COINS OF THE CHANNEL ISLANDS.

Although the coins of what is known as the Jersey or Channel Islands type belong more properly to the Gaulish series, yet in a work professing to treat of the ancient British coinage they cannot be passed over without notice, as not only are the islands in which they most frequently occur British possessions, but the coins themselves are from time to time found in Britain. The general character of these coins may be gathered from an inspection of Plate I, in which twelve of the principal varieties of the large and small pieces are delineated. The latter are much rarer than the former, and appear to have been, as is usually the case with the small gold coins, quarters of the larger pieces.

The type of the obverse is, on all, a head in profile, nearly always to the right, though in a few exceptional cases, as on No. 11, to the left. The hair is represented in a very peculiar manner, being arranged in curved bands, usually three, springing from S-shaped coils in the region of the ear; each of the bands consists of a number of curled locks, the spiral ends of which fringe the head. On some of the coins the features are fairly represented, but on many the nose is formed by a detached figure, like the astronomical sign ♈, or the ℳ on Mercian coins, while on others it is formed by a crosier-like figure in front of the eye and forehead. There is usually a low or bracket-shaped figure ⌒ in front of the face, or else double spirals, or dolphin-shaped objects.

On the reverse is a very peculiarly formed horse, with hind-legs at each end of the body, so that at first sight it is often difficult to say in which direction it is going. It has sometimes a bird-like head, at other times it is human-headed. In the latter case there are occasionally what appear to be reins proceeding from the mouth of the centaur, if so it may be termed, as on No. 12. A comparison of this coin with No. 8 will show that these reins were originally the arms of a Victory guiding the horse. Even on No. 8 the transition into the human face has commenced, and the eye and nose may be recognised above the head of the Victory. The head having thus been attached behind the original horse accounts for the anthropocephalous animal having a pair of hind-legs in front. Above the horse are found different objects, sometimes a figure like the head of an ichthyosaurus, a rosette, a cross, and other objects. Below there is usually a boar, or the lyre-shaped object, which is also found on the gold coins, Plate D, Nos. 2, 3, 4.

The metal of which these coins are formed is billon, or base silver, which appears to vary considerably in the amount of its alloy. From an analysis made by De Caylus[*] of two coins, their composition was found to be as follows:—

	A	B
Silver	·0413	·1770
Copper	·8414	·7954
Tin	·1168	·0265
Iron	·0003	·0009
Gold	·0002	·0002
	1·0000	1·0000

The weight of the larger pieces ranges from 80 to 105 grains, being usually 95 to 100 grains, and that of the smaller coins about 25 grains.

A large number of these coins was found at Mount Batten, near Plymouth (Num. Journal, vol. i. p. 224), where also the gold coin, Plate C, No. 4, and a silver coin

---

[*] Donop, Médailles Gallo Gasliques. p. 24.

of the type Plate F, No. 9, were found (Hawkins, p. 12). Other coins of the same class were found near Portsmouth (Hawkins, pl. i. 13), and I have a coin like No. 8, found in Devonshire. A specimen like No. 9, engraved in the Num. Chron., vol. iii. p. 153, No. 5, is said to have been found at Hexham, in Northumberland; and another, said to have been found at Lesmahago, Lanarkshire, has been communicated to me by Mr. Pettigrew. In the Arch. Assoc. Journal, vol. iii. p. 62, is an account of a find of these coins at Avranches, by Mr. C. Roach Smith, who remarks that they are often found on the southern and south-western coasts of England.

It is, however, mainly in the Channel Islands and Armorican Britain that these coins occur. In the year 1820 a hoard of nearly 1,000 was discovered in Jersey, of which no less than 760 are represented in De Donop's Médailles Gallo-Gaëliques (Hanover, 1838). His description of the coins is a farrago of learned nonsense, which it is needless to quote, though his discovery that the mane of the boar is a *cuneiform inscription* is worth recording. Numerous other specimens of the same class of coins will be found engraved in Lambert, pl. v., some of which were found in Jersey in the year 1787, and others at various times in the Armorican district.

The types are so closely allied to those of some of the Gaulish coins in gold, that though in a different metal these coins may be regarded as derivatives of the Macedonian stater, and may probably be classed among the latest of the Gaulish coins.

CHAPTER IX.

INSCRIBED COINS.

I now come to by far the most important portion of the Ancient British series—the coins bearing inscriptions upon them. The arrangement I have here adopted for them is, as far as possible, geographical, for any attempt at a chronological arrangement would be futile, on account of the absence, in nearly all cases, of any historical record of the princes who struck the coins. But besides this, there is reason to suppose that the coinage of several rulers of various independent tribes in different parts of Britain was contemporaneous, though it would appear that the introduction of inscriptions upon the coins took place at very different periods in different districts.

The various divisions of Britain to which distinct coinages may be referred I have classified as "districts." They are as follows :—

Western District—Somersetshire, Wilts, Gloucestershire, and part of Oxon and Berks.
South-Eastern District—Hampshire, Sussex, and Western Surrey.
Kentish District—Kent and Eastern Surrey.
Central District—Bucks, Beds, Herts, Middlesex, Essex, Northampton, and parts of Berks, Cambridgeshire, Hunts, and Oxon.
Eastern District—Norfolk, Suffolk, and parts of Cambridge and Huntingdon.
Yorkshire District—Yorkshire, and parts of the adjacent counties to the south.

It will be observed that these districts nearly coincide with those to which it appeared safe to assign various classes of uninscribed coins; and further, that there are no inscribed coins peculiar to the South-western district of Cornwall, Devonshire, and Dorset.

A classification of the coins, under the names of the various British tribes mentioned in history, would, as I have before observed, have been more satisfactory than the merely geographical arrangement now proposed. Unfortunately, however, it is now almost, if not quite impossible to ascertain the extent and position of the territory of the different tribes at the time these coins were struck.

The Western district might, for instance, have been called that of the Dobuni; the South-eastern that of the Belgæ, Regni, and Atrebatii; the Kentish that of the Cantii; the Central that of the Catyeuchlani and Trinobantes; the Eastern district that of the Iceni; and the Yorkshire that of the Brigantes. And in most instances we should probably have been right in assigning the coins peculiar to each of the districts mentioned to the tribes above cited; but when it is considered that the inscribed coinage ranges from about the time of the invasion of Julius Cæsar until the days of Claudius, it becomes evident that by the alliance or subjugation of different tribes there was probably a considerable alteration in the territorial division of the country under the different reguli during that period. In fact there are some tribes mentioned by Cæsar, such as the Ancalites and Bibroci, who are not enumerated among those who occupied territory in Britain in the time of Ptolemy. Such being the case, I have thought it better to adopt a modern terminology, rather than an ancient, for the names of the various districts, and to reserve the question of attribution to any tribe for discussion when each of the various inscriptions comes under examination.

In attempting to interpret the legends of the coins, I have, as far as possible, abstained from advancing beyond the limits of comparatively safe speculation. The scantiness of the information within our reach, as to the names of those who at different periods have held the supreme command over the various tribes, has been not only a negative but a positive evil, for it has led many antiquaries to adopt a sort of Procrustean method with the inscriptions on the coins, by which they have adapted them, as best they might, to suit some name recorded by Cæsar or Tacitus, Suetonius or Dion.

It is no doubt a tempting achievement to find Boadicea in BODVOC, Cassivellaunus in TASC, Mandubratius in ANDO, or Caractacus in EPATI; or, still farther, to reduce an obdurate CRAB into "the Community of the Belgic Regni;" but the real antiquary will not forget that the Roman historians did not pretend to write British annals, or to chronicle the succession of Hampshire or Sussex potentates. He will bear in mind that the number of the recorded names of British chiefs during the first century after Cæsar's invasion bears no proportion to that of the British tribes; and that the sole memorial of many a powerful chieftain may be the three or four letters we find upon one of his coins.

"Vixere fortes ante Agamemnona
Multi, sed omnes illachrymabiles
Urgentur ignotique longâ
Nocte, carent quia vate sacro."

But though history has dealt hardly with their names, "Time, which antiquates antiquities, and hath an art to make dust of all things, hath yet spared these minor monuments," and the name, title, and territory of more than one unrecorded British chief has been, and yet may be, rescued from oblivion by his coins.

Much more might, however, have been done, had proper attention been always paid to recording the places of finding of the various types; and though the present most unsatisfactory state of the law of treasure-trove too often interferes to prevent the finder of a coin from divulging the place of its discovery, yet the number of facts amassed during the last twenty years affords a good promise of a largely increased amount of knowledge before another such period shall have elapsed.

CHAPTER X.

COINS OF THE WESTERN DISTRICT.

To this district may be assigned coins inscribed BODVOC, CATTI, COMVX, VO-CORIO - AD (?), ANTEDRIGV., SVEI, and INARA (?). The only metals in which they are at present known to occur are gold and silver, no copper or brass coins having been discovered. In character they differ considerably from the coins of any other district, the gold coins having usually a remarkable ornament, somewhat like a fern-leaf, on the obverse, and the silver coins an extremely barbarous head in profile. The former are closely allied to the uninscribed gold coins, Plate C, No. 4, and the latter to those in Plate F, Nos. 4 to 9. The metal of which they are composed is extremely base, so much so that some of the gold coins have more the appearance of being of brass or copper. It is difficult to assign any chronological order to the coins with the different legends; but probably those with BODVOC are the most ancient, and those with SVEI and ANTEDRIGV the most recent among them. These latter, it will be seen, must belong to the time of Claudius, and probably none of the series date back beyond the Christian era. If, as is probable, this class of coins was struck by the Dobuni, they must have been among the latest of the tribes in the southern part of Britain to adopt a coinage, though those of the Brigantes in the north commence probably at even a later date.

BODVOC.

PLATE I., No. 1.

Obv.—BODVO[C] in large letters across the field.

Rev.—Disjointed three-tailed horse to the right; above, two ring ornaments and a crescent; below, a wheel; behind, a pellet; in the field, three small pointed crosses. From some specimens the whole appears to have been surrounded by a circle of pellets set at a little distance apart. Æ. 83 to 84½ grains.

PLATE I., No. 2.

Obv. & Rev.—The same as No. 1, but reading [B]ODVOC.

Of these, No. 1 is in the British Museum, and No. 2 in the Ashmolean collection at Oxford. The second coin is engraved merely for the purpose of completing the legend; it varies, however, slightly from the first in having the letters rather smaller, and in being flatter and less dished. On both varieties there is a slight indentation round the edge of the letters, showing that they were not engraved, but punched into the dies, and that the *burr* thus occasioned was not removed from the face of the dies, having been probably left with the view of giving greater apparent relief to the letters on the coins. Though the legend upon them occupies the same position as the TINC and COM. F. on the coins of the South-eastern district, yet there is this material difference, that it is not placed within a sunk recess, like a countermark, but stands up in relief on the field. Looking at the uninscribed coins, such as Plate B, Nos. 8 and 10, it will at once be perceived that the plain obverse offers the most eligible place for an inscription on coins struck after that pattern, and the reverse of these BODVOC coins testifies to some such prototype as these anepigraphous coins having been used. The small crosses on the field are found also upon the coins reading CATTI and VO-CORIO-AD(?), as well as on those of Antedrigus. The same cross appears under the horse's head on the allied coin (Plate C, No. 4), which was found at Mount Batten, near Plymouth, and on the silver coins, both inscribed and uninscribed, of this district. The earliest coin on which it appears is Plate A, No. 6, which weighs fully 10 grains more than these.* In workmanship these coins are neater than the other inscribed coins of the same district. They are heavier, and of finer gold than those of Antedrigus, though some few of the coins inscribed CATTI and VO - CORIO - AD (?) exceed them in weight.

In the following notice of the places where these coins have been found, and the works in which they are mentioned, I have not attempted to discriminate between the two varieties already referred to, but have regarded the coins as being all of one type.

One specimen was found at Rodmarton, Gloucestershire (Arch. Journ., vol. i. p. 388), where also Roman remains have been discovered; another at Birdlip, in the same county (Arch. Assoc. Journ., vol. ii. p. 336); and a third at Stanlake, Oxon, which is now in the Ashmolean collection, at Oxford. An account of this coin was communicated to the Ashmolean Society of Oxford by Dr. Ingram, who regarded it as a coin of Boadicea (Gentleman's Mag., 1840, p. 620). Mr. Webster has lately sent me impressions of another, like No. 2, found in a quarry at Stow, Gloucester-

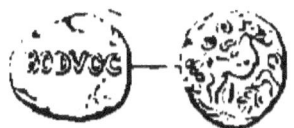

shire. Another, of which a woodcut is here given, was found, in November, 1861, at Birkhill, near Dumfries, and is now in the Museum of the Society of Antiquaries of Scotland (Num. Chron., N.S., vol. ii. p. 159; Num. Soc. Procs., January 16, 1862). The occurrence of a British coin so far north is very unusual, though of course there are

* The small cross on the gold coins of Cunobeline (Plate IX., No. 8) differs in character from these, and has more the appearance of being a sort of mint-mark.

exceptions to the general rule that British coins are only
found in the district in which they were originally struck.
Another coin, engraved in the Archæologia, vol. xxxiii. pl. ix.,
is erroneously stated to have been found at Beckford, Gloucestershire, where the silver coin, No. 3, was found.

Engravings of these coins are also given in Ruding,
Appendix, pl. xxix. 3; Hawkins, pl. ii. 28; Akerman,
pl. xxiv. 19; Beale Poste, p. 20; Arch. Assoc. Journ.,
vol. ii. p. 12; Gibson's Camden, pl. i. 8; Stukeley, pl. xi. 9,
and pl. xx. 10; Speed, p. 34; Vetusta Mon., vol. i. pl. viii.;
Taylor Combe, pl. i. 17; and Lelewel, pl. viii. 18.

PLATE L, No. 3.

Obv.—BODVOC. Bare, beardless head in profile to the left.
Rev.—Horse galloping to the right; above, a ring ornament and
two crescents; below, a rosette of pellets; in the
field various small crosses and pellets. Æ. 16 grains.

The obverse type of this coin is evidently connected with
that of Plate F, No. 4, though of much better art, and turned
in the other direction. The horse on the reverse closely
resembles that of Plate F, No. 9. This coin, which was
formerly in the collection of Mr. Huxtable, is now in that
of Captain Murchison. From a privately printed plate we
learn that it was ploughed up in a field in the parish of
Beckford, in the county of Gloucester, A.D. 1805. It is
engraved in Ruding, Appendix, pl. xxix. 4; Akerman,
pl. xxiv. 20; Lelewel, pl. viii. 19; and C. Roach Smith's
Coll. Ant., vol. i. p. 181, where a few interesting remarks
upon it will be found. It is mentioned by Beale Poste,
p. 27, as having been engraved by Taylor Combe, but this
is an error. I have another specimen, weighing 11¼ grains,
and found near Cirencester. It is, however, in but poor
condition, and shows only slight traces of the legend.

The gold coins have long been known, having been engraved by both Camden and Speed. Most of the earlier
writers on British coins, and some of the more recent who
have not gone deeply into the subject, have been inclined to

assign them to Boadicea, Queen of the Iceni, the leader of the revolt against the Romans in A.D. 61, which is described by Tacitus, and by Xiphilinus in his Epitome of Dion Cassius. There can, however, be no doubt that such an attribution is erroneous; as not only have the types no connection with those of the coins which are usually found within the Icenian territory, but the recorded places of finding of the coins inscribed DODVOC are all on the opposite side of Britain. These coins, moreover, form only a part of a series peculiar to the Western district, of which probably they are the earliest, while the latest were in all probability struck some years before the revolt under Boadicea. There is indeed no ground for supposing that any coins were struck by Boadicea, who never seems to have exercised the queenly power, unless as the leader of a short-lived revolt, and whose chief complaint against the Romans was that the kingdom left by her husband, Prasutagus, to which possibly she may have hoped to succeed, was overrun and pillaged by their troops, she herself scourged, and her daughters put to shame. There are not even any coins which can safely be attributed to Prasutagus, her husband, who was far more likely to have struck coins, both from his wealth and the peaceful possession of his territory in which during his lifetime he was left by the Romans.

There is much more probability of truth in the supposition which originated with Camden, that the inscription on these coins bears some relation to the Boduni or Dobuni, a tribe whose capital, according to Ptolemy, was Corinium (*Cirencester*), and who were located in and around Gloucestershire, the county in which the coins have principally been found.

The passage in Dion Cassius relating to this tribe is rather obscure. He says (lib. lx. s. 20) that Aulus Plautius, in A.D. 43, brought to terms of peace a part of the Boduni, who were under the dominion of the Catuellani, "μέρος τι τῶν Βοδούνων ὧν ἐπήκοον Κατουελλανῶν ὄντες," from which it is difficult to determine whether the whole tribe of the Boduni were subject to the Catuellani, or only that portion which

submitted to Plautius.* From numismatic evidence, I should
be inclined to think that the latter was the case, as coins of
Cunobeline are of not unfrequent occurrence as far west as
Oxfordshire, while I have no record of any having been
found in Gloucestershire. Besides this, a distinct coinage
appears to have been maintained in Somersetshire, and what
I have called the Western district, up to at least as late a
period as the time of Claudius.

However this may have been, the form BODVOC can
hardly be intended simply to represent the name of the
tribe, but more probably that of some prince, whose name
may possibly indeed have borne an allusion to the tribe over
whom he reigned; and the legend occurring round a head on
the silver coins rather favours this regal attribution. It is
possible that the discovery of some other specimens may
supply the termination of the legend, unless BODVOC is
the complete form.

In Camden's Britannia (ed. 1637, p. 645; Gough's ed.,
vol. iii. p. 123) is a notice of an inscription at Mynydd
Margan, in Glamorganshire, of which a rude woodcut is
given. It runs as follows:—

   BODAOC HIC IVCIT
   FILIAS CVTOTIS IRNI
   PRONEPOS ETERNVLI
   VE DOMVV.

The last words are read by Camden "Æternali in domo;"
but in whatever manner the inscription is to be read, it
would seem as if it were in memorial of a BODVOC who
spelt his name in precisely the same way as it appears on
these coins, as there can be no doubt that the fourth letter
is a V, from its recurring in the same form in FILIVS.

---

* Dr. Latham, writing in Smith's Dictionary of Geography, appears to be
doubtful whether the Carualiani are to be identified with the Catyeuchlani, or
not; but there seems much probability that the same tribe is intended by
both names. His doubts appear in part to have arisen from not recognising
Baline and Urolanium, the two chief towns of Ptolemy's Catyeuchlani, as
possibly Sandy, in Beds, and certainly Verulam, in Herts. (See also under
Plate X., No. 7.)

The A's are also reversed in the same manner. The coincidence in the name is very remarkable, though some centuries must have elapsed between the two Boduocs whose names are preserved on the coins and on the stone of Maen Llythyrog. Some remarks, both on the inscription and the coin, are given in the Archæologia Cambrensis, vols. iv. and v., by Professor Westwood.

BODVOC F (BODVOC FECIT) occurs also among the potters' marks from the *Allier*, of which an account is given by M. Tudot (see Smith's Coll. Ant., vol. vi. p. 72). BODVACVS* is likewise found among the names of Gaulish warriors sculptured on the Roman triumphal arch at Orange, in the department of Vaucluse.

The supposed connection between BODVOC and the Boduni may therefore after all be purely imaginary, as besides finding the name on these inscriptions, we meet with the same syllables entering into the composition of some Gaulish names, such as Boduognatus, a prince of the Nervii, mentioned by Cæsar (to whom these coins have by some been attributed), and Boduogenus, whose name occurs on the handle of an elegant bronze vessel, discovered in the Isle of Ely, and engraved in the Archæologia, vol. xxviii. p. 436, and who must probably have been of Gaulish or British origin.

Unsatisfactory as it may appear, the whole that can with certainty be predicated of these coins is that they were struck in the Western part of England at a rather late period of the British coinage. To this may be added the probability that on them is preserved a portion, or possibly the whole of the name of some prince, and that he reigned over the Boduni.

CATTI.

Plate I., No. 4.

Obv.—Convex, an object like a fern leaf or spike of flowers.
Rev.—CATTI. Disjointed, three-tailed horse to the right; above, a solid crescent between two pellets, and a

* Num. Chron., vol. iv. p. 119; Revue Arch., vol. v. p. 300.

small pointed cross; below, a wheel and a small cross; another in front; behind, three pellets. On some specimens the cross beneath the horse assumes the form of a pellet, and there are other pellets in the field.

N. 83 grains. Others 81, 83½, and 85½ grains.

This coin is in the British Museum. It is difficult to say precisely what the device on its obverse and on that of the three following coins is intended to represent. It is in all cases formed by a straight stem, having five branches issuing from it at nearly a right angle on either side, and gradually decreasing in length as they approach the point. At the lower end of the stem, and where the branches cease, are pellets, and at its point, and at those of the ten branches, are other pellets, with small spikes beyond them. On some of the VO - CORIO - AD (?) coins these spikelets are absent. It is more like a spike of some flowering plant in bud than anything else; but what plant, I leave to botanists to determine.

Whatever it was intended to represent, there is little doubt that it is a legitimate descendant of the wreath of Apollo upon the earlier uninscribed coins, though some of the links in the chain of successive copies of copies are still wanting. The three-tailed horse on the reverse is very similar to that on many of the uninscribed coins, both with plain obverses and with portions of the rude head upon them, such for instance as Plate B, Nos. 9 and 10. The small crosses, as before remarked, are peculiar to the coins of this district.

Two coins of this type were in the hoard found at Nunney, near Frome, so frequently cited; another from Frome was in the cabinet of the late Mr. Cuff, and is engraved in the Numismatic Journal, vol. i. pl. i. 8 ; another, showing only the letters ATT, was found in the neighbourhood of Chepstow (Arch. Assoc. Journ., vol. iv. p. 257, and vol. x. p. 224). The Frome coin is figured in Hawkins, pl. i. 7 ; Ruding, pl. A, 61 ; Revue Numismatique, vol. iv. pl. xiii. 8; Lelewel, pl. viii. 17 ; Arch. Assoc. Journ., vol. iii. pl. iv. 8 ; and Beale Poste, pl. iv. 8. The Chepstow coin is given by Beale Poste,

p. 120, and there attributed to the Attrebates; but this error is corrected by him in his Celtic Inscriptions, p. 125.

It is impossible to say to what part of the series of coins of the Western district these coins belong chronologically, but those found at Nunney with the coins of Claudius and Antonia show but little wear. They are, however, probably anterior to the coins of Antedrigus; and whether, like them, they are to be regarded as bearing a portion of the name of some British chieftain, or whether CATTI represents the name of some tribe, such as the Cassii or Catyouchluni, has been a subject of discussion. Finding, however, as we do, so many coins so closely resembling each other in type, yet varying in legend, though all belonging to the same district, and apparently to nearly the same period, I am inclined to think we must regard the legends upon them as representing the names of the princes by whom they were struck, rather than as giving the names of the tribes among whom they were current; though there is always a possibility of some of the legends representing the names of towns. The government of the British tribes appears to have been regal and hereditary, rather than republican, and this strengthens the assumption that these coins bear upon them the names of princes rather than of tribes. Were it not for these reasons, and for the fact that the coins have only been found quite in the West of England, we might regard them as having been struck by the Catyouchlani for circulation among the Boduni, a portion of whom at least were under their dominion, as we learn from the passage in Dion Cassius already cited.

COMVX.

Plate L, No. 5.

Obv.—As No. 4.

Rev.—COMVX. Horse, &c., as on No. 4, but with trefoils instead of the small crosses. Æ. 80½ to 82 grains.

The coin here engraved is in the British Museum, and was found near Frome, in Somersetshire (Archæologia, vol. xxx. p. 180, pl. ix.). It is also engraved in the Num.

Chron., vol. xiv. p. 71, No. 2. I have two other specimens, one from the same neighbourhood, and the other from Disley, near Stroud, Gloucestershire. A fourth, found at Churchill, on the western border of Oxfordshire, is in the collection of Captain Murchison.

I am not aware of the existence of any other specimens, but the places where these were found are all within the district to which the coins would have been assigned from their type, had the places of their discovery not been known.

It will be remarked that the legend reads inversely, or with the lower part of the letters towards the rim of the coin. Mr. Birch (Num. Chron., xiv. p. 70) thought there were traces of some letters before COMVX on the Museum coin, but from other specimens it appears that they are portions of the ring of pellets set at some little distance apart, with which the device on the reverse of most coins of this class is surrounded.

As to the meaning of the word COMVX, I must confess myself entirely at a loss. I cannot, however, accept Mr. Poste's conjecture (p. 170) that it designates the COM(munitas) VX(aeona), or VX(ella), partly because I have yet to learn that Communitas, or Commios, is ever found in the sense of a community or people on British coins; partly because there is no sign of any division between the COM and the VX, and partly because none of the coins have been found in Shropshire or Cornwall (or Devonshire), the counties in which Uxacona and Uxella appear to have been situated.

The only argument in favour of the name of some town being intended by this inscription, is that the syllable VX, or VSC, which is supposed to be the same as *Uysg*, and to signify a place on the banks of a stream, has a local rather than a personal signification. It must, however, be borne in mind that X is substituted for S on some of the coins of Tasciovanus, and certainly COMVS .... seems more likely to have formed the name of some British regulus than COMVX ....

VO - CORIO - AD (?)

Plate I., No. 0.

Obv.—As No. 5.

Rev.—VO-CORIO. Horse, &c., as on No. 4. The small crosses are sometimes replaced by trefoils or pellets, and are occasionally though rarely altogether absent. The two pellets above the horse are sometimes ornamented. The letters VO are often larger than those of the rest of the legend, and the O is sometimes above and sometimes below the level of the horse's tail.

N. 80 grains. Others $80\frac{7}{8}$, $81\frac{1}{2}$, 85, and 86 grains.

This coin is in my own collection. I have others, which were found at Radstock, near Frome, and at Llanthony Abbey, Monmouth. Another was purchased by Mr. Mayer, at Worcester, and was not improbably found in that neighbourhood (Num. Soc. Proc., Nov. 24, 1859). Other specimens are engraved in Wise, pl. xvi. 3; Beale Poste, pl. iv. 8; and Arch. Assoc. Journ., vol. iv. pl. ii. 8. The type was published by Mr. Birch in the Num. Chron., vol. xiv. p. 78. The metal of these coins is generally yellower, and apparently finer, than that of the others with the same obverse. It is much to be regretted that we are at present unable to complete the legend upon them, the first portion of which, from a comparison of several specimens, appears to have been VO-CORIO. On a coin in the Hunter collection at Glasgow are the letters AD in front of the horse's head, but running in the contrary direction to the VO-CORIO. The same arrangement of the legend occurs on the coin reading TIN-DV, No. 12 in this Plate. On the coin from Radstock there is the letter D in front of the horse's legs, preceded apparently by two other letters, which may be an A and a D. In this case the legend is continuous, VO-CORIO-ADD (?). In what manner this inscription is to be interpreted is a mystery, which the fact of there being apparently three words in the legend tends to complicate.

Many Gaulish and British names are compounded with VO, CORI, and ADD; and VOSII[NOS] and ADDEDO-MAROS, and possibly VOLISIOS, occur as the names of princes on British coins. Under neither of these, however, were the present coins struck, as they reigned in quite a different part of the country from that in which the coins were found. For a similar cause the CORIO cannot refer to the Coritani. It seems much more probable that it may refer to Corinium (*Cirencester*), the chief town of the Boduni, among whom the coins circulated; but even were this accepted as the meaning of CORIO, the VO and ADD would still remain to be interpreted.

ANTEDRIGVS.
PLATE L, No. 7.

Obv.—As No. 6.

Rev.—ANTEDRIGV. As No. 4, but sometimes more crosses in the field. The concluding letters of the legend are scattered, the R being beneath the nose of the horse, the I between his fore-legs, the G in the space between the fore-legs and the wheel, and the V beneath the tail. *N*. 69, 71, 73, 77½, 79, 81, and 83 grains.

The coin here engraved was found at Nunney, near Frome, and is in the collection of Captain R. M. Murchison. It is also figured in the Num. Chron. N.S., vol. i. pl. i. 2. Another variety, reading ANTEO.I.OV, was found in 1842 at Bourton, about two miles from Banbury, on the Southam road (Num. Soc. Procs., Dec. 22, 1842). A woodcut of it is given in the Arch. Assoc. Journ., vol. ii. p. 24; and Beale Poste, p. 38, where it is erroneously stated to have been found near Danbury, Oxfordshire. An absurd letter upon the subject of this and allied coins will be found in the Gent.'s Mag. for 1843, p. 30. See also Num. Chron., vol. vii. p. 44. The legend has been misread as QVANTEΘ, or OVANTEΘ. Another specimen is engraved by Wise, pl. xvi. 0, and in the Num. Chron., vol. xvi. p. 80, No. 6. Mr. Vaux has mentioned to me the discovery of one of these coins at Chepstow; but by far the most important find was that at Nunney, near Frome, of which I have given an account in the Num Chron. N.S., vol. i. p. 1.

The types of these coins are so similar to those of the

preceding coins that they do not require any further notice. The arrangement of the legend on the reverse is, however, singular. The ANTED or ANTEΘ above the horse is always conspicuous enough, but the other letters which are placed in front of the horse, and under his legs, might readily escape observation. The sickle-shaped form of the G is worthy of notice. It generally approximates to the form of the written G, but in some instances the terminal stroke or handle of the sickle has been put on at the wrong end, giving the letter the form of the figure 2 reversed, like the Lombardic ꝗ. The form is in either case quite different from that of the G on the Yorkshire coins, Plate XVII., No. 3, which afford the only other instance at present known of the occurrence of this letter on British coins.

It is curious to observe how the form of the D varies upon different specimens, being sometimes a simple D, at others a barred D, like the Saxon Ð, and at others, again, a perfect Θ, thus affording a commentary on the "*Græcis literis utuntur*" of Cæsar,* in his account of the Druids.

The metal of which some of these coins are composed is extremely base, so much so as to give them the appearance of being merely copper plated with gold. This, as well as the lightness of their weight, points to a late period in the British coinage, but their date and attribution will be best considered after describing the silver coins with the same legend.

Plate I., No. 8.

Obv.—Extremely barbarous head in profile, to the right, as on Plate F, No. 7.

Rev.—ANTEO (on some ANTED). Three-tailed horse to the left, much like that on Plate F, No. 7; below and behind, ring ornaments; various pellets in the field. The whole within a circle of pellets set at a considerable distance apart.

Æ. 13 to 21 grains. Average weight, 17½ grains.

The coin engraved is in the collection of Captain R. M. Murchison. The first that was known of this type was

* De Bell. Gall., vi. 14.

procured by the late Mr. Bateman, of Youlgrave, at Lincoln, and was published by me in the Num. Chron., vol. xx. p. 172, No. 11. The next coin was obtained by Captain Murchison, and was reported to have been found at Freshford, about seven miles from Bath; but the find of coins at Nunney, near Frome, comprised at least sixteen of these coins, on one of which the legend appears to be ANTEORL, the RL being beneath the up-turned tail of the horse.

The type, which is precisely that of the uninscribed coins, Plate F, Nos. 7 and 8, has already been commented on. It is the same, too, as that of the coins reading SVEI, No. 9 in this Plate, of which several were found associated with those at Nunney.

With regard to the meaning of the legend ANTEDRIGV, which we find in full on the gold coins, and in a more or less abbreviated form on those in silver, there can be but little doubt that it was intended to represent the name of some British *regulus*. Whether ANTEDRIGV,* or, as on the Banbury coin, it may possibly stand, ANTEDRIGOV, is intended to present a nominative or a genitive inflexion, or whether the final S has been omitted for want of space, we are fully justified in adding the name of ANTEDRIGVS to the roll of British kings. On the gold coins of Epaticcus, Plate VIII., No. 12, the same absence of the final S may be observed; unless possibly the letter has in that case been merged in the tail of the horse.

Whether the British name of Victory "Andate" enters into the composition of the name of Antedrigus; whether by any possibility the name of this prince is to be traced in that of Arviragus, mentioned by Juvenal,† and whether RIGV. may represent Regulus or Rex, are questions I will not attempt to determine.

ANTEBROGIUS, the ambassador of the Rhemi to Cæsar,‡ and ANDECOMBOS,§ a name occurring on Gaulish coins which

---

* It appears that several old Celtic nominatives terminate in U. See Max Müller's Science of Language, 1862, p. 246, note.
† Sat. iv. 127.　　‡ De Bell. Gall., ii. 3.　　§ Duchalais, No. 358.

have been attributed to the Andecavi, and ANDEBROOTRIX, a name occurring in an inscription at Vienne (Isère), may be mentioned as presenting somewhat analogous forms; but the most remarkable coincidence is that of the legend ANTED, or ANTEO (with the letters linked into a monogram), which occurs on coins of the Iceni (Plate XV., Nos. 9, 10, 11). It would seem either that there was among this tribe another prince whose name commenced with ANTED, or else that possibly the same Antedrigus had dominion both in the western and eastern counties. The latter hypothesis affords much matter for speculation.* There is, in the first place, great probability of the Icenian coins with this inscription belonging to about the same period as those of the West of England, though they may indeed be rather earlier. In the deposit of coins found at Weston, in Norfolk, there were consular denarii of the Antonia and Cassia families; while in the find at Nunney, out of four denarii which accompanied the British coins, three were of the same class, being of the Æmilia, Julia, and Servilia families. In the latter case there were, however, a denarius of Caligula and several brass coins of Claudius and Antonia. This might seem to be evidence of the deposit at Nunney having been many years subsequent in date to that at Weston, though it is by no means conclusive on this point. All that is actually proved by the circumstances of the case is, that the coins found at Nunney were deposited after the commencement of the reign of Claudius, or subsequently to A.D. 41; and it might have been entirely fortuitous that no imperial coins were deposited with those found at Weston, as the family coins found there show considerable signs of wear. Still, the fact that the coins of Antonia are barbarous imitations of those of Roman fabric, seems to prove that it could not have been until some years after the accession of Claudius—by whom the coins of Antonia were struck—that the coins of Antedrigus, some still fresh from the mint, were buried. It appears by no means improbable that this took place during the wars with the

* See also under Plate XV., No. 11.

Romans, when Ostorius Scapula was propraetor in Britain, A.D. 50 to 55; and if so, it becomes a question whether a prince named Antedrigus, whose original dominion was over the Iceni, may not have been appointed the chieftain of some British league, and as such, have had coins struck in his name, both in the Western and Eastern parts of Britain with the characteristics in each case of the local coinage.

The Cangi and Iceni are mentioned by Tacitus as the two most powerful tribes with whom Ostorius had to contend; and whether or not we are to fix the seat of the Cangi in Somersetshire, as has been done by some antiquaries, there is reason to suppose, from the account of Tacitus, that the various tribes of Britons were to a great extent acting in concert, and the supposition that they may have elected Antedrigus as their common chief, though purely hypothetical, carries with it some slight degree of probability. It must, however, have been prior to the time when Caractacus obtained the pre-eminence over the rest of the British leaders, and after all there is but little stress to be laid on such conjectures. Under any circumstances it would appear that with the coinage of Antedrigus and Suci . . . the native currency ceased in the Western part of Britain, though possibly it was continued until a rather later period in the Yorkshire district.

That an uninscribed coinage was co-existent with the inscribed is a remarkable fact, to which, however, attention has already been called under Plate F, No. 8. The same is the case with the Icenian coinage.

The relative value of the silver and gold coins cannot of course be now ascertained, though possibly three of the silver coins were equivalent to the Roman denarius, being about equal in weight, though of considerably baser metal.

While this work has been passing through the press, Mr. H. Durden, of Blandford, has most obligingly communicated to me another coin of the same class as those of Antedrigus, but presenting upon it a new and unpublished legend. It was found in the curious earth-work at Hod Hill, near Blandford, in 1862. The metal of which it is composed is so base that it is covered with a beautiful green patina, but from the type I think that it was probably intended to pass muster as a gold coin, though the weight is only 60 grains. Its character will be seen from the annexed woodcut.

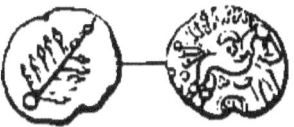

The legend appears to be INMA, or INAM, or INARA, unless possibly it is to be read the reverse way, as the termination of some word ending in VNL. I am, however, of opinion that INARA is the preferable reading, though we must await farther discoveries before this point can be established. Were Dr. Stukeley alive, he would unhesitatingly read the legend as INMA, and attribute the coin to Imanuentius, the father of Mandubratius, who, according to Cæsar,* was killed by Cassivellaunus. The coin must, however, belong to a period nearly a century after Cæsar's invasion, though if bearing the name of a prince, and if its legend be correctly read as INMA, it may have been struck under some later INMANUENTIUS, who, like the Divitiacus of Cæsar's days, would seem to have derived his name from a chieftain of a previous generation.

SVEI.

Plate I., No. 9.

Obv.—Rude head in profile to the right, as on No. 8, but even more barbarous, and with more ring ornaments in front of the face.

Rev.—SV-EI below and above a horse to the left, with a streaming triple tail; the head, shoulder, and hind-quarters, formed with ring ornaments. In the field various pellets, and in front of the horse there is generally a ring ornament. On some specimens there is a

* De Bell. Gall., lib. v. 20.

Y-shaped figure, or star of three points, above the horse. Æ. 14½ to 21½ grains.

The coin engraved is in the collection of Captain R. M. Murchison. Coins of this type were unknown until the discovery of the large hoard of British coins at Nunney, near Frome, in October, 1860, already mentioned, of which I have given an account in the Numismatic Chronicle, N.S., vol. i. p. 1. In the hoard were twenty-seven coins of this class, all of very base silver, and of the average weight of 17⅞ grains. Numerous other British coins, both inscribed and uninscribed, but all belonging to the same district, as well as some Roman coins, were found at the same time. I have another specimen of this type, said to have been found near Worcester. These coins nearly coincide with those of Antedrigus, Plate I., No. 8, and the uninscribed coins, Plate F, Nos. 7 and 8, but are, if possible, even more barbarous. It is this close agreement with the former, on which there is AN below, and TED above the horse, that determines their proper reading to be SVEI rather than EISV, which would certainly have appeared preferable had there been no such analogy to guide us.

From the same cause we must regard these coins, like those of Antedrigus, as having been struck by some British regulus, possibly of the Boduni, whose name commenced with SVEI, and the termination of which the future discovery of some of his gold coins may possibly enable us to supply. There are not wanting examples of names with a very similar commencement among the princes of Gaul and Germany. In the celebrated inscription of Augustus, at Ancyra, mention is made of SVEBO, a prince of the Marcomanni; and SUTICUS, a prince of the Veliocasses, is known by his coins. The word SUICCA also occurs on tetradrachms apparently of Pannonian origin. The Suessiones, the Suessetani, the Suevi, and the Suciones are all instances of the names of tribes compounded with this prefix. The question of the date to be assigned to these coins has already been discussed under those of Antedrigus, with which they must be, as nearly as possible, contemporary.

CHAPTER XI.

COINS OF THE SOUTH-EASTERN DISTRICT.

THE inscribed coinage of what I have termed the South-eastern district, as far as it is at present known, extends over but a comparatively short period. This district, which comprises the counties of Hampshire and Sussex, and Western Surrey, was at the time of Cæsar's invasion occupied, for the most part at all events, by Belgic tribes who had crossed over from the continent for the purposes of war or plunder. Most of these retained the same names as the parent states, and had apparently but a short time previously been subject, in connection with many Gaulish tribes, to Divitiacus, a prince of the Suessiones. Among these Belgic tribes may be mentioned the Atrebates, or Atrebatii as Ptolemy calls them, whose chief town was Calleva, probably *Silchester*, and the Regni, whose chief city was Noviomagus. In the days of Ptolemy, who furnishes the names of these towns, the Belgæ proper were located more to the west, their chief towns being Ischalis, *Ilchester* (?); Aquæ Solis, *Bath;* and Venta, *Winchester*. In the time of Cæsar, however, it is possible that the Atrebates and other Belgic tribes had not extended their territory so far inland and westward as they subsequently did; but, under any circumstances, the alliance between the tribes in Britain and the parent tribes on the continent was closely maintained, and not only did the league, of which the Veneti were the chief tribe, obtain assistance from Britain in their war with Cæsar, but when the latter determined to invade this country, the fact was immediately made known, through

the commercial intercourse between the two countries, among
the British tribes, who sent ambassadors to Cæsar to make
peace, B.C. 55. These ambassadors were sent home with
liberal promises, and Commius, whom Cæsar had made king
over the vanquished Atrebates of the continent, and who
had great influence in part of Britain (cujus auctoritas in
iis regionibus magni habebatur), was sent over with them,
to exhort the Britons to tender their allegiance to the
Romans.

As the history of this Commius appears to be intimately
connected with that of the inscribed coinage of the South-
eastern part of Britain, it will be well to trace it, as far as
practicable, from Roman sources, and see what countenance
is afforded for the supposition of his having founded a
kingdom in this country, to portions of which three of his
sons succeeded. When sent on this message by Cæsar,
Commius was seized on his landing, and cast into prison, and
only liberated after the defeat of the Britons. He was also
in Britain at the time of Cæsar's second invasion, B.C. 54,
and introduced the ambassadors of Cassivellaunus to him.
He afterwards returned to Gaul, as he is said to have been
left with a detachment of cavalry as a guard over the
Menapii while Cæsar proceeded against the Treviri, in
B.C. 53. In the following year, however, he forsook his
allegiance to the Romans, and became one of the leaders
of the Gallic league against Cæsar. So active was he, that
Labienus attempted to take his life by treachery; but
Commius escaped, though severely wounded. It is uncertain
to what exact period the anecdote related by Frontinus[*] is to
be referred, when Commius fled before Julius from Gaul
into Britain, and escaped by the stratagem of hoisting the
sails of his vessel while still high and dry on the shore, and
thus leading Cæsar, who was hotly pursuing at a distance,
to believe that he had safely embarked. In B.C. 51 he was
again one of the leaders of an alliance formed between the
Bellovaci, the Atrebates, and other tribes, against the

[*] Lib. ii. cap xiii. s. 11.

Romans, but he finally made his subjection to them, promising that he would go and act where and how Mark Antony prescribed; but on the condition that he should never come within sight of another Roman, "ne in conspectum veniat cujusquam Romani."*

This is all that history teaches us concerning Commius; the subsequent events of his life are merely matters of conjecture. I think, however, that this dread of the Romans, which even Mark Antony considered to be genuine, was not unlikely to cause Commius to retreat from Gaul, where his former subjects, both Atrebates and Morini, were now completely reduced under the Roman sway, and to take refuge in Britain, whither, as we learn from Frontinus, he had already once fled, and where there were some of his fellow-countrymen, the Atrebates, still in the enjoyment of freedom, and where also, as we have already seen, his influence in former times had been so great. His hatred of the Romans during the last few years, and his vehement antagonism to them, which had induced him to carry on the warfare with them after others had succumbed, and to prolong a hopeless contest until nearly all his followers had perished, may well have reinstated him in that position in the eyes of the Belgic tribes which his former submission to Cæsar had in some degree caused him to lose. At all events we hear no more of him in Gaul, while we have what appears to be sufficient numismatic evidence, not only of his having taken up his abode in Britain, but of his having, in all probability, again become the head of a confederation of tribes.

There are, as we shall shortly see, numerous coins, struck by three different princes, nearly, if not quite, contemporary, though each apparently having a distinct territory of his own, all of whom place upon their coins the title of C. F., COM. F., or COMMI. F. Now, looking at the workmanship of these coins, many of which bear strong traces of foreign art, and have the shape of the letters upon

* De Bell. Gall., viii. 48.

them purely Roman, and taking into account the constant occurrence of the title DIVI. F. on the contemporary coins of Augustus, we cannot well do otherwise than accept Mr. Birch's interpretation of these legends as COMMI. FILIUS (the son of Commius).[*]

Still it does not of necessity follow that the Commius of the coins is the same person as the Commius of Cæsar. There may have been more than one prince of that name, in the same manner as there was more than one Divitiacus; and as one Divitiacus ruled over the Suessiones, and another over the Ædui, so also possibly there may have been one Commius, prince of the Atrebates in Gaul, and another, prince of the Regni, or some British tribe upon the South-eastern coast. It is also possible that though the Commius of Cæsar had been chief of the continental Atrebates, he may have ruled over some other tribe than the Atrebates in Britain, in the same manner as he had been also chief of the Morini on the continent; though in that case the two tribes of Atrebates and Morini may have been united under his rule.

But, whether there were only one Commius or two, the district we must assign, on numismatic authority, to the Commius who reigned in Britain, seems to agree with what, from historic grounds, might have been assigned to the Commius of Cæsar, had it been certain that on his retirement from public life in Gaul he obtained the chieftaincy of any British tribe or confederation.

When we consider the position of these South-eastern counties with regard to Gaul, and the consequent facility for their being brought under the influence of Roman civilisation, it is evident that an inscribed coinage must have been adopted in them earlier than in districts further inland. We find, however, that Tasciovanus, the father of Cunobeline, whose capital was Verulam (near St. Alban's, in Herts), had an inscribed coinage probably dating as far back as B.C. 30, and we are therefore justified in assigning to the coins of the

[*] Num. Chron., vol. vii. p. 82.

sons of Commius a still earlier date. This circumstance
enhances the probability of the Commius of the coins and
of Cæsar being one and the same.

The suggestion of Mr. Beale Poste, that COMMI. F. means
COMMIOS FIRBOLG (the community of the Firbolgs, or
Belgæ), seems hardly to require refutation. It is enough to
say that Fir meaning nothing more than "viri," men, and
Fir-Bolg, even in the days of Irish literature, never having
assumed the form of a true proper name,* but having the
Fir declined while the Bolg remained uninflected, the initial
F could never have been used to represent the Belgæ. As
well might we now use the letter M to represent "the Men
of Ireland."

Having then what appear to be the names of three sons of
Commius on British coins, the question at once arises, Are
they peculiar to the district in which Commius had such
influence in the days of Julius Cæsar? and the answer is
distinctly in the affirmative. There has hitherto not been a
single recorded instance of one of these coins having been
found except in Hampshire, Sussex, Surrey, or Kent, and
possibly Wilts.

But each of these three supposed sons appears to have
had a separate territory—one in Hampshire and Sussex, the
second in Sussex and Surrey, and the third in Kent. The
coins of the first and second will be discussed immediately;
those of the third will be treated of under the coins of Kent,
which for various reasons I have thought better to constitute
a separate district, or rather sub-district.

As therefore there are these three distinct coinages, which,
as before observed, there is every reason to regard as contemporaneous,† and all of which bear the title of COM. F.
most frequently in the place of honour on the obverse, it
seems no unreasonable supposition that Commius may have
held the sovereign power over the various tribes of the
district, and that at his death his dominions were divided

---

* See Smith's Geographical Dict., sub voce, Belgæ.
† See also under Plate III., No. 14.

among his three sons, possibly as rulers of the Regni, the
Atrebates, and the Cantii.

It may be objected that we do not find any coins that can
be indisputably attributed to Commius, but it must be
remembered that the introduction of a legend on British
coins does not appear to have taken place until about the
period of the accession of his sons, as some of their coins
are formed strictly on the model of the old uninscribed
coinage, with a few letters inserted in the field. There are,
moreover, two coins in my collection of precisely the same
character as those of the sons of Commius, which, as will
shortly be seen, there are some grounds for attributing to
Commius himself.

As to the period of the death of Commius and the accession
of his sons, there is nothing to guide us; he could not,
however, have been past the prime of life at the time of his
submission to Antony, so that he may have lived many
years after that event. The names of his sons were
TINC[OMMIUS], VIRICA or VERICA, and EPPILLUS. With the
two former the coinage of the South-eastern district appears
to have ceased, unless possibly the coins inscribed CRAB
belong to this district. In Kent, which seems to have
formed the dominion of Eppillus, the coinage was probably
continued to a later period. The reason why it should have
ceased in this Southern part of Britain sooner than in the
districts farther removed from the continent is, like that of
its early origin, perhaps to be found in the intercourse
with Gaul, which under Augustus had become rapidly
Romanised, and where the native coinage had ceased. This
must have made the Britons who traded with Gaul acquainted
with Roman money; and if Strabo's account be true, that
under Augustus the Britons paid duties to the Romans on
their exports and imports to and from Gaul, it is possible
that the use of Roman coins may have superseded the necessity
of a native coinage.

The inscribed coins of the South-eastern district have as
yet been found in gold and silver only, as the brass coins

of Tinc[ommius] appear to be ancient forgeries of those of gold, though of Eppillus there are several types known in copper.

The following is the coin that may possibly be assigned to Commius:—

COMMIUS (?).

Plate L, No. 10.

Obv.—Portions of the laureate bust to the right, the same as on Plate D, No. 5, with an object like the head of a serpent above the decoration of the neck.

Rev.—. .MMIOS. Three-tailed horse to the right, with wheel beneath, and trefoil ornament above. A second specimen shows an arm (?) terminating in a crescent and pellet above the tail of the horse, and an oval ring ornament below. *N*. 82 and 83½ grains.

The type which is published in the Numismatic Chronicle, vol. xviii. p. 44, No. 1, is so like that of Plate D, No. 5, that probably the latter, if it had been sufficiently spread, would have shown the same legend. The place of finding of either of the inscribed specimens, both of which are in my own collection, is not known, but the uninscribed were found at Farley Heath, and between Odiham and Basingstoke, Hants. The close resemblance between this and the next two coins also proves them to belong to the same district. The ornament above the horse is remarkable, as it appears to have been formed with the puncheon employed for the nose of the horse when turned to the left. The same device is to be observed on the coins of Addedomaros (Plate XIV., Nos. 5 and 6). The type of the obverse is allied with that of Plate D, No. 9, on which, however, the locks of the back hair have not yet degenerated into crescents.

With regard to the legend, it will be observed that the coin here engraved only shows the letters MMIOS. My second specimen only gives doubtful traces of an O preceding this, so that the legend is still incomplete. I think, however, that we are justified in assuming it to have been COMMIOS, but whether or no there was on the die another syllable preceding this must remain an open question until more perfect specimens are discovered. If there was another syllable, it was probably TIN, making the whole legend TINCOMMIOS, which there are some grounds for supposing was the name of the prince whose coins we shall next examine, though his name is usually abbreviated to TIN or TINC. Should there have been a TIN in the legend, the coin will have to be transferred from Commius himself to his son; but in the meantime, to use the words of Camden and Philemon Holland with reference to another coin, "Both I and some others are pleased with this conceit, that it is a coin of Commius Atrebatensis, whom Cæsar mentioneth."* An objection to this pleasing "conceit" may however be found in the presumption that if Commius actually struck inscribed coins, we ought to find all three of his sons commencing their coinage on the same model as the coin of their father, whereas it is only on some of those of Tinc[ommius] that this type appears.

TINC[OMMIUS].

The coins of this prince present numerous varieties, on nearly all of which he assumes the title of COMMI. F. or C. F., a title which, on coins showing traces of Roman art, can hardly by any sound rules of criticism be interpreted otherwise than as COMMI FILIUS, "the son of Commius." With the exception of two specimens found in Surrey and Westmoreland, the whole of his coins, as far as is recorded, have been discovered in Hunts and Sussex, principally in the latter county. The coins bearing the name of VERICA, COMMI. F., have also been found in the same counties, occasionally in company with the coins inscribed TINC; but they have, in addition, occurred in some numbers in Surrey. Whether the two brothers were joint rulers over the same district, or whether the one held the dominion of the Regni and the other that of the Atrebates, cannot now be determined.

* Holland's Camden, p. 60.

One thing appears certain, that during, at all events, some portion of their reigns, they were contemporary princes; for not only, as before observed, have their coins been found together, but in some cases the coins of both are identical, except as regards the legend. There is, however, some reason for supposing that Tinc[ommius] commenced the issue of inscribed coins earlier than Verica, as it is on his coins alone that the archaic type of the laureate head and the three-tailed horse is preserved. If the coin No. 10 is to be transferred from Commius to Tinc[ommius], and the inscribed coinage originated with the latter, we might infer that Tinc[ommius] held the maritime state of the Regni, and was thus brought in more immediate contact with the Gauls and Romans, from whom he, first of all the Britons, learned the practice of inscribing his name upon the coinage, and employing foreign artists, or those who had had the advantage of an education in some province under the Roman rule, to engrave his dies—a practice which was afterwards imitated by his two brothers, Verica and Eppillus. It is, however, possible that Tinc[ommius] succeeded, in the first instance, to the whole of the dominions, whatever they may have been, of Commius, which he subsequently shared with his brothers.

It is a curious fact that the coins of Tinc[ommius], as far as at present known, appear to have been struck in gold alone (unless, indeed, Plate II., No. 7, was intended for a brass coin), while both his brothers coined also in silver, and one of them in copper. Possibly some of his coins in the baser metals may eventually be found, as that in silver engraved in Plate III., No. 14, seems to bear the names of all three brothers. They cannot, however, have been plentifully struck, or they would ere this have occurred. As might have been expected, there does not appear to be any mention of such a prince in history, though possibly it is his name which is preserved in the form of TIM,[*] in company with that of Dubnovellaunus, in the inscription at Ancyra commemorating the deeds of Augustus. I should, however, regard Tinc[ommius] as belonging to a

---

[*] See p. 110, and Mon. Hist. Brit. cvi.

rather earlier period than Dubnovellaunus, though both
must have been contemporaries of Augustus, even if they
were not among the suppliants who came to his imperial
throne.

The name of Tinc[ommius] does not offer any decided
analogy with any other British or Gaulish name. There was,
however, a town called Tinconcium, or Tincollo, in Gaul,
between Avaricum and Decetia.

Plate I., No. 11.

Obv.—Portions of the laureate bust to the right, as on No. 10,
but with a small annulet at the end of one of the
open crescents.

Rev.—TINC COMMI. F. Barbarous three-tailed horse to the
right; above, a triangle of pellets or annulets (?);
below, a ring ornament and annulet; behind, a ring
ornament. *N.*

This coin, which is in the Hunter collection at Glasgow, is
hitherto unpublished. The obverse so closely corresponds
with that of the previous coin, as to raise a presumption that,
whether No. 10 be rightly ascribed to Commius, or not, No. 11
must be as nearly as possible contemporary. The differences in
the reverse are slight, but the neck of the horse is more deeply
slit, and the adjuncts in the field are different. The legend
on the reverse is interesting, as giving the title COMMI. F.
at full length, instead of in a more abbreviated form. It is
the only coin of this prince on which it occurs, though the
same form is found on some of the silver coins of Verica.
This and the next coin would, from their types, appear to be
among the earliest of those struck by Tincommius.

Plate I., No. 12.

Obv.—Portions of the laureate bust, as on No. 10.

Rev.—Rude three-tailed horse to the right; above, TIN; in
front, DV. Above the horse, a crescent and pellet;
below, a wheel; in front, another crescent; and
behind, an oval ring ornament. The whole seems to
have been surrounded by a beaded circle.
N. 83½ grains.

The coin here engraved is also given by Mr. C. Roach Smith in the Coll. Ant., vol. i. pl. lvi. 1. It was found in the neighbourhood of Steyning, Sussex, where also a coin of Verica, of the type Plate II., No. 10, was discovered. See also Arch. Assoc. Journ., vol. iv. p. 157. Another, not showing the DV, was found at Alfriston, Sussex, in company with coins of the type Plate I., No. 14, and Plate II., No. 1. This is engraved in Akerman, pl. xxi. 13; in the Numismatic Chronicle, vol. vii. pl. iv. 2; Coll. Ant., vol. i. pl. vii. 3; Deale Poste, p. 23; and Arch. Assoc. Journ., vol. i. p. 304. Another coin was found at Brumber Castle, Sussex (Böcke's Sale Catalogue, March 22, 1850).

The type of the obverse is precisely like that of No. 10, and much like that of No. 11, and the same remarks apply to it. The reverse differs, not only in the legend, but also in the adjuncts. It approaches more nearly to that of Plate B, Nos. 9 and 10. As far as workmanship goes, these coins may rank with the rudest of the uninscribed varieties, from some of which, indeed, they differ in little more than having a few letters inserted in the field.

Though apparently much more ancient than the two next coins, there is no doubt of their belonging in fact to as nearly as possible the same period, for it will be remembered that one was found in company with some of the type Plate I., No. 14, and presented no marked difference in point of wear.

The legend TIN is not, as far as at present known, accompanied on this type, as it is on most others, by the title COM . F., though there may have been this or some other legend below the horse on the die. There are, however, the letters DV in front of the horse, which are visible on the Steyning coin alone, and to which attention is now for the first time called.

From their position upon the coin, it is impossible to say whether they may not be merely the termination of some legend running beneath the horse, rather than complete as they stand. In either case it seems probable that they

M

may form a portion of the name of some town, such as
DVROBIOVAR or DVRNOVARIA if the letters are initials, or
SORBIODV[NVM] if terminals. But it is unsafe to speculate
upon this subject until specimens showing the legend in a
more perfect form have been brought to light. The occurrence of the name of a town on coins in conjunction with
the name of the prince is of frequent occurrence in the
British series, especially among the coins of Tasciovanus and
Cunobeline. The coin of Amminus, Plate V., No. 1, reading
DVN on the reverse, may possibly be connected with this
coin of Tinc[ommius] reading DV.

PLATE I., No. 13.

Obv.—Convex, TINC on a sunk tablet.
Rev.—Horseman poising a javelin and charging to the right;
below, C.F.; above, a star of six points. The whole
within a beaded circle.
N. 82 grains; another 81½ grains.

This coin is in the British Museum. A coin of this type
was found on Titchfield Downs, Hants (Akerman, p. 185,
pl. xxi. 12; Arch. Assoc. Journ., vol. i. p. 300; Deale Poste,
p. 23; Numismatic Chronicle, vol. vii. pl. iv. 6; Num. Soc.
Proca., November 23, 1843). The same coin is also engraved
in the Archæologia, vol. xxxiii. pl. ix., but is there erroneously
stated to have been found at Alfriston. Mr. C. Roach Smith
has communicated to me impressions of another found at
East Wittering, Sussex.

The type of the obverse is peculiarly British in its character, the inscription on a sunk tablet being not only
common on the coins of Tinc[ommius] and Verica, but
inscriptions in the same position and style being frequent
on the coins of Tasciovanus and Cunobeline.

The horseman now takes, for the first time, his place on
the reverse of the British gold coins, and the style of workmanship, which exhibits a marked contrast to that of the
preceding coin, shows that foreign aid must have been called
in to assist native art at the British mints. The probability

is that we have here the work of some Roman artist, or of some Briton trained under a Roman moneyer. The form of the inscription on the obverse is exactly the same as that of the countermarks so common on the earlier Imperial coins. It has not, however, been produced upon these British coins by means of a small punch, as was the case with the Roman coins, but the tablet and letters have been formed upon the dies. Mr. Beale Poste (p. 206) adduces a second brass coin of Agrippa, according to his reading countermarked TIN, and found, as supposed, at Slenford, Sussex, which he thinks belongs to this class of coins. The countermark is, however, in all probability merely the usual TI. N., with the AV for AVGVSTVS in monogram. The horseman has by some been thought to have been copied from the coins of Tarentum; he bears, however, to my eye, a much closer resemblance to the figure on the reverse of the denarii of the Crepusia family (Cohen, pl. xvi.), as shown in the annexed woodcut. The letters C. F. are, beyond all doubt, merely an abbreviated form of COM. F. (Commii filius), which is given in the same form on the small coin, Plate II., No. 4. The star in the field is of the same character as that on the coin of Verica, Plate II., No. 12, suggesting that the dies were the work of the same engraver. Another specimen of this type, but of ruder workmanship, and with a large C only, instead of the C. F., below the horseman, and no star above, is engraved in Plate II., No. 8. The place of finding is not known.

PLATE L, No. 14.

Obv.—Convex, COM . F on a sunk tablet.
Rev.—Horseman with javelin to the right; below, TIN; behind the horseman a star; behind the horse three pellets conjoined in a peculiar manner. The whole within a coarse beaded circle. Æ. 81 1/2 grains.

PLATE II., No. 1.

Obv.—Convex, COM . . . on a sunk tablet.
Rev.—TIN, &c., as on the last coin. Æ. 83 grains.

These two coins are, in fact, but varieties of one and the same type. There has been a flaw in the die of the obverse of No. 14, which runs across part of the coin just behind the C of the inscription, giving it so much the appearance of a K, that it has usually been considered to read KOM. F. Plate II., No. 1, has also been generally thought to have had no more than COM on the obverse; but this merely arises from the part of the coin where the F. would have been having never been struck up, or else from the letter having been subsequently obliterated by a heavy blow upon the edge of the coin, of which there appear to be marks on both obverse and reverse.

Both the coins here engraved were found at Alfriston, Sussex, together with a coin of the type Plate L, No. 12. The former is in the British Museum; the latter in my own collection, having been presented to me by Mr. J. D. Dergne. I have another specimen, which was purchased at Swindon, Wilts, and was probably found in that neighbourhood. It is from the same dies as No. 14, but struck before the flaw on the obverse had become so fully developed.

The Alfriston coins are also engraved in the Numismatic Chronicle, vol. vii. pl. iv. 3 and 4; Coll. Ant., vol. i. pl. vii. 1 and 2; Akerman, pl. xxi. 10 and 11; Beale Posto, p. 22; and Arch. Assoc. Journ., vol. i. p. 303.

The type of the reverse is the same in design as that of the preceding coin, but the execution is much ruder. The star occurs on the field of some of the coins of Verica (Plate II., Nos. 11 and 12). On the brass (?) coin of Tinc[ommius], Plate II., No. 7, it is placed beneath the horse's tail. It is also found on the reverse of some of the small gold coins of the Bognor hoard. (See Plate E, Nos. 6 and 7.)

PLATE II., No. 2.

Obv.—TINCOM, and a zigzag ornament in the spaces between three corded lines across the field.

Rev.—Horse to the left; above, a wheel and annulet; in front, three annulets braced; below, what is probably the degenerate representation of the hind legs of the second horse of the biga. Æ, 18½ grains.

PLATE II., No. 3.

Obv.— . . NCOM, as on the last coin.
Rev.—As last. Æ, 18½ grains.

Both these coins are of the same type, but the latter is of ruder workmanship than the former. No. 2 was formerly in the collection of the late C. W. Loscombe, Esq., but is now in the British Museum. No. 3 is in my own cabinet, and was formerly in that of Mr. John Trotter Brockett. It is said to have been found near Brough, Westmoreland, but if so, it had travelled far from its original home. They are both engraved in the Numismatic Chronicle, vol. xvi. p. 80, Nos. 9 and 10. No. 3 is also engraved, though incorrectly, in the Numismatic Chronicle, vol. i. p. 80, No. 12; Lelewel, pl. viii. 42; and the Revue Numismatique, vol. iv. pl. xiii. 4.

The legend was at first strangely misread, and was considered to be a barbarous attempt to give the name of Cunobeline. By Lelewel it is made to read CIMONMVA, the zigzag below the inscription forming the last three letters.

There seems good reason for reading this as TINCOM, and not as forming part of the legend TIN . COM . F; for, firstly, there is no division or stop between the TIN and the COM; secondly, the coin No. 3 appears to show the termination of the inscription, and bears no sign of an F; and, thirdly, we know from Plate I., No. 13, that the name of the prince who struck these coins commenced with TINC. I was at one time inclined to regard the annulet near the head of the horse on the reverse as a C, and to suppose that on a better spread coin we should find C . F. This is, however, very doubtful. Still there is enough to justify us in regarding these coins as presenting us with a more extended form of TIN or TINC, which suggests TINCOMIUS or TIN-COMMIUS as the name of the prince who struck them.

The method of placing the inscription would appear to be

intermediate between a mere wreath and a legend on a sunk tablet. Such coins as Plate D, No. 9, and Plate E, No. 5, may well have been the prototypes. The coins of this type may be regarded as belonging to the first coinage of Tinc[ommius], like Plate L, Nos. 11 and 12, of which they are the quarters. The presence of a curved figure, significant of a reminiscence of the hind-legs of the second horse of the biga, is also to be observed on some of the coins of Tasciovanus (Plate V., Nos. 8 and 9).

PLATE II., No. 4.

Obv.—TINC on a tablet; C above and F below. The whole within a beaded circle.

Rev.—Full-faced winged head of Medusa, surrounded by snakes, and occupying nearly the whole of the field, within a beaded circle. N. 13 grains.

This unique coin, which formerly belonged to the late Mr. Cuff, is now in my own collection. It was found on the sea-coast, near Bognor, in company with a coin of Verica, Plate III., No. 1, and numerous uninscribed coins of the types Plate E, Nos. 6, 7, 9, 10, 11, and 12.

It is engraved in the Coll. Ant., vol. i. pl. vii. 13; in the Numismatic Chronicle, vol. vii. pl. iv. 9; and in Dixon's Geology of Sussex, p. 32, No. 1. An account of this Bognor find is given in the Num. Soc. Procs., December 23, 1841. When first published, the inscription on the tablet was considered illegible, but as I have already stated in the Numismatic Chronicle, vol. xviii. p. 46, I can pronounce it with certainty to be TINC.

The type of the obverse is thoroughly British in character, though of good workmanship; while the type of the reverse appears to be purely classical, and may be appealed to as an evidence of the influence of foreign artists upon our native coinage. There is, it is true, a somewhat similar head upon a Gaulish coin in brass, found near Amiens, and published by the late Dr. Rigollot, in the Revue Num., vol. iii. pl. viii. 2, and Lelewel, p. 294; but it is doubtful whether, in that case, the head is not rather that of Minerva than of Medusa. A full face occurs also on some other Gaulish coins, such as Lelewel, pl. vi. 56, and even on coins of Cunobeline (Plate XI., No. 10); but in no case does it approach this head of Medusa, in the classical character of the design.

The question of course arises, in what manner are we to account for such a subject appearing on a British coin? We find the head of Medusa, sometimes in profile and sometimes full-faced, on Roman coins of the Aquillia, Cossutia, and Cordia families, as well as on many Sicilian coins, but, unlike the head in profile on the coins of Cunobeline, Plate XII., No. 6, from none of these does the head upon the present coin appear to have been directly derived. Its origin must, therefore, be sought elsewhere, and may, I think, without much difficulty be found. As has already been observed, there is little doubt that about the period when the inscribed coinage of Tinc[ommius] commenced, Roman artists, or possibly native artists who had had the benefit of Roman instruction, were for the first time employed in the British mints. This new school of engravers did not, however, immediately introduce entirely new types or forms of coins, but continued to strike the coins upon the old model, as far as regarded their usually dished form, and merely modified and adapted the existing types; as for instance, by placing an inscribed tablet on what had been formerly the plain convex side of a coin, and converting the rude horse on the reverse into a well-formed equestrian figure. Now, among the coins found at Bognor in company with this coin of Tinc[ommius], were many coins of the same module belonging to the old uninscribed series, and among these it is but natural to look for the prototype of the present coin. The obverse presents no difficulty, as we find that among the anepigraphous coins it was in many cases quite plain and convex, presenting a suitable field for the addition of a tablet and inscriptions. The derivation of the reverse is not at first sight so apparent; but any one who will examine the reverse of the coin found at Bognor, and engraved in Plate E, No. 10, will see how readily the device upon it assumes the form of a full face. But in addition to this, the central tree-like object which forms the nose expands at the top into two wing-like projections occupying just the position of the wings above the forehead of the Medusa. The comparison of the actual coins is even more conclusive than that of the mere engravings; and I cannot but come to the conclusion that the head of Medusa was suggested to the mind of the engraver by some of these rude coins, and the original device was improved by him into a subject more in accordance with classical mythology.

Viewed in this manner, the coin is doubly interesting, both as affording the earliest example of the introduction of a purely classical subject upon the British coinage, of which we find many subsequent instances, and also as showing the manner in which an old type may, under certain influences, be so completely metamorphosed, that it is only under peculiar and even fortuitous circumstances that it can possibly be recognised.

It has already been suggested that the type of the reverse of Plate E, No. 10, is but the degenerate representation of the type of the charioteer; and here we find it reconverted into the head of Medusa—a transformation far beyond the power of the Gorgon's head itself.

PLATE II., No. 5.

Obv.—COM F on a sunk tablet.

Rev.—TIN; above, a bridled horse prancing to the right. The whole within a beaded circle. Æ. 17¾ grains.

This coin, formerly the late Mr. Cuff's, is now in my own collection. It probably formed part of the Bognor find, but this is by no means certain. There is a similar coin in the British Museum, of the same weight, the legend on which was mistaken by Taylor Combe for VI. My coin is engraved in the Num. Chron., vol. xviii. p. 44, No. 2. In type it bears a general resemblance to that of the larger coins of Tinc-[ommius] (Plate I., No. 14, and Plate II., No. 1), and also to that of the small coins of Verica (Plate III., Nos. 1 and 2).

Plate II., No. 6.

Obv.—COM F on a sunk tablet.
Rev.—Bridled horse prancing to the right; above, TI; below, N. The whole within a beaded circle. Æ. 16¼ grains.

This coin, which was found at Kingston, in Surrey, is in my own collection, and differs from the preceding only in the arrangement of the letters and in showing the beaded circle. It has not before been published. It is worth noticing that the horses on these coins are represented as bridled, though they have no rider, like those on the larger coins.

Plate II., No. 7.

Obv.—COM F on a sunk tablet.
Rev.—TIN; horseman galloping to the right; behind, a star. The whole within a beaded circle. Æ.

I have copied this coin from Akerman, pl. xxi. 14. A cast which I have of it does not show the inscription on the obverse quite so clearly. It is also engraved in the Num. Chron., vol. vii. pl. iv. 5, and was found in the immediate vicinity of Winchester. In the Num. Soc. Procs. for April 27, 1843, it is said to have then been in the possession of Mr. W. R. Bradfield, of that town. Though always described as being of brass, I am doubtful whether this coin ought properly to be regarded as of that metal. The type is evidently that of the gold coins, and though the weight is not recorded, the module is much larger than that of the copper coins of Eppillus, which we should expect any brass or copper coins of Tinc[ommius] to resemble in size. It must, therefore, I think, be considered either as being of extremely base gold, or else as being a contemporary forgery in brass of the gold coins Plate I., No. 14, and Plate II., No. 1, from which it differs only in the position of the star behind the horseman. I have seen the impression of a brass coin of Verica, of the type Plate II., No. 10, which was found on the Downs near Lancing, and which is also apparently an ancient counterfeit of the gold coins.

PLATE II., No. 6.

Obv.—As Plate I. No. 13.

Rev.—As Plate I. No. 13, but without the star in the field, and with a large C beneath the horseman, instead of C.F.

Æ. 76 grains.

This coin, in my own collection, is merely a variety of the type engraved in Plate I., No. 13, and has been already mentioned at page 163.

VERICA OR VIRICA.

Of this prince no mention whatever is made in history, and all the information that can be obtained concerning him must be derived from numismatic evidence. Upon coins his name appears under various forms: VI, VIII, VIRI, VERIC, and VERICA, in nearly all cases accompanied by the title COMMI. F, in a more or less abbreviated form, and occasionally with that of REX. As might have been inferred from the appearance of this latter title, some of his coins, such for instance as those with the cornucopiæ (Plate III., Nos. 5 and 6), show unmistakable signs of the influence of Roman art upon them, and nearly all are of superior workmanship. Though none of them are struck on the same archaic pattern as some of those of his brother Tinc[ommius], yet in other cases the coins of the two brothers are identical in type, and vary only in having the legend VIR and TIN respectively. This, when taken in connection with the fact that the coins of both have been found together, without showing any perceptible difference in the amount of wear, proves that Tinc[ommius] and Verica were, during some portion of the reign of each, contemporaries, and gives additional reason, if any such were necessary, for interpreting the legend COMMI . F. as Commii Filius. It also shows that these coins cannot, as was first suggested by Mr. Akerman (Numismatic Chronicle, vol. xi. p. 155), have any connection with the Bericus mentioned by Dion Cassius, who cannot have been expelled from Britain much before A.D. 43, or at all events until after the death of Cunobeline; whereas the coins of Tinc[ommius] and Verica evidently belong to the earliest period of the inscribed British coinage, and are decidedly more ancient than those of Cunobeline. In fact, there is no evidence that the Bericus of Dion Cassius (lib. lx. 19) ever occupied the position of a king; he is spoken of as simply Βέρικος τις ἐκπεσὼν ἐκ τῆς νήσου κατὰ στάσιν, and not as one of the kings to whom the Britons were subject, ἔαν ᾖ οὐκ ἀυτονόμοι ἀλλ' ἄλλοις βασιλεῦσι προστεταγμένοι. Still the evident similarity of name between this Bericus or Vericus of history and the Verica of coins is well worthy of notice. There are, however, many names, both British and Gaulish, into the constitution of which the syllable VER or VIR enters, such as Vergasillaunus, Vercingetorix, Viridovix, Arviragus, Verulamium, Virosedum, &c. On some Gaulish coins we have a very close approximation to the name of Verica or Virica in the VIIRICO and VIRICO* which occurs upon them.

The title of REX, which appears for the first time on the coins of Verica, is also found on some of those of Eppillus and Cunobeline, but not on any others of this series. It is that which is also usually applied by Cæsar and the other Roman historians to the petty princes of the various British tribes, though occasionally they are termed *Reguli*.

The extent of territory over which Verica had the dominion is extremely uncertain. His coins have been found associated with those of Tinc[ommius] in more than one instance in Sussex, while in Surrey they have been found without any such admixture. There is only one instance in each county of their discovery in Hampshire and Kent. Such being the case, it is possible that Verica may have been the ruler over the Atrebates, though, as it will be subsequently seen, there is some reason for supposing that eventually Eppillus may have ruled over that tribe as well as over the Cantii. There is, however, some probability,

* Rev. Num., 1863, p. 67.

if the coin, Plate III., No. 14, which seems to read TC. VI. EP, is rightly interpreted, that the three brothers at one time held the joint rule over the whole of the South-eastern district, including Kent, though each had a separate province more immediately under his own control. In the days of Julius Cæsar there appears to have been a united sovereignty of this kind in Kent, where there were four kings who, if they had not some sort of joint rule, at all events acted in perfect accordance, the one with the other, when appealed to by Cassivellaunus; but this point will be better reserved until I come to treat of Eppillus.

From the abundance of silver coins of Verica as compared with those of Tinc[ommius], of whom indeed there are none with his sole name upon them, it is probable that Verica survived him. This appears all the more probable from the silver coin, Plate III., No. 7, bearing the joint names of Verica and Eppillus, while that of Tinc[ommius] is absent. At the same time, from the occurrence of copper coins of Eppillus, of several types, while there is but one doubtful specimen of either Tincommius or Verica, it would seem that they were both outlived by their brother Eppillus.

PLATE II., No. 9.

Obv.—VI — RI on either side of an expanded leaf.

Rev.—CO. F; horseman leaping to the right. From other specimens it is seen that the horse is springing from a square stage beneath his hind-feet, while there is another similar stage immediately beneath his fore-feet. The horseman carries behind him a long oval pointed shield, above which appears what may be a quiver or club, for it does not seem to be pointed at the end like a spear. There is a beaded circle round the whole. Æ. 82 grains.

This coin is in the British Museum, and was found at Romsey, Hants (see Archæol., vol. xxxiii. pl. ix.; Arch. Assoc. Journ., vol. iv. p. 157; Coll. Ant., vol. i. pl. lvi. 8). Another was found in Pagham Harbour, Sussex (Num. Chron., vol. xv. p. 105), and I have been informed that a third was found at Shoreham, Sussex. The place of finding of the coin engraved in Akerman, pl. xxi. 15, is not known.

These coins are usually of extremely fine work, the leaf on the obverse being, on some of them, engraved with the highest skill, and on all there is great spirit combined with delicacy of execution in the horseman on the reverse. The leaf appears to be that of the vine, but whether this was an original type to signify the fertility of the soil in respect of vines, or adapted from some other source, it is hard to say. An acquaintance with the vine might probably result from the intercourse with the Romans; and the permission of the Emperor Probus[*] for Spain, Gaul, and Britain to cultivate the vine and make wine, implies its existence and use in all three countries at that time. At any rate, the device of the vine leaf does not appear to have been borrowed from any Roman coin, but the obverse of these British coins bears a strong resemblance to that of some of the coins of Selinus. On these latter, however, the leaf is that of the wild parsley, and not of the vine.

The horseman on the reverse is springing from a sort of stage, much in the same way as the Dioscuri and other equestrian figures are represented on many of the Roman family coins. He appears to be naked, though wearing some sort of cap. His long oval shield is carried diagonally behind his back, and above it appears the quiver or club, if such it be. On some specimens this object closely resembles the letter I, and would in that case make the legend CIO F. On others, however, it is in so slanting a position, that it can hardly be intended for a letter. The shield is much the same in shape as that carried by the horseman on the reverse of the coins inscribed TASCIO-RICON, &c. (Plate VIII., Nos. 6 to 9). It is, however, smaller, and shows a beaded line along its centre. The silver coin of Tasciovanus, Plate VI., No. 2, affords another instance of a somewhat similar shield on the British coinage. Some further remarks on the subject of these shields will be found in the description of

[*] Fl. Vopiscus, de Probo, c. 18.

that coin. The weapon that usually accompanies these shields seems to be a short sword, though apparently it is not so in the present instance.

This is the only gold coin on which the name of the king is found in the form VIRI, though it occurs in this form on some of the silver coins mentioned farther on. At first sight it might appear probable that the coins reading VI., VIR, and VIRI, were to be assigned to some other prince than those with VERIC and VERICA; yet it must be borne in mind that both classes of coins are found in the same part of the country, and, as in the find at Lancing Downs, even associated together, and both give the same titles, COM. F and REX; while at the same time they are of similar art, and present similarities in some of their details. We also find I and E interchanged on some of the coins of Verulam.

PLATE II., No. 10.

Obv.—Convex; COM. F, on a sunk tablet.
Rev.—VIR REX; horseman charging to the right, holding in his right hand a short dart; behind the horse a lituus-shaped object, and beneath this an open crescent reversed. The whole within a beaded circle.
N. 82 grains.

This coin is in my own collection, but I do not know where it was found. Another was found near Steyning, Sussex, where also was discovered a coin of Tinc[ommius] of the type Plate I., No. 12 (Coll. Ant., vol. i. pl. lvi. 2; Arch. Assoc. Journ., vol. iv. p. 157). Another is engraved in Akerman, pl. xxii. 1, on which there appear to be some pellets instead of the crescent beneath the horse's hind-feet.

The type was engraved by Camden (pl. ii. 10, ed. 1637; pl. i. 30, Gibson's ed.), and by Speed (pp. 29, 44, &c.), but as only giving COM on the obverse and REX on the reverse. The same is repeated by Stukeley, pl. xxiii. 2, who represents the coin as of brass. It is, however, worth notice, that Nicolas Fabri de Peiresc, in a letter to Camden, dated

May, 1608 (Camd. Ep., p. 105, col. 1091), says that the coin appears to read COME rather than COM. The crescent and *lituus*, which are engraved with considerable accuracy in Speed, prove that the coin known to these early antiquaries was of the same type as that here engraved, but less perfectly struck or preserved. It is not, therefore, another variety which has still to be rediscovered, as has by some been supposed.

The obverse is precisely that of the gold coins of Tinc[ommius] already described (Plate I., No. 14; Plate II., No. 1). The horseman is also very similar in character to that on the reverse of those coins, but the accessories in the field and the legend are different. These accessories are peculiar to this type, and it is difficult to say what they are intended to represent. The *lituus* is of the form usual by the Augurs, and not the cavalry trumpet, and is exactly the same as on some Roman coins; such, for instance, as the gold coins of Julius Cæsar and Mark Antony; but why it should appear in this position on a British coin I cannot imagine. I have already remarked on the title REX.

Plate II., No. 11.

Obv.—COM . F as on No. 10.

Rev.—VIR, beneath a horseman galloping to the right, with a short dart in his hand; behind him a star of five points, and behind the horse an annulet (?). The whole within a beaded circle. N. 80,3/10 grains.

The coin here engraved was formerly in the Dimsdale and Huxtable collections, and is now in my own. Its place of finding is not known. It is engraved in Akerman, pl. xxi. 10. The horseman on the reverse is very similar to that on the coin last described, but he appears to hold the javelin in his left hand, and to have his right arm drawn back. The reins are not shown to extend behind the horse's neck, and apparently are not held by the rider.

The star, which occurs also on other coins of Verica, is found in precisely the same position as on this coin, on those of Tinc[ommius], Plate I., No. 14; Plate II., No. 1; and the design and workmanship of the coins of both princes are so nearly identical, that there can be no doubt of their having been contemporaries. In each case only the three first letters of the name are given, and in precisely the same relative position to the horse. In the catalogue of Baron Dimsdale's collection, sold in 1824, this and the preceding coin are attributed to Vergasillaunus, one of the chiefs of Alesia during the siege by Julius Cæsar.

Plate II., No. 12.

Obv.—Convex: VERIC COM F in two lines across the field; above, a crescent or annulet (?); below, a star of six points.

Rev.—REX beneath a horse walking to the right; above, a star of six points. The whole within a beaded circle.

N. 20.$\frac{6}{8}$ grains.

The coin here engraved was found on Farley Heath, near Guildford, and is now in the British Museum. It is engraved in the Num. Chron., vol. xi. p. 92, No. 2; Tupper's Farley Heath, No. 1; and in the Archæologia, vol. xxxiii. pl. ix. At the same spot was found a silver coin of Epaticcus (Plate VIII., No. 13); and a number of uninscribed coins of the types Plate D, Nos. 4 to 11, have been found in the same neighbourhood. Another of these coins of Verica was found at East Wittering, Sussex, for an impression of which I am indebted to Mr. C. Roach Smith. They are, of course, quarters of the larger pieces.

The arrangement of the legend on the obverse is remarkable, and shows that the VERIC. and COM. F. are closely connected with each other, and are to be read together. The title REX on the reverse is the same as we find on No. 10, where the name of the king is represented by VIR only. The R has interfered with one of the hind-legs of the horse, which the engraver in consequence left out altogether. Still the art displayed on the coin is very good. The stars of six points are of quite a different character from that on the preceding coin, but are precisely the same as that on the coin of Tinc[ommius], Plate I., No. 13, and form another point of connection between the coins of that prince and of Verica.

Plate II., No. 13.

Obv.—COM.F on a sunk tablet. The whole within a beaded circle.
Rev.—VI.; bridled horse pacing to the right, upon an exergual line, within a beaded circle. *N.*

This coin, which is hitherto unpublished, was, I believe, one of the hoard found at Bognor, already mentioned. It differs from Plate III., No. 2, in the tablet being distinctly sunk, and having no raised line round it, and also in there being no ring ornaments above and below the tablet, and in the beads of the circle being coarser and better defined. I am indebted for a cast of it to Mr. C. Roach Smith.

Plate II., No. 14.

Obv.—COM.F on a sunk tablet with a raised border; above and below, a ring ornament.
Rev.—VIR (?); a horseman to the right, as on No. 10, but with the lance horizontal; behind, a small star of six points, of the same character as on No. 13; below, a small cross of four pellets. *N.* 81¼ grains.

This coin is in the collection of Mr. Samuel Sharp, of Dallington Hall, Northampton, but its place of finding is not known. It differs from the other large coins in having the ring ornaments on the obverse, but is in this respect all the more closely allied with the small pieces, Plate III., Nos. 1 and 2. The coin was exhibited to the Numismatic Society, October 24, 1861.

Plate III., No. 1.

Obv.—COM.F on a tablet having slight projections at each end; above and below, a ring ornament.
Rev.—VIR; bridled horse prancing to the right, upon an exergual line. There is a beaded circle on both obverse and reverse. *N.* 12½ grains.

This coin is in my own collection, and was found, with

others, at Bognor, Sussex. One of them is engraved in the Coll. Ant., vol. i. pl. vii. 12, but the final F on the obverse has been accidentally omitted, and the legend on the reverse is but imperfectly shown. This has been copied by Beale Poste, p. 23, and in the Arch. Assoc. Journ., vol. i. p. 303. The coin is engraved more correctly in Akerman, pl. xxii. 3; in the Archaeologia, vol. xxxiii. pl. ix; and in the Numismatic Chronicle, vol. vii. pl. iv. 7. It is also given, though inaccurately, in Dixon's Sussex, p. 32, No. 2.

Plate III., No. 2.

Obv.—COM F, as on No. 1., but without the small projections at the ends of the tablet.

Rev.—VI; horse galloping to the right, upon an exergual line. The beaded circle is more apparent on the obverse than the reverse. *N.* 16½ grains.

The place of finding of this coin is not known. It is in the British Museum, and was engraved by Taylor Combe, pl. i. 7, who, however, read COMI on the obverse, and assigned the coin to Commius. He mentions another coin (p. 11) as having "OMI vel OMB intra quadratum scriptum," with S below the horse on the reverse. This latter coin, which weighs 17¾ grains, is, however, one of Tinc[ommius] of the type Plate II., No. 5, and the supposed S is merely the leg of the horse.

Both came from the Cracherode collection. The former is also engraved in Akerman, pl. xxii. 2, and Lelewel, pl. viii. 9.

The type of both No. 1 and 2 is so intimately connected with that of the coins of Tinc[ommius], Plate II., No. 5, that there can be no reasonable doubt of their belonging to precisely the same period.

Plate III., No. 3.

Obv.—VERICA COMMI F around an object probably intended to represent a circular shield or target.

Rev.—REX; a lion running to the right; above a narrow crescent. *R.* 13½ grains.

This unique coin was found on Farley Heath, and was communicated by Mr. Martin F. Tupper to the Numismatic Chronicle, vol. xii. p. 174. It is now in the cabinet of Mr. Whitbourn, of Godalming. The engraving here given is copied from the woodcut in the Numismatic Chronicle, and it will be observed that the legend is partially restored, though there can be no question as to its giving the correct reading. Mr. Akerman, who describes the coin, observes that the Roman style and formula of legend on this coin are sufficiently obvious, and remarks that on many Gaulish coins there are terminations in A. If BRICCA, which we find on coins of the North of Gaul, be the name of a chief, it presents a very close analogy with the name of Verica. We have here, as on the gold coins, the title REX occurring on the reverse, while the designation COMMI F. accompanies the name on the obverse.

The device of the obverse appears to be a circular target, such as we know to have been in use among the Britons, though the shields which are usually represented on their coins are long and oval. The arrangement of the device on some of the silver coins of Tasciovanus may however be intended to convey the idea of a circular shield, with a ring of small bosses between two raised circles around the rim. The circular buckler found near Dorchester, Oxon, and engraved in the Archæologia, vol. xxvii. pl. xxii., shows a central hollow boss, large enough to hold the hand at the back, and surrounded by a double row of smaller bosses. Its diameter is only fourteen inches. The large circular shield which belonged to Sir Samuel Meyrick (Archæologia, vol. xxiii. pl. xiii.) had also an umbo to receive the hand, but the bosses around were much smaller, and in many more rings. It was the same with two circular bucklers from the bed of the Thames, described in C. Roach Smith's Catalogue of London Antiquities, p. 80. One of these had eleven concentric circles of small circular studs, and the other no less than twenty-six. Just such a shield, showing three rings of studs, occurs on denarii of Augustus of the

Julia family (Cohen, pl. xxiii. 66), and of the Carisia family (Cohen, pl. x. 10). On a quinarius of the same family (Cohen, pl. xx. 14), commemorative of the victories of Julius Cæsar, there is a trophy on which is a circular buckler with bosses upon it, and a long shield, in form like an 8, at the side. Possibly this coin, like that with the chariot upon it (Cohen, pl. xx. 13), records the conquests of Julius in Britain. Some of the coins of Eppillus, CRAB, and Verulam, as well as those of Tasciovanus above mentioned, and some of the uninscribed coins from Lancing Downs, have a shield-like device on the obverse. The lion is of frequent occurrence on Gaulish coins, and was possibly derived from thence. It occurs also on coins struck at Lyons by Mark Antony, one of whose coins it will subsequently be seen served as a prototype for another coin of Verica. Certainly the lion cannot be regarded as an indigenous type, for the original British lion, whether the fossil Machairodus or the Felis Spelæa, had been long extinct even in the days of Verica. The addition of the crescent above is of a more truly British character. We find it in the same position above a horse or centaur on coins of Cunobeline and Tasciovanus, and it forms the principal type on the next coin, and on a coin of Eppillus (Plate IV., No. 1), as well as being of frequent occurrence on the uninscribed series. A herald would suggest that it is the sun that is represented on the gold coins of Verica, and the moon upon the silver, as being the proper representatives of the metals, especially on regal coins.

Plate III., No. 4.

Obv.—COM.F. between two open crescents above and below, the horns facing each other, and with a pellet opposite the centre of each. The whole within a beaded circle.

Rev.—Uncertain legend, possibly VI; lion (?) to the right, upon an exergual line; above, a star. Æ. 15$\frac{3}{5}$ grains.

Unfortunately this coin, especially the reverse of it, is in but poor preservation, and the legend cannot in consequence be deciphered with certainty. There is however no doubt of its having been struck by one of the sons of Commius; and from what appears of the legend, and from the type of the reverse, which is in general character so similar to that of the coin last described, probably by Verica. It was, moreover, found at Albury, close to Farley Heath, where also coins of both the preceding and succeeding types have been discovered. It was first published in the Numismatic Chronicle, vol. xii. p. 67, and subsequently by Beale Poste, p. 154, and Arch. Assoc. Journ., vol. v. p. 157, from whence my engraving of the reverse has been copied. In the Numismatic Chronicle the animal has more the appearance of a wild boar than of a lion, and it is also described as such by Mr. Beale Poste. The coin is now in the possession of Mr. Whitbourn, of Godalming, and from examination of it I think the animal may have been intended for a lion. The type of the obverse may be compared with that of the reverse of the coin of Eppillus, Plate IV., No. 1.

PLATE III., Nos. 5, 6.

Obv.—VERICA; a draped, or partly draped figure seated to the right.

Rev.—COMMI F; a kind of sceptre (?) between two horns of plenty issuing from a vase with two handles. A beaded circle around the device on both obverse and reverse. Æ. 19½ grains; 17½ grains.

Of these coins, which together nearly complete the type, No. 5 was found at Richborough, and was formerly in the collection of the late Mr. Rolfe, of Sandwich, but is now in my own; and No. 6 was found at Farley Heath, and presented to the British Museum by the late Mr. Henry Drummond, of Albury. The former is engraved in the Numismatic Chronicle, vol. xiii. p. 134, and in C. Roach Smith's Richborough, p. 120; the latter in the Arch. Assoc. Journ., vol. v. p. 137, and Beale Poste, p. 154, from whence I have copied it. In both cases the convex side, or obverse, has been represented as the reverse, an arrangement which I have here unintentionally followed.

Until some more perfect specimen is discovered it is difficult to say whom the seated figure is intended to represent. The device is, however, of classical origin, and may possibly be a seated Victory, such as is seen on coins of the Porcia family. The device on the other side of the coin may, I think, be traced beyond all doubt to the reverse of a denarius of Mark Antony (Cohen, pl. iii. 10), on which there is a winged caduceus between two cornua-copiæ, issuing from a globe, instead of, as on these British coins, from a diota. Mr. C. Roach Smith observes, "The device, an emblem of abundance and prosperity, is purely Roman, as is the workmanship of all the coins of the British princes at this period." "The cornua-copiæ and caduceus form the tasteful design on one of the terra-cotta lamps recently discovered at Colchester." The presence of this Roman type on this coin of Verica, taken in conjunction with the style of art, affords strong evidence of intercourse with Rome, and justifies us in regarding the inscriptions upon these British coins as Latin, both in language and form.

PLATE III., No. 7.

Obv.—VIRRI; diademed, beardless head to the right.
Rev.—EPPI COM F; Capricorn to the left. A beaded circle round both obverse and reverse. Æ.

This coin, which is in the Hunter collection at Glasgow, has been engraved by White, No. 2, as reading VIRCO on the obverse, in which he has been followed by Gough, pl. i. 18, who has again been copied by Beale Poste, pp. 22 and 42, and Arch. Assoc. Journal, vol. i. p. 303, and vol. ii. p. 28. There is another coin of this type engraved in Stukeley, pl. xxi. 2, in which the legend of the obverse is given as V—JO, but the legend on the Hunter coin is as I have given it, VIRRI. It is struck in bold relief, and is of fine execution, and in remarkably good condition. The head on the obverse is much like that on No. 14, but turned in the opposite direction. The Capricorn on the reverse is doubtless copied from the coins of Augustus, such as that shown in the woodcut, though without the cornucopiæ, rudder, or globe. There is a silver coin of Augustus (Cohen, No. 56) on which also the Capricorn appears without the adjuncts. Here again we have an instance of a British type derived from the Roman; but the most remarkable feature of the coin is its presenting the names of both the brothers Verica and Eppillus upon it, as if struck by their joint authority. This, at all events, proves Verica and Eppillus to have been contemporaries, and not, as has been supposed by Mr. Poste,* divided by an interval of nearly a century. When we come to No. 14 in this Plate it will be seen that it was probably struck in the name of all three brothers, Tinc[ommius], Verica, and Eppillus, and it may be inferred that at the time when No. 7 was struck, the first named of these three princes was dead, and that it is therefore subsequent in date to No. 14.

Beside the coins engraved in the Plates there are some other coins of Verica with which I have lately become acquainted, and for impressions of most of which I am, as I have been in so many other instances, indebted to Mr. C. Roach Smith. They were all found on the Downs, near Lancing, Sussex, but I am not in possession of all the particulars of the discovery. The find appears to have comprised at least one specimen of each of the two large coins, of which I have given woodcuts; and I think two of the small coins with the head. Of the other four small coins there were, I believe, two of No. 1, two of No. 2, one of No. 3, and four of No. 4. Besides these there was a small silver coin of the type of Plate F, No. 12, and three brass or copper coins—one of them, apparently, an ancient forgery of the gold coin, Plate II., No. 10; the other two nearly undecipherable, but one of them possibly Gaulish, of GERMANUS INDUTILLI L., and the other with a horse on the reverse. Some mention

* Celtic Inscriptions, p. 45.

of the discovery is made in Smith's Coll. Ant., vol. i. p. 93, and in Dallaway's Sussex, vol. ii. part ii. p. 389. In the latter work is a woodcut of one of the coins, which I have

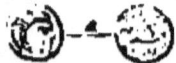

here reproduced. On the obverse is a bare head in profile to the right, and on the reverse a horse galloping to the right, with a legend which may be VIII . F . CO, or possibly VIRRI . CO. Though the head is turned in the opposite direction, the general character of the coin is not unlike that of the silver coins inscribed Boduoc, which are, however, in all probability of a later date. The coins which follow are all now published for the first time.

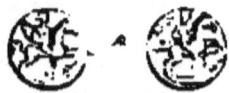

Of these the most remarkable is one with, apparently, COM . F. on the obverse, and with VERICA on the reverse, and armed horsemen on either side. That on the obverse will at once be recognised as being as nearly as possible identical with the horseman on the reverse of Plate II., No. 9; but the horseman on the reverse differs from that on any other British coin, as he appears to be charging like a mediæval knight, with his lance in rest. Altogether, his attitude is much like that of one of the Dioscuri on the Roman family coins.

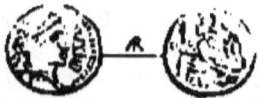

The next type presents on the obverse a draped bust, apparently with a diadem, and possibly winged, with the legend VIRL; and on the reverse a seated figure (also apparently winged), draped, and wearing a sort of helmet, holding in her right hand a branch with a pellet on either side, and in her left a sceptre (?).

This coin is struck in high relief, and the workmanship, like that of the coin last described, is good, though the style is rather rude. The head has much the appearance of having been copied from the denarii of the Carisia family (Cohen, pl. x. 1), and the figure on the reverse may be a seated Victory; but the die from which the coin was struck had been injured, so that there is great difficulty in making out the details.

The other types of the smaller coins, which seem to be quarters of the larger, are shown in the annexed woodcut. Of these No. 1 shows the legend VIRI on a sort of

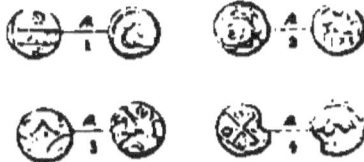

tablet between two stars of pellets above and below, and on the reverse an object the nature of which it is difficult to determine, but which seems to be connected with that on the reverse of No. 4. On the obverse of No. 2 are two squares interlaced, with a pellet in the centre, forming an ornament much like that on some of the copper coins of Verulam, and the silver coin reading DIAS, Plate VI., No. 14. On the reverse is a horse to the right, with a legend apparently VIRI. The device on the obverse of No. 3 is a hollow square, with the sides curved inwards; in the centre a pellet, and opposite each side a ring ornament. On the reverse is a horse galloping to the left; above, a wheel; below, a ring ornament. The obverse type is closely connected with that of the small coins of Verulam, Plate VIII, No. 1. No. 4 presents on the obverse a cross with irregular figures in each angle, and has an unintelligible device on the reverse. The obverse is in general character very like the reverse of some of the silver coins of Southern Gaul (Lelewel, pl. iv. 1, &c.), which were probably derivatives of some of the coins of Massilia with the wheel on the reverse. In this case, however, it is probable that the cruciform device is only a modification of the hollow square, No. 3, and that that was originally derived from the head on the small coins like Plate F, No. 12, which on some specimens shows a great tendency to assume the form of a square with concave sides. The similarity of the reverse of No. 3 to that of the gold coin of Tinc[ommius], Plate II, No. 2, is striking. The resemblance of the obverse types of Nos. 2 and 3 to those of coins of Verulam is also very curious, especially as there is, as will subsequently be seen, a close connection between some of the types of the coins of Eppillus (the brother of Verica) and some of those of Verulam struck under Tasciovanus. Looking at the size of the coins, which shows that very small denominations of money must have been requisite for the purposes of trade, and that there must in consequence have been a considerable degree of civilisation in the part of the country where such a currency existed, I think that most of these pieces must be assigned to the latter portion of the reign of Verica, and that the uninscribed, as well as the inscribed pieces may have been struck by his authority.

CHAPTER XII.

COINS OF THE KENTISH DISTRICT.

I now come to the coins that are principally found in Kent, the inhabitants of which part of Britain are by Cæsar said to have been the most civilised of the British tribes, and differing but little in their mode of life from the Gauls. It is, however, possible that the district which was by Cæsar called Cantium may have comprised a part of Sussex, as we have his own evidence of much of the south-eastern seaboard being occupied by Belgic tribes, and he does not contrast the civilisation of Kent with theirs, but with the state of tribes in the interior, who did not sow corn, but lived on flesh and milk, and clothed themselves with skins. As far as numismatic evidence goes, there is nothing to distinguish Kent from the other south-eastern counties, except the greater comparative abundance of copper coins, from which it may be inferred that the native coinage was probably continued there to a later period than in Hants and Sussex. Of the four kings of Kent mentioned by Cæsar—Cingetorix, Carvilius, Taximagulus, and Segonax—no coins are known, though, as will be subsequently seen, some have been erroneously attributed to the latter. It was probably not until after their days that inscriptions began to appear upon the British coinage.

Of those whose names we find on coins discovered almost exclusively in this county, the principal is EPPILLUS, one of the sons of Commius, and brother of the princes whose coins have just been described; and the next, DUBNOVELLAUNUS,

whose territory appears also to have comprised a portion
of Essex. Besides these there was a prince whose name
appears to have been VOSENOS. The coins of AMMINUS are
also probably Kentish; and those inscribed CRAB may belong
either to this or some adjoining district.

EPPILLUS.

This prince, like all the others of whom I have hitherto
treated, except Commius, is entirely unknown to history;
and all that is ever likely to be ascertained concerning him
must be gathered from his coins. That Eppillus is his full
and correct name is certain, as, unlike Tinc[ommius], we
have not to supply the final syllables by conjecture, but meet
with the name, not only as EP, EPP, EPPI, and EPPIL,
but also in full, EPPILLVS. That he reigned in a part at
least of Kent may also be regarded as an established fact,
for there is no recorded instance of a single coin bearing his
name having been found beyond the limits of that county.
We further learn from his coins that he was a son of
Commius, and, as such, brother of Tinc[ommius] and
Verica, and that, like the latter, he had the title of REX.
The coins also afford some ground for supposing that at
one time there was a sort of joint sovereignty or close
alliance between the three brothers, and after the death of
Tinc[ommius], between Eppillus and Verica. The more
classical style of his gold coins—on none of which either
the pure archaic type of the rude head of Apollo, and
the degenerate bigæ (such as on the coin of Tinc[ommius],
Plate I., No. 12), nor even the sunk tablet (such as on
those of Tinc[ommius] and Verica), is to be seen—renders
it probable that he did not attain to the kingly power
at so early a period as either of his brothers. At the same
time, the greater number of his copper coins seems to prove
that he survived them both. Whether at any time he
became chieftain of the Atrebates, as well as of the Cantii,
is an open question; but the word CALLE, which is found

on some of his silver coins, seems to refer them to Calleva, the chief town of the Atrebates, as their place of mintage. Though, as before observed, the archaic type of the degenerate Macedonian stater is not found on the coins of Eppillus, as on those of Tinc[ommius], yet one at least of his types is derived from the uninscribed coinage on which the head of Apollo had arrived at the cruciform stage. This type, as will hereafter be seen, rather tends to connect his coinage with that of the Central district, while many of his coins bear a strong general resemblance to those of Tasciovanus and of Verulam. He must, indeed, probably have been a contemporary of Tasciovanus, as well as of Vose[nos] and Dubnovellaunus, during a portion of their reigns, for, as will subsequently be seen, there is some reason for supposing that these chiefs occupied a part of Kent, while Eppillus had possession of some other part of the same district. The chronology and extent of territory of these three princes last mentioned cannot, however, as yet be ascertained with any approach to certainty.

The name of Eppillus presents analogies, both in its commencement and termination, with many British and Gaulish names—Epaticcus, Epasnactus, Eporedorix, Cavarillus, Celtillus, may be cited as instances. Many more names ending in ILLUS, from Gaulish inscriptions and other sources, will be found in the Revue Numismatique, Nouv. Sér., vol. v. p. 185.

PLATE III., No. 8.

Obv.—EPPIL COM F in two lines across the field. The whole within a beaded circle.

Rev.—Pegasus springing to the right; below, a ring ornament. *N.*

This coin, which is in the Hunter Museum, at Glasgow, is now published for the first time. On the obverse we have the name of the prince in a slightly abbreviated form, followed by the title COM F, corresponding exactly with the inscription on the coin of his brother Verica, Plate II., No. 12. On the reverse is the classical type of the Pegasus, which may, however, have been derived from some Gaulish coin. In character, this Pegasus resembles that on the small gold coin of Tasciovanus, with whom Eppillus appears to have been contemporary, as there are so many analogies between the coins of the two chiefs. Like Nos. 12 and 13, this coin represents the quarter of the larger pieces, Nos. 9, 10, and 11.

PLATE III., Nos. 9, 10.

Obv.—Convex, COM.F within a circular wreath.

Rev.—EPPILLVS; naked and unarmed horseman galloping to the left; in front, a ring ornament; behind, a star; below, an ornament formed of four leaves and four pellets, between two ring ornaments. The whole within a beaded circle. *N.* 81½ grains, 83½ grains.

In order to show the entire type, I have engraved the only two specimens at present known, the one of which gives the inscription, and the other the details below the horseman on the reverse. No. 9 is in the British Museum, and is engraved as Gaulish in Taylor Combe, pl. i. 11. It is also given by Akerman, pl. xxi. 3; and in the Archæologia, vol. xxxiii. pl. ix., where its place of finding is said to have been Sandwich; but this is possibly an error, as there is no record of the fact preserved at the Museum. The same coin is engraved by Lelewel, pl. viii. 8. No. 10 was found in cutting the railway from Chatham to Sittingbourne, and is now in my own collection. It is engraved in Smith's Coll. Ant., vol. v. pl. xxviii. 1.

These coins differ from any others of the sons of Commius in having the inscription on the obverse placed within a wreath. In the next coin the wreath appears much in the same manner, but there encircles a Victory. Improbable as it may at first sight appear, there is some reason for supposing the type of the circular wreath to be a descendant of the often cited laureate bust, for among the uninscribed coins found at Bognor is one of small size with a circular wreath surrounding a pellet on the obverse (Plate E, No. 6). As I have before remarked, some of the Gaulish and German derivatives of the Philippus also show the wreath assuming a circular form. It will be remembered that coins of Tinc[ommius] and Verica were found in the Bognor hoard, though I believe none of Eppillus. There is, however, a wreath surrounding the device on many of the Roman family coins, and it occurs also on coins of Ammimus and of Cunobeline. The horseman on the reverse is turned in the opposite direction from those on the coins of Tinc[ommius] and Verica, and, unlike them is entirely unarmed. The quatrefoil beneath the horse is peculiar to the coins of Eppillus, and occurs again on the small coin No. 12, but the star behind the horseman is found also on the coins of both his brothers. The nearest approach to the quatrefoil is that beneath the horse on some of the Whaddon Chase coins, see Plate C, No. 8.

PLATE III., No. 11.

Obv.—Winged and draped Victory marching to the left holding a garland and palm branch. The whole within a wreath.

Rev.—EPPI . COM . F ; horseman springing to the right, holding the carnyx over his shoulder. The whole within a beaded circle. *N.* 82¾ grains.

This unique coin was found at Staple, near Ash, in Kent, in the year 1837, and was formerly in the collection of the late Mr. Rolfe, of Sandwich, but is now in my own. It is engraved in Akerman, pl. xxi. 4. It is also given by Beale Poste, p. 21, and in the Arch. Assoc. Journal, vol. i. p. 302.

The device of the obverse, though decidedly British in its manner of treatment, is probably derived from a Roman prototype, as on several of the Roman coins of the time of Augustus we find a winged and draped Victory with the wreath and palm-branch. It is indeed evident that such a type could hardly have been adopted in this country until the intercourse with the Romans had made them acquainted with the goddess under these attributes, for the native Andate or Andraste cannot be conceived as carrying a palm-branch. She is here, however, represented as far more of a virago than on the Roman coinage. The inscription on the reverse shows the manner in which the legend on all these coins is to be read—EPPI. COM. F., not COM. F. EPPI., and proves the analogy of this formula with that of CAESAR. DIVI. F. The object held by the horseman is well worthy of close attention. Though not brandished in the same manner, there is no doubt of its being precisely the same object as that on the reverse of the coins of Tasciovanus, Plate V., Nos. 10 and 12, only in this case there appears to be a fillet attached to its end. This object had been variously described as a club, a battle-axe, or a pedum, but has been shown by the Marquis de Lagoy,* to be the carnyx, or Celtic war-trumpet, one of which forms a conspicuous object on the left side of the trophy on the reverse of a coin of Julius commemorative of his victories in Gaul and Britain (Cohen, pl. xx. 11), of which a woodcut is annexed. It occurs also on some Gaulish coins, such as that engraved in the Revue Num., vol. xx. pl. v. 9. Whether, like the lituus among the Romans, this instrument was peculiar to cavalry, as the tuba was to infantry, cannot be determined. On British coins it is found only in the hands of horsemen. I am not aware of any other instance of a fillet or streamer being attached to the end of the carnyx, as is the case on this coin.

PLATE III., No. 12.

Obv.—COM F within a small beaded circle.
Rev.—EPPI above a horse at liberty, galloping to the right; below a quatrefoil like that on No. 10. The whole within a beaded circle. *N.* 20 grains.

This coin, which is now in my own collection, was found near Margate, and is engraved in the Num. Chron., vol. xvi. p. 80, No. 13.

The type of the obverse is very like that of the silver coins

* Recherches Numismatiques sur l'armement, &c., des Gaulois. 1848, p. 18.

of Verulam with VIR within a beaded circle, Plate VII., Nos. 1 and 2; and the horse on the reverse is of much the same character as that on the small gold coin of Tasciovanus, Plate V., No. 13, as well as that on the coin of Verica, Plate III., No. 2. The quatrefoil beneath the horse is precisely the same as that on the larger piece, No. 10, of which this is the quarter. They both, therefore, probably must belong to the same coinage, and have been issued together.

Plate III, No. 13.

Obv.—EPPI in the compartments of a cross formed by a wreath and a band of three lines, the middle one beaded; with two thin crescents in the centre.

Rev.—A horse walking to the left; above, a ring ornament between three pellets; below, a star of pellets; another pellet between the fore-legs. *N*. 23½ grains.

The place of finding of this coin is not known. It is in the British Museum, and is engraved in the Num. Chron., vol. xvi. p. 80, No. 4. The same coin probably, is engraved by Stukeley, pl. xx. 3, and is described by Beale Poste, p. 47, and in the Arch. Assoc. Journ., vol. vii. p. 404.

The type of the obverse testifies to a reminiscence of the original laureate head, and may be compared with Plate C., No. 14, among the uninscribed coins, and those of CRAB — Andoco[mius], and Tasciovanus, Plate V., Nos. 3, 5, and 13, among the inscribed. The horse on the reverse, though turned in the opposite direction, closely resembles that on the coin of Verica, Plate II., No. 12, even to the absence of one hind-leg, and strengthens the conclusion that Verica and Eppillus were contemporaries.

In White's Plate of British Coins (1773), No. 8, and in Gough's Camden, pl. i. 9, is engraved a gold coin, with COME between four branches forming a cross. Assuming this coin (which is not at present known) to have been genuine, there is no doubt that the inscription was COM. F, and though the reverse is shown as uninscribed, it was probably a coin either of Eppillus or of Verica.

PLATE III., No. 14.

Obv.—TC VI (?); diademed, beardless head to the left. The whole within a beaded circle.

Rev.—EP; naked winged Genius or Victory holding a wand or sword. The whole within a beaded circle.

Æ. 20 grains.

The coin here engraved is in the British Museum, and was purchased in December, 1853, from the collection of the late Rev. Bryan Faussett. It was found in Kent. Another specimen, but not showing more than faint traces of the letters on the obverse, was found at Birchington, in the Isle of Thanet, and is engraved in Smith's Coll. Ant., vol. I. pl. xxiii. 1; it weighs 18 grains, and is now in my own collection, having formerly belonged to the late Mr. Rolfe. This coin is also engraved in Akerman, pl. xxi. 7, and is mentioned in the Num. Soc. Procs., 25th April, 1844.

Though the inscription on the obverse is not perfectly plain, yet I have but little doubt that I have read it correctly. The coin, therefore, would seem to have been struck in the joint names of the three brothers, Tinc[ommius], Verica, and Eppillus, whose names are represented by the TC, VI, and EP upon it, two letters being assigned to each, though in the case of Tinc[ommius] they are not the two first letters of the name, but a still more suggestive abbreviation of it. In Latin we find the word TUNC abbreviated in the same manner, as TC.* If this interpretation of the legend be correct, this coin must be regarded as one of the most remarkable of the ancient British series, as proving the joint authority of the three brothers, at all events in their issue of money, and as affording the only instance of the names of three British princes being preserved on a single coin. The presumption that it is correct is to some extent increased by the coin engraved in Plate III., No. 7, which shows, I think indisputably, that it was issued by the joint authority of Verica and Eppillus.

I cannot say for whom the head on the obverse is intended,

* Gerrard Siglarium Romanum, p. 581.

but it seems to be the same as that on No. 7. The winged figure on the reverse of No. 14 is carrying a sword or staff at its waist; in my coin from Birchington it is carried over the shoulder. I am inclined to think that the figure is intended for Victory, though represented more in accordance with British, than classic mythology.

Plate IV., No. 1.

Obv.—EPP; an eagle to the right with expanded wings.
Rev.—REX CALLE; an open crescent between two stars of pellets. A beaded circle round both obverse and reverse. Æ. 17,⁵⁄₈ grains, 16,⅝ grains.

There is no record of the spot where any of these coins have been found, though they have been often engraved. Both Camden (No. xi., Ed. 1637) and Speed (p. 36) were acquainted with them, though the former had not noticed the EPP upon them. The latter ascribes these coins to Calgacus, or Galgacus. Stukeley, pl. xi. 7, makes them to have been struck by *Cælius Rex*. Taylor Combe (pl. i. 5) got no farther than to read IP on the obverse, and placed the coins among those of the Gaulish reguli. His engraving is copied by Lelewel, pl. viii. 40. Mr. Akerman was the first to read EPP upon them, and engraved two in pl. xxi. Nos. 8 and 9, of his Coins of Cities and Princes. He was inclined to regard the legend as standing for REX CALLE EPPilli (filius). Mr. Beale Poste, p. 125, concludes that the full legend intended was (K)ERR(ATIK) Caractacus, as with curious infelicity he reads the legend, "in Greek letters ERR."

I think myself that the EPP must have been intended to designate Eppillus, especially as we find the type of the eagle on his next two coins, and there is such a strong general analogy between the side on which there is the crescent (which being convex ought properly to have been termed the obverse) and that of the coin, Plate III. No. 4, which I have ascribed to Verica. The double P proves, I think, that it cannot have been struck by Epaticcus, to whom possibly it might otherwise have been assigned. The title REX, however, affords another argument for placing it to Eppillus, for following the analogy of the coins of Verica, Plate II., No. 12, and Plate III., No. 3, this title is to be read in conjunction with the name upon the other side of the coin as EPP . REX. It remains then only to assign a meaning to CALLE, which I am ready to agree with Camden, " is not much unlike the name of that famous and frequented citie *Callena*," or rather *Callera*. The objection to considering Calleva (*Silchester*) the place of mintage of these coins, is its distance from Kent, where the coins of Eppillus, as far as at present known, are exclusively found. This is not, however, insuperable, and possibly future discoveries may prove that the dominions of Eppillus extended as far west as Calleva. Assuming him to have outlived his brother, Verica, and to have succeeded to his dominions, this becomes the more probable, as so many of the coins of Verica have been found near Guildford, within 25 miles of Silchester. If their father, Commius, was the Commius of Cæsar, there is additional probability of a connection between Eppillus and the Atrebates. The analogy of the coins of Eppillus with those of Tasciovanus might also lead us to suppose that, as in the one case Verulamium is represented by VER, so in the other Calleva may be by CALLE. It is, however, unsafe to enter farther into the regions of speculation.

The type of both obverse and reverse of these coins must, I think, be regarded as purely British. The crescent certainly is so, and the eagle can hardly have been adopted out of compliment to the Romans. We find it already on the apparently uninscribed coin Plate G., No. 9, as well as on those of Epaticcus, CRAB, and probably Verulam, as well as on numerous Gaulish coins.

PLATE IV., No. 2.

Obv.—EPPI COM F between the limbs of a cruciform ornament formed by four scrolls, with a circular disc in the centre. The E and F indistinct.

Rev.—An eagle standing to the left, but looking to the right, its wings expanded; ring ornaments in the field.
Æ. 34 grains.

Plate IV., No. 3.

Obv.—EPPI COM, as on No. 2.
Rev.—An eagle, as on No. 2. Æ.

Of these two coins, which are varieties of the same type, the first was procured with many Roman coins from the hill above Kits Coty House, near Maidstone, by the late Mr. Thomas Charles, and the second was found at Bapchild, Kent, with Roman urns and coins, on the site of what had been a Roman burial-place (Archæol., vol. xxix. p. 220). They are both engraved in Smith's Coll. Ant., vol. i. pl. v. 7, and vi. 2; in Akerman, pl. xxi. 5 and 6; Beale Poste, pp. 21 and 22; and the Arch. Assoc. Journ., vol. i. p. 302. A representation of the first is also given in the Num. Chron., vol. i. p. 84, and Lelewel, pl. viii. 59; and of the second in the Archæol., vol. xxxiii. pl. ix.

There is a shield-like character about the obverse, which has led some to connect this type with the shield on the Macedonian coinage. It is certainly allied with the obverse type of some of the copper coins of Verulam, Plate VII., Nos. 3, 4, and 5, Plate VIII., No. 1, and with the silver coin at page 185, No. 3. The eagle on the reverse is in a different attitude from that on the silver coin No. 1 in the Plate, and is more like those on the coins of Epaticcus, Plate VIII., Nos. 13 and 14, though apparently it does not hold a serpent in its claws.

Plate IV., No. 4.

Obv.—EPPI (?); rude bearded head in profile to the left. The whole within a beaded circle.
Rev.—Horse galloping to the right; above, a ring ornament with a large central pellet; below, an uncertain legend (?). Æ.

This coin, which is unfortunately in bad preservation, is in the Hunter collection at Glasgow, and has not before been

published. The bearded head on the obverse is of the same
character as that on the coins of Tasciovanus struck at
Verulam, given in Plate VII., though it is turned the other
way. The horse on the reverse resembles that on the small
silver coin of Verica, page 184. Both types are purely
British, and that of the obverse appears to be the same as
that of the coin, Plate XIII., No. 6, which I have placed
among the uncertain coins, though there appears good
reason to regard it as having been struck by Eppillus.

PLATE IV., No. 5.

Obv.—EPPIL (?) above a bull to the right. The whole within
a beaded circle.

Rev.—An eagle, as on No. 2.

This coin is also in the Hunter Collection. I have another
weighing 33½ grains which was formerly in the collection of
the late Mr. Rolfe, of Sandwich, and was probably found in
Kent, but I have no record of the exact place. This type is
now published for the first time, but both coins are unfortunately in such poor preservation that some of the details
cannot be accurately made out. The legend on the obverse
appears to be EPPIL. The device on the reverse is precisely
the same as that on the other copper coins of Eppillus, but the
bull affords another instance of the connection of the coins
of this prince, with those of Tasciovanus and of Verulam ;
such, for instance, as that engraved in Plate VII, No. 4.
As has been before observed, Eppillus is the only one of the
three sons of Commius of whom, as yet, copper or brass
coins, intended to be current as such, have been discovered ;
and as copper was no doubt the last metal introduced into
their coinage, it is probable that he was the last survivor of
the three brothers, and that these coins were issued towards
the end of his reign.

DUBNOVELLAUNUS.

Though the name of this prince is unknown to history, it
has still been preserved, not only by coins, but by a lapidary

inscription, found, it is true, not in Britain, but at the other extremity of the Roman empire, at Ancyra, in Galatia. By the last will of Augustus* an abstract of the events of his reign was to be engraved on brazen plates and placed before the mausoleum which contained his ashes. The inhabitants of Ancyra, who had erected a temple to his honour, appear to have engraved a transcript of this chronicle, in Greek and Latin, on the walls of this temple, a considerable portion of which has been preserved and published. The Latin portion had been made known in the sixteenth century, but our knowledge of the Greek version is mainly due to the exertions of Mr. W. J. Hamilton.

The portion relating to Britain is as follows:—

ΠΡΟΣ ΕΜΕ ΙΚΕΤΑΙ ΚΑΤΕΦΥΓΟΝ ΒΑΣΙΛΕΙΣ ΠΑΡΘΩΝ ΜΕΝ
ΤΕΙΡΙΔΑΤΗΣ ΚΑΙ ΜΕΤΕΠΕΙΤΑ ΦΡΑΑΤΗΣ ΒΑΣΙΛΕΩΣ
ΦΡΑ[ΑΤΟΥ ΥΙΟΣ ΜΗΔΩΝ Δ]Ε ΑΡΤΑ . . . .
. . . . . [ΒΡΕΤΑΝ]ΝΩΝ ΔΟΜ[ΝΩΝ ΒΕ]ΛΛΑΥΝΟΣ [ΤΕ]
ΚΑΙΤ[ΙΜ] . . . .

AD ME SVPPLICES CONFVGE[RVNT]REGES PARTHORVM
       TIRIDA[TES ET POSTEA PHRATES]
REGIS PHRATIS [FILIVS] MEDORVM ARTA
[REG]ES BRITANN[ORVM] DAMNO BELLA[VNVS QVE] ET
TIM.

In filling up the *lacunæ* in this inscription I have followed the Monumenta Historica Britannica. I think, however, that the restoration of the Greek name ΔΟΜΝΩΝ ΒΕΛΛΑΥΝΟΣ is erroneous. The Archæologische Zeitung, 1843, p. 20, makes it ΔΑΜΝΩΝ ΒΕΛΛΑΥΝΟΣ, but following the Latin, ΔΑΜΝΟ ΒΕΛΛΑΥΝΟΣ would appear more likely. It will be observed that both in the Greek and Latin versions the TE and QVE are supplied, but assuming that TIM also designates some British prince, it by no means follows that Damno and Bellaunus are two different persons, even supposing the restoration of the inscription to be correct. I have already remarked that the TIM may possibly refer to

* Suet. in Aug. 101.

Tinc[ommius], but of the identity of the Dumnobellaunus of the inscription and the Dubnovellaunus of coins, I have not the slightest doubt. The difference in the spelling of the first part of the name is very trifling, and may be paralleled to a certain extent by the case of Dumnorix, who is so called by Cæsar, but whose name appears as Dubnorix on his coins. There can, moreover, be no doubt of the date to which the coins of Dubnovellaunus are to be assigned; and had not the inscription at Ancyra been known, they would have been referred to the days of Augustus. Such being the case, we must assume him to have been one of those princes who in some manner sought the protection of the Roman power, though, unlike Tiridates and Phraates, his name has not been preserved by contemporary historians. Still the Ode of Horace, Carm., lib. iii. 5—

> "Præsens Divus habebitur
> Augustus, adjectis Britannis
> Imperio, gravibusque Persis,"

may possibly allude to the submission of Dubnovellaunus, as it certainly does to that of Phraates.

But though the names of the British princes are not recorded, historians with one consent relate, how, when Augustus[*] was about to lead an expedition against Britain, the British reguli sent an embassy to desire peace. Indeed Strabo says that some of them having gained the friendship of Augustus, dedicated their offerings in the Capitol, and brought the island into a friendly connection with the Romans.

The result of this intercourse we have already traced on the coins of other princes; let us now see what light the finding or the types of the coins of Dubnovellaunus throw upon his history.

The types of the gold coins of Dubnovellaunus are two in number; the one having a plain obverse, with merely a raised band across it; the obverse of the other presenting a wreath with two open crescents in the centre. Now it is

[*] Dion Cassius, lib. liii. 22.

not a little curious, that, as far as has at present been observed, the coins of the former type have been found exclusively in Kent, while those of the latter have been principally found in Essex. Of the two types, that with the plain obverse is to my mind the earlier, and approximates to other Kentish coins, while the other type comes nearer to the coins of Cunobeline, struck in Essex. The bucranium on the reverse of the former type is analogous with that on the coins of Vose[nos], while the palm-branch on the latter, though in a different position, occurs on the coins of Cunobeline. The one type is in fact such as might have been struck in Kent in the middle of the reign of Tasciovanus; the other such as might have been struck in Essex just before the time of Cunobeline. Now it will be shown hereafter that the majority of the coins of Tasciovanus were struck at Verulam (*St. Albans*), while the bulk of those of his son Cunobeline were coined at Camulodunum (*Colchester*). To account for this change of capital is difficult, unless we suppose that Cunobeline, having been left in possession of the eastern portion of his father's dominions (as his brother Epaticcus was of the western), extended them farther east by conquest or annexation, and then found it desirable to make Camulodunum his capital. Or else, which is perhaps more probable, he may have been an independent prince even in his father's lifetime, and absorbed the eastern half of the dominions left by his father, without finding it necessary to make the town which had been his father's capital his own seat of government. But however this may have been, I am inclined to regard Cunobeline as the immediate successor, and that probably by conquest, of Dubnovellaunus in Essex. We have seen, however, that what appear to be his earlier coins are peculiar to Kent. It would seem, therefore, that originally he was a Kentish prince, the successor possibly of Vose[nos] (see p. 207), but who, from some cause or other, either was driven out of Kent into Essex, or else annexed a portion of the country north of the Thames to his dominions in Kent. He must too, I think, have been a contemporary of Eppillus, though his coins do not show so much of Roman influence. It is by no means impossible that Dubnovellaunus may have been expelled from his Kentish dominions by Eppillus, and compelled to take refuge in Essex, from whence he was subsequently driven out by Cunobeline. If this were the case we could see good reason why he should have been among those who sought redress for their wrongs at the hand of Augustus. It must, however, be confessed that there are but slender grounds on which to build this history of Dubnovellaunus, though the evidence of his gold coins, as to their having been issued at two different periods and in two different districts, is sufficiently strong. His silver and copper coins are too scarce for them to be of much assistance, but the silver are apparently Kentish, and the copper allied to those of Cunobeline.

It was not till 1851 that any coins were attributed to this prince, which was done simultaneously by Mr. Birch and myself, and I have since had the satisfaction of adding to the gold coins then first made known others both in silver and copper. The name of Dubnovellaunus is connected with that of Dubnorix, Togodumnus, Cassivellaunus, and many others; but on this subject see Mr. Birch, in the Num. Chron., vol. xiv. p. 76. The DVMNO on the Yorkshire coins seems to be a portion of some similar name. It is also allied to the Dunwallo and Dyfnwal of the Welch chroniclers.

PLATE IV., Nos. 6, 7, 8, AND 9.

Obv.—Two crescents in the centre of a sort of wreath terminating in ring ornaments; on either side other ring ornaments. There are generally depressions along the field on either side of the wreath.

Rev.—DVBNO ...., [DV]BNOVELL ..., DVBNOVIILLA, [DVBNO]VIILLAVN; a horse galloping to the left; beneath, a branch and two ring ornaments; above, a ring ornament; pellets in the field.

N. 81, 81½, 82,⁵⁄₇, 84, 84½, and 86 grains.

No. 7 was found at Walton-on-the-Naze, in November, 1850 (Num. Chron., vol. xiv. p. 74), and is now in the

British Museum. Nos. 8 and 9 are in my own collection. The latter was found at Colchester, and the Rev. J. H. Pollexfen possesses an ancient forgery, of copper plated with gold, found at the same place. I have another coin found at Canterbury, the legend on which apparently terminates in LLAN..., as was also the case on a coin in the collection of the late Mr. Huxtable. Another specimen is recorded to have been found in Essex (Arch. Assoc. Journ., vol. xvii. p. 69), and one in the Ashmolean Museum, at Oxford, was found at Dorchester in that county. Mr. C. Roach Smith has communicated to me a specimen found at Mark's Tey, Essex, in 1850.

Engravings of these coins are given in the Num. Journ., vol. i. pl. ii. 7; Ruding, pl. A, 93; Num. Chron., vol. xiv. pp. 71 and 70; Arch. Assoc. Journ., vol. vii. p. 402; and Beale Poste, p. 232.

Their obverse presents a curious derivative from the laureate bust. It is much the same as some of the cruciform devices, but with two limbs of the cross removed. The horse on the reverse, with the long thin tail, and horn-like ear, resembles those on some of the coins of Tasciovanus, Plate V., Nos. 8 and 9, though turned in the opposite direction. The branch beneath the horse occurs on no other British coins except those of Addedomaros, but is found on a smaller scale above the horse on the gold coins of Cunobeline.

The variation in the legend on these coins of the same type is remarkable, and can hardly be paralleled in the British series. The use of the double I for E is, however, of frequent occurrence on the coins of Addedomaros, and is also to be found on coins of Verulam, and on some few Roman coins (see p. 238). The small gold coins of Dubnovellaunus have not as yet been discovered.

PLATE IV., No. 10.

Obv.—Plain, with a raised band across it.
Rev.—DVBNO[VELLA]VNOS; a horse at liberty, prancing to

the right; above, a bucranium, between two pellets and two ring ornaments; below a serpent and another ring ornament; in front and behind, three pellets. *N*. 79, 81, 81½, 82, and 82½ grains.

The coin engraved is in the British Museum. Others of this type have been found near Gravesend (Smith's Coll. Ant., vol. i. pl. v. 11), apparently with a coin of Tasciovanus. I have specimens found near Canterbury, at Sevenscore, near Ramsgate, and at an unknown locality also in Kent. Engravings of other coins will be found in the Num. Journ., vol. i. pl. ii. 5 and 6; Ruding, pl. A, 91 and 92; Num. Chron., vol. xiv. pl. i. 3, 4, and 9; Arch Assoc. Journ., vol. iii. pl. iv. 3 and 4, and vol. iv. pl. ii. 9. The latter are also in Beale Poste. A coin of this type, showing only the latter part of the legend, has been altered so as to read CVNO, and pass for a coin of Cunobeline. It is engraved in Stukeley, pl. ix. 9; Pegge, class I a; and Arch. Assoc. Journ., vol. iii. p. 121.

The obverse resembles that of the coins of Vose[nos], Nos. 13 and 14, as well as that of many of the uninscribed coins, such as Plate D, No. 12, Plate D, No. 10, and Plate E, Nos. 13 and 14. The raised band is the last surviving trace of the wreath on the head of Apollo.

The reverse is remarkable for the serpent beneath the horse, which occurs also on the coins of Vose[nos], though on the latter it has horns, which is not the case on the coins of Dubnovellaunus. Its introduction upon the coins has been thought to be connected with the Ophite worship of the Druids, and possibly may be so, though in a secondary degree. I cannot, however, but connect the serpent on these coins with the object beneath the horse on some of the coins of Tasciovanus (Plate V., No. 9), which probably represents the hind-legs of the second horse of the biga on the Macedonian staters. There is also on these coins of Tasciovanus, as well as on those of Vose[nos] and Andoco[mius], a bull's head above the horse. The not unfrequent occurrence of the whole or part of the head of the ox in British barrows (as the late Mr. Bateman* remarked) goes far to prove the existence of some peculiar superstition connected with it, of which no notice has reached modern times.

Plate IV., No. 11.

Obv.—DVBNO; laureate beardless head to the left, the hair braided in a straight line from above the eye to the ear, and apparently surmounted by a sort of tiara.

Rev.—A griffin, or ornithocephalous winged horse, springing to the right; above, a star; below, a trellised compartment and another star; in front, a pellet and small cross; behind, a ring ornament.

Æ. 17½ and 14½ grains.

This type was published by Stukeley, pl. xi. 1, and attributed by him to Cogidumnus. It had previously been engraved in Gibson's Camden, pl. ii. 10, where it is suggested that it may be a coin of Dumnorix. This attribution is followed by Taylor Combe, pl. i. 8, and his engraving is copied by Lelewel, pl. viii. 20. In the Num. Chron., vol. xvi. p. 178, I have given reasons why the coin belongs rather to Dubnovellaunus than to Dumnorix, which it is needless here to repeat. Even Lelewel considered it to have been found in England. The coin here engraved is in the collection of Captain R. M. Murchison, and there is some reason for believing it to have been found in Kent. It formed part of a collection of coins "from the country" sold by Sotheby and Co., 20th Nov., 1847, and was subsequently in the collection of Captain Hoare, of Cork.

The head on the obverse is very peculiar, though not altogether dissimilar in character from that on the coin of the sons of Commius, Plate III., No. 14. There is also an analogy between the dotted work on the wings of the griffin, and on those of the Victory on the reverses of the two coins. The trellised compartment on the reverse appears to be peculiar to British coins, and occurs in the same relative position to the horse on the gold coin found near Maidstone, engraved in Plate B, No. 12. The griffin is much the same

* Ten Years' Diggings, p. 130.

as that on the silver coin of Cunobeline, Plate XI., No. 1, though in a different attitude. It may have been derived from a Gaulish source, or may have been suggested by the reverse of some Roman coin, as, for instance, that of the Papia family (Cohen, pl. xxx. 1); or, again, it may have been adopted as sacred to Apollo, whose head possibly we find on the obverse.

Plate IV., No. 12.

Obv.—An animal somewhat resembling a dog or a wolf, running to the right, his head turned back and tail erected.

Rev.—DVBN on a tablet; beneath, a lion (?) springing to the left; behind, a star. Æ. 41 and 36½ grains.

The coin here engraved is in the collection of Captain Murchison, and is the same as that published in the Num. Chron., vol. xx. p. 170. Its place of finding is not known. I have two other specimens, one of which is reported to have been found at Brighton, but I am not satisfied of the fact. It gives the legend very distinctly DVBN, but none of the coins are in fine preservation, especially on the obverse or convex side, so that it is difficult to determine what animal the artist intended to represent upon it. A lion crouching above a tablet inscribed CAMV is found on the coins of Cunobeline, Plate XIII., No. 2, and in style of work and general appearance these copper coins of Dubnovellaunus approach very nearly to those of Cunobeline, though the silver coins have more of the Kentish character about them.

VOSE[NOS].

Of this prince, whose name is now for the first time published, but little can be said. There is even some doubt whether his name is correctly given, as his smaller coins have hitherto only supplied the commencement of his name, VOSII, and his larger coins only the termination, NOS. There may, therefore, have been some intermediate letters, such for instance as would make the name VOSIILLAVNOS.

or VOSELLAVNOS; but under any circumstances I am inclined to regard the double I as representing an E, in the same manner as on the coins of Dubnovellaunus and Addedomaros. Whatever may have been the exact form of his name, I have little hesitation in placing his dominions in some part of Kent, as not only have three out of the five coins of this prince with which I am acquainted been found in that county, but the type of the larger coins approximates most closely to the Kentish type of Dubnovellaunus. Whether the two princes were contemporaries, or Vose[nos] was the predecessor of Dubnovellaunus, and in what relation he may have stood to Eppillus, are questions beyond solution. At present his gold coins only are known. Both his large and small coins are the production of the same artist, and all those of the larger size are from the same dies. The inference is that his reign was short and his dominions but of small extent. The first syllables of his name may be compared with those of VOSICVNNVS,[*] on the red glazed ware probably manufactured in Gaul.

PLATE IV., No. 13.

Obv.—Convex, with a raised band across the field.
Rev.—. . . . . NOS; horse galloping to the left; above, a bucranium and a ring ornament; below, a horned serpent and a small wheel. The nostril of the horse is much exaggerated, and there is a ring ornament on his shoulder. *R.* 82¾ and 83¼ grains.

I have met with but three coins of this type, all of which have passed through my hands. One of them was found at Moldash in Kent. The second, which formerly belonged to the late Mr. Rolfe, was found at Goshall, in the parish of Ash, near Sandwich, in 1844, and is engraved in C. Roach Smith's Coll. Ant., vol. i. pl. iv. 0. The third was in the same collection, and probably found in Kent. The obverse of these coins is the same as that of the coins of Dubnovellaunus, No. 10. The reverse is also of much the same

[*] C. Roach Smith, Cat. Lond. Ant., p. 46.

character, though the horse is executed in a very different style, and the serpent beneath it is horned. The occurrence of this horned serpent on a British coin affords much matter for speculation. I have already made a few remarks upon it at p. 204.

PLATE IV., No. 14.

Obv.—Similar to No. 13.

Rev.—VOSII; horse galloping to the left; above, a star within a circle between two small ring ornaments; in front, a pellet. *N*. 18 and 20 $\frac{1}{2}$ grains.

Coins of this type are engraved in Stukeley, pl. xiv. 4, and in the Num. Chron., vol. i. p. 88, No. 5. The latter does not attempt to give the inscription. That here engraved is in the Museum collection, but there is no record of where it was found. The same coin was published by Mr. Birch in the Num. Chron., vol. xiv. p. 77, but he gives the legend as only VOS. From the very peculiar workmanship and drawing of the horse there can be no doubt of the dies of these small coins having been engraved by the same artist as the large coins. Both the bull's head and the *Cerastes* are, however, absent, and the legend occupies a different position. The ring enclosing a star may possibly be only a wheel, like that on the large coins, which is of frequent occurrence above the horse.

AMMINUS.

Nothing certain is known of the history of this prince, and it is only on account of the coins here engraved, that his name has been inserted in the list of British princes. The coin on which his name appears at full length is in the collection of Mr. Wigan, and was first published by Mr. Beale Poste, and was by him attributed to Adminius, the son of Cunobeline, on the suggestion of the Marquis de Lagoy.* There is, however, no reason to suppose that any coins were ever struck in the name of Adminius, as the only

* Beale Poste, p. 85.

record we have of him is that he was driven out of Britain[*] by his father, Cunobeline: and he could hardly have coined money while his father was alive, unless he held some separate dominion, of which there is no mention. But whether or not the Amminus of the coin is to be identified with the Adminius of history, the style of workmanship and the size of the coin tend to the presumption that it is of British origin, and if so, the DVN on the reverse is probably significant of some British town. But here again conjecture is at fault, as the only town of which there is any record whose name commences with DVN, is Dunium, or Muridunium, among the Durotriges, and in a part of the country where no coins of this character appear to have been struck. It is barely possible that among the various towns whose names are compounded with Dunum, some one may have been so well known, that its ordinary prefix may have been dropped by its inhabitants, in the same manner as St. Edmund's Bury is in Suffolk known as Bury. In the magnificent collection of M. de Saulcy is another silver coin of the same module, and very similar fabric, reading AMMI on the obverse, and SE. on the reverse. As will be seen by the woodcut, there is on the obverse a bare head, to the

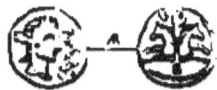

right, not unlike that on the coin of Cunobeline, Plate X., No. 8; and on the reverse, apparently the front view of a bign, with a small head above. It is uncertain in what order the letters on the reverse ought to be read—whether as ES or SE.,—but M. de Saulcy suggests the latter, and is inclined to refer it to the Segontiaci, as he considers the coin to be British, and not Gaulish, though the collection out of which it came into M. de Saulcy's hands was formed

---

[*] Suetonius in Calig. c. 44. See also Orosius, vii. 5, where he is called Minocynobellinus.

in Germany, on the borders of the Rhine. Besides these, there is a third silver coin, which I formerly thought bore the legend CAM, but which on close examination proves to read AM on the reverse. It has the letter A in the centre of the obverse, and I have little doubt was also struck by Amminus. This coin, Plate XIII., No. 7, has a Capricorn or hippocampus on the reverse; the same as the copper coin, Plate V., No. 2, which also reads AM. Another copper coin, Plate XIII., No. 10, seems to have the same letters on the obverse. As both these latter coins were found in Kent, and as the character of all the coins well accords with those of the Kentish district, I am disposed to consider that the territory of Amminus was in that part of Britain. From the style of work on his coins, they are probably of rather later date than those of Eppillus, to a portion of whose dominions he may possibly have succeeded.

PLATE V., No. 1.

Obv.—AMMINVS around a sort of plant with seven buds or berries.

Rev.—DVN beneath a Pegasus walking to the right on an exergual line. There is a beaded circle on both obverse and reverse. Æ 14½ grains.

As has already been said, this coin is engraved in Beale Poste, p. 51, and in the Arch. Assoc. Journ., vol. iii. p. 33. Its place of finding is unfortunately not known. The device upon the obverse is to some extent analogous with that on the gold coins of the Western district, Plate I., Nos. 4 to 7, but the small branches are fewer in number; the berry-like ends are somewhat in the shape of acorns, but the plant seems to be a botanical puzzle. The Pegasus on the reverse is not unlike that on coins of Tasciovanus and Cunobeline, Plate V., No. 14, Plate X., No. 7, though in a slightly different attitude. It has already been observed that the inscription DVN possibly refers to some town. It may be compared with the DV on the coin of Tinc[ommius], Plate I., No. 12, and appears to be of equally difficult interpretation.

The weight of the coin, which is in good preservation, is rather less than that of the silver coins of Tasciovanus and Cunobeline, which usually exceed 18 grains; but the difference of three or four grains in a single specimen, and that of silver, cannot afford any safe indications of its date, or of its connection with other coins.

Plate V., No. 2.

Obv.—Head in profile to the right.
Rev.—AM; Capricorn or hippocampus to the right.
 Æ. 22½ grains.

This coin, which is in my own collection, and was kindly presented to me by Mr. C. Roach Smith, was found, with several other coins, both British and Roman, at a place called the Slade, near Boughton Montchelsea, Kent. (See Coll. Ant., vol. i. p. 5; Archæologia, vol. xxix. p. 414; Num. Soc. Proce., 1842, p. 40.) It is unfortunately in bad preservation, but I am pretty confident that I have read the legend on the reverse correctly. It is curious that the reverse of this coin agrees both in type and legend with the silver coin, Plate XIII., No. 7, which must also be attributed to Amminus. The brass coins, Plate XIII., Nos. 10 and 12, likewise probably belong to the same prince. The device of the Capricorn, like that on the coin of Verica and Eppillus, Plate III., No. 7, was in all probability derived from some of the coins of Augustus, with whom, or Tiberius, Amminus appears to have been contemporary.

CRAB.

Up to the present time only a solitary coin bearing this legend has been published, to which I am now, by the kindness of Mr. H. Durden, of Blandford, able to add a second. The meaning of the inscription has not been hitherto fathomed, though it has been suggested by Mr. Beale Poste (p. 235, and Arch. Assoc. Journ., vol. vii. p. 405) that it is the abbreviated form of C[ommios] RA[ignus] B[voilan] or C[ommunitas] RA[ignorvm] B[elgis]. Whether there ever was such a community, whether it could have had such a title, and whether that title could ever have been abbreviated in such a manner, I will leave for others to determine. There is, however, no doubt of the coins being British, as both the specimens at present known were found in this country, and the types have little or no analogy with those of Gaul. It is not easy to say to what district they belong, for though one of the coins was found near Portsmouth, and the other near Blandford, Dorsetshire, the types of the larger coin appear connected with those of coins of Eppillus and Tasciovanus, while those of the smaller seem more nearly allied to those of Verica. At the time when I was acquainted with the larger coin only, I was inclined to assign it either to the Kentish or Central district, but it would now appear that the coins may not improbably belong to the South-eastern district. Of the two coins known, which are both in silver, the smaller appears to be the quarter of the larger, and as we first find the silver coinage thus subdivided, in what there is reason to believe must have been the latter days of Verica, it seems possible that these coins may have been struck under his successor.

It is to be hoped that, eventually, some gold coins may be discovered which may enable us to complete the name of this prince, for there can be but little doubt that in CRAB we have the commencement of the name of some British regulus. It is not altogether impossible that it may have been Crabilius, as we find a Kentish king called Carvilius mentioned by Cæsar, whose name, by a slight metathesis, would be converted into Cravilius or Crabilius. But even were this so, the coins could hardly have been struck by the prince recorded by Cæsar, unless he survived the Roman invasion many years, in which case we should probably have had a greater abundance of his coins. The question, therefore, of the name and the territory of the prince who struck these coins must for the present remain unanswered.

Plate V., No. 3.

Obs.—C R A B in the angles formed by a cruciform ornament. Each limb of the cross consists of a corded line, with a beaded line on either side, and in the centre is a large boss with a smaller roundel upon it.
Rev.—An eagle with expanded wings, its head turned back. Beaded circles around both obverse and reverse.

Æ. 16 $\frac{1}{10}$ grains.

This coin, which is now in the British Museum, is engraved in Hawkins, pl. i. 12, but the eagle is erroneously described as having a wreath in its beak. It was formerly in the collection of Mr. Cuff, who in a MS. note, which was kindly shown me by Mr. Webster, has recorded that it was found near Portsmouth. The type of the obverse much resembles that of some of the gold coins of Andoco[mius] and Tasciovanus, but instead of having crescents in the centre, it has a circular boss, more like that on the coins of Verica and Eppillus. It presents, however, the closest analogy with the coin engraved as Plate VI., No. 10. The whole device is of course a derivative from the head on the earlier gold coins. On some of those found at Whaddon Chase, Plate C, No. 7, and on some of the small gold coins of the Southeastern district, we also find a central boss instead of the usual crescents. The eagle on the reverse is precisely the same as that on the copper coins of Eppillus, Plate IV., Nos. 2 and 3; but there do not appear to be any ring ornaments in the field. It is also much like that on the silver coins of Epaticcus, Plate VIII., Nos. 13 and 14. The coin has suffered a little by wear and oxidisation, so that it must originally have weighed from 18 to 20 grains, or about the same as most of the inscribed British coins in silver.

The second coin of this class was communicated to me by Mr. Durden, of Blandford, since the plates were engraved. It was found in the earthwork at Hod Hill, near that town, where also some uninscribed coins of the type Plate F, Nos. 1 and 2, and a coin in tin of the same class as those in Plate II, as well as a large number of British and Roman antiquities, have been found. It is represented in the woodcut on the next page.

Obv.—CRAB on a tablet; above, an annulet; below, an S-shaped figure.

Rev.—Star formed of six arcs of circles, with a triangle of pellets opposite each, and with a ring ornament in the centre. The whole within a beaded circle.

Æ. 4½ grains.

This little coin is of the utmost importance, as establishing the reading of the larger coin as CRAB, which might otherwise have been regarded as ABCR, or RABC. The type of the obverse is very similar to that of the small gold coins of Verica, Plate III., Nos. 1 and 2; and the copper coin inscribed RVFS (?), Plate VII., No. 14. It is also like that of the silver coin of Cunobeline, Plate X., No. 5. The tasteful shield-like device on the reverse is very neatly executed, and is related to those on the smaller silver coin from Lancing Downs, p. 185, No. 3, and on the copper coins of Verulam, Plate VII., Nos. 3 and 4, and of Eppillus, Plate IV., Nos. 2 and 3, though different in the details of the pattern, in which it approaches more nearly to some of the Macedonian coins. From the weight, it is evident that this was the quarter of the larger coins, and the fact of there being two denominations of silver coins at the time when these were struck, implies a considerable degree of civilisation, and renders it probable that it was not until many years after the invasion of Julius, that they were issued.

CHAPTER XIII.

COINS OF THE CENTRAL DISTRICT.

That portion of Britain which I have included under the above designation is of considerable extent, and comprises the counties of Bucks, Beds, Herts, Middlesex, Essex, Northampton, and parts of Cambridge, Hunts, Berks, and Oxfordshire. It may be again subdivided into a Western and an Eastern Central district, in which the principal tribes were the Catyeuchlani and the Trinobantes respectively. Besides these two tribes, it will be seen that a portion, if not all, of the country of the Segontiaci was connected at one time with the Central district, more properly so called, as far as its coinage was concerned. The chief towns of the Catyeuchlani, as recorded by Ptolemy, were Salinæ (possibly Sandy, in Beds), and Urolanium or Verulamium (near St. Alban's, in Herts). The chief city of the Trinobantes was Camulodunum (Colchester). The name of Londinium (which is placed by Ptolemy within the territory of the Cantii), and which became the most important city of Britain at an early period of the Roman domination, does not appear upon any British coins. Indeed, at the time of the issue of the inscribed series, London cannot have been of the same importance as either Verulamium or Camulodunum, though the site of the former is now covered by corn-fields, and the latter ranks as a second-rate county town. The Cassii, a tribe mentioned by Cæsar (Bell. Gall., v. 21), are not improbably the same as the Catyeuchlani of Ptolemy, and the Catuellani of Dion Cassius.

It is a question whether the territory of the Ancalites, another tribe mentioned by Cæsar, was not also situated within this district. Their exact position has never been determined, though it has been suggested by Camden, that it was in the hundred of Henley, in Oxfordshire; but for this supposition there appear to be no grounds beyond the slight resemblance between Ancalites and Henley. The coins which are assigned to the Central district are those of Andoco[mius], and those of Tasciovanus and his family, including some on which the names of the towns of Verulamium and Segontium (?) occur alone, as well as a few uncertain coins. The coins of Dubnovellaunus, some of which appear to have been struck in this district, have already been described.

ANDOCO[MIUS] (?).

Although it is at present impossible to complete this name with certainty, as is unfortunately the case with so many of the names which are found on British coins, yet, from the analogy of the coins on which it appears, with those of Tasciovanus, there is good reason for regarding ANDOCO as a portion of the name of a prince, rather than of that of any town or people. We are also able to point out, with some degree of certainty, the position of the territory over which this prince ruled, as out of the five or six of his coins at present known, all, whose places of finding are recorded, came from the counties of Bucks, Beds, or Northampton. The style and types of his coins prove him to have been a contemporary of Tasciovanus and Eppillus; and as, from the rarity of his coins and the paucity of the types, his reign would appear to have been of short duration, it is by no means improbable that he was subjugated by the former, whose coins are found over much the same district. With regard to the completion of the name, I have, in the Num. Chron., vol. xvi. p. 82, called attention to the fact, that Mandubratius, a chief of the Trinobantes, mentioned by Cæsar, is, by the later writers, called Androgeus, or Androgorius, so that possibly an error might have crept into the text of Cæsar, and the name have been originally written Andubratius. But, even if so, the coins reading ANDO. belong to a much later period than the invasion of Julius, and must be placed towards the middle or end of the reign of Tasciovanus, rather than at the beginning; and their places of finding sanction their attribution to a prince of some other tribe adjoining the Catyeuchlani, rather than of the Trinobantes. The reading, Mandubratius, is moreover supported by the analogy of the names Cartismandua, the Mandubii, &c., while Ando . . . finds its equivalent in the ANDOB . . of the Gaulish coinage, the potter's mark ANDORN, and Andoboles, or Indibilis, the well-known chief of the Hergetes, in Spain. The attribution to Mandubratius cannot, therefore, be sustained; and, moreover, the discovery of the silver coin engraved in Plate V., No. 6, proves that the name commenced with ANDOC, while the copper coin engraved in Stukeley, pl. iv. 7, which there appears good reason for considering to have been a genuine coin of this prince, carries his name as far as ANDOCO. Under these circumstances, it seems probable that his name, when complete, presented some such form as ANDOCOMIUS, or ANDOCOMBOS, and I have adopted the former, provisionally, until some further discovery may enable us to complete the name in a more authentic manner. As I have little doubt of Stukeley's engraving having been made from a genuine coin, I have here reproduced it on a reduced scale.

Should another specimen be discovered, it will probably turn out to be even smaller than here shown, as the gold and silver coins of Andoco[mius] agree in size with those of Tasciovanus.

PLATE V., No. 4.

Obv.—Cruciform ornament of four wreaths, ending in ring ornaments, with two thin crescents in the centre, the horns ending in pellets. In the alternate angles Y-shaped figures, between two ring ornaments; and open crescents with bracket-shaped — — figures springing from them between two pellets.

Rev.—AND. beneath a horse galloping to the right; above, a peculiarly formed bucranium between two annulets, one of which is surrounded by pellets. In front another annulet and traces of another bucranium. The annulet in front of the horse may possibly be an O, which would make the legend ANDO.

N. 84½ grains.

This coin, which was kindly presented to me by Mr. Z. D. Hunt, was found, in 1855, on the side of the road leading from Ellesborough (near Wendover, Bucks) to Dunsmore Farm, and is engraved in the Num. Chron., vol. xx. p. 172, No. 10. Another specimen, with the letters rather larger, is engraved in the Num. Chron., vol. xvi. p. 80, No. 3, and was probably found in the neighbourhood of Chesham, Bucks. A third, in my own collection, came from the neighbourhood of Biggleswade. Another seems to be mentioned by Mr. Hawkins (Silver Coins, p. 11), as having been found at Ecton, Northamptonshire; but this coin I have not seen.

The type of the obverse, which is one of the numerous derivatives from the laureate head, is precisely the same as that of some of the coins of Tasciovanus (Plate V., No. 9), and proves that Andoco[mius] was a contemporary of that prince. The reverse is also very similar to that of some of his coins, such as Plate V., Nos. 8 and 9. The mane of the horse is, however, represented in a different manner, and the bucranium is of a different character. The latter also differs from that on the coins of Dubnovellaunus and Vose[nos]. The occurrence of the bull's head on the coins of so many British princes points to some superstition in connection with it, as I have already suggested, at p. 204.

Plate V., No. 5.

Obv.—ANDO between the limbs of a cruciform ornament, with two open crescents in the centre.
Rev.—A horse galloping to the left; above, a bucranium; below, a wheel. *N.* 21$\frac{11}{16}$ grains.

This unique little coin was purchased for the British Museum at the sale of Lord Holmsdale's collection, in 1850. It is not known in what part of the country it was found. An engraving of it is given in the Num. Chron., vol. xvi. p. 80, No. 2; in the Arch. Assoc. Journ., vol. vii. p. 307; and Beale Poste, p. 227. It is also described by Mr. Birch in the Num. Chron., vol. xiv. p. 73.

Like the preceding coin, this shows an extreme similarity to a coin of Tasciovanus, No. 13 in the same Plate, the only difference, except that in the legend, being, that the horse is to the left instead of to the right, and has a wheel beneath it. This coin may also be compared with that of Eppillus, Plate III., No. 13. The extreme accuracy of the adjustment of its weight to that of the preceding larger piece is worth notice. The one was intended to represent the fourth part of the other, and the weights of the two, which are in nearly equal preservation, are 21$\frac{1}{16}$ grains and 84$\frac{1}{4}$ grains respectively. The workmanship of both this and the preceding coin is very neat.

Plate V., No. 6.

Obv.—A - behind a bearded head in profile, to the left, the hair forming a sort of club behind; the whole within a looped circle formed of a plain and beaded line interlaced.
Rev.—ANDOC (the N and D in monogram). Bridled Pegasus springing to the left. Æ. 18$\frac{1}{4}$ grains.

I am indebted to Mr. Fairholt for the acquisition of this coin, which has not before been published. It was not improbably found in the neighbourhood of Evesham. The head on the obverse appears to be the same as that on the silver coin of Tasciovanus, Plate VI., No. 3, though of better execution. It also resembles that on the coins of Verulam,

Plate VII., Nos. 9 to 13. It is impossible to say for whom it is intended. The Pegasus is of frequent occurrence on the coins of Tasciovanus, but is usually unbridled. The repetition of the name of the prince under two forms, A and ANDOC, on this coin, may be compared with the A and AM on the coin of Amminus, Plate XIII., No. 7, and the T and TASC of the coin of Tasciovanus, Plate VI., No. 12. The looped or twisted circle occurs also on the coins inscribed SEGO and SOLIDV, Plate VIII., No. 10, and Plate XI., No. 6. In Stukeley, pl. iv. 7, is given a copper or brass coin attributed to *Androye Rex*, of which I have given a representation at p. 217. Mr. Beale Poste, p. 228, considers it to belong to the Gaulish Andecavi, but the coin is not known in France, and I have no doubt was struck by the same prince as the gold and silver coins.

TASCIOVANUS.

This prince, whose name has given rise to an infinity of speculations among those who have written on the subject of the ancient British coinage, is another of those who are unrecorded by history, but concerning whom numerous particulars are afforded by numismatic evidence. But before entering into the medallic history of Tasciovanus, it will be well to glance at some of the opinions of antiquaries of different periods, as to the meaning of TASCIA or TASCIO, forms under which his name frequently appears upon coins.

Camden, adopting the opinion of " Master David Powell, a man most skillfull in the British language," considered that TASCIA betokened a *" Tribute Penye,"* and that it was derived perhaps of the Latin *Taxatio*.

Wise, however, saw the utter improbability of a coinage for the sole purpose of taxation, and thinks TASCO (for so he assumes it to have been sometimes written) must designate some people or state, and finds, as he says, most opportunely in Pliny[*] the Tascodunitari, a people of Gallia Narbonensis, on whom he fathers these coins.

[* Lib. iii. c. 4.]

Dr. Pettingal, who wrote a dissertation upon the TASCIA, agrees with Camden that the word does relate to the tribute which was paid by the British princes to the Romans, but derives it from *Tag*, a prince or chief. Pegge, in his essay on the Coins of Cunobeline, comes to the conclusion that "in respect of the common notion concerning the word TASCIA it cannot be the true one," and he is "led naturally into a persuasion that the coins are the productions of TASCIO, a provincial artist, entertained in the service of the British prince Cunobeline."

Others again considered that the word meant a king or chief, and this view of its being a titular designation is still retained by Mr. Poste. Ruding,* however, showed that such a meaning was improbable, as the name is found on the reverse of a coin of Cunobeline, who is styled CVNOBELINVS REX on the obverse.

Mr. Hawkins† judiciously observes that the word has occasioned much controversy, but has never been explained; and Lelewel, ‡ with no slight assurance, regards it as "*hors de toute controverse;*" that this inscription related to a town whose geographical position was not known, but which was called Tasciovania or Tasciovanium.

Such was the state of the question until 1844, when Mr. Birch§ communicated a paper to the Numismatic Society on a proposed new reading of certain coins of Cunobeline, in which he showed that the true readings of some of his coins (instead of being TASCE, TASCHOVANIT, and TASCIOVANIT, as they had formerly been considered to be) were really TASC. F., TASCHOVANI. F., and TASCIOVANI. F. This made the complete legend CVNOBELINVS TASCIOVANI. F., and arguing by analogy from the contemporary coins of Augustus, with the legend AVGVSTVS DIVI F., Mr. Birch felicitously interpreted it, "Cunobeline the son of Tasciovanus." Such an interpretation has everything to recommend it. The types of the coins of Cunobeline are in

* Vol. i. p. 180. ‡ Type Gauloise, p. 405.
† Page 155. § Num. Chron., vol. vii. p. 78.

numerous instances derived from those of Roman coins. The divinities which are represented upon them all belong to the classical Pantheon, and the workmanship is that either of Roman artists, or of those who had profited by Roman instruction. The appearance of such a formula is, therefore, entirely in accordance with the other circumstances of this coinage; and as, from the number of the coins of Tasciovanus, and the probable extent of his territory, he was evidently a chief of great importance, we may well see reasons why Cunobeline should make political capital of his relationship to him, in the same manner as Augustus did by his adoptive father Julius, and as the sons of Commius did in Britain by assuming the title COM. F. But besides the coins already mentioned, Mr. Birch also cited that engraved in Plate XII., No. 4, the legend on which he showed to be, in all probability, TASC. FIL, though the final letter is eroded, and nothing but a honey-combed perpendicular stroke remains. This reading, if thoroughly substantiated, would be conclusive; but I will reserve any remarks upon it until I come to the description of the coin, merely observing that to my mind the legends TASC. F., TASCIOVANI. F, in conjunction with the name of Cunobeline, speak for themselves as to the correctness of the views of Mr. Birch, and require no further corroboration.

As to the suggestion that the F is a contraction of Firbolg —a presumed name of the Belgæ—it is not worth a moment's consideration. We may, therefore, at once accept Tasciovanus as the father of Cunobeline, and see what light his coins will enable us to throw upon his history.

And first with regard to the period when he lived. To ascertain this there are two criteria: the one, the character of his coins; the other, the era of his son Cunobeline. What we know with regard to the latter is, that he was already dead in A.D. 43,[*] having left several sons, all of mature age. He cannot, therefore, have been by any means a young man at the time of his death; and, indeed, the number and

[*] Dion Cass., lib Ix. c. 20.

variety of his coins prove that his reign extended over a very considerable period. If we may believe Geoffrey of Monmouth, Cunobeline was brought up by Augustus, and it was in his days that the birth of our Saviour took place. Matthew of Westminster fixes his accession in B.C. 5; and taking into account that Augustus died A.D. 14, and that not only tradition but the derivation of the types of many of the coins of Cunobeline tend to prove that he was a contemporary of Augustus during some considerable portion of his reign, I think we shall not greatly err in assuming this date to be somewhere near the truth. There are, however, reasons for supposing that Cunobeline (whose capital was Camulodunum, while that of Tasciovanus was Verulamium) acquired the rule over the Trinobantes in his father's lifetime. Assuming this to have taken place about B.C. 5, it is evident that the commencement of the reign of his father, Tasciovanus, might not unreasonably be placed some twenty-five years earlier; while they may have ruled together, the one over the Catyeuchlani, and the other over the Trinobantes, during another period of ten years. Geoffrey of Monmouth fixes the accession of Tenuantius, the father of Cunobeline, seven years after Cæsar's second invasion, or B.C. 47; but this is probably too early. That the reign of Tasciovanus did not terminate until after B.C. 13, is proved by one of his coins being an imitation of a coin of Augustus which first appeared in that year (see Plate VI., No. 5). Taking all things into account, we may assume that Tasciovanus died about the year A.D. 5, and there can be no valid reason shown, why his reign should not have commenced about B.C. 30; though, of course, such a chronology is purely conjectural. This would be about twenty-four years after the invasion of Cæsar; and we will now see how far the character of the coins bearing his name agrees with such a date. In looking through the series of gold coins of this prince, the fact becomes at once apparent that the obverse types of all are, without exception, derivatives from the degenerate laureate bust of the uninscribed coins; and as we know that the introduction of letters

upon British coins must have commenced not long after the
invasion of Julius, such a prevalence of the archaic types
would point to an earlier period even than B.C. 30, were it
not that the coinage belongs to an inland and not a maritime district; so that the introduction of legends upon
the coins would probably take place later in the case of
these coins, than in those of the South-eastern part of
Britain. In treating of the coinage of that district, I have
shown how frequent is the analogy between the coins of
Eppillus and those of Tasciovanus. I have also shown the
probability of the former having been the last survivor of the
sons of Commius, and of his not having attained to the
dignity of a chieftain so early as his brothers, Tinc[ommius]
and Verica. If, therefore, we date the inscribed coinage of
Tasciovanus as commencing about twenty-four years after
Cæsar's invasion, he may well have been a contemporary of
Eppillus, as from the style of his coins appears to have been
the case. Another chief, who must be mentioned as a contemporary of Tasciovanus, is Andoco[mius], who appears to
have ruled over contiguous territory to his, and may possibly
have been subjugated by him. Yet another contemporary is
Dubnovellaunus, who, from the occurrence of his name in
the inscription at Ancyra, is known to have been among
those who fled as suppliants to the court of Augustus. It
would seem, moreover, probable, that some few years before
the death of Tasciovanus, Dubnovellaunus was either dis-
possessed of his dominions in Essex, or succeeded in them
by Cunobeline. The numismatic evidence, therefore, as far
as it goes, concurs in placing the reign of Tasciovanus at or
about the period I have mentioned. It is of course possible
that some uninscribed coins may have been struck in the
earlier part of his reign, and if so, it may be thought necessary to carry its commencement further back than B.C. 30,
though any attempt to fix an absolute, rather than an
approximate date, is open to objections. Under any circumstances there is so great a variety, both in the types and
workmanship of the coins of Tasciovanus, that we cannot do

otherwise than assume that his reign extended over many years.

Let us now see what portion of Britain was probably under his rule. There can be no doubt that Verulamium was his principal city, for its name is found on a very considerable number of his coins. On other coins again, the name of TASCIO is found associated with the word RICON or RICONI, and also with the word SEGO. It would appear probable that both these words are intended to designate towns within his dominions, especially as SEGO occurs on the obverse of a silver coin, having precisely the same reverse as a coin of Verulam in the same metal, but with VER on the obverse. The identification of RICONI[VM] has not yet been achieved. It must not, however, be confounded with Uriconium, as will be seen when the coins thus inscribed come under consideration. The word SEGO seems plainly to point to the tribe of the Segontiaci, whose chief city appears to have been known as Segontium, or by the Britons as Caer Segont. Henry of Huntingdon thus identifies the town, "Kair-Segent quae fuit super Tamesin non longe à Redingo et vocatur Silcestre." As will be subsequently seen, there is some doubt as to this identification being correct. But wherever the town was situate, it seems pretty clear that the tribe was one of those which were under the rule of Tasciovanus. The other principal tribe was that of the Catyeuchlani, the name of whose chief town was Verulamium. It is doubtful whether the Trinobantes may not also have been subject to him, at all events during the latter part of his reign, though none of his coins bear the name of Camulodunum upon them as their place of mintage; but the probability seems to be rather with the view that the Trinobantes were brought under the dominion of Cunobeline by conquest or otherwise, than that they had been among the subjects of his father.

With regard to the family and connections of Tasciovanus, it has already been shown that Cunobeline assumes the title of Tasciovani Filius upon his coins; but it appears from numismatic evidence that there was another son named Epaticcus, who on his coins bears the same title. It is, however, remarkable that all his coins, at present known, seem to have been found either in Surrey or the eastern part of Wilts, while those of Cunobeline appear to have been minted exclusively at Camulodunum. The fact of Tasciovanus having had two sons, who at his death may have divided his dominions between them, helps materially to explain a difficulty which would otherwise have been felt in attempting to explain why the mint of the father was at Verulamium, and that of the son at Camulodunum. If, however, we assume, as we are fairly entitled to do, that either Tasciovanus towards the end of his reign, or his son Cunobeline before his father's death, had obtained the sovereignty over the Trinobantes, and that after the death of Tasciovanus his dominions were divided between his two sons—Cunobeline taking the eastern portion, and Epaticcus the western—we can see a reason why Segontium should become the capital of the latter, and Camulodunum of the former, while Verulamium would cease to be the chief town of either portion.

The types of the coins of Tasciovanus show much less of Roman influence than those of Cunobeline, though some may be traced to a Roman source. His gold coins of the earlier types are purely indigenous in their character; but the Pegasus on the later types, the centaur and hippocampus on the copper coins, and, in one instance, a type in silver borrowed from a coin of Augustus, indicate their derivation from a foreign original. This point will, however, be better reserved for the descriptions of the coins.

It has been suggested that possibly the Cassivellaunus of Cæsar may lurk disguised under the Tasciovanus of coins; but such a supposition involves considerable chronological difficulties, as the coins bearing this name can hardly be of so early a date, and were it the case, we should have the father a chieftain in B.C. 54, and the son reigning down to nearly A.D. 43. The name of the father of Cunobeline, as given by Geoffrey of Monmouth, is Tenuantius: he is also called

Themantius, Theomantius, Tenancius, &c., all of which bear some slight likeness to the real name, which, in its British form, must have been Tascio-van, or something like it. That it was so, is proved by the fact that on the coins of Cunobeline it appears Latinised under three different forms— Tasciovanus - i, Tasciovanius - ii, Tasciovans - vantis. On some coins the name commences TAXCI instead of TASCI. Its analogy with Taximagulus, a king of Kent mentioned by Cæsar, Tasgetius, King of the Carnutes, and Moritasgus, one of the Senones, is apparent, so far as the TASCIO is concerned. TASCONVS and TASCILLA appear among the potters' names on the red-glazed ware which has been termed Samian, though apparently made in Gaul. TAS-CIACA (now Thescé*) occurs as the name of a town on the Peutingerian Tables. The termination VANVS is not common among Gaulish and British names, though the name ADIETVANVS is found on Gaulish coins; but it is worth notice that among the names given by the British or Welsh chroniclers to the father of Cunobeline, occurs that of Teneuvan.

PLATE V., No. 7.

Obv.—Cruciform ornament formed of wreaths, with crescents and ring ornaments in the centre, and V-shaped objects and open crescents in the angles, the same as on Plate C, No. 12.

Rev.—TASCIOVAN. Horse galloping to the right; above, a ring ornament surrounded by pellets; below the horse and above its head, a ring ornament; pellets before and behind. *N*. 83 grains.

The coin here engraved is in the British Museum, and was found at High Wycombe, with ten other coins, in an oblong hollow flint, about the size of a swan's egg, by a boy who was trying to dig out a mole. There was a hole at one end of the flint, out of which two of the coins fell, and nine more were found inside. The place where the coins were discovered is called Keep Hill, and there are vestiges of earthworks upon it. An account of the discovery is given in

* Coll. Ant., vol. iv. p. 2.

the Gent.'s Mag. for 1827, p. 493, and also in the Archæol., vol. xxii. p. 297, No. 5, where this and four others of the coins are engraved. They are all of the same prince, and include the coins I have shown in Plate V., Nos. 8 and 10; and Plate VI., No. 12; as well as one of the same type as Plate V., No. 9. The six coins not engraved are stated by Mr. Norris, who furnished the account to the Society of Antiquaries, to bear a general resemblance to the types, Plate V., Nos. 7, 8, and 9. The hoard of coins found at Wonersh, near Guildford, was also enclosed in a hollow flint, see p. 85. The coin now under consideration is also engraved in Hawkins, pl. i. 10, and in the Mon. Hist. Brit., pl. i. 3, but erroneously, as it is there made to read TASCIOVANI, instead of TASCIOVAN.

In treating of the uninscribed coins, Plate C, Nos. 9 to 12, I have shown how the type of the obverse of this and the following coins is a derivative from the primitive laurelled bust. That of the reverse is also a descendant of the biga, though all traces of the second horse of the chariot are gone. The head of the horse bears a great resemblance to that on some of the coins of Dubnovellaunus. The legend, TASCIOVAN, is of great importance, as proving that the TASC, TASCIAV., &c., of the coins, with nearly the same devices upon them, may be thus extended, and showing that the coins bearing the name alone must have been struck by a prince whose Latinised name would be TASCIOVANVS, the exact form in which the name appears upon the coins of Cunobeline, who proclaims himself to have been TASCIOVANI.F.

PLATE V., No. 8.

Obv.—Similar to No. 7, but the wreaths less curved, and with pellets in the field.

Rev.—[T]ASCIAV. Horse to the right; above, a bull's head between two pellets; below, a curved object and a ring ornament; over the horse's head a rosette of pellets; behind, two pellets. *N*. 85 grains.

This coin, from the Museum collection, was found with

No. 7, at High Wycombe, as before mentioned, and is engraved in the Archæol., vol. xxiii. p. 297, No. 3. It is also figured in the Num. Journ., vol. i. pl. ii. 6; and Ruding, pl. A, 94. Another specimen, from the Hunter collection, weighing 82¼ grains, is engraved in Ruding, pl. ii. 37; but the artist does not seem to have recognised the letters upon it. It would, however, appear as if the legend were continued in front of the horse, making it TASCIAVAN. Beale Poste has engraved it in pl. iii. 0; and Arch. Assoc. Journ., vol. iii. pl. iv. 0; and, singularly enough, seems to regard it as a coin of one of the sons of Cunobeline rather than of his father. In Gough's Camden, vol. ii. p. 52, mention is made of a British gold coin, with TASCIA, found at Sandy, in Bedfordshire, and exhibited to the Society of Antiquaries, in 1720, by Mr. Degge, which must, probably, have been of this type. The devices of both obverse and reverse have already been considered: that of the reverse under Plate C, No. 12, which is probably one of these self-same coins, though not showing the inscription. The bull's head above the horse connects these coins with those of Dubnovellaunus, Vose[nos], and Andoco[mius].

PLATE V., No. 9.

Obv.—Similar to No. 7, but with annulets and pellets in the field, and one of the wreaths curved in the opposite direction.
Rev.—TASCI .... Horse galloping to the right, with nearly the same adjuncts as on No. 8, but with a loop (qy. a serpent?) above the bull's head; below the horse a crooked-shaped figure and an annulet. Ring ornaments before and behind the horse. *N*. 82½ grains.

This coin was found at Dorchester, Oxon, and is engraved in the Num. Chron., vol. xiv. p. 71, No. 10. It is described also by Beale Poste, p. 234, and in the Arch. Assoc. Journ., vol. vii. p. 404. Another specimen, weighing 84 grains, either of this or of the preceding type, was found at Shorne, near Gravesend, and is engraved in Smith's Coll. Ant., vol. i.

pl. v. 12. Another, not showing the legend, and weighing 64 grains, was found at Brentwood, and has been communicated to me by Mr. C. Roach Smith.

One of the coins found at High Wycombe, and engraved in the Archaeologia, vol. xxii. p. 207, No. 4, appears to be of this type, though the legend is not distinct. Compare also Num. Journ., vol. i. pl. ii. 11; and Ruding, pl. A, 07. I have a specimen of this type, with the annulets on the obverse, and the loop above the bucranium on the reverse, but reading TASCIA . . . Another specimen in my collection, of the reverse of which a woodcut is here given, shows so much of the field in front of the horse as to prove that the dies from which these coins were struck were at least an inch in diameter, while the coins themselves are rarely as much as three-quarters of an inch. It shows, too, that the legend was continued in front of the horse, apparently as TAXCIAVANI; but these last letters are uncertain. In front of the horse's head is a singular object, like a head in profile with a pointed cap; beyond that again a wheel. Beneath the wheel is a curved line, like a long horn, and reaching to the first object mentioned, giving the whole somewhat of the appearance of the *carnyx* or *lituus* held by the horseman on No. 12. It cannot, however, be intended for this, as, on some coins, a ring ornament occupies the place of the curved line. See, for instance, Plate VI., No. 13. I am unable to say what the object is, though the head-like figure is much like that beneath the horse on some coins of the type, Plate C, No. 14. The curved figure which so constantly occurs beneath the horse on the coins of this class is of equally difficult interpretation. But whatever they were intended immediately to represent, I have little doubt, from the general position and shape of these objects, that they are the degenerate representatives of the head and hind-legs of the second horse of the biga on the Macedonian stater. For though possibly no other instance of the kind can be pointed out, yet the appearance upon coins of Cunobeline (see Plate IX., Nos. 1 and 2) of two horses side by side, shows that the remembrance of the original type of the biga subsisted until even a later period.

The form of the legend TAXCIA is very remarkable, and affords a contradiction to the dictum of Camden,* that "the Britans acknowledge not X for their letter." The workmanship of the coins of this type is generally ruder than that of the coins of the two preceding types, and they are also usually flatter and more spread. I am inclined to consider them as among the earliest of the gold coins which bear the name of Tasciovanus, and to regard those with the horseman as again subsequent to those with the horse without a rider.

PLATE V., No. 10.

Obv.—Similar to that of No. 7, but with three pellets between the crescents in the centre; the open crescents in the angles of the cross have become nearly oval in form, and there are numerous ring ornaments as well as pellets in the field.

Rev.—TASC. Horseman galloping to the right, brandishing the *careyx* (?). In front of the horse, a wheel and three pellets; behind, a wheel. There is an exergual line, but nothing in the space below. *N.* 85 grains.

The coin here engraved was among those found at High Wycombe, as previously mentioned, and is now in the British Museum. It is engraved in the Archæologia, vol. xxii. p. 297, No. 2; Num. Journ., vol. i. pl. ii. 12; Hawkins, pl. i. 11; Beale Poste, pl. iii. 7; Arch. Assoc. Journ., vol. iii. pl. iv. 7; Mon. Hist. Brit., pl. i. 1; and Ruding, pl. A, 98. The type was originally given by Speed, p. 30, who, however, seems to have read the legend CAS, and attributed the coin to Cassivellaunus. It is also engraved in Gibson's Camden, pl. i. 19, and pl. ii. 4; and reproduced by Pegge, class v. 2 and 3; and in Henry's Britain, vol. ii. class v. 2 and 4. See also Whitaker's Manchester, vol. i. pp. 301 and 304; and Stukeley, pl. iv. 5, and xix. 5. Another coin

---

* Page 97. Ed. 1637.

is engraved in the Num. Journ., vol. i. pl. ii. 10; and in Ruding, pl. A, 90.

The type of the obverse of this coin, though preserving generally the device of the preceding coins, is much more elaborated, all the vacant spaces having been filled with pellets or ring ornaments. The horseman on the reverse is executed in a spirited manner, and seems to have been engraved without any regard to the legend, the four letters of which appear to have been subsequently inserted wherever an unoccupied space could be found, and regardless of their relation to each other—the T occupying the place of the antipodes to the following letter, A. The horseman, who appears to be naked, is holding a long instrument in his hand, which by some has been regarded as a battle-axe, a club, or as a *pedum* or shepherd's crook.* The Marquis de Lagoy, in his " Recherches Numismatiques sur l'Armement, &c., des Gaulois," has, as has already been observed, when treating of a coin of Eppillus with a somewhat similar reverse (Plate III., No. 11), shown that it is the *carnyx* or military trumpet of the Gauls and Britons. In the case of that represented on the present coin, there are several projecting rings at intervals along it, the same as on that shown on the trophy of the coin of the Julia family, Cohen, pl. xx. 15.

PLATE V., No. 11.

Obv.—Similar to that of No. 8, but with three pellets in the centre between the crescents, and some ring ornaments in the field.

Rev.—[T]ASC. A horseman to the right, as upon the last coin; in the exergue, a ring ornament. *N*. 84½ grains.

The coin here engraved is in my own collection, but I do not know where it was found. It formerly belonged to the late Mr. Cuff. Another specimen of the same type, in the collection of Mr. Fairholt, was found near Sevenoaks. A third, in the British Museum, found in the Victoria Park,

* See also Beale Poste, p. 166.

and weighing 85¾ grains, presents some slight variations, and I have, therefore, given a woodcut of its reverse. There is but one pellet in the centre of the obverse, and the letters on the reverse are arranged in the same manner as on No. 10; but the most remarkable feature is, that the horseman appears to wear a sort of cuirass with circular bosses upon it, instead of being naked, as is generally the case on these coins. This appearance of defensive armour is curious, but owing to the minute size of the figure the details cannot be accurately made out. Apart from the interest attaching to it as exemplifying the armour of the Ancient Britons, it is of great value in a numismatic point of view; for the horseman on these coins is, in respect of his body armour, precisely the same as that on the coins inscribed TASCIOV RICON, TASCI RICONI, &c., Plate VIII., Nos. 6, 7, 8, and 9, and this fact affords the strongest presumptive evidence that these latter coins were struck by the same prince, Tasciovanus, whose name appears on those now under consideration. It will be observed, too, that the body of the horseman on both classes of coins presents the same triangular form. Beside thus linking these two classes together, the reverse of these coins is, to some extent, a connecting link between the coins inscribed TASCIO NEGO and those with TASC alone, as will be seen on comparing it with Plate VIII., No. 9, on which the device appears to be identical, even to the ring ornament in the exergue, and the only difference is in the legend.

Plate V., No. 12.

Obv.—Similar to that of No. 10, but with the crescents longer, and with more ring ornaments in the field.

Rev.—TAS. Horseman to the right, between two wheels, as on No. 10. *N.*

This coin, which differs slightly from No. 10 in the arrangement, and possibly in the number of letters on the reverse, is in the collection of Mr. R. Grove Lowe, of

St. Alban's. It was found in the neighbourhood of that town —the modern representative of Verulamium, the capital of Tasciovanus, where most of his coins appear to have been struck. The form of the bridle is worth notice, and is evidently adapted for giving the rider a most powerful command over his horse. It calls to mind the account given by Cæsar* of the skill of the British charioteers, how even in steep and precipitous ground they could stop their horses at full speed, and check and turn them in a small space. The wheels on these coins are more probably merely reminiscences of the pristine biga, than intended to represent the British war-chariots.

Plate V., No. 13.

Obv.—TASCI between the limbs of a cruciform ornament, proceeding from two crescents in the centre, and terminating in ring ornaments.

Rev.—[T]ASC. A horse galloping to the right; above, a bucranium. N.

This very pretty little coin was found at Reculver, in Kent, and is now, together with many other coins and objects of antiquity collected there by Dr. Battely, in the library of Trinity College, Cambridge. It is engraved on an enlarged scale, and described as being of electrum, in pl. vi. of the Antiquitates Rutupinæ. From thence it was copied by Pegge, class v. 5, who takes no notice of the size being exaggerated, and calls the metal silver. In this he was followed by Henry, in his History of Britain, vol. ii. pl. ii. The coin is engraved of its real size in the Num. Chron., vol. xvi. p. 80, No. 1.

The type of the obverse is singularly like that of the coin reading ANDO, Plate V., No. 5, with which there is also considerable analogy in the reverse. This coin may likewise be compared with that of Eppillus, Plate III., No. 13, though the horse is more like that of Plate III., No. 12. From the occurrence of the bull's head above the horse, and

* De Bell. Gall., iv. 33.

the general similarity of type, it would appear to have been minted for the quarter of No. 8, in the same manner as No. 5 for the quarter of No. 4.

I have seen another coin of much the same type, but presenting a new and apparently unique variety, in the collection of Mr. Beal, of Oundle. It was found near that town, and has on the obverse a cruciform ornament, with the limbs of the cross curved, with letters between them, of which one appears to be a V. On the reverse is a horse to the right, standing on an exergnal line, and below the horse TASC.

Plate V., No. 14.

Obv.—TASC within a compartment placed across a triple band or wreath, the centre line of which is beaded. There are curved lines on either side of the wreath, and also at the ends of the compartment, which is placed between two ring ornaments; at the end of the wreath are three pellets following the sweep of the coin.

Rev.—Pegasus springing to the left, his tail in the air; in front (and behind), a small ring ornament; above, two pellets; and below, a small star. *N* 28,$\frac{1}{2}$ grains.

I have a coin of this type found at Thrapstone, Northamptonshire, and weighing 20¼ grains. Two specimens are engraved in Akerman, pl. xxii. 5 and 6, and though the former is described as bearing a horse and not a Pegasus, I have no doubt of the identity of the type, and that the wings would have been visible on No. 5 had the coin been struck from the centre of the die. The same coin is engraved in Ruding, Appendix, pl. xxix. 6, and there also erroneously described as having a horse upon it. The specimen I have engraved is in the British Museum, and is also given in the Mon. Hist. Brit., pl. i. 5.

The type of the obverse is another of the derivatives from the primitive type of the wide-spread laureate bust, of which the only trace remaining is the wreath. By comparing the obverse with that of Plate E, No. 5, it becomes obvious how such a transformation has taken place. The coins of Cunobeline, Plate IX., Nos. 1 and 2, illustrate the same metamorphosis, and the connection of the type of the present coin with that of Plate VIII., Nos. 6, 7, 8, and 9, is another link between the coins with the name of Tasciovanus alone and those with TASCIOV RICON, &c. Indeed, it appears by no means improbable that these small coins, with the inscription on a tablet, are the quarters of the larger coins on which the inscription is arranged in a similar manner. The Pegasus on the reverse seems to indicate the influence which the intercourse with the Romans was beginning to have on the types of the British coinage, which becomes more evident on some of the silver and copper coins. The same Pegasus occurs also on the coins of Eppillus, Animinus, Andoco[mius], and Cunobeline, as well as on some of the silver and copper coins of Tasciovanus. It must, however, be observed, that a Pegasus is found also on many of the Gaulish coins, such, for instance, as the imitation of the quarter Philippus, Lelewel, pl. iv. 54, and the coins of CRICIRV and TASGETIVS, Lelewel, pl. iv. 56 and 57.

Plate VI, No. 1.

Obv.—TASC on a tablet, the same as on Plate V., No. 14, but with pellets instead of the curved lines at the sides of the wreath.

Rev.—Pegasus springing to the left; behind the wing a small star; in the field, numerous pellets. Æ. 18¾ grains.

The only specimen I have seen of this type is that now engraved for the first time, from my own collection. I am not aware of the place of its finding. Though the obverse has been dreadfully battered, it still shows some traces of the inscription; but the correspondence with the gold coin last described proves the correctness of its attribution to Tasciovanus. At the same time, there are slight differences in the details, which seem to show that this is not a silver coin struck from the dies intended for the gold coinage. The horn-like projections from the head of the Pegasus are very remarkable. I have never observed them in any other instance, and am unable to offer any suggestion as to their meaning. It will be observed that, unlike that on the former coin, the animal has no mane, and though the body is that of a horse, the head and neck are more like those of an antelope.

Plate VI., No. 2.

Obv.—TASC, on a tablet, placed within a triple circle, the centre one beaded.

Rev.—Horseman galloping to the left, his body and legs entirely hidden by a long shield; and with two hands streaming backwards from his shoulder. There is an exergual line. Æ. 18, 23, 24 grains.

Coins of this type have been engraved in Stukeley, pl. xix. No. 7; Pegge, cl. v. 4; White, No. 7; Henry's Britain, vol. ii. pl. ii. cl. v. 5; Pembroke Coins, pt. ii. pl. 94; Akerman, pl. xxii. 9; Ruding, pl. v. 35; and Mon. Hist. Brit., pl. i. 0. One is also described by Taylor Combe, p. 15, No. 19; but in no instance is there any record where any genuine coin of this type was found. I have a plated specimen, an ancient forgery, found in the neighbourhood of Biggleswade. The reverse is precisely the same as that of the coin engraved, which is also in my own collection, but the inscription on the obverse is retrograde, ƆSAT. The weight is 25 grains, or fully that of a genuine coin, and though the silver has now to a great extent peeled off, the coin must, when new, have been a very successful counterfeit. It is a proof of a higher civilisation than we are wont to attribute to the ancient Britons, not only that they possessed this faculty of plating, but that there should have been a sufficient circulation of silver coins to make it worth the trouble to counterfeit them.

The type of the obverse of these coins may be compared with that of Plate VII., No. 14; Plate VIII., No. 10; and the coins of Cunobeline, Plate X., Nos. 4 and 5; as well as with the small coin inscribed CRAB, at p. 214. There are many other instances where the inscription is placed on a tablet, a plan much in favour among the Britons. The triple circle occurs on some other coins of Tasciovanus, both in silver and copper, see Plate VI., No. 6, and Plate VIII., No. 4. The representation of the horseman on the reverse is singular, for though a long shield of somewhat similar character accompanies the horseman on other coins of the same prince, as well as of Verica and Cunobeline, yet in no case is the warrior so completely hidden by it. The shield has rather more of a diamond form than usual, and, except that it has a raised border, appears to be perfectly plain. The shields on the Gaulish coins of Verotalus are often of much the same form, but far more highly ornamented; the warriors who hold them are, however, on foot (see Rev. Num., N.S., vol. v. pl. vi.). None of the British shields which have hitherto been discovered are of the shape here shown, the long shields not being pointed, but square at the ends. The shield on the coin of the Julia family, Cohen, pl. xx. 11, already referred to at p. 192, as having the *carnyx* upon it, and those on Nos. 15 and 16 of the same plate, approach very nearly in form to this; they are, however, more truncated at the ends, and slightly ornamented. Still the resemblance is such that, taken in conjunction with the *carnyx* and the *caerdum* on No. 13, we are justified in supposing that these coins refer to the conquests of Julius in Britain.

In the description given by Herodian [*] of the Northern Britons of a later period, about A.D. 210, they are spoken of as carrying a small or narrow buckler and a spear, with a sword girt about their naked bodies, and opposed to the use of a cuirass or helmet. This description, however, is at variance, in most points, with the figures of what appear to be British warriors on the coins of the Southern Britons at an earlier period. On these we have not only the long shield, but the cuirass and helmet, though it is true that the buckler also occurs, and that the warriors are frequently represented naked. Xiphilinus [†] also speaks of the use of a buckler, and short spear and dagger. On a silver coin, engraved by Lambert, pl. viii. 17, a Gaulish horseman is

[*] Lib. iii. c. 14.   [†] Lib. lxxvi. c. 12.

represented partly hidden by a round buckler, and with a weapon of some sort showing above his shoulder.

I am at a loss to explain the object which seems to proceed from the shoulder of the horseman of this coin of Tasciovanus. Were it a little higher, it would seem to be a diadem, the same as on Plate VII., No. 2. As it is, it gives the warrior the appearance of riding on a Pegasus rather than on a horse. We can, however, hardly expect to find Bellerophon armed with such a shield even on a British coin.

Plate VI., No. 3.

Obv.—Bearded head to the left; in front two small crosses; the whole within a beaded circle.

Rev.—TASCIO. Horseman galloping to the right, and holding a javelin (?). Before and behind him a star of pellets.
Æ. 16⅞ grains.

This coin, which is in the British Museum, appears to be the same as that engraved in Ruding, pl. v. 33, from the Hebello collection. It is also given by Akerman, pl. xxii. 11; Lelewel, p. 406; Beale Poste, p. 35; and Arch. Assoc. Journ., vol. ii. p. 21. In type it is almost identical with the succeeding coin, from which I am by no means sure that it differs in the legend. I will therefore pass on to No. 4 before making any remarks upon the type.

Plate VI., No. 4.

Obv.—The same as No. 3, but of even ruder work.

Rev.—TASCIA. A horseman as on No. 3, but shewing only one star and several pellets in the field.
Æ. 11¾ grains.

I have copied this coin from Ruding, Appx., pl. xxix. 9, not having seen the original. It is also copied by Akerman, pl. xxii. 12 (No. 10 in the description); and another of the same type seems to be described under No. 14. As all these authorities concur in giving the legend TASCIA, and there appear to be some slight differences in the adjuncts of this and the preceding coin, I have engraved them both. It has already been seen on the gold coins how the name of the

prince is written indifferently TASCIOVAN and TASCIA-
VAN. I have a specimen of the same type as these coins,
found in 1863 at Gayton, near Blisworth, and kindly procured for me by Mr. Samuel Sharp, of Northampton. The
obverse is much the same as that of No. 3; but there are
three C-shaped locks of hair at the temple and two behind
the head. The reverse shows only as far as TASC of the
legend, but gives another star of pellets beneath the horse's
tail. The weight is 17 grains.

Though the execution of the hair and beard on the obverse
of these coins is very peculiar, the locks of hair being rendered by lines of pellets touching each other, yet the horseman, on the reverse, is fairly drawn, and the art is certainly by
no means so extremely barbarous as some have stigmatised it.
The resemblance of the horseman on the reverse to that on
some of the coins of Cunobeline, Plate X., Nos. 1, 2, 3, affords
an argument against these being regarded as the earliest
silver coins of Tasciovanus. Whether the bearded head was
intended for that prince, or, as seems more probable, for that
of some local divinity, it appears to be the same as that
which occurs on so many of the types in copper, struck at
Verulam, such as Plate VII., Nos. 9 to 13, though on these
the small crosses are absent. It seems hardly probable that,
like the X on the Roman denarii, the XX should have been
symbolical of the value of the coin, as compared with those
in copper. The crosses are quite different in form from
those on the coins of the Western district; but like them
may have been intended merely to fill up blank spaces. Had
the crosses been intended for XX with a numerical value,
they would probably have been made more closely to resemble
the letters on the reverse. The horseman on the reverse,
with the short dart, reminds us strongly of the coins of
Tinc[ommius] and Verica, but occurs also on some of the
copper coins of Tasciovanus. On the Gaulish series the
horsemen generally appear to be holding a spear or lance,
rather than a javelin. The body of the horseman on these
British coins is made up of small bosses, which may have

been intended to represent a cuirass, the same as on the
gold coins already mentioned.

Plate VI., No. 5.

Obv.—TASCIA. Laureate headless head to the right, within a
beaded circle.

Rev.—A bull butting to the left; above, a pellet. There is an
exergual line, and some specimens show a beaded
circle. Æ. 18½ grains.

This coin, in the British Museum, is engraved in the
Mon. Hist. Brit., pl. i. 7, and described in Taylor Combe,
p. 15, No. 18. The type was first engraved by Camden,
No. 17; but in Gough's edition it is given, pl. i. 12, as
having the bull to the right. This appears to have been
copied from White's plate, No. 12; but I have never met
with a coin showing the bull in that direction. The engravings in Stukeley, pl. ix. 8; Pegge, class v. 1; and Henry's
Britain, appear to be copies from Camden.

In Ruding, pl. v. 34, the reverse of a coin of this type
(the original of which I have seen in the Hunter collection) is
engraved, as showing a horse to the left beneath a tree, but
in the description of the plates it is spoken of as an ox (?).
Akerman, however, who has copied Ruding's plate, describes
it (pl. xxii. 13) as a horse feeding beneath a tree. This is,
however, an error, arising from the artist who drew the
coin having mistaken the preternaturally bushy tail of the
bull for a tree, and its head for that of a horse.

A coin of the type of Ruding, pl. v. 34, is said to have
been among those found at Chesterford, by the late Lord
Braybrooke (Archæol., vol. xxxii. p. 355; Proc. Soc. Ant.,
vol. i. p. 170); but there is, I believe, some mistake in the
reference. Whether we regard the head upon this coin as that
of Tasciovanus or not, the types of both obverse and reverse
may be traced to a Roman source. There can indeed be but
little doubt that they are derived from the silver coins of
Augustus, with his laureate head on the obverse and a butting

bull on the reverse, of one of which a woodcut is here given. These coins seem to have been struck not earlier than B.C. 12, nor later than B.C. 10, and probably those of Tasciovanus are not many years later in date: from their style and their

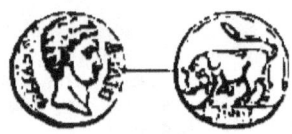

resemblance to the coins of his son Cunobeline, they probably belong to quite the latter part of his reign. The bull occurs on the copper coins of Verulam, probably struck under Tasciovanus, but it is not in this butting attitude. It was such a favourite type on the Gaulish coins, as for instance, on those of Massilia and innumerable uninscribed brass coins, that it might have been regarded as derived from a Gaulish rather than a Roman source, had it not been for its peculiar attitude, and its being accompanied by the laureate head, so like that of Augustus, on the obverse. It will be noticed how different this head is from that on the preceding coins, and indeed from that on any of the coins of Tasciovanus or Verulam, except the large coin, Plate VI., No. 8, and perhaps No. 9 in the same plate. This difference can hardly have arisen from any other cause than from a Roman prototype having been taken for imitation.

PLATE VI., No. 6.

Obv.—TAS. Pegasus walking to the left within a beaded circle.
Rev.—Winged griffin springing to the right. Around, three circles, the centre one formed of pellets.
Æ. 20$\frac{5}{10}$ grains.

This beautiful little coin, which I believe to be unique, after belonging successively to the White, Rebello, Thomas, and Huxtable collections, is now in my own cabinet. It has been engraved in White's plate, No. 9; Stukeley, pl. xx. 8; Pegge, cl. v. d.; Henry's Britain, cl. v. 9; Gough's Camden,

pl. i. 17; Ruding, pl. v. 30; and Akerman, pl. xxii. 10.
There is no record of where it was found. The Pegasus on
the obverse differs in treatment from that on the gold and
silver coins already described, in showing both wings, that on
the off-side being rather in advance of the other, the same as
on the copper coin No. 8. The legend, unlike that on most
other coins of Tasciovanus, has the top of the letters towards
the rim of the coin. The griffin on the reverse occurs also
on the silver coins of Dubnovellaunus, Plate IV., No. 11,
though the wings are there differently rendered; and also on
the next coin, and on silver and copper coins of Cunobeline,
Plate XI., No. 1, Plate XII., No. 8, though in different
attitudes. Although probably of classical origin, this animal
occurs on Gaulish coins, such as those of PIXTILOS, so
that it was possibly introduced from thence to the British
coinage. It seems, however, more probable that its appearance is due to the employment of foreign artists, or to some
acquaintance with the classical mythology which made this
animal sacred to Apollo. In the present instance it is
difficult to fix on any prototype combining the Pegasus and
griffin, but there is a small silver coin of Leucas, in Acar-
nania (Combe, Hunter Coins, pl. xxxiii. 10), which bears a
curious general resemblance to this coin of Tasciovanus.
The treble circle, with the centre one formed of pellets, is
found also on Plate VIII., No. 4, and appears to be peculiar
to the coins of this prince.

Plate VI., No. 7.

Obv.—TASCIA. An eagle standing to the left, its head turned
to the right. The whole within a beaded circle.

Rev.—Griffin walking to the right, on an exergual line; in front,
a ring ornament; beneath, a triangle of pellets.
Æ.

This curious little coin is in the Bodleian Library at Oxford,
and has not before been published. From the general
appearance of the bird upon the obverse, it is probably an
eagle, though the beak is by no means aquiline. It may be

compared with that on the copper coins of Eppillus, Plate IV., Nos. 2, 3, and 5. An eagle holding a snake forms the reverse type of the coins of Epaticcus, Plate VIII., Nos. 13 and 14, and of the uninscribed copper coin, Plate G, No. 9, so that this bird is a favourite device on British as it also is on Gaulish coins. The griffin on the reverse is beautifully executed, and must have been the work of an artist educated abroad. It is of frequent occurrence on Greek coins, and is found in a springing attitude on the common denarii of the Papia family (Cohen, pl. xxx. 1). For other instances of the griffin on British coins, see under No. 6.

Plate VI., No. 8.

Obv.—TASCIAVA. Beardless bare head to the right.

Rev.—TAS. Pegasus to the left, his fore-leg raised. Beaded circles on both obverse and reverse, and an exergual line on reverse. Æ. 60½ grains.

This coin, in my own collection, was found near Cambridge. The obverse is, however, in hardly such good condition as shown in the drawing, which has been partly taken from the Hunter specimen. This latter weighs 88$\frac{2}{10}$ grains, and is engraved in Ruding, pl. v. 37, and in the Mon. Hist. Brit., pl. i. 8. These engravings show only TA on the reverse, though the S exists on the original. Another specimen was found in Berkshire, and has been communicated to me by Mr. C. Roach Smith. From the large module and the weight of these coins, they seem to have been current for twice the value of the smaller pieces, which in general weigh from 30 to 40 grains. The head, though probably imitated from coins of Augustus, may be intended for that of Tasciovanus, whose name is here spelt with an A instead of an O. The Pegasus on the reverse, it has already been seen, was a favourite device for his coins. It is curious that we should have the head of Medusa on the coins of Tinc[ommius] and Cunobeline, Perseus on a coin of the latter, and the Pegasus on so many other British coins.

PLATE VI., No. 9.

Obv.—TASCIAV (?). Beardless head to the right.
Rev.—Horse galloping to the right, within a double circle, the outer one beaded. Æ.

This coin was found at Springhead, Kent, in a field abounding in foundations of Roman houses. It is engraved as reading TASCIO in C. Roach Smith's Coll. Ant., vol. i. pl. v. 10, from whence I have partly copied it. The head on the obverse bears some resemblance to that on the preceding coin. From a rather imperfect cast of this coin, kindly sent me by Mr. C. Roach Smith, it appears that there may have been an inscription beneath the horse, possibly VER, in which case it belongs to the class of coins struck at Verulam.

PLATE VI., No. 10.

Obv.—. . IR. (?) in the angles of a cruciform ornament formed of triple wreaths, with a square figure in the centre, its sides curved inward, and with diagonal lines across it. The whole within a beaded circle.
Rev.—Boar springing to the right. Æ.

This curious coin, which has not before been published, is in the Bodleian Library at Oxford, and formed part of the collection of the late Rev. Dr. Ingram. It is unfortunately much injured, and its place of finding not known. From its analogy with the coins of Verulam, Plate VIII., No. 5, I have inserted it here, to fill a blank space which I had left in the Plate, though the attribution of the coin to Tasciovanus or to Verulam is purely conjectural. Even the two letters visible of the legend are uncertain, and the obverse type is more like that of the coin reading CRAB, Plate V., No. 3, than any other; the boar, however, occurs on at least two of the coins of Verulam, so that possibly the discovery of a better preserved specimen, may justify my having given this type its present place in the Plates.

COINS STRUCK AT VERULAMIUM.

The name of the capital of the Catyeuchlani appears under somewhat different forms in early writers. By Ptolemy it is called Οὐρολάνιον; in the Itinerary of Antoninus it is Verolamium; and in Tacitus, Verulamium, which appears to me to be the preferable form. On coins the name is found in the locative case as VERLAMIO. It has by some been considered as the Oppidum Cassivellauni mentioned by Cæsar, but this is of difficult proof. It must, however, in all probability, have been at that time a place of importance, as shortly after, in the reign of Tasciovanus, we find its name not only on coins bearing the name of that chief, but also on some of an apparently autonomous character. It appears to have been seized by the Romans, on their occupation of this country, as one of the principal cities, and was raised to the rank of a *municipium* as early as the time of Nero, or possibly earlier; and in the revolt under Boadicea, in A.D. 61, this place, in common with Camulodunum and Londinium, was ravaged by the Britons, when seventy thousand Roman citizens and their allies perished. Its subsequent history need not here be traced, but some account of it, as illustrated by coins found upon the spot, has been given by me in the Num. Chron., vol. xx. p. 101. Its site close to St. Alban's, in Hertfordshire, is well known; and, as will be seen, several of the coins struck at Verulam have been found among or near its ruins.

It is as the place of mintage of Tasciovanus that its name first appears upon coins—on the gold in extremely small characters, but more conspicuously upon the silver and copper pieces. On some of these latter we have the name of the town alone, without that of the prince, but still the types are so connected with those which bear the name of Tasciovanus, that it is evident that the apparently autonomous coins must have been issued during his reign. There is great probability that the majority of these coins of Tasciovanus, which do not indicate their place of mintage, were minted at Verulam, and indeed in some instances the types are such that I have felt justified in placing coins among those struck in that town, without any further warrant.

But besides these pieces with the name of Tasciovanus, or that of Verulam, or both, or neither, upon them, there is another class of coins which must be attributed to this town, bearing the mysterious legends DIAS and RVFS (?) upon them. It seems at the present time impossible to find any satisfactory interpretation of those legends, but it is to be hoped that future discoveries may throw some light upon their meaning. In the meantime we cannot be far wrong in classing them among those struck at Verulamium. The coins inscribed VER BOD or VRE BOD are all modern fabrications (though I was at one time induced to accept them as genuine), as is also the gold coin with VERO on the obverse, engraved by White, No. 12, and in Gough's Camden, pl. i. 4.

PLATE VI., No. 11.

Obv.—VER in minute letters, among ornaments as on Plate V., No. 10, but with only two pellets between the crescents in the centre.

Rev.—As Plate V., No. 10. *N.* 84$\tfrac{9}{10}$ grains.

This coin, formerly in the Cuff collection, and now in the British Museum, is said to have been found at Old Sarum.[*] It is engraved in the Num. Journ., vol. i. p. 91; Revue Num., vol. ii. p. 22; Lelewel, pl. viii. 50; Ruding, pl. A, 100; Akerman, pl. xxii. 7. A *false* coin with the same obverse, and a disjointed horse on the reverse, disgraces pl. i. of the Mon. Hist. Brit., in which it stands No. 50.

I have a specimen of this type from the find at High Wycombe, on which, however, only the V is legible. I have also one from the same dies as the one here engraved, but on which the letters have become very indistinct through the

---

[*] Sale Catalogue, 6th June, 1854, lot 253. Arch. Assoc. Journ., vol. xv. p. 267.

wear of the dies. The letters on the coins are even more minute than shown in the engraving, and may be regarded rather as forming a mint-mark than as presenting prominently the name of the town. In this respect they differ materially from the CAMV on the coins of Cunobeline. The occurrence of the VER on these coins raises a strong presumption that all the gold coins with the horseman bearing the *carnyx* were struck at Verulam.

Plate VI., No. 12.

Obv.—Similar to Plate V., No. 10, but with T in the centre between the crescents, and V in the field.

Rev.—TASC. As Plate V., No. 10, but without the wheel behind the horseman, who also appears to wear a cuirass.
N. 81 grains.

The coin here engraved was among those found at High Wycombe (see p. 227), and is now in the British Museum. It is figured in the Archæol., vol. xxii. p. 207, No. 1. The V, however, was mistaken for an A by Mr. Norris, who communicated the account of this find. Another is engraved in the Num. Journ., vol. i. p. 91; the Revue Num., vol. ii. p. 22; Ruding, pl. A, 09; and Akerman, pl. xxii. 8. In the latter instance the V has been accidentally omitted. There can be no doubt that this letter represents the name of Verulam, as the central T does in all probability that of Tasciovanus, whose name is found in a somewhat similar manner on both obverse and reverse of Plate V., No. 13, like that of Amminus, on Plate XIII., No. 7. The letters on these coins are so minute, that possibly the whole VER may yet be found on some coin of this type which is better spread, and which happens to have been struck when the dies were less worn.

Plate VI., No. 13.

Obv.—The same as Plate V., No. 9, but with a small V in the field.

Rev.—TA . . . As Plate V., No. 9. *N*.

The letter V on this coin, in my own collection, is so small and indistinct, that I should not have ventured to insert it in the Plates, had I not seen two specimens on which it was just visible. It seems probable, therefore, that on some coins, struck when the dies were in fresher condition, the letter may have been more distinct. As the case stands I cannot refer to it with any great confidence; but if the V be really on the coins, it is of great interest, as showing that this earlier type of Tasciovanus was struck at Verulam, and bears the mint-mark of that town upon it, as well as the later type with the horseman.

PLATE VI., No. 14.

Obv.—DIAS on a tablet, with an annulet or ring ornament above and below, in the centre of a star formed of two squares interlaced,—the one beaded, and with the sides curved inward; the other plain, with straight sides.

Rev.—VIR, or possibly VER, beneath a horse galloping to the left; above, a curved object of doubtful import.

Æ.

This coin ought properly to have come rather later in the series, but was inserted here to fill a blank space left in the plate. The type was first published by Camden (No. 13, Ed. 1637), but without the VIR on the reverse. In Gibson's Ed., pl. i. 13, the horse is shown to the right instead of to the left, in which direction it is also in Stukeley, pl. vii. 7. Gibson's plate has been copied by Beale Poste, p. 91, and in the Arch. Assoc. Journ., vol. ii. p. 17; but since the days of Camden there is no record of any coin of this type having been seen. In 1857 I remarked,* with regard to the gold coin of Epaticcus, that so convinced had I been of the existence of such a type "that I had inserted it in a catalogue of ancient British coins I had in course of preparation, in company with that reading DIAS in the centre of two interlaced squares, a specimen of which still remains to be found, which I hope Mr. Whitbourn's or my own researches

* Num. Chron., vol. xx. p. 3.

may yet be able to produce." I have now the pleasure of seeing this hope realised, as the engraving is taken from a well-preserved coin of this type, found, I believe, upon the borders of Essex and Herts. Besides proving the existence of such coins as that described by Camden, it establishes the fact of their having been struck at Verulam. The close correspondence of the type of the obverse with that of the copper coins of Verulam, Plate VII., Nos. 3 and 4, might, indeed, have raised a presumption that such was the case, but it is extremely satisfactory to have the presumption converted into a certainty, by the name of the town being placed on the coin. The interlaced squares occur also on the silver coin, which is probably of Verica, given in the woodcut at p. 185, No. 2; but the character of the horse on the reverse, as well as the place of finding, tend to prove that the inscription on the reverse of the present coin relates to Verulam, and not to Verica. It is hard to say whether the name of the town is given as VIR or VER, but if it be the latter, the E must be excessively narrow. VIR appears to occur on several other coins of Verulam (see Plate VII., Nos. 7 and 9). The horse has much the same character as that on several of the coins of Tasciovanus. The curved object above, cannot, I think, be explained until other coins of this type have been found. What I have described as an annulet, above the tablet on the obverse, has much more the appearance of the letter C. I think, however, that my description is correct, and that half of the ring has been destroyed by corrosion, as the coin has in parts suffered from oxidisation. I cannot offer any probable conjecture as to the meaning of the word DIAS. Whatever its import may be, it seems evident, from the character and style of the coins, that they were struck either under Tasciovanus, or within a very short period after his reign. DIAS can, however, hardly be only another way of writing TAS. The legend DIAOVLOS occurs on Gaulish coins, and the Diablintes were a people of Gaul.

PLATE VII., No. 1.

Obv.—VER within a beaded circle.
Rev.—TASCIA. Horse cantering to the right; the exergual line is sometimes double. Æ. 21½ and 21¾ grains.

The coin here engraved is in the British Museum,[*] and is also engraved in Ruding, pl. v. 1; Hawkins, pl. ii. 25; Akerman, pl. xxii. 10; Mon. Hist. Brit., pl. i. 11; and Lelewel, pl. viii. 48. The type was however long since known, having been engraved by Camden, No. 4 in his plates, and also in his description of Verulam. A representation of it, apparently taken from this identical coin, is also given by Speed. Stukeley has it under different degrees of misrepresentation—in pl. iv., 3, 4, and 10; and in the Vet. Mon., vol. i. pl. viii. In Pegge, and in Henry's Britain, it figures as class vi. 1.

I have a coin of this type, with rather smaller letters on the obverse, which was found at Verulam, and was presented to me by the Rev. Dr. Nicholson, Rector of St. Alban's.

Although Wise (p. 227) was unpatriotically inclined to assign these coins to Vernometum, or Verbinum, or Veronum, in Belgic Gaul, there can be no doubt of the VER meaning Verulamium. Had any doubt existed, the finding of the coin on the spot, and the combination of the name of the town with that of the prince Tasciovanus, would have been sufficient to remove it. The type of the obverse, with the legend within a small beaded circle, is the same as that of the gold coin of Eppillus, Plate III., No. 12. On the next two coins the name of the town appears alone.

PLATE VII., No. 2.

Obv.—VER. As No. 1.
Rev.—Uninscribed. Naked horseman prancing to the right, wearing a diadem, with the long ends streaming behind him. There is an exergual line, and the whole is within a beaded circle. Æ. 20¼, 16¼ grains.

This coin is in my own collection. Other specimens are

[*] Taylor Combe, p. 19, No. 1.

engraved in Combe, Hunter Coins, pl. lxii. 11; Ruding, pl. v. 2; Akerman, pl. xxii. 17; and Mon. Hist. Brit., pl. i. 51 and 52. No. 51 has two pellets in the field, above and below the fore-legs of the horse. It is in the Hunter collection, and is probably that which is described by Combe, p. 353, as being of brass, though there is little doubt it is of silver.

These coins are remarkable, as not presenting the name of Tasciovanus, under whom, from the identity of the obverse with that of No. 1, there is every reason to believe they were struck. It would seem that, in certain cases, the name of the town was allowed to take precedence over that of the prince, as, for instance, on the coin of Cunobeline, Plate XII., No. 9, with CAMVLODVNO at full length on the obverse, and only CVNO in the exergue on the reverse. But the most remarkable, and indeed perfectly analogous case, is that of the coin, Plate VIII, No. 10, where we have, in all probability, the name of Segontium, or the Segontiaci, on the obverse, combined with precisely the same reverse as there is on these coins of Verulam. In fact, these two types seem to have been emitted at the same time, in what we have already seen to have probably been the two principal cities within the dominions of Tasciovanus. Probably the horseman on the reverse is intended for this chieftain, whose sovereignty is denoted by the regal diadem. It is certainly a curious circumstance, that this decoration, apparently of Eastern origin, should be found on the British coinage.

PLATE VII., No. 3.

Obv.—VERLAMIO between the rays of a star-like ornament, formed of two interlacing squares, the one plain, the other beaded; in the centre, a boss with a raised rim. The sides of the squares are curved inwards, and the corners, or rather points, terminate in annulets. There are a number of small pellets in the angles formed by the intersections. From other specimens it appears that the whole is surrounded by a sort of wreath, like that on No. 1.

Rev.—Bull to the left, his fore-leg raised, and his tail in the air; surrounded by a wreath.

Æ. 32$\frac{1}{2}$, 25$\frac{1}{2}$, 26, 25$\frac{1}{2}$, 33$\frac{1}{2}$ grains.

This coin, in the British Museum, is engraved in Hawkins, pl. ii. 20; and Mon. Hist. Brit., pl. i. 53. The same type is given by Ruding, pl. v. 3 and 4; Akerman, pl. xxii. 18 and 19; and Lelewel, pl. viii. 49. It does not appear to have been known by the earlier writers. I have a specimen, found within the site of ancient Verulam; another was found in "the Black Grounds," at Chipping Warden (Arch. Assoc. Journ., vol. ii. p. 101); another at Harlow, Essex (Gent.'s Mag., 1821, p. 66); and one or two were discovered by the late Lord Braybrooke, in his excavations at Chesterford.

The type of the obverse is closely connected with those of the silver coin reading DIAS (Plate VI., No. 14); that engraved as No. 2, on p. 185; and the two succeeding copper coins. The single square occurs on Plate VIII., No. 1, and on No. 3, at p. 185. Taken as a whole, the device has very much the appearance of some sort of buckler, and reminds those conversant with the Greek series, of the coins with the Macedonian shield. The copper coins of Eppillus, Plate IV., Nos. 2 and 3, have a device of much the same character on their obverse. I have already made some remarks as to the shield-like appearance of the obverse of some British coins, when describing the coin of Verica, Plate III., No. 3 (p. 179).

The bull is in rather a different attitude from that in which it appears on the silver coin of Tasciovanus, Plate VI., No. 5, and is more like that on the Gaulish coins of GER-MANUS INDUTILLI. L., but with its tail in the air. The manner in which the devices are surrounded by continuous wreaths is peculiar to the coins of Verulam, though similar wreaths occur round the legend and device on two of those of Eppillus. Although the name of Tasciovanus does not appear on these coins, I have little doubt that they were struck during his reign, and under his authority.

Plate VII., No. 4.

Obv.—A ring ornament in the centre of a star formed by two interlacing squares, the whole within a kind of wreath.

Rev.—Bull, as on the last coin, but to the right, standing on an exergual line, and within a braided circle.
Æ. 33½ grains.

This coin was published by me in the Num. Chron., vol. xvi. p. 80, No. 11. Another specimen was found at Harlow, Essex (Gent.'s Mag., 1821, p. 66), and I have one, said to have been found in Herts. Although uninscribed, the types of both obverse and reverse are such that there can be no doubt that it belongs to the same place, and was issued at much the same time as the preceding coin. The recorded places of finding also corroborate the attribution of these coins to Verulam. The absence of the inscription makes the shield-like character of the device of the obverse very apparent.

Plate VII., No. 5.

Obv.—Ornament formed by a square, with loops at the corners, interlacing with another square with curved sides. There are crescents and pellets outside two of the corners of the latter, and ring ornaments within the other two. In the centre is a small cross, and the whole is surrounded by a braided circle.

Rev.—TASCI. Horse galloping to the left; above, a ring ornament and trefoil; the whole within a braided circle.
Æ. 30½ grains.

This coin is in the Hunter collection, and is also given in Ruding, pl. v. 5, and Akerman, pl. xxii. 20. I have another specimen, but it is unfortunately broken at the edge. The type of the obverse, though somewhat more fanciful than those of the two preceding coins, is hardly so symmetrical or pleasing. It is, however, so closely allied to them in form and character, that it must, in all probability, have been struck at the same place, while the legend of the reverse shows it to belong to Tasciovanus. Taking the three coins, Nos. 3, 4, and 5, together, the evidence seems to me conclusive of all having been struck by that prince in the mint of Verulam. The horse on the reverse is of much the same stamp as on some of the gold coins of Tasciovanus, and the device above, consisting of a ring ornament and trefoil, is, as will shortly be seen, one of the characteristics of the coins struck at Verulam, occurring, as it does, on Nos. 8, 10, and 11, in this Plate, all of which, there is good reason to suppose, were struck in that town.

PLATE VII, No. 6.

Obv.—.. R. (?) Two heads in profile, side by side, the upper one bearded, the hair crisped in a double row of locks; the whole within a beaded circle.

Rev.—TASC. Ram standing to the left, on a beaded exergual line; in front and below, rosettes of oval pellets.
Æ. 31½ grains.

This coin, in my own collection, was, I believe, found near Biggleswade, and was published by me in the Num. Chron., vol. xviii. p. 44, No. 4. A coin of the same type is engraved in Ruding, App., pl. xxix. 10; but the second profile has escaped attention. The same oversight has occurred in a woodcut of a similar coin, in the Mechanics' Magazine for 1820, p. 40. The absurdly drawn coin in Stukeley, pl. v. 5, is also probably intended for one of this type.

From the coin being as usual smaller than the die, it shows only the final letter of the inscription upon the obverse. This appears to be an R, and leads to the inference, that in its perfect state it may have been VER, a point which future discoveries must decide; but in the meantime I have placed the coin among those of Verulam. I am at a loss to explain the two "*têtes accolées*" on the obverse, which are not to be found on any other British coin, and differ materially from those on the Gaulish coins inscribed HPOMILAOC and RICOM, which are young and beardless as well as farther apart. The animal on the reverse appears to be certainly a ram or a sheep, and not a horse, as described by Ruding and Akerman, p. 180, No. 10. On

Plate VIII., Nos. 2 and 4, there are a goat and a boar, so that we have, on the coins of Tasciovanus, struck at Verulam, representations of all the larger domesticated animals—the horse, ox, goat, sheep, and pig—as well as various mythical creatures, such as the centaur, pegasus, and hippocampus.

Plate VII., No. 7.

Obv.—TASC[IA . .] Bare head to the right, with short, crisp hair and beard; the whole within a beaded circle.

Rev.—VIR or VER (?). Centaur prancing to the right, playing on the double flute; above, a solid crescent, and in front a ring ornament; the whole within a beaded circle. Æ. 25 $\frac{1}{5}$, 26 $\frac{1}{8}$, 25, 21$\frac{1}{4}$, and 20$\frac{1}{2}$ grains.

This type has already been published by Taylor Combe, p. 15, No. 30; Ruding, pl. v. 38; Akerman, pl. xxii. 15; and in the Mon. Hist. Brit., pl. i. 9; but in no instance had the legend of the reverse been given until I engraved a specimen in the Num. Chron., vol. xi. p. 157, No. 5. I have three coins of this type (one of them said to have been found in Huntingdonshire), two of which show the legend on the reverse; but, as was the case with Plate VI., No. 14, I am not certain whether the middle letter is an I or a very narrow E. In order to show the type more fully, I have engraved the obverse of one coin and the reverse of another. I have not as yet been able to complete the legend on the obverse, but I think it was TASCIAVA. The head differs from that on most of the succeeding coins, in having the beard short and crisp, instead of its being as usual long and flowing. It is, however, of much the same character as that on No. 8. The type of the Centaur occurs on one other British coin, that of Cunobeline, with the legend TASCIO-VANI . F (Plate XII., No. 1), but in that case he is merely blowing a single horn, and not playing on the double flute. It is singular that we should find such a purely classical device upon a British coin, and it is difficult to say from whence it was derived, unless from the fertile imagination of some Roman artist who was employed to engrave the dies.

It is just possible that it may be a reminiscence of the
androcephalous horse so common on the Gaulish coinage.
On Roman coins of a later period we occasionally find the
centaur represented, but then as an archer rather than a
musician. On a coin of Julia Domna,* struck at Nicæa,
there is a bacchanalian chariot drawn by two centaurs, male
and female, the latter, as on this British coin, playing the
double flute. Among earlier coins, centaurs appear as
drawing a chariot on a denarius of the Aurelia family
(Cohen, pl. vii. 6), but in that case holding olive branches.
On coins of Prusias, King of Bithynia, a centaur is represented
as playing on the lyre; but nowhere, that I am aware of,
does he appear singly, and playing on the double pipe, except
in this instance. The reputed proficiency of the centaurs in
music is well known, and Chiron is celebrated as having been
the instructor of Achilles in that art. The performance of
a duet by a single player is an accomplishment perhaps to
be reckoned among the lost arts; but nothing was more
common among the Romans than this feat of playing on the
double pipe, as may be seen by its constant occurrence in the
representations of their *tibicines*, and the use of the expression, " tibiis cantare," instead of " tibiâ." The sort of cap
or head-dress, whatever it be, worn by the centaur, is the
same as that of the horseman on No. 12 in this Plate.

PLATE VII., No. 8.

Obv.—Bare head to the right, within a beaded circle.
Rev.—VER (?). Pegasus to the left; above, a ring ornament and
trefoil; the whole within a beaded circle. Æ.

This coin was formerly in the collection of the late Mr.
James Brown, F.S.A., of St. Alban's, and was, in all probability, found upon or near the site of ancient Verulam. I
have already published it in the Num. Chron., vol. xviii.
p. 44, No. 7. The head on the obverse, though more rudely
executed than that on the preceding coin, is of much the

* Seguin, Sel. Num., p. 103, ed. 1684.—Spanheim, vol. I. p. 240. Micaut,
vol. ii. p. 458, No. 210.

same character. The legend, which was probably there, does not show, owing to the coin having been struck towards the side of the die. I have, however, seen another specimen, found at Oundle, Northamptonshire, and in the collection of Mr. Beal, of that town, which shows the legend TASC in front of the head. The Pegasus has already been noticed on gold and silver coins of Tasciovanus, and the trefoil and ring ornament occur on several other coins of Verulam and of that prince.

PLATE VII, No. 9.

Obv.—Rude head in profile to the right, with flowing beard.

Rev.—VIR or VER (?). Hippocampus to the left. There is no exergual line, and another specimen shows a beaded circle round both obverse and reverse.

Æ. 31, 32 grains.

PLATE VII, No. 10.

Obv.—Head to the right, as on No. 9.

Rev.—VIIR. Hippocampus to the left; above, a trefoil and ring ornament. Æ. 35 grains.

Both these coins are in my own collection, and were found in the neighbourhood of Biggleswade. They have already been published by me in the Num. Chron., vol. xviii. p. 44, Nos. 5 and 6. I have another specimen like No. 9, which was kindly presented to me by the Earl of Verulam, and found near the site of the ancient city, from which he derives his title. There has been a legend on the obverse in front of the face, but on none of the coins can it be deciphered, though I fancy I can trace VIR. The variations in the legend on the reverse are interesting, as showing the use of the double II for the E on these coins, in the same manner as on the coins of Dubnovellaunus, Voso[nos], and Addedomaros, and on many Gaulish coins. The same substitution frequently occurs in Roman inscriptions, and occasionally on Roman coins, such, for instance as that of Mark Antony,* with the legend COS. DIISIG. ITIIR. IIT. TIIRT.

* See Eckhel, Doct. Num. Vet., vol. vi. p. 46.

IIIVIR II.P.C. Whether among the Gauls and Britons this use of the double II for E originated from their having derived their knowledge of letters from a Greek source, in which alphabet the H so closely resembles the II, is a matter for speculation. There is some doubt as to the correct reading of the passage in Cæsar where he mentions the Gauls as using Greek letters, but it is certain from their coins that they did so; and, moreover, we find the Θ passing through the form of the barred D into that of the ordinary Roman D on British coins. It is worthy of notice that in an alphabet incised on a fragment of pottery, and published by M. Tudot (Collection de Figurines en Argile, Paris, 1860), the letter E is represented in the same manner as here, by two straight strokes.

That the horse, so frequent on the coins of this series, should, on these coins, assume its marine form of hippocampus, is certainly a cause for surprise, though possibly it may have been considered as typical of the insular condition of Britain. The device of some of the coins I have ascribed to Amminus seems to be a hippocampus rather than a capricorn, though differing in form from these, which retain a good deal of the horse even in their hind-quarters. The winged hippocampus is occasionally found on Greek coins of maritime states, and especially on the copper coins of Syracuse, and a quadriga of wingless hippocampi appears on some of the large and second brass coins of the Præfects of Mark Antony (Sempronia, Cohen, pl. lxvi. 6 and 7; Oppia, pl. lxi. 7).

The combination of the trefoil and ring ornament on the reverse appears, as has already been observed, to be peculiar to the coins of Verulam.

Plate VII, No. 11.

Obv.—V (?) behind a bare bearded head to the right.
Rev.—TAS. Hippocampus to the left; above, a trefoil and ring ornament. An exergual line. Æ. 37½, 38 grains.

At the time when I first published this type in the Num.

Chron., vol. xviii. p. 44, No. 3, the coin I then possessed gave me the impression that the head upon it was diademed. The Rev. Mr. Christmas has, however, since presented me with a second specimen of this type, which shows clearly that the head is bare, and that what I had taken for the ends of a diadem are, in all probability, the letter V. It also shows traces of a beaded circle round the obverse. I am not aware of the place of finding of either coin.

The head on the obverse differs from that of the preceding coins, in the hair being represented by a number of short locks, instead of being in long tresses like those of the beard. It is in fact the same head which appears on the two subsequent coins. The reverse is the same as that of the preceding coins, except in having the name of the prince instead of that of the town upon it. Apart from the doubtful letter V on the obverse, this shows that the coin No. 11 must have been struck at Verulam, and at much the same time as Nos. 9 and 10, which bear the name of Verulam upon them. It may also be inferred from this coin that the two other coins just mentioned, though they apparently do not give the name of the prince, were struck under Tasciovanna.

Plate VII, No. 12.

Obv.—RVFI (?) or RVLI (?). Bare bearded head to the right, the whole within a beaded circle.

Rev.—No legend visible. Horseman to the right, holding a sword (?) in his right hand; in front of him a pellet; the whole within a beaded circle. Æ. 34 grains.

Plate VII, No. 13.

Obv.—As No. 12, but not showing the legend.

Rev.—VIR (?) or VER (?). Horseman, &c., as No. 12.

Both these coins, which are of the same type, have already been published in the Num. Chron., vol. xx. p. 157, Nos. 6 and 7. No. 12 was found at Creslow, near Aylesbury, and was most kindly presented to me by Mr. Z. D. Hunt. No. 13 is in the collection formed by the late Mr. T. Bateman, of Youlgrave. I have another badly preserved specimen, with the head apparently beardless, found at Dorchester, Oxon, and have seen others found near Harlow, Essex, and Upper Stondon, Beds. The legend on the obverse is very perplexing, but will be best considered after the description of No. 14. Whatever may be its true reading, or the meaning of the legend, the identity of the head on the obverse with that on the preceding coin, as well as the legend on the reverse, prove these coins to have been struck at Verulam. The slim-waisted horseman closely resembles that on the gold coins reading TASCIOV RICON, &c., Plate VIII., Nos. 6, 7, 8, and 9. The silver coins of Tasciovanus, Plate VI., Nos. 3 and 4, may also be referred to. The horseman appears to wear a sort of cap similar to that of the centaur, Plate VII., No. 7. On a specimen in Lord Braybrooke's collection there appears to be an R beneath the horseman, so that possibly the legend on the reverse is the same as on the obverse, RVFI, or RVLL*

PLATE VII., No. 14.

Obv.—RVPS on a tablet; above and below, an annulet; the whole within a beaded circle, with a sort of milled or engrailed circle beyond it.

Rev.—Uncertain animal to the left. Æ.

This coin, in the collection of the late Lord Braybrooke, was discovered by him, with numerous Roman coins, in April, 1853,† during his excavations near the Fleam Dyke, Cambridgeshire, among the foundations of an ancient building at the base of a tumulus known as Muttilow Hill. It is represented in a woodcut at p. 87, vol. xiii., of the Arch. Journ., from whence I have copied it, both here and in the Num. Chron., vol. xx. p. 157, No. 8. The surface of the coin is considerably eroded, but the inscription appears to be exactly as it is shown in the engravings.

In the Revue Num., N.S., vol. v. p. 175, is an interesting

---

* The Harlow coin also seems to have this R.
† Arch. Journ., vol. ix. p. 231.

article on the form of the letter F, by M. Adrien de
Longpérier, in which he conclusively shows that on various
lapidary inscriptions, potters' marks, and on some Gaulish
coins, the letter F is represented under the form P. It
would appear, then, that the legend on this coin is to be read
as RVFS., while that on No. 12 appears to be RVFI, a form
which seems also to be found upon Plate VIII., No. 1, so
that some such name as Rufus or Rufinus may possibly be
intended. A name like this has much more the appearance
of being Roman than British, but it at once calls to mind the
Rufinus mentioned by Martial*—

"Claudia cœrulcis cum sit Rufina Britannis
Edita, cur Latiæ pectora plebis habet?"

Though here the question would be, how a name apparently
of Latin origin comes to be found on a British coin? But
in the present state of our knowledge it is useless attempting
to assign a meaning to this legend. Whatever it may
eventually prove to be, I think I shall not have erred in
attributing these coins to Verulam. The legend on the
tablet reminds us of the equally mysterious DIAS on the
silver coin, Plate VI., No. 14, and the TASC and TASCIO
on the silver and gold coins, Plate VI., No. 2, and
Plate VIII., No. 11. The whole type, with the legend on a
tablet, a ring ornament or annulet above and below, and the
whole within a beaded circle, is curiously similar to that of
one of the gold coins of Verica, Plate III., No. 2, so that this
is another instance (if my attribution of this coin to Verulam
be correct) of the analogy to which I have before alluded
between the coins struck at Verulam and those of the sons of
Commius.

The animal on the reverse can hardly have been intended
for a horse, but would seem more probably to have been meant
for a deer, or possibly a goat, though no horns are visible.
It seems possible that there was originally an inscription on
the reverse as well as on the obverse.

* Lib. xi., Epig. 54.

Plate VIII., No. 1.

Obv.—A square, with the sides curved inwards, including within it a smaller similar square with an annulet in the centre; the whole within a circle.

Rev.—RVFI (?). Eagle (?) to the left, its wings partly expanded its head turned to the right, and holding a branch (?) in its beak. Æ. 14, 10 grains.

The two coins here engraved are in my own collection, and I have never seen any others like them. They were both found in the neighbourhood of Biggleswade, and have been published in the Num. Chron., vol. xviii. p. 44, Nos. 8 and 9. From their small size and weight, they seem to have been intended to represent the half of the larger coins, and this seems to give a reason for their having the single square upon the obverse instead of the two squares interlaced, as on Plate VII., Nos. 3, 4, and 5, though both single and double squares occur on the silver coins of Verica, Nos. 2 and 3, p. 185, which are both of one size. It certainly betokens a much higher degree of civilisation than that for which we are wont to give the Britons credit, that they should have coins of so many denominations, and some of them so small as these, current among them. There is, for instance, in the class of coins now under consideration, the gold stater and its quarter, of the weight of about 84 and 21 grains respectively; the silver piece of about 21 grains; and three sorts of copper money, the normal weights of which appear to have been about 68, 34, and 17 grains respectively. There was, however, less care taken originally in adjusting the weights of the silver and copper coins than of those in gold, and the inferior metals being so liable to suffer from erosion, there is considerable variation in the weight of such coins as have come down to our time.

There is still very much of the shield-like character about the obverse of these small coins, and indeed they are almost identical in appearance with the shields at the foot of the trophy on the coins of the Antonia family (Cohen, pl. iv. 31, 32, and 33). They differ from those of the Cæcilia family (Cohen, pl. viii. 6 and 7) in having a square instead of a pentagon upon them. The same sort of shield occurs also on coins of l'acetum. Though there is no legend on the obverse, there is a strong resemblance between it and that of the coins of Eppillus, Plate IV., Nos. 2 and 3. This resemblance also extends to the reverse, though the eagle on the coins of Eppillus has nothing in its beak. The eagle occurs also on the coin inscribed CRAD, Plate V., No. 3; on those of Epaticcus, Plate VIII., Nos. 13 and 14, and on the uninscribed (?) coin, Plate G, No. 9, which was found in the same neighbourhood as these small coins. The legend RVFI (?) appears to be the same as that on Plate VII., Nos. 12 and 14, but requires farther illustration from better preserved coins.

Plate VIII., No. 2.

Obv.—VER. Male head to the left, with a double row of locks and a short beard.

Rev.—Goat to the right; above, a rosette; below, a ring ornament; behind, a cross of pellets; other pellets in the field. Æ.

This curious little coin was among those found by the late Lord Braybrooke, in his excavations at Chesterford (Proc. Soc. Ant., vol. i. p. 176; Archæol., vol. xxxii. p. 355). It has, however, been described as having the goat on the reverse standing to the left; while in the Arch. Journ., vol. iv. p. 29, the coin has been, through accident, drawn with the devices to the right; and again, in another representation of a coin found at Chesterford (of the same type and possibly the same specimen), Arch. Journ., vol. vi. p. 20, the artist seems entirely to have misunderstood the obverse, though the reverse is correctly given. My engravings of this and the two succeeding coins are taken from impressions which Lord Braybrooke kindly allowed me to make, and their accuracy may be relied on. The head of the obverse has been considered, by Mr. C. Roach Smith, to be that of Hercules, derived from some consular coin. In treatment, it certainly differs from that on any of the preceding coins. The device of the reverse is also new, and affords the only known instance of the occurrence of the goat on the British copper coinage, though it is found on the silver coin, Plate G, No. 4. In treatment it much resembles that of the sheep on Plate VII., No. 6, the body of the animal being covered with globular projections. The occurrence of so many domesticated animals on the coins of Tasciovanus and Verulam seems to indicate that the Catyouchlani were among the tribes of whom Pomponius Mela says, they were " pecoru ac finibus dites," * and reminds us that cattle were among the exports of Britain mentioned by Strabo.†

PLATE VIII., No. 3.

Obv.—TAS (?). Bare beardless head, with short hair, to the right; behind, a curved object, possibly the end of a fillet or diadem, and a pellet; the whole within a circle of pellets.

Rev.—V. beneath a horseman to the right, wielding a long staff. Æ.

This coin was found at Wenden, near Saffron Walden, and is in the collection formed by the late Lord Braybrooke. It is, I believe, unpublished. The head on the obverse is rather like that on the next coin. It may also be compared with that on the silver coins of Cunobeline, Plate XI., Nos. 2 and 3. The horseman on the reverse is identical with that of Plate VII., No. 12, except that he wields a long staff or spear, instead of the short sword. (See also the reverse of Nos. 6, 7, 8, and 9.) The V beneath the horseman is perfectly distinct, so that there can be no doubt about the attribution of this coin to Verulam. I am not, however, quite certain as to the reading of the legend on the obverse. The object behind the head may possibly be a *lituus*, in imitation of that on some of the Roman coins. See, for instance, the obverse of that of Mark Antony (Cohen, pl. iii. 10), the reverse of

* Lib. iii. c. 3.   † Lib. iv. p. 270; Ed. 1867.

which we have already seen imitated on the coin of Verica, Plate III., Nos. 5 and 6.

PLATE VIII., No. 4.

Obv.—[VE]R (?). Bare head to the right; the whole within a triple (?) circle, the centre one beaded.

Rev.—Pig to the right; above, an annulet; at its feet in front, a cluster of pellets. Æ.

This coin, which has not hitherto been published, was found in the excavations made at Chesterford, by the late Lord Braybrooke. Unfortunately that part of the obverse, on which there is the legend, has suffered considerably by erosion, so that only the letter R can be distinguished. I have, however, little doubt that it originally stood as VER. The head is not unlike that on the preceding coin, but better executed. The triple circle by which it is surrounded is peculiar to the coinage of Tasciovanus. The pig on the reverse does not show its mane, like that on the next coin; but possibly this may be partly due to corrosion, or it may be intended for the domesticated, and not the wild animal. The representations of the latter are of frequent occurrence, both on the Gaulish and British series, and what appear to be domesticated swine occur on some of the coins of Cunobeline. (See Plate XIII., No. 1.)

PLATE VIII., No. 5.

Obv.—A triple wreath, divided by two solid crescents back to back, with annulets and scrolls on either side, forming a sort of cruciform ornament.

Rev.—VER. Boar running to the right; above, a crescent (?). Æ. 30 grains.

A coin of this type, weighing 30⅜ grains, is engraved in Ruding, pl. iii. 54, from the Hunter collection. It does not, however, show the inscription. That here engraved was found at Amiens, and was most generously presented to me by M. F. de Saulcy. It is of great interest, not only as affording an instance of an undoubtedly British coin being found in France, but as proving this type, which has hitherto been regarded as uninscribed, to belong to Verulam. A fine specimen, in the Bodleian Library, at Oxford, from the collection of the late Dr. Ingram, shows the type of the obverse more distinctly, and I accordingly give a woodcut of it. The device is singular, as being evidently one of the derivatives from the laureate head on the Macedonian stater, yet appearing on a copper coin. It may be compared with the gold coin of Tasciovanus, Plate V., No. 14, and others of the gold series, such as Plate C, No. 14; Plate III., No. 13, &c. But while retaining so many of the characteristics of the usual cruciform ornament, there is a general resemblance to the device on Plate VII., No. 5, and consequently to the other star-like devices, Nos. 3 and 4. Taking this into account, I am inclined to regard this type as earlier in date than those just cited. The boar on the reverse seems to be a fiercer animal than that on the last coin, and is drawn with much spirit. I have already made some remarks on the occurrence of this boar on British coins, under Plate G, No. 12 (p. 121).

COINS INSCRIBED TASCIO-RICON, &c.

The classification of the coins thus inscribed has afforded considerable matter for controversy among numismatists. Upwards of twenty years ago, Mr. Haigh, in the Gent.'s Mag., 1838, and Num. Chron., vol. iv. p. 27, proposed to attribute them to Uriconium (*Wroxeter*), on the strength of a coin with the legend $\frac{\text{TASCIO}}{\text{VRICON}}$ upon it "very distinct." But at that time Mr. Akerman most properly remarked, "When coins bearing this legend are known to have been dug up on the site of the ancient Uriconium," we will "award to our correspondent the merit of having appropriated another British coin to its locality; but until we have authenticated accounts of such discoveries, we shall continue to think that the coins with these legends were struck in a more central part of Britain." In addition to this, the legend on the coin in the Gent.'s Mag. is not, as Mr. Haigh stated, TASCIO / VRICON but TASCIOV / RICON as will be seen from the accompanying facsimile of the woodcut. The coin is in fact the identical specimen which I have engraved in Plate VIII., No. 8.

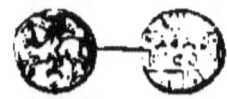

This notion of the coins having been struck at Uriconium has been lately revived by Mr. Beale Poste (who by the way entirely ignores Mr. Haigh's priority in the suggestion) in the Arch. Assoc. Journ., vol. xviii. p. 76.

Satisfactory as it would be to add the name (now so well known) of Uriconium to those of Verulamium, Camulodunum, and Segontium, which are preserved on British coins, there are, I am afraid, no valid arguments whatever, by which the attribution of these coins to Uriconium can for an instant be maintained. In the first place the name, whatever it may be, is RICON or RICONI, never VRICON, and when we consider what an essential part of the name of VRICONIVM was the commencing V, as testified by the modern names, Wroxeter and Wrekin, this objection is of great weight. But, in the next place, among the coins discovered at Wroxeter, whether formerly or during the recent excavations, not only have no coins of this type been found, but, I believe, no British coins whatever. The recorded places of finding of these coins are, moreover, on the opposite side of England, in Essex, Hunts, and Norfolk, corresponding well with the range of the other types of Tasciovanus, whose name indeed appears on these coins. Taking into account their types, weight, and workmanship, there can be no question of their having been struck by the same Tasciovanus of whom such a number of coins have already been described. His name appears under the same forms

TASCI, TASCIO, TASCIOV—(and though in this instance combined with RICON or RICONI), in just the same fashion, on a tablet in the centre of a wreath, as we find it on the small gold and silver coins with TASC only, Plate V., No. 14; Plate VI., No. 1. The horseman on the reverse, with his peculiar cap and taper waist, is much the same as that on the copper coins, Plate VII., Nos. 12 and 13, but in addition to this, wears the embossed cuirass, the same as has already been described on the gold coin of Tasciovanus, Plate V., No. 11. In weight they exactly coincide with the ordinary gold coins of this prince, and as far as workmanship is concerned, they might have been engraved by the same artists. The evidence, therefore, in favour of their being coins of Tasciovanus, is irresistible. The meaning, however, of the word RICON has still to be ascertained. Analogy would certainly lead to the conclusion that it has a local signification, and though it cannot well have been Wroxeter, it seems possible that there may have been some important town within the territories of Tasciovanus, the name of which, RICONIUM, has escaped alike geographers and historians. The names of RIGODUNUM, a town of the Brigantes, and RIGOMAGUS, in Gaul, are both compounded with much the same prefix. We must, however, leave this an open question, in the hope that future discoveries may possibly afford some means of solving it.

PLATE VIII., No. 6.

Obv.—TASCIO RICON in two compartments of a tablet with curved ends, placed across a five-fold wreath of alternately plain and corded lines; the line of division of the tablet is extended across the coin, and there are curved lines which spring from the angles of intersection of the wreath and tablet. From another specimen it appears that there are ten or twelve pellets ranged round the whole.

Rev.—Horseman to the left, armed with a sword, shield, and cuirass, and looking backwards; below, a ring ornament, and, on another coin, an annulet in front. The whole within a braided circle. *N*. 84 grains.

This coin, in my own collection, is said to have been found at St. Ives, Huntingdonshire. I have engraved it in the Num. Chron., vol. xx. p. 50, in company with the false coins inscribed VER BOD, which at that time I had been induced to regard as genuine. The late Mr. Huxtable possessed a coin of the same type, reported to have been found near Norwich. Another, which was procured by the Rev. E. Trafford Leigh from a peasant at Rome, is engraved in the Num. Chron., vol. iii. p. 153, No. 1. Its weight is 84 grains. This coin is reproduced in Akerman, pl. xxii. 4; Beale Poste, p. 95; Arch. Assoc. Journ., vol. ii. p. 21, and vol. xviii. p. 70. I have taken some of the details of the description from this specimen. A coin engraved in Stukeley, pl. xv. 0, reads TASC RICO, but of course no confidence can be placed in it. Another coin, in the Museum at Rouen, has been engraved by Lambert, pl. xi. 21, who considered it to read TASSIE RICON. I find, however, on inspection of the coin, that the legend is in fact TASCIO RICON, the same as here. The weight is 102 French grains = 83½ troy grains. The consideration of the devices of this coin will be best deferred until the next three pieces have been described.

PLATE VIII, No. 7.

Obv.—TASCI RICONI, as No. 6.
Rev.—As No. 6, but no annulet in front of the horseman. *N*.

This coin, in the Hunter collection at Glasgow, is engraved in the Mon. Hist. Brit., pl. i. 4. The O and N are, however, hardly so distinct upon it as I have made them. The reverse is in beautiful condition, and gives the whole type in a most satisfactory manner.

PLATE VIII, No. 8.

Obv.—TASCIOV RICON, as No. 6.
Rev.—Horseman, as on No. 6. *N*. 82 grains (?).

PLATE VIII., No. 9.

Obv.—TASCI RICON, as No. 6.
Rev.—Horseman, as on No. 6.

No. 9 was found near Biggleswade, and Mr. Warren, of Ixworth, informs me that he formerly possessed one with the same legend, found at Castle Hedingham, Essex, about 1850. No. 8 was found near Epping, and is described in the Gent's. Mag. for 1821, p. 60. The weight is there said to be 5 dwts. 10 grains, or about 48 grains more than usual. This weight of 130 grains, according to Mr. Beale Poste, who ascribes the coins to Uriconium,* "may remind us of the proximity of gold mines, which it is believed did formerly exist in North Wales;" but it is, in fact, simply due to a typographical error, by which 5 dwts. was printed for 3 dwts. This coin is mentioned as having been found at Harlow, in the Arch. Assoc. Journ., vol. iv. p. 150, but, it would seem, erroneously. Both it and the preceding coin are described in Akerman, p. 187, Nos. 2 and 3.

The type of the obverse has been described by Mr. Beale Poste as follows:—"A row of five spears, placed upright against, apparently, some framework, and from one side of these projects another representation of the Celtic carnyx, or war trumpet," with a double tablet "in front of the row of spears." The fact of the alternate "spears" being wreathed or corded, seems to have been unnoticed by Mr. Poste, or he might possibly have recognised in this group of spears the ordinary five-fold wreath which occurs on many of the uninscribed coins, such as Plate D, Nos. 6, 7, 8, and Plate C, No. 9, as well as on the coins of Dubnovellaunus, Plate IV., Nos. 6 to 9.

The gold coin of Cunobeline, Plate IX., Nos. 1 and 2, has much the same type on the obverse, while the reverse still retains the two horses of the original biga. On several of the silver and copper coins of Cunobeline we have the legend placed in the same manner in two compartments of a tablet, though no longer associated with a wreath.

The horseman on the reverse, looking backwards, and defending himself apparently from a pursuing foe, is peculiar to these coins as far as this attitude of defence is concerned.

* Arch. Assoc. Journ., vol. xviii. p. 78.

On the coin of Cunobeline, Plate XII., No. 3, and on that of Epaticcus, Plate VIII., No. 12, he is however armed in precisely the same manner, though apparently charging the enemy. The practice of making a feigned retreat, so as to separate their pursuers from the main body of the opposing army, is attributed to the Britons by Cæsar,* but his account refers to the *essedarii* rather than the cavalry.

It is remarkable that both Tacitus and Herodian make the Britons unacquainted with the use of the *lorica*, or cuirass, whereas there can be but little doubt that the horseman on these coins is represented as thus armed. The best method of accounting for this contradiction seems to be, to consider the accounts of the historians as referring only to the more northern and barbarous tribes of Britain. If any dependence can be placed on these representations, the cuirass must have been ornamented with circular bosses, in the same manner as was the case with some of the British shields. I have already observed that the horseman on some of the other coins of Tasciovanus wears a similar cuirass. The slenderness of waist for which all these horsemen seem remarkable, was much aimed at by the Gauls as well as the Britons.

The covering of the head would seem to be some form of hat, or possibly of helmet, not unlike that on some of the Gaulish coins (see Lelewel, type 51, pl. x.), but not showing any crest. The same writers who deny the use of the thorax, deny also the use of the helmet, but, as we shall subsequently see, it is of by no means uncommon occurrence on the coins of Cunobeline.

COINS OF TASCIOVANUS INSCRIBED SEGO.

The coins bearing the word SEGO upon them—of which there are two types, one giving that word alone, and the other bearing it in conjunction with TASCIO, have—like the class of which I have just been treating, been the subject of

* De Bell. Gall., v. 10.

some controversy among those who have occupied themselves about the British coinage.

The first to engrave one of these coins (that in silver) was Stukeley, who, on the strength of reading FV on a variety not now known (and which was indeed probably a coin of Cunobeline of the type Plate XI., No. 6), attributed them to a King Fulgenius, one of the race of British heroes described by Geoffrey of Monmouth, who was killed in a battle with the Emperor Severus, in A.D. 211!!

The next to delineate the silver coin (Plate VIII., No. 10) was John White, who, in the account of his plate of British coins, assigns it "to Segontium, now Silchester." Gough, who in his edition of Camden has copied this coin from White, simply remarks that he has attributed it to the Segontiaci. Ruding, however, who engraves both types, assigns them to Segonax, one of the Kentish kings mentioned by Cæsar, in which he is followed by Hawkins and Akerman, though the latter considered the attribution very doubtful. Beale Poste assigns the coins to Segontium and the Segontiaci, as did also Mr. Haigh,* but the latter under the impression that Segontium was Caernarvon. There is no record of the place of finding of any of the coins bearing the inscription SEGO, so that their *provenance* affords no assistance in the inquiry as to their attribution. The types and workmanship of the coins speak, however, with sufficient distinctness, to give a complete denial to the claims of Segonax to them. Unless that chief had lived for a considerable number of years after the invasion of Cæsar, it is certain that his coins must have more closely approximated to those of the uninscribed series than do these; but when we take into account that, with the exception of the legend, the reverse of the gold coins is identical with that of the coin of Tasciovanus, Plate V., No. 11, and that we also find his name under the form of TASCIO on the obverse, it is evident that it is to Tasciovanus they must be assigned, whatever meaning we may put upon the word SEGO. We

* Num. Chron., vol. iv., p. 28.

find, moreover, that the reverse of the silver coins is absolutely identical with that of a silver coin (Plate VII., No. 2) which can almost be demonstrated to have been struck under Tasciovanus at Verulam; and under these circumstances we are led to the conclusion that as the VER on the analogous coin undoubtedly denotes Verulam, so also the SEGO on this must have a geographical signification. Whether, as was the case on the coins of Verulam, it stood for the name of a town—Segontium—or whether merely for the name of the tribe of the Segontiaci, like the ECEN for the Iceni on their coins, must, to a certain extent, remain an open question.

The first, and indeed the only mention of the Segontiaci among the classical writers, is by Cæsar,[*] who records that they were one of the British tribes, who sent embassies and made submission to him. Their name appears to have been unknown to Ptolemy, but seems to have been preserved in a votive inscription found at Silchester,[†] inscribed DEO HER[CVLI] SAEGON. Camden locates the tribe on the north edge of Hampshire, in Holeshot hundred, and makes Vindonum to have been their chief city, but on what authority, is by no means clear.

It would seem probable that he did so, in consequence of having identified Silchester with Vindomum, and of having found, from Henry of Huntingdon, that that city was anciently called Kair Segont, or the city of the Segontiaci. There is, however, a preponderance of evidence in favour of identifying Silchester with Calleva, the chief town of the Atrebates, so that possibly Henry of Huntingdon, who wrote as late as about A.D. 1140—50, may have erred in fixing Kair Segont at Silchester, though he may have been correct in saying that it was "super Tamesim non longè a Redingo." Certainly, if the CALLE on the coins of Eppillus refers to Calleva, and that town was known long afterwards as Calleva Atrebatum, the SEGO on the coins of Tasciovanus does not refer to the same place. My own opinion is that

---

[*] De Bell. Gall. v. 21.   [†] Gough's Camden, vol. I. p. 204.

the Segontiaci must have been settled farther north than they are placed by Camden, and that they probably had some chief town known by the name of Segontium, the site of which has still to be ascertained. The Segontium mentioned in the Itinerary of Antoninus must not in any way be confounded with this, its site being fixed on valid grounds at Caernarvon. It is not, however, of much importance whether we find on these coins the name of the tribe or that of their chief town. They certainly seem to establish the fact of the Segontiaci having been one of the tribes who were under the rule of Tasciovanus; and, as will shortly be seen, it is probable that their territory fell, at his death, to the share of his son Epaticcus, while the eastern part of his dominions came under the dominion of Cunobeline.

At present there are no copper coins known with SEGO upon them, and those in gold and silver are of extreme rarity.

PLATE VIII., No. 10.

Obv.—SEGO on a tablet within a circle formed of two lines twisted into a sort of guilloche pattern.

Rev.—Uninscribed. Naked horseman prancing to the right, wearing a diadem, with the long ends streaming behind him. There is an exergual line, and the whole is within a beaded circle. Æ 19 grains.

This coin is in the British Museum, and has been engraved in Stukeley, pl. xii. 10; White, No. 9; Gough's Camden, pl. i. 36; Taylor Combe, pl. i. 18; Ruding, App., pl. xxix. 5; Lelewel, pl. viii. 47; Mon. Hist. Brit., pl. i. 40; Akerman, pl. xxi. 2; Beale Poste, p. 28; and Arch. Assoc. Journ., vol. ii. p. 14. Its place of finding is not known. A coin with a similar obverse, and on the reverse a standing figure with the legend FV, is given by Stukeley, pl. xiii. 2. It was probably drawn from a badly preserved coin of Cunobeline, with SOLIDV on the obverse, such as Plate XI., No. 6.

The general appearance of the obverse of this coin is much like that of other coins of Tasciovanus, with TASC on a tablet, instead of SEGO (Plate VI., No. 2); but the twisted circles are the same as on the coin of Cunobeline just mentioned, and that of Andoco[mius], Plate V., No. 6, though on the latter, one ring is beaded and the other plain. As has already been observed, the type of the reverse is identical with that of the coins of Verulam, Plate VII., No. 2.

PLATE VIII., No. 11.

Obv.—TASCIO on a tablet; above and below, a wheel, with annulets and pellets on either side.

Rev.—SEGO. Horseman galloping to the right holding a trumpet; behind, a wheel; below the exergual line, a ring ornament. *N.* 82 7/8 grains.

This coin is in the Hunter collection, at Glasgow. Another, which gives the horseman more perfectly and shows the *carnyx* which he is holding, though it does not give the legend on the reverse, is in the British Museum. Both coins are engraved in the Mon. Hist. Brit., pl. i. 10 and 2. The Hunter coin is also given in Ruding, pl. iv. 1; Hawkins, pl. ii. 18; Akerman, pl. xxi. 1; Beale Poste, p. 28; and Arch. Assoc. Journ., vol. ii. p. 14. The obverse, though differing from that of any of the other coins of Tasciovanus in most of its details, still resembles the preceding coin, and that in Plate V., No. 14, in having the name upon a tablet.

The reverse is almost identical with that of Plate V., No. 11, even to the ring ornament in the exergue, and the trumpet is of precisely the same form as on Nos. 10 and 12 in the same Plate. The only real difference is in the legend.

EPATICCUS.

The history and even the name of this chief were unknown until the discovery of one of his gold coins near Guildford, in 1857, of which I communicated an account to the Numismatic Society in May* of that year. The type of the coin then discovered, though new to numismatists of the day,

* Num. Chron., vol. xx. p. 1.

had, however, long since been described; and not only so, but upwards of two hundred years ago, in the dawn of antiquarian knowledge in this country, engravings were made from two specimens, one evidently in fine preservation, and the other apparently abraded, as a variation is made in the legend. This latter was given by Camden, and is to be found in all the earlier editions of the Britannia. He gives the devices pretty correctly, but makes the legend TASCIE and CEARATIC, and describes the coin as follows:* — "The ninth, wherein is represented an horseman with speare and shield, and these letters in scattering wise, CAERATIC, I would deeme to be a Coine of that warlike prince, Caratacus, whose praises Tacitus highly extolleth." Nicolaus Fabri de Peiresc, in a letter to Camden (Camd. Ep., p. 105, ed. 1691), suggests, however, that there is a mistake in this reading, and considers the legend to be rather C.VERATIC. The engraving of this coin was expunged in Gough's edition of 1806, as not then known, and wonderful to relate, a coin of Carissa, in Hispania Bætica, was made to take a place among the ancient British coins in its stead.

Camden's version of the coin was copied by Pegge,† who ascribed it to Cunobeline, and imagined CEARATIC to be the name of some town within his territory. Wise,‡ however, was inclined to refer the coin to the Curretani, (Carpetani?) a people of the Vascones, in Spain!

Stukeley copied the coins into his plates, but made the legend CARATIC, the better to suit its supposed attribution to CARATICVS, as he calls the chief usually known as Caractacus. In this attribution of the coins to Caractacus, Stukeley is followed, even at the present day, by Mr. Beale Poste; with what reason will subsequently be seen. We can hardly find a better example of the danger of interpreting coins in accordance with preconceived opinions than we have here. The name of Caractacus—if that indeed be the correct version of the name of that brave chief—has,

* Ed. 1637, p. 184.   † Coins of Cunob., p. 78.
‡ Bodleian Coins, p. 25.

of course, been long familiar to the students of British
history, and it has been solely from the desire to attribute
coins to him, that the legend on this piece has been so much
abused; for it may be regarded as a certain fact that had the
name of Caractacus been unknown, the legend on these gold
coins would never have been read as CAERATIC. In
reading it thus, it is evident that the antiquaries I have
mentioned sinned against light, for Speed,[*] in his Chronicle,
has engraved a specimen from the collection of Sir Robert
Cotton, of Cunington, with the legends distinctly TASCI F
and EPATIC—V.[†] To get over this, Mr. Poste actually
proposes to regard the legend as CAEPATIC (CAERATIC),
in mixed Greek and Roman letters, notwithstanding the
improbability of such a mixture, and regardless of having to
commence the legend in a place where no one would, under
ordinary circumstances, dream of commencing it, and unmindful
of the inverted position of the A, for which the V is made
to do duty. The improbability of this interpretation is, however,
far outdone by that by the same author, when he treats
of the silver coins with the type of the head of Hercules in
the lion's skin, the paws meeting under his chin, and with
the legend EPAT or EPATI. He first of all converts the
lion's paws into the letter K, then reads the whole as in
Greek letters, and makes the KEPATI thus obtained to
stand for Caractacus. It seems needless to refute such
assumptions; but it may be as well to remark, that when
any coins of Caractacus are discovered, if such an event ever
takes place, we may, at all events, expect to find that Roman
letters will have been used upon them, as they always are,
without exception, on the coins of his father, Cunobeline,
and his grandfather, Tasciovanus.

But to return to the coins of Epaticus, which at present
are known only in gold and silver, and on which his name

---

[*] Ed. 1623, pp. 34 and 63.

[†] "Others read it Epatica, which may keep its native signification, since we
find parsley, the palm, vine, myrtle, cynoglossum, leucopiteon, and other plants
sometimes figured, sometimes only named, upon coins."—Walssa, in Gibson's
Camden, p. xcii.

occurs under the forms EPATICCV, EPATI, and EPAT, accompanied, on the gold coins, by the legend TASCI . F. This legend, which is identical with that which occurs on some of the coins of Cunobeline, and which, in its extended form, was TASCIOVANI . F, proves that Epaticcus was also a son of Tasciovanus, and consequently a brother of Cunobeline. Had no such legend been upon the coin, there could have been no hesitation about regarding Epaticcus as a contemporary of Cunobeline, as the obverse type of his gold coin corresponds exactly, even to the number of grains in the ear of corn, and the shape of the leaflets on its stem, with the common gold coins of Cunobeline; while the horseman on the reverse is exactly similar to that on some of the copper coins of the same prince, even to the shape of the shield, and the short dart or staff. The workmanship is also similar to that of the coins of Cunobeline, and the weight the same.

When treating of the coins of Tasciovanus, I have mentioned that there is some reason for supposing that, on his death, his dominions were divided between his two sons, Cunobeline taking the eastern portion, and Epaticcus the western. With regard to Cunobeline's share there can be little doubt; we know perfectly well, from his coins, that Camulodunum (Colchester) was his capital, as Verulamium (near St. Alban's) had been that of his father; but with regard to Epaticcus the evidence is much less conclusive. It seems, however, likely that he eventually succeeded to some part of his father's dominions, though probably to a much smaller portion than that which fell to the lot of his brother Cunobeline. The small number of his coins, which are far rarer than those of Cunobeline, and the limited number of his types, of which only two are known, would seem to point not only to a smaller extent of territory, but to a more limited duration of reign.

The date of the coin of Tiberius, found with those of Epaticcus, at Savernake Forest, might lead us to doubt whether the coins of the latter were minted so early as

A.D. 5, the assumed date of the death of Tasciovanus; but the discrepancy is not of many years. It is, however, of course possible that Cunobelin succeeded to the whole of his father's dominions at his death, and that subsequently some tribe may have revolted from Cunobeline, and made Epaticcus their chief. Or, again, Epaticcus may have acquired the rule over some tribe which was never subject to his father. However this may have been, the places where his coins have been found are, as far as is hitherto known, confined to the western part of Surrey, and the eastern part of Wilts. If we are to judge from their having been found in these localities, it would seem probable that the Segontiaci, among whom we have seen that Tasciovanus struck coins, were the tribe over whom Epaticcus reigned. It must, however, be confessed that at present this is purely conjectural. His name, which bears no great analogy to that of any other British prince, may be compared, as to its commencement, with the Gaulish Epasnactus (or EPAD of coins) and Eporedorix. The final TICCVS is to be found in the name of Casticus, a prince of the Sequani mentioned by Cæsar, and in Suticcos, a name which appears on Gaulish coins. Among the names occurring on the red-glazed ware, which in many cases appear to be Gaulish, we find EPPA., BELINICCUS, and DOVICCUS.

PLATE VIII., No. 12.

Obv.—TASCI F. Ear of bearded corn placed vertically, with two leaflets springing from its base.
Rev.—EPATICCV. Naked horseman prancing to the right, in his right hand a short lance or staff, and on his left arm a large oval shield. The whole within a beaded circle. *N.* 82 grains.

This coin, in the collection of Mr. Whitbourn, of Godalming, is believed to have been found in the neighbourhood of Guildford. Reference has already been made to the various works in which coins of the same type have been engraved. The type of the obverse, with the ear of bearded corn, consisting of eleven grains, is identical with that of the gold coins of Cunobeline, Plate IX., No. 3, &c. It is difficult to say what particular cereal it was intended to represent, but it is more probably bearded wheat than barley. Even in Strabo's time, both corn and cattle were exported from Britain, so that possibly the device may have been adopted as emblematic of the fertility of the soil. At the same time I have no doubt that one of the principal reasons for its adoption, was the similarity of the ear of corn to the laurel wreath, which, under one form or another, was so persistent upon the British coins, long after all other traces of the head of Apollo on their prototype had disappeared.

The horseman on the reverse has, as has already been observed, a great likeness to that on some of the coins of Cunobeline. It also resembles, in a greater or less degree, the warriors on the coins of Tasciovanus, Tinc[ommius], Verica, and Eppillus, though the shield occurs only once on the coins of the sons of Commius (Plate IL, No. 9).

I was at one time doubtful whether the legend was not intended to be EPATICCVS, with the final S merged in the horse's tail. I am, however, now of opinion that it is EPATICCV only, a form of which we have another example in the coins inscribed ANTEDRIGV.

The metal of which this coin is composed is a red gold, much the same as was generally used by Cunobeline and Tasciovanus.

Plate VIII, No. 13.

Obv.—EPATI. Head of Hercules in the lion's skin, the paws projecting beneath his chin; behind, a curved object with a pellet in the centre of its looped end. The whole within a beaded circle.

Rev.—Uninscribed. Eagle standing upon a serpent, its wings expanded, and its head turned to the left; above its neck a ring ornament. A beaded circle surrounds the whole. Æ. 17½ grains.

Plate VIII., No. 14.

Obv.—EPAT. As No. 13.
Rev.—As No. 13. Æ. 18¼ grains.

A coin of this type, from the Cracherode collection, in the British Museum, was first engraved by Taylor Combe, pl. i. 10, but attributed by him to some Gaulish regulus, whose name began with EPAT. Akerman, p. 185, in a note, cites it as probably of British origin; but singularly enough, when describing a coin of this type in the Num. Chron., vol. xi. p. 99, fell into the error of regarding the lion's paw as the letter M, and made the legend MEPATI. Under this name

"Young Mepati, come of the Comian stock,"

and his supposed father, brave King Verio, are the heroes of a tale, by Martin F. Tupper, in the "Seven Tales by Seven Authors."

The coin which gave rise to this mistake was found at Farley Heath, near Guildford, a spot where many other British coins, especially those of Verica, have been found. It is now in the British Museum, as are also two other coins of this type, found in Savernake Forest, near Marlborough.

I have also two coins like No. 13, weighing 19 and 19¾ grains respectively, which came from the find in Savernake Forest, as well as an uninscribed gold coin of the type of Plate D, No. 1, and a denarius of Tiberius, which were, I am informed, discovered at the same time. The coin of Tiberius is of the common type (Cohen, No. 2), with PONTIF. MAXIM. on the reverse, and has somewhat suffered from wear. Assuming Cohen's date for this type (A.D. 15) to be correct, the coin can hardly have been deposited before A.D. 20 or 25; and as the coins of Epaticcus show but little signs of wear, it would seem probable that they were struck subsequently to A.D. 15. There will, however, always be difficulties in assigning exact dates to the coins of princes of whose existence we have no direct historical testimony, and as yet but a very limited amount of numismatic evidence; and it is always possible that coins, though found at the same place and on the same day, may not have been in actual association.

Engravings or notices of coins of this type will be found

in Tupper's Farley Heath; the Revue Num., vol. xv. p. 240; Lelewel, pl. viii. 10; Num. Soc. Proc., January 25, 1849; Gent.'s Mag., 1848, p. 71; Beale Poste, p. 164, &c.; and the Arch. Assoc. Journ., vol. v. p. 374, as well as in the works before cited.

It is difficult to say from whence the type of the head of Hercules, enveloped in the lion's skin, was immediately derived. It is, however, of such common occurrence on both Roman and Greek coins, that on the adoption of classical types for the British coinage, it must have been one of the most obvious. The annexed woodcut shows the obverse of a denarius of the Cornelia family, Cohen, pl. xv. 22. We find the full length figure of Hercules on several of the silver coins of Cunobeline, so that though Diodorus Siculus informs us that Hercules never made war in Britain, his worship would appear to have been introduced into this country by the time of Epaticcus. Assuming that my view of his having been a prince of the Segontiaci is correct, it seems possible that we have, on these coins, the head of the "DEVS HERCVLES SAEGONTIACVS," to whom a votive inscription was found at Silchester, as has already been stated. The object behind the head has much the appearance of being a sling, and though there appears to be no mention in history of this weapon having been in use among the Britons, it seems most probable that they were acquainted with it.

The eagle holding a serpent in its claws, the ancient ensign of the Spartans, may possibly have been taken from some Greek coin. Much the same device, however, appears on the bronze coin, Plate G, No. 9. It is doubtful whether the eagle which occurs so often on the coins of Eppillus has a serpent in its claws or not. It is, however, remarkable that some of these coins seem to have been coined at Calleva, which must have been close upon the borders of the territory of Epaticcus, so that much the same device would appear to have been adopted by conterminous tribes. We have already seen that Eppillus must have been a contemporary of Tasciovanus, and it seems by no means improbable that he may have survived him, and thus have been a contemporary of Epaticcus also. The peculiar dotting under the wings of the eagle is much the same as that on the wings of the eagles, Victories, and Pegasi, on the coins of Eppillus, Dubnovellaunus, and Tasciovanus, but the head on some of these coins of Epaticcus is in bolder relief than is common on British coins.

CUNOBELINUS.

Of this prince, whose name, under the form of Cymbeline, has become a household word since the days of Shakspere, there is a great variety of coins known in all the metals. As, notwithstanding the cavils of some of the older school of foreign numismatists, and the doubts raised by some even of our own antiquaries, their attribution is perfectly certain and satisfactory, they have always been regarded as of the highest interest by most students of British history. At a time when the coins of many other British princes were either assigned to some of the chieftains of Gaul, or were even treated with contempt, coins bearing the name of Cunobeline were held in high repute, and, as l'egge says, " were purchased by our antiquaries at a vast expense." The coins of Cunobeline, Pinkerton * affirms, " are the only ones probably British ; " and even so lately as 1848, were we to judge from a work issued at vast expense under the auspices of the British government, and professing to contain the materials for the History of Britain, there were no coins of any of our native chiefs which were considered worthy of a place in the British series, except those of Cunobeline and Tasciovanus ; and, in this instance, the coins of the latter appear to have been admitted, only because they were supposed to have been struck by the former. Out of the fifty-one† British coins

* Vol. i. p. 309, ed. 1809.
† I purposely omit two coins—the one, No. 30, *false*, and the other, No. 48, erroneously ascribed to Cunobeline.

engraved in the Monumenta Historica Britannica, no less than thirty-six are of Cunobeline, and the remainder were struck by Tasciovanus at his various places of mintage.

It is in a great degree owing to the coins of this prince having been so long popular among collectors, that so many varieties of them are known, as every piece on which some of the letters of his name could be traced, was prized accordingly; while the coins of unknown chiefs were held in little esteem, and many were in consequence allowed to pass into oblivion. It results, I think, from the diligence with which these coins were collected, that it is so rare at the present day to meet with any of them of new and unpublished types; and though, since I commenced this work, I have been able to fill many gaps that I had left in some of the Plates, on the chance of new types occurring while it was still in progress, the vacancy in Plate X., No. 6, still remains to be filled.

Before proceeding to discuss the nature of his coinage, it will be well to lay before the reader such notices of Cunobeline as are to be found in the Roman historians, and such facts with regard to the nature and extent of his dominions as may be deduced from their narratives, and from the localities in which his coins have been found.

From Suetonius,[*] who probably wrote his history of the twelve Cæsars about A.D. 120, we learn that Adminius (who by Orosius, is called Minocynobellinus), a son of Cinobellinus, having been driven out by his father, fled with a small band of followers, and surrendered himself to the Romans, and that the emperor in consequence sent a grandiloquent letter to Rome, describing the whole island as having been given up to the Roman power; and, moreover, gave the messengers orders to drive into the Forum, and not to deliver his letter except in the Temple of Mars, and in a full assembly of the senate. This must have taken place in A.D. 40, at which time, therefore, Cunobeline must have been still alive. That he was evidently the most powerful

[*] Vit. Cali. Cæs., cap. xliv.

chieftain in Britain at the time, appears from the exaggerated importance attached by Caligula to the nominal surrender of his territory by one of his sons. Suetonius, indeed, calls him "Britannorum Rex," as if he held the sovereign power over all the British tribes; but makes no further allusion either to him, or to his sons, when relating the conquest of Britain, under Claudius. Dion Cassius,* however, whose history was composed A.D. 200—220, furnishes us with some additional particulars. We learn from him, that when at the instigation of one Bericus, who had been driven out of Britain by an insurrection, Claudius sent an expedition, under Aulus Plautius, against this island, in A.D. 43; Cunobeline was dead. Plautius found the Britons not "autonomous" (which, taking the Roman signification of the word, may mean that they had not the power of electing their own chieftains), but subject to different kings. Of these he conquered, "first, Cataratacus, and then Togodumnus, sons of Cynobellinus, for he was then dead." On their flight, he brought to terms of peace a certain part of the Doduni, who were under the rule of the Catuellani. After a severe battle with the Britons, we next hear of the death of Togodumnus, and subsequently, on the arrival of Claudius in Britain, of the passage of the Thames by the Romans, and the capture of Camulodunum, the royal city (βασίλειον) of Cynobellinus. Of the history of this town I shall subsequently have occasion to speak; at present our concern is with Cunobeline and his history. Taking the accounts of Suetonius and Dion Cassius together, we learn that he had at least three sons—Adminius, who fled to the Romans; Togodumnus, who was killed, or died, in A.D. 43; and Cataratacus, or Caractacus, whose subsequent history may be learnt from Tacitus. Some † other brothers of Caractacus are mentioned by Tacitus, though not by name, and it seems possible also that the Bericus who was driven out of Britain by an insurrection was another son of Cunobeline. Whether this were the case or not, it appears that both Togodumnus

* Lib. lx. s. 10—23. † Ann., lib. xii. c. 35.

and Caractacus had, on the death of their father, assumed the regal power, and had each some portion of the territory of Cunobeline under their rule.

Such a division of the territory of Cunobeline between his sons, as may be inferred from the narrative of Dion Cassius, affords an analogous instance to that which, from numismatic evidence, appears to have taken place on the death of his father, Tasciovanus, whose dominions seem to have been divided between Cunobeline and his brother Epaticens. I have already mentioned that it was the eastern part of the territory of Tasciovanus, which seems to have fallen to the share of Cunobeline, and have suggested that it was probably in consequence of this partition, combined with the annexation of the Catyeuchlani to the Trinobantes, that Camulodunum became the chief town of his dominions instead of Verulamium, which had been the capital city of his father. Whether Cunobeline may not have become the ruler of the Trinobantes, even during his father's lifetime, is a question well worthy of consideration. We have no coins of Cunobeline which can be proved to have been struck at Verulamium, and it will be seen, from what has been said with regard to the coins of Dubnovellaunus, that there is some colourable foundation for the hypothesis which I have advanced, as to his dominions in Essex having been brought by conquest under the rule of Cunobeline, before the death of Tasciovanus. Where history fails, conjecture is, to a certain extent, allowable, but must only be taken for what it is worth.

But apart from mere speculation, looking at the important position which, from the accounts of the Roman historians, it is evident that Cunobeline held in Britain, it would seem probable that he exercised a sovereign power over all the south-eastern part of the island; that is to say, over that part of the country with which the Romans came in more immediate contact, after the conquest of Gaul; though probably the tribes which formed no part of his father's dominion were still, to a certain extent, under independent chieftains who, however, looked up to Cunobeline as their sovereign ruler. His own peculiar territory was that of the Trinobantes, and probably the Catyeuchlani, and part, at all events, of the Boduni; and it is principally within the limits of these tribes that his coins have been found, though occasionally also in neighbouring districts, especially Kent. Some of them have been found in each of the counties of Norfolk, Suffolk, Cambridge, Nottingham, Essex, Herts, Beds, Bucks, Oxon, Middlesex, and Kent; but Essex, as might have been expected, seems to be the most prolific of them. Their number and variety, especially of the silver and copper coins, proves that the reign of Cunobeline must have extended over many years; but though we are able to fix the year of his death as between A.D. 40 and 43, we have no certain guide as to the date of the commencement of his reign. Every circumstance, however, that is known concerning him seems to point to his having arrived at extreme old age at the time of his death. The number of his coins, the defection of his sons, the concurrent testimony of the British chroniclers, all tell the same story.

The history given by such men as Geoffrey of Monmouth must, of course, be taken with due allowances. But according to him, Cassibellaunus* died seven years after Cæsar's second expedition into Britain, and was succeeded by Tenuantius, who, it would seem, must be identified with the Tasciovanus of coins. This would give B.C. 47 for the accession of Tenuantius, "who governed the kingdom with diligence," "was a warlike man and a strict observer of justice. After him Kymbelinus, his son, was advanced to the throne, being a great soldier and brought up by Augustus Cæsar. He had contracted so great a friendship with the Romans that he freely paid them tribute when he might have very well refused it. In his days was born our Lord." "Kymbelinus, when he had governed Britain ten years, begat two sons, the elder named Guiderius, the other Arviragus." After his death the "government fell to Guiderius. This prince refused to pay tribute to the

* Brit. Hist., Lib. iv. c. 11, 12.

Romans; for which reason Claudius, who was now Emperor, marched against him," &c. The general outline of the events thus stated by Geoffrey of Monmouth seems fairly in accordance with both historical and numismatic evidence, though the dates may require correction. We know from the coins that the reigns of both Cunobeline and his father must have each been of great duration, and though probably that of Tasciovanus did not commence so early as B.C. 47, yet there seems a probability in favour of that of Cunobeline having commenced before the birth of our Saviour. In speaking of the coins of Tasciovanus, I have assumed that the date of his death was about A.D. 5, and shown that the character of his coins accords well with an extended reign, terminating at about that epoch. If, as has been suggested, Cunobeline became ruler of the Trinobantes, with Camulodunum for his capital, in his father's lifetime, we might place his accession to power some ten years earlier. This would well coincide with the date B.C. 5, assigned by Matthew of Westminster for that event,* and would allow him a reign of about forty-seven years. Such a duration of reign, though no doubt far above the average, is still by no means extraordinary, for had he been thirty at the time of his accession, he would only have attained the age of seventy-seven; and we have already seen that there is a concurrence of testimony, both direct and circumstantial, in favour of his having arrived at a great age at the time of his death.

The coins of Cunobeline present a considerable range of types, some few of them being purely British in their character, but the majority of them showing the influence of Roman art, and many of them bearing devices borrowed from Roman coins. Even on the coins of Tasciovanus we have seen that this was, to a certain extent, the case, especially with what are supposed to be his later coins. But under Cunobeline it seems pretty evident that Roman

---

* Other chroniclers assign a still earlier date. See Poste's Britannic Researches, p. 227, et seqq., where there is a good collection of the pedigrees of the British kings, as given by different chroniclers.

engravers, or engravers brought up in the Roman workshops, were employed in the mint of Camulodunum. It would indeed appear that Cunobeline must have been one—and probably the principal one—of the princes alluded to by Strabo when he says,* "At the present time, some of the princes in Britain having, by their embassies and court, gained the friendship of Cæsar Augustus, have dedicated their offerings in the Capitol, and have brought the whole island into a state little short of intimate union with the Romans" (οἰκείαν σχεδὸν παρεσχήκασαν). His adoption of the formula TASCIOVANI. F. in imitation of the DIVI. F. on the coins of Augustus and Tiberius, is one evidence of this Roman influence, but the number of divinities borrowed from the classical mythology which we find upon his coins, as well as the character of the workmanship of many of them, are even more conclusive. Jupiter Ammon, Hercules with his club, and with the trophies of some of his labours, Apollo Musagetes, Diana, Cybele on a lion, and many other devices which will hereafter be noticed, prove how completely the Roman mythology must have taken root in this country, before such types would have been adopted for the native coinage, unless we are to suppose that the types were purely arbitrary, and left to the mere fancies of the engravers.

It must, however, be observed that this adoption of classical types is confined to the silver and copper coinage, for the gold coins of Cunobeline still retain the original British types, though in a somewhat modified form. On some indeed (Plate IX., Nos. 1 and 2) we find a close approximation on the obverse, to the cruciform ornament formed of two wreaths, while on the reverse, the second horse of the biga reappears. On the majority of them, however, the sole remembrance of the original laureate bust is the wreath-like ear of corn, and a single horse is all that is left of the biga on the reverse. On some few of the silver and copper coins the types are also either purely British (Plate X., Nos. 1, 2, and 3; Plate XI., Nos. 10, 11, &c.), or else more nearly

* Lib. iv. p. 280. Ed. 1807.

allied to coins of other British princes than to those of
Rome. (See, for instance, Plate X., No. 4; Plate XI.,
Nos. 1 and 9; Plate XII., Nos. 8, 11, &c.) The workmanship of the coins, in all the metals, is also very variable in its
character, some of them being executed with all the finish
of Roman coins, and others again being of inferior work,
while some few are almost barbarous. This diversity of
type and execution appears to afford conclusive proof that
the reign of Cunobeline must have been of long duration,
especially when it is taken into account that nearly all the
coins were minted in the same place. In the case of the
gold coins the name of Camulodunum, in a more or less
abbreviated form, appears upon every one of them, and
though it is of less frequent occurrence upon the silver and
copper coins, there is every probability that by far the
greater number of them were minted in that town, which,
as we have already seen from Dion Cassius, was the
Βασίλειον of Cunobeline. The name of this town, which
was subsequently a Roman colony, is mentioned by many of
the writers of antiquity under different forms of spelling, but
there can be no doubt that the preferable form is that given
on the coins, CAMULODUNUM. By Pliny* it is called
" CAMALODUNUM Britanniæ oppidum," or as some copies
have it, CAMALODUNUM. By Ptolemy† ΚΑΜΟΥΔΟ-
ΛΑΝΟΝ, the city of the Trinobantes. The geographer of
Ravenna‡ gives it as CAMULODULUM; and Dion Cassius§
as ΚΑΜΟΥΛΟΔΟΥΝΟΝ and ΚΑΜΑΛΟΔΟΥΝΟΝ in
different copies. In an inscription given by Gruter‖ and
Camden¶ it is CAMALODUNUM. In the Itinerary of
Antoninus, the Tabula Peutingeriana, and Tacitus,** it is
spelt as on the coins. Its site has been supposed by Camden
and others to have been at Maldon, in Essex; but there can
be no doubt that Colchester is its modern representative.
Dr. Latham, writing in Smith's Dictionary of Greek and

* Nat. Hist., lib. ii. c. 75. ‡ Lib. v. ‖ cxxxxix. 5.
† Lib. ii. c. 3. § Lib. lx. c. 21. ¶ Brit., p. 447; ed. 1637.
** Ann., lib. xii. c. 32; xiv. c. 31.

Roman Geography, expresses an opinion that the Colonia and the Camulodunum of the Itinerary are to be separated, and that the first was Colchester and the second Maldon, name for name in each case. It must, however, be borne in mind that though the name Colonia in the Itinerary stands alone, yet in Tacitus, and in the inscription already cited, it is coupled with Camulodunum, so that one and the same place must be intended. That the Camulodunum of Cunobeline was situate at Colchester and not at Maldon there is ample numismatic evidence. I have recorded no less than fifteen of the types of his coins as having been found there, while I am not aware of a single specimen having been found at Maldon. In Cromwell's History of Colchester* it is affirmed that more of Cunobeline's coins have been found at this place than at any other part of the island.

The name of the town appears to be compounded of Camulus and Dunum, the former being apparently the British name of Mars, as we learn from an inscription† found near Kilsyth, and preserved in the Hunter Museum at Glasgow; and the latter being the equivalent of "town," making the signification of the whole "the Town of Mars." The name of the only other town where the coins of Cunobeline are thought to have been struck appears to have been SOLIDUNUM, which, on similar grounds might be interpreted as the town of Minerva,‡ as SUL or SULI appears, from inscriptions, to have been a name applied to her in Britain. It is not, however, absolutely certain that the SOLIDV on those coins has a local reference, though there appears much probability that it has. If so, however, the town of Solidunum, which

* Page 572.

† DEO MAR..
CAMULO
III C
O
SC.

Hough's Camden, vol. iv. p. 101. Camulus also enters into the composition of the name of Camulogenus, a Gaulish chief mentioned by Cæsar, Bell. Gall. lib. vii. c. 57. See also Revue Num., N.S., vol. viii. p. 301.

‡ DEAE SULI –DEAE SULIMINERVAE, &c. See Arch. Assoc. Journ. vol. xiii. p. 10; Crania Britannica, c. 5, &c.

is not mentioned by any of the ancient historians, has still to be identified. It cannot for a moment be admitted that Aquae Solis, or Bath, is intended, as not only are no coins of Cunobeline found so far west, but there was, as has already been seen, an indigenous coinage in that part of Britain, of a totally different character from that of Cunobeline, though probably contemporary with it. If a conjecture is to be hazarded, I should be much more inclined to place it at Salinae, or as some copies of Ptolemy give it, Σαλιοῦαι, one of the cities of the Catyeuchlani. The whole subject is, however, involved in obscurity.

The silver and copper coins of Cunobeline may be divided into three classes. 1st. Those on which his name appears alone. 2nd. Those on which it appears in conjunction with that of his father Tasciovanus. 3rd. Those on which it is found in conjunction with the name of the place of mintage. They are arranged in the Plates in accordance with this subdivision, which was originally suggested by Pegge. The weight of the gold coins is moderately uniform, and in well preserved specimens of the larger size it is usually from 83 to 84 grains. The small pieces, which were, no doubt, quarters of the larger, generally weigh about 20 grains. I have, however, one specimen weighing 29¼ grains, which would appear to have been intended for the third or possibly three eighths of the larger pieces. The silver coins range from 12¼ to 30¼ grains, but by far the greater number are from 17 to 20 grains. It is, therefore, probable that their weight was intended to be the same as that of the small gold coins; and assuming the relative value of gold to silver to have been as ten to one, forty of the silver coins were equivalent to the larger coin in gold. The usual weight of the copper coins is from 34 to 35 grains; but there is considerable range, partly owing to difference in the state of preservation, some coins being as light as 17 grains, and others as heavy as 40 grains. It will be seen from this, that though the gold coins of Cunobeline are, as a rule, rather lighter than those of Tasciovanus, yet that the silver and copper coins approximate closely to his, and the currency of both was founded on the same principles. The gold coins are generally considerably alloyed, apparently with copper, but I have no exact analysis.

The name of Cunobeline is evidently compounded of the prefix Cuno, and of the name Belinus, Bellinus, or Belenos, under which Apollo was worshipped in Gaul, and even in Norica, and which, in the form Vellaunus, enters into the names of Cassivellaunus and Dubnovellaunus. The prefix, Cuno, has been generally supposed to mean "king" or "ruler;" but whatever was its meaning, it occasionally enters into the composition of British and Gaulish proper names, of which examples have been given by Camden. It is curious to find it recurring in Wales and Cornwall after the lapse of several centuries; but on a stone[*] of the Christian period with Runes incised along its edge, found at Trallong, Brecknockshire, is the following inscription:—CVNOGENNI FILIVS CVNOGENI HIC IACIT. On the Mên Scryfa,[†] an inscribed stone, a few miles from Penzance, we meet with the name Cunoval, RIALOBRAN CVNOVAL FIL., and on another we have CIRVSIVS HIC IACIT CVNOMORI FILIVS.

Up to the present time, no coins of any of the sons of Cunobeline are known; as the attribution which has been made of various types to Caractacus and Togodumnus cannot be sustained. At the death of Cunobeline there would appear to have been a general ferment throughout Britain, and probably intestine wars; a state of affairs which may very likely have led to a cessation of the native coinage in what had been the dominions of Cunobeline, if not elsewhere. Of his two sons, whose names are preserved, and who, on his death, appear each to have ruled over some portion of his territory, Togodumnus reigned but a very short time, and Caractacus, after the Roman invasion, appears to have occupied the position of a general

---

[*] Quart. Journ. Kilkenny Arch. Soc., vol. iii. p. 308.
[†] Borlase, Ant. of Cornwall, p. 396.

rather than that of a king, so that it is not probable that either of them struck coins. Caractacus, after his defeat by Plautius, appears to have fled from his former dominions, and when next he appears on the stage, it is as the general of the Silures, a tribe which was not under his father's rule, and which does not appear to have ever possessed a native coinage; while his father's capital, Camulodunum, had been converted into a Roman colony. What he had been doing between A.D. 43 and A.D. 50, history does not inform us; but the war between the Romans and Britons was carried on during all that period; and Tacitus incidentally mentions, that the many changes and prosperous turns of fortune had, in the meantime, advanced Caractacus to a pre-eminence over the rest of the British leaders, so that it would appear that he had taken an active part in the war during the whole period. Of his subsequent fate I need not speak; but some notice of him was necessary, to explain why the coinage of this district of Britain appears to have ceased with Cunobeline.

GOLD COINS OF CUNOBELINUS.

Plate IX., Nos. 1 and 2.

Obv.—CAMVL on a tablet with beaded edges, placed across a five-fold wreath; in the angles are V-shaped figures, alternately plain and wreathed; in each of the plain ones is an oval between two round pellets. The tablet is placed between two ring ornaments, and its ends are curved inwards. The ends of the wreath, next the tablet, are formed by narrow crescents, and the lines of which the wreath is composed are alternately beaded and plain.

Rev.—CVNOBELI.. Two horses galloping to the left; above, a large leaf and a pellet, another pellet below the tail; under the horses, a wheel of four spokes, with pellets between them. A curved exergual line separates the legend from the field, and the whole is surrounded by a beaded circle.

N. 84¾, 82$\frac{7}{8}$, 83½ grains.

Of these two coins, which are both of one type, though

presenting different portions of the device on the reverse, the first is in the British Museum, and was found near Colchester; and the second, which was found near Cambridge, is in my own collection, having been formerly in that of the late Mr. Huxtable. Mr. Warren, of Ixworth, informs me that he once possessed a coin of this type, found at Colne, near Halstead, Essex, about 1847. Another coin of the same type is in the Hunter collection, and is engraved inaccurately, as regards the legend on the obverse, in Ruding, pl. iv. 1; and Hawkins, pl. ii. 10. It is given more correctly in the Mon. Hist. Brit., pl. i. 31. Representations of my coin are given in the Num. Journ., vol. i. p. 222; Akerman, pl. xxiii. 5; Archæol., vol. xxxiii. pl. ix.; and Lelewel, pl. viii. 51. It is also mentioned in the Gent.'s Mag. for 1832, p. 213. It was at one time supposed that the legend was partly in Greek characters, CVNOBHL, but such is not the case. Had Greek letters been used, the name of Cunobeline would still have been spelt with an E, and not with an H.

The type of the obverse is an evident derivative from the original laureate head, and may be compared with Plate D, Nos. 6, 7, and 8, and others among the uninscribed series. Among the inscribed, it comes nearest to that of the coins of Tasciovanus, Plate VIII., Nos. 6, 7, 8, and 9. On the reverse there is a very remarkable recurrence to the original type, as *both* horses of the biga are given distinctly, of which indeed this is perhaps the only instance, as, with the possible exception of Plate A, No. 1, the horse on the earliest uninscribed coins, though showing eight legs, has but one head or body. The leaf above the horse is also peculiar to these coins. Whether there existed some uninscribed type, which, in the device on its reverse, came nearer to the original Macedonian stater than any of those at present known, is a question which future discoveries may solve. From the analogy of the obverse with the coins of Tasciovanus already mentioned, as well as from the strong general reminiscence of the original prototype exhibited on these coins, it would seem that they must be regarded as the earliest productions of the mint of Cunobeline. Their resemblance to his father's coins rather favour the view of his having obtained the dominion over the Trinobantes in his father's lifetime.

Plate IX., No. 3.

Obv.—CA-MV on either side of an ear of bearded corn, the stalk springing from an ornament shaped like a Gothic trefoil.

Rev.—CVNO beneath a horse galloping to the left; above, an ornament, in shape like the Prince of Wales' plume, resting on a reversed crescent. There is an exergual line, and the whole is within a beaded circle.

N. 82?, 81? grains.

The coin here engraved is in the British Museum, but I am not aware of its place of finding, nor of that of any other specimens of this type. I have published it in the Num. Chron., vol. xx. p. 157, No. 1. The obverse is much the same as that of the ordinary gold coins of Cunobeline which follow, though the ear of corn is rather more widely spread than usual; but the reverse is remarkable, as having the horse to the left, instead of to the right. The ornament above the horse is also singular, and may be intended for a flower on a long stalk, between two waving leaves. It is, however, in some degree allied to, or derived from, the bucranium, which occupies a similar position above the horse on coins of Tasciovanus, Dubnovellaunus, Andoco[mius], and Vose[nos]. An ornament of much the same character, but reversed, appears on a Gaulish gold coin, Rev. Num., N.S., vol. viii. pl. xvi. 2. The horse itself is remarkably well drawn, and the whole execution of the coin is extremely good. Though I have placed it in the Plate among the first of the gold coins of Cunobeline, I am, from the skill with which it is engraved, inclined to assign it to the latter part of his reign. I have already remarked that the type of both obverse and reverse is probably derived from the degenerate Philippus. The ear of corn on all these coins differs from that on the coins of Metapontum, in having only two rows of grains instead of three.

PLATE IX., No. 4.

Obv.—CA·MV. Ear of bearded corn with leaflets at the stem and a pellet on either side.

Rev.—CVNO. Horse prancing to the right; above, a branch. There is an exergual line, and the whole is within a beaded circle. Æ. 81 grains.

This specimen is in the British Museum. The more usual variety of this type does not show the pellets on the obverse. I have specimens, found at Weston, near Loys Weedon, Northamptonshire (84¼ grains); at Nottingham (81¼ grains); and at Lawshall, near Bury St. Edmund's (83¼ grains). Another, found near Dorchester, Oxon (83¼ grains), was in the collection of the late Rev. Trafford Leigh. One found at Colchester is engraved in Morant's Essex, pl. i. 1, as reading CVNOB on the reverse. The final B is probably inserted in error.

This type is engraved in Ruding, pl. iv. 2; Hawkins, pl. ii. 20; Akerman, pl. xxiii. 3, showing scrolls on each side of the stem; and in the Mon. Hist. Brit., pl. i. 32 and 33, the former showing traces of ring ornaments in the same position. It is also engraved in the Encyclop. Metrop., pl. i. 14. The coin engraved in Camden, No. 3; Pegge, cl. ii. 2; Stukeley, pl. vi. 6; and Lagoy, No. 2, probably belongs to this type. It differs from the succeeding coins principally in the character and execution of the horse, which is generally more spirited and in better drawing. The absence of adjuncts, in addition to the branch on the reverse, is also a characteristic. All the grains in the ear of corn on the obverse are bearded. Their usual number on all these coins is eleven.

PLATE IX., No. 5.

Obv.—CA·MV. Ear of bearded corn.

Rev.—CVNO. Horse prancing to the right; above, a branch between two pellets, and other pellets in front of the breast and beneath the tail. There is an exergual line, and the whole is within a beaded circle. Æ. 81 grains.

On some coins of this type there is also a pellet beneath the horse, and that above the branch is absent. There are two such in my collection, the one found at Biggleswade, the other at Cuddington, near Aylesbury, both 84 grains. In the collection of the late Mr. Bateman, of Youlgrave, is another, found near Colchester. Coins of this type are engraved in Ruding, pl. iv. 4; Mon. Hist. Brit., pl. i. 35; White, No. 2; and Gough's Camden, No. 2. They are characterised by a peculiar stiffness in the drawing of the horse, as well as by the numerous pellets in the field. On the obverse the stem is not shown running up the middle of the car as on the preceding coins.

Plate IX., No. 6.

Obv.—CA-M[V]. Ear of bearded corn.
Rev.—CVNO. Horse prancing to the right; above, a star of five points; between the fore-legs, a heart-shaped figure. There is an exergual line, and the whole is within a beaded circle. *N.* 82½ grains.

This coin, in the British Museum, is engraved in Ruding, pl. iv. 6, and in the Mon. Hist. Brit., pl. i. 34. It is described by Akerman, p. 100, No. 6, and Taylor Combe, p. 14, No. 7.

Its principal characteristic is the heart-shaped figure between the fore-legs of the horse, the meaning of which I am at a loss to discover. The shape of the O, which is almost of a diamond form, and the absence of beard or "haulms" from the grains of corn below the inscription, are also to be noticed. There is no appearance of the stem running up the car. A coin of nearly the same character, but with the stem running up the car, and not showing the heart between the horse's legs, has been communicated to me by Mr. C. Roach Smith. It was found at Colchester, and weighs 80 grains.

Plate IX., No. 7.

Obv.—CA-MV. Ear of bearded corn.
Rev.—CVN (or possibly CVNO). Horse prancing to the right;

above, a branch and a star of five points; below, a
ring ornament. The whole is within a beaded circle.
N. 73 grains.

This coin is in the British Museum, and has lost weight
by being filed on the reverse. It is engraved in Hawkins,
pl. ii. 21, but the central pellet of the ring ornament
has been accidentally omitted. Another coin, engraved in
Ruding, pl. iv. 5 (83½ grains); Pembroke Coins, pt. ii.
pl. 94; Pegge, cl. ii. 8; and Lagoy, No. 1, shows that there
is an exergual line. A third is engraved in the Mon. Hist.
Brit., pl. i. 30. The ear of corn on the obverse is sometimes
partly, and sometimes entirely bearded. I have a specimen
of the former sort, weighing 82½ grains. The horse on the
reverse is usually of rude execution, with a very large body
and a remarkably small head. The occurrence of the star on
the field of this and the preceding coin, shows that from
some cause or other this was a favourite symbol with the
Britons, as the same is found on the gold coins of all the
three sons of Commius, though, in those cases, in conjunction
with a mounted horseman.

PLATE IX., No. 8.

Obv.—CA·MV. Ear of bearded corn, with leaflets at its base;
in the field a small cross.

Rev.—CVN. Horse prancing to the right; above, a branch between two pellets. No exergual line, and the whole
within a beaded circle. *N*. 83½ grains.

This coin, in my own collection, was found at Childerley
Gate, near Cambridge, in 1854. Another of precisely the
same type, but not showing the small cross, was found near
Potton, in Bedfordshire, about 1858, and is in the collection
of Mr. W. Allen. Its weight is 82½ grains. I have another
specimen (80½ grains), which was found at Quainton, near
Aylesbury, likewise without the cross, but with the letters
rather larger, and the horse on the reverse bridled. Possibly
the coin found at Aston Rowant, Oxfordshire, described in
the Arch. Assoc. Journ., vol. xv. p. 290, was of the same
character. No mention is made of the cross upon it, and on

some other specimens the cross is wanting. In that engraved in Ruding, pl. iv. 3 (80½ grains); Akerman, pl. xxiii. 2; Archæol., vol. xxxiii. pl. ix.; and Mon. Hist. Brit., pl. i. 37, the cross is below the CA. The coin is said to have been found at Colchester.

On these coins the central stem of the ear of corn is shown all along it, and the lower grains are not bearded. They are characterised by the legend on the reverse being CVN, instead of CVNO, by the absence of an exergual line, and by the mane of the horse being rendered in a peculiar manner, like the posts and rail at the side of a bridge. The workmanship is very neat, but wants the spirit displayed on Nos. 3 and 4. The small cross would appear to be a private mark of the engraver, as it occurs in various positions on the coins, and even upon the horse, as will be seen in No. 9. It differs in this respect, and in the limbs not being so pointed, from the cross on the coins of the Western district, Plate I., Nos. 1 to 9, and on the uninscribed coins, Plate A, No. 8, and Plate C, No. 4.

Plate IX., No. 9.

Obv.—CA·MV. Ear of corn, as on No. 8.
Rev.—CVN. As No. 8, but a small cross on the hind-quarters of the horse. *N.*

This coin is engraved in Akerman, pl. xxiii. 1, from whence I have copied it.

There can be little doubt that the dies from which it was struck, were engraved by the same artist as those for the last coin. The horse, however, is represented as bridled.

Plate IX., No. 10.

Obv.—CA·MV. Ear of corn.
Rev.—CVN beneath a horse prancing to the right; O in front; above, a branch. There is an exergual line, and the whole is surrounded by a beaded circle.
N. 84½ grains.

This coin is in my own collection, but I do not know where it was found. A coin of this type was, however, found at

Wood Eaton, Oxfordshire, where also a coin of the type Plate E., No. 11, was discovered, and is engraved by Plot, pl. xv. 19. It is repeated in Gibson's Camden, pl. i. 28 (where it is erroneously described as brass); and in Pegge, cl. ii. 4. From its correspondence with the engraving in some of its minor details, it appears probable that mine is the identical coin drawn by Plot. The grains in the ear of corn are small, and all bearded; they are thirteen in number, instead of eleven as usual. The arrangement of the legend on the reverse is peculiar, as are also the form of the branch, and the mane and head of the horse. The O, from a flaw in the die, is tore-shaped, but was probably intended for the letter, and not for a mere adjunct. Another specimen of the same type is in the British Museum. In workmanship this coin is more nearly allied to No. 7 than to any of the other types.

I have, however, another coin found near Daklock, and weighing 84¼ grains, which is probably the work of the same engraver. The ear of corn on the obverse has the thirteen grains, but there is a pellet above the M in CAMV. On the reverse, the whole of the legend CVNO is below the horse; the final O being, as it is on most of these coins, more like a *vesica piscis* than a circle in shape.

We now come to the small gold coins of Cunobeline, which, like those of other British princes, appear to have been in nearly, if not quite all cases, the quarters of the larger coins.

PLATE IX., No. 11.

Obv.—[C]AM CV[N] on either side of an ear of corn.
Rev.—[CVN]. Horse prancing to the right; above, a branch. The whole within a beaded circle. *N*.

This curious little coin, in the collection of the Rev. J. H. Pollexfen, was found at Colchester, and shows rather more of the N on the obverse than in the engraving. Another coin with the same legend, and found near the same town, is mentioned in Cromwell's History of Colchester, p. 303. Though the legend is given in an unintelligible form, a coin of the same type is engraved in Gibson's Camden, pl. ii. 12, and Pegge, cl. ii. 5, from which it appears that there is the legend CVN, and an exergual line below the horse on the reverse. Mr. Beale Poste,* reading the legend on the obverse WICV, attributes this coin to the Huiccii, whose capital city, Huiccum, he says, Cunobeline honoured, by striking coins with their name. Huiccum, he adds, was the ancient Wigornia, or modern Worcester! I need only observe, that the Huiccii, or rather Wiccii, are first mentioned by Saxon historians, and that their name is evidently of Saxon origin. It seems curious that the name of Cunobeline should appear on both obverse and reverse; but such is the case also on one of his silver coins, Plate X., No. 5. In the present instance, it is not impossible that it originated in a mistake of the die-sinker, who put AM-CV for CA-MV, and then corrected his error by adding a C and N, making the legend CAM CVN. There are seven grains in the ear of corn, and the horse is much like that on No. 13.

Plate IX., No. 12.

Obv.—CA-M[V]. Ear of corn.
Rev.—CV[N]. Horse prancing to the right; above, a branch with three pellets beneath it, like berries; the whole within a beaded circle. *N.* 20½ grains.

This coin, found near Oxford, is in my own collection. It is peculiar from the horse upon it being in high relief, and from its having the pellets beneath the bough. The beaded circle is rather coarser than usual, and the grains in the ear of corn are eight in number.

Plate IX., No. 13.

Obv.—CA-M[V]. Ear of corn.
Rev.—CVN. Horse prancing to the right; above, a branch. *N.* 20 grains.

This is the commonest type of the small gold coins of Cunobeline, and has several minor varieties. I have a

* Celtic Inscriptions, &c., p. 93.

specimen, found near Oxford, reading CVNO on the reverse, and have seen another with the same legend, which was found at Oundle, Northamptonshire. Another, found at Reculver, engraved in Battely's Antiquitates Rutupinæ, pl. vi., shows a crescent in front of the horse and a pellet above. I have seen another specimen found near Tring, Herts. Another was found at Chingford, Essex (Arch. Assoc. Journ., vol. xiii. p. 334). Mr. Godwin, of Newbury, has a specimen found in that neighbourhood. The type is engraved in White, No. 5; Gough's Camden, No. 30; Ruding, pl. iv. 7; Akerman, pl. xxiii. 4; and Mon. Hist. Brit., pl. i. 38. Stukeley's pl. xix. 2, and pl. xx. 7, are also probably intended for this type. It is also described by Duchalais, No. 713, who compares it with that of the coins of Metapontum.

I have a coin of this type, but of rude workmanship, which is of fine gold, weighing 29¼ grains, and would appear to represent three-eighths of the larger pieces. It cannot, however, be regarded as an established fact, that coins were issued to represent that value.

PLATE IX., No. 14.

Obv.—CA-M[V]. Ear of corn.
Rev.—CVN. Horse prancing to the right; above, a branch; the whole within a beaded circle. N. 20¼ grains.

This coin, in my own collection, was found at Garlington, near Oxford. I have another, weighing 21 grains, found at Swaffham, Cambridgeshire. The ear of corn upon them has seven grains (the lower ones not bearded), and has leaflets at the base; the stalk is shown all the way up the ear. Another, with nine grains in the ear, found at Debden, Essex, weighing 20 grains, has been communicated to me by Mr. C. Roach Smith. The horse on the reverse has a peculiar mane, the same as on Nos. 8 and 9, so that these coins, though not, as far as has hitherto been observed, showing the small cross as a mint-mark, are probably by the same engraver. It is difficult to assign any chronological order to these small gold coins; but possibly No. 12 is the earliest, and No. 14 the latest among them.

SILVER COINS OF CUNOBELINUS.

Plate X., No. 1.

Obv.—CVNO-BELI in the two compartments of a tablet; above and below, a small star; the whole within a beaded circle.

Rev.—CVN. Horseman galloping to the right. There is an exergual line, and the whole is within a beaded circle. Æ. $16\frac{7}{8}$ grains.

This coin, from the Hunter collection, is engraved in Ruding, pl. iv. 13, but the tablet is not faithfully given. This is copied by Akerman, pl. xxiii. 11, and Lelewel, pl. viii. 53. Another coin of the same type is engraved by White, No. 13, and repeated in Gough's Camden, pl. i. 20. This, however, reads CVNO-BELIN, while another in Ruding, pl. iv. 12, for which "White" is given as the authority, reads CVNO-BEL only. This latter coin is also engraved in Akerman, pl. xiii. 10; its weight is $30\frac{1}{8}$ grains. The types of both obverse and reverse are essentially British. The placing of the legend on a tablet on the obverse is common on the coins of Tinc[ommius] and Verica, as well as on coins of Tasciovanus. On those of the latter with TASCIO RICON, &c., we have the two compartments, which occur also on several other coins of Cunobeline, both in silver and copper. The horseman on the reverse probably carries a short lance or staff, and may be compared with that on the coins of Tasciovanus, Plate VI., Nos. 3 and 4. The repetition of the name of Cunobeline upon the reverse is worthy of notice. It occurs also on No. 5. It has been suggested that the CVN on the reverse is significant of the town of CVNETIO (*Marlborough* ?). But it is to be observed, first, that had coins of Cunobelius been minted there, the name of the town, if it was intended to be given, would have been placed upon them in a less ambiguous form;

and, secondly, that there is no proof of the dominions of Cunobeline having extended so far west as Cunetio. The type is moreover most intimately connected with that of the succeeding coins, which there is some reason for supposing were minted in another locality.

PLATE X., Nos. 2 AND 3.

Obv.—CVNO - BELI (*retrograde*) in two compartments of a tablet; above and below, a star; the whole within a beaded circle.

Rev.—LDA(?) Horseman to the right, holding a short lance or staff. The whole within a beaded circle.
Æ. 13,$\frac{3}{5}$ grains.

Of these coins No. 2 is in the Hunter collection, and is engraved in Ruding, pl. iv. 14; Akerman, pl. xxiii. 12; Stukeley, pl. xiv. 6. It is also cited in Whitaker's History of Manchester, vol. i. p. 305, as exhibiting a hat on the horseman, which "corresponds pretty well to the form and appearance of the modern." No. 3 is in the British Museum, and is engraved in Hawkins, pl. ii. 24, and in the Mon. Hist. Brit., pl. i. 24.

The type is precisely that of the preceding coins, but the legend on the obverse is retrograde. The A-like form of the L is worth notice. The horseman wears a cap much like that which is found on some of the coins of Tasciovanus. The legend on the reverse has hitherto been regarded as illegible. It appears to me, however, that in all probability it is, like that on the obverse, retrograde. If so, it is possible that the letters are LIDV, and are the termination of the word SOLIDV, which occurs on the silver coin of Cunobelino, Plate XI., No. 6; in which case these coins are to be referred to the same place of mintage. Under any circumstances, I think that they are to be ranked among the earlier coins of Cunobeline, both from their general resemblance to some of the coins of Tasciovanus, and from their showing none of those signs of Roman influence in their designs, which are visible on what are probably the later coins.

PLATE X., No. 4.

Obv.—CVN. on a tablet within a beaded circle.
Rev.—Wolf (?) springing to the left. Æ. 20 grains.

This coin, in the Hunter collection, is engraved in Ruding, pl. iv. 10; Akerman, pl. xxiii. 14; and Mon. Hist. Brit., pl. i. 23. Another is engraved in Wise, pl. xvi. 23; and Pegge, cl. i. 4, as being of brass, but on inquiry I was informed by the late Dr. Dandinel that the coin in the Bodleian collection is silver.

The type of the obverse is extremely simple, and may be compared with that of the coin of Tasciovanus, Plate VI., No. 2, though it has not the peculiar triple circle. The animal on the reverse has been variously described by different writers, and affords a good instance of the unsettled character of the zoology of British coins. By Ruding it is called a dog, by Akerman a griffin, by Wise a horse, by Pegge a sheep or dog, while in the Mon. Hist. Brit. it is called a wolf! I think that it was intended for the latter animal, which seems also to occur on some of the uninscribed gold coins, Plate C, Nos. 2 and 3. Like the foregoing coins, this appears to be purely British in its types, and may, therefore, be referred to the early part of the reign of Cunobeline.

PLATE X., No. 5.

Obv.—CVN. on a tablet; above and below, a ring ornament.
Rev.—CV—N. Hercules walking to the right, and carrying his club upon his shoulder; in the field, three pellets. A beaded circle on both obverse and reverse.
Æ. 15½ grains.

This coin, from the Pembroke and Huxtable collections, is now in my own cabinet. It has been engraved among the Pembroke coins, pt. ii. pl. 94; in Pegge, cl. i. 3; and Lugoy, No. 5; but in all these cases erroneously as Æ. instead of Æ. The coin in Stukeley, pl. v. 10, appears to have been a badly preserved specimen of the same type. That engraved in Gibson's Camden, pl. ii. 23, and Pegge, cl. i. 2, does not show the ends of the tablet, nor the beaded circle on the obverse. My coin is engraved also in the Mon. Hist. Brit., pl. i. 20; the Arch. Assoc. Journ., vol. v. p. 152; and Beale Poste, p. 152.

The type of the obverse is very much the same as that of the preceding coin, and differs only in having the ring ornaments above and below the tablet. It may be compared with the coins of Verica, Plate II., No. 14; Plate III., Nos. 1 and 2; and that reading RVFS, Plate VII., No. 14.

It is difficult to say from whence the figure of Hercules on the reverse was derived, as I do not remember to have seen Hercules in this attitude on any Greek or Roman coins, and the temptation is strong to regard it as a representation of the DEVS HERCVLES S. EGONTIACORVM recorded on the inscription found at Silchester. The same deity appears with more classical attributes on Nos. 11, 12, and 13 of this Plate; but I think that the appearance of Hercules on the present coin is a sign of the intercourse with Rome having begun to exercise an influence on the productions of the British mints, though not nearly to the same extent as it it did on coins which will subsequently be described.

When speaking of No. 1, I have alluded to the occurrence of the CVN on both sides of this coin, and shown the improbability of either of them designating CVNETIO. Should any one be inclined to adopt that hypothesis, I still think that they will pause before adopting Mr. Poste's * view, that the rings on the obverse may possibly have had a reference to the Druidical circles abounding in the neighbourhood of Marlborough.

No. 6 in this Plate is blank.

PLATE X., No. 7.

Obv.—CVNO, on a tablet in the centre of a wreath. The whole within a beaded circle.

Rev.—TASC.F. Pegasus prancing to the right. There is an exergual line, and the whole is surrounded by a beaded circle. Æ. 18½ grains.

* British Coins, p. 152.

This coin was found at Sandy, Bedfordshire, in 1837, and is engraved in the Num. Chron., vol. vii. pl. v., No. 1; Mon. Hist. Brit., pl. i. 15; Archæologia, vol. xxxiii. pl. ix.; and Akerman, pl. xxiii. 13. A coin of the same type was published by Camden (Gibson's ed., pl. i. 18), who, however, read the legend on the reverse as TASCE, and this error is repeated in Stukeley, pl. viii. 6; and Pegge, cl. iii. 2.

This coin, like those which follow, belongs to the second of the classes into which the coins of Cunobeline may be divided; viz., those which bear the name of his father, Tasciovanus, in addition to his own. There can be no reasonable doubt that the TASC.F. upon it is analogous with the DIVI.F. on the coins of Augustus and Tiberius; and, indeed, this coin was among those cited by Mr. Birch,[*] when he first propounded his views as to the interpretation of "the TASCIA" on British coins. Though still, to a great extent, preserving the character of a purely British coin, yet the introduction of the wreath around the tablet, and the Pegasus on the reverse, as well as the great neatness of the workmanship, seem to testify to Roman influences having been at work. The type of the obverse is identical with that of the silver coin, Plate XI., No. 1, though the wreath in that case appears to be of olive, and in this of laurel. In both, the junction of the two branches forming the garland is on the left side of the tablet, and not below it. The same may be remarked of the copper coin, Plate XII., No. 13, which has a similar obverse. The wreaths round the coins of Eppillus and of Verulam are continuous. The Pegasus is of much more frequent occurrence on the coins of Tasciovanus than on those of Cunobeline.

In Morant's Essex, pl. i. 2, and Stukeley, pl. viii. 7, a silver coin is engraved as of Cunobeline, but anepigraphous. On the obverse is a head in profile, to the right, possibly of Ammon, and on the reverse a Pegasus to the right. The type is not now known, but possibly may yet be re-discovered.

---

[*] See Num. Chron., vol. vii. p. 75, and Arch. Journ., vol. iv. p. 5.

PLATE X., No. 8.

Obv.—CVNOBELINI. Beardless head to the right; the whole within a beaded circle.

Rev.—TASCIO. Horse galloping to the right; above, an open crescent; there is an exergual line, and the whole is surrounded by a beaded circle. Æ. 20½, 18¾ grains.

This coin, from the Pembroke collection (pt. ii. pl. 94), is now in my own cabinet. It has been engraved in Lagoy, pl. i. 8, and Mon. Hist. Brit., pl. i. 10. Other representations of the same type will be found in Gibson's Camden, pl. ii. 39; Stukeley, pl. x. 6; Pegge, cl. iii. 4, 8; Ruding, App. pl. xxix. 7; and Akerman, pl. xxiii. 20.

I have another specimen, weighing 18¾ grains, which was found at Sandy, Beds, and kindly presented to me by Mr. James Wyatt, of Bedford. A coin of the same type, but not showing the TASCIO on the reverse, has been figured in Gibson's Camden, pl. i. 5; Pegge, cl. i. 1; Stukeley, pl. x. 4; Ruding, pl. iv. 10; Akerman, pl. xxiii. 8; and Mon. Hist. Brit., pl. i. 25.

From the arrangement of the hair, it seems not altogether improbable that the head is laureate, and from its resemblance to that on the copper coin, Plate XII., No. 1, with which this coin corresponds in the genitive termination of the legend, it is possible that we have here the portrait of Cunobeline. From the execution of the coin, there can be but little doubt of its being the work of some Roman artist, or of some one brought up in a Roman school of engraving. At the same time, the type of the reverse, the ever recurring horse, with a crescent above it, like that on the uninscribed coin, Plate D, No. 10, shows that the indigenous types were by no means forgotten.

PLATE X., No. 9.

Obv.—CVNO. Winged bust, with bare beardless head to the right, the shoulders draped. The whole within a beaded circle.

Rev.—TASCIO. Sphinx seated to the left, upon an exergual line. The whole within a beaded circle. Æ. 17½, 18¾ grains.

This coin is in the national collection. The type has long been known, having been engraved by Speed, though from an imperfect coin. It is engraved in Gibson's Camden, pl. i. 20; Gough's Camden, pl. i. 16; Stukeley, pl. vi. 8, and xxi. 7; Pegge, cl. iii. 3 and 7;[*] Pettingal, No. 5;[*] Pinkerton, vol. i. pl. ii. 5; Ruding, pl. iv. 8; Akerman, pl. xxiii. 6; and Mon. Hist. Brit., pl. i. 12. See also Whitaker's Manchester, vol. ii. p. 11. A coin of this type, found at Colchester, is given by Morant, and in Cromwell's Colchester, p. 373.

The types appear to have been borrowed from Roman sources. The bust on the obverse, though it has much more of a masculine than a feminine appearance, is probably that of Victory, whose draped bust occurs on coins of the Carisia and Mussidia families (Cohen, pl. x. 1, 2, 4; pl. xxix. 3), and also on those of the Titia and Valeria families (Cohen, pl. xxxix. 3; pl. xl. 3 and 4). The quinarius of the Titia family is that which comes nearest, both in size and in the character of the bust, to this British coin, which, however, has still distinctive features of its own. The sphinx on the reverse is in precisely the same attitude as that on the denarii of the Carisia family (Cohen, pl. x. 8). It is, however, to the left instead of to the right, and the wings, which in character resemble those of the Pegasus on coins of Tasciovanus and Cunobeline, are turned upwards instead of downwards. The seated sphinx occurs also on coins of Augustus (Cohen, Nos. 249 and 250), and Stukeley[†] refers to one of the coins of this emperor, struck in Egypt, for the origin of this type. It has been thought by some that the sphinx, which is also found on other coins of Cunobeline, was adopted by him out of compliment to Augustus, with whom it was a favourite device. We learn, indeed, from both Suetonius[‡] and Pliny[§] that it was the device upon his seal, before he changed it for that of the head of Alexander the Great. His reason for using it appears to

[*] Erroneously as reading TACIO. [†] Vit. Aug. cap. I.
[‡] Plate VI. [§] Nat. Hist., lib. xxxvii. c. 1.

have arisen from his finding, among his mother's jewels, two seals with this device, so much alike that they could not be distinguished, one of which he carried with him in the Civil War, while with the other his friends sealed the edicts issued in his name at Rome. As these latter, like those sealed with the frog of Mæcenas, were frequently demands upon the purses of the citizens, the seal of the sphinx got into bad odour, and this led to its being changed for that with the head of Alexander the Great. That this type on the coins of Cunobeline should have been adopted out of compliment to Augustus, is therefore very doubtful. Had there been any such intention of flattery, the capricorn, such as we find on the coins of Verica and Eppillus, would have been a much more suitable device.

Some further remarks on the sphinx, in connection with these coins, will be found at p. 339.

Plate X., No. 10.

Obv.—TASCIIOVAN. Female bust, the hair gathered into a roll and tied with a fillet behind; the shoulders draped; the whole within a beaded circle.

Rev.—CVNOBELI. Apollo seated, naked, except round the loins, and playing the lyre; behind, a tree. There is an exergual line, and the whole is surrounded by a beaded circle. Æ. 19½ grains.

This coin, here engraved from a specimen in the British Museum, was also known to Speed and Camden, though the obverse legend was misread as TASNOVANE and TASC VANIT.

It is engraved in Gibson's edition of Camden, pl. i. 7 and 23, and in Gough's, pl. i. 7. The type is also given in Stukeley, pl. vi. 4; Pegge, cl. iv. 1 and 3; Ruding, pl. iv. 9; Hawkins, pl. ii. 23; Akerman, pl. xxiii. 7; Mon. Hist. Brit., pl. i. 14; Arch. Assoc. Journ. vol. v, p. 152; and Beale Poste, p. 153.

The execution of this coin is admirable; indeed, both in drawing and workmanship it is superior to many of the

Roman coins of the period. The devices on either side appear to be purely classical. On the obverse the head is apparently that of Diana, of much the same character as that on the common silver coins of Massilia. There is hardly enough shown of the head to see whether it has the diadem and crescent, with which the head of this goddess is usually represented on the Roman family coins. The figure of Apollo on the reverse, as Stukeley long since pointed out, is copied from a coin of Augustus (Cohen, No. 70), on which the god is represented naked, seated on a rock, and playing the lyre. The device differs, however, in some of its details, a tree being introduced behind the figure, which also, instead of being on a rock, is seated on a cylindrical object, possibly the *cortina*. Both Diana and Apollo* were held in especial reverence by Augustus, as he considered that two of his principal victories had been won under their auspices—that over Sextus Pompeius at Artemisium or Dianium, near Mylæ; and that over Antony, off Actium, where there was a celebrated temple of Apollo. The Actian Apollo is frequently represented on the coins of Augustus, who enlarged his temple and restored the ancient games in his honour. He is, however, usually clad in a *stola* flowing down to his feet.

Though in the present instance this stola is wanting, we have seen that on one at least of the coins of Augustus, the Apollo Citharœdus is naked; and looking at the types of this coin of Cunobeline, there seems fair ground for supposing that the friendship or flattery of Augustus may have conduced to their adoption.

Plate X., No. 11.

Obv.—CV—NO. Hercules standing, his club held downwards in his right hand; behind, to his left, a lion (?). There is an exergual line, and the whole is within a beaded circle.

Rev.—TASCIIOVA. Female seated on a lion (?). The whole within a beaded circle. Æt. 10,¾ grains.

---
* Eckhel, Doct. Num., vi. 93.

This coin has also long been known, and is engraved in
Pettingal, No. 4; Pegge, cl. iv. 5; Gough's Camden,
pl. i. 15; Ruding, pl. iv. 15; Hawkins, pl. ii. 22; Akerman,
pl. xxiii. 13; and Mon. Hist. Brit., pl. i. 13. There are
specimens both in the British Museum and Hunter collec‑
tions. The devices on these coins stand out in bold relief,
and there is considerable spirit in the figures, especially in
that of Hercules. The animal behind him appears to have
been intended for a lion (though it may possibly be only
the lion's skin); but, as was the case with the former
coin, on which the same deity appears (No. 5), it is hard to
point out the exact source from which the type was derived.
Ruding* suggests that it is possibly from one of the coins of
Tiberius—I presume a colonial coin. He regards the figure
on the reverse as Europa on the bull, and considers the type
to have been derived from another coin of that emperor. It
might, too, have been taken from a coin of the Valeria
family (Cohen, xl. 7). On the Museum coin the animal has,
however, much more the appearance of being a lion, so that
the figure is probably that of Cybele, the mother of the gods.
It seems more in conformity with what we find on the
preceding and following coins (which are linked with this by
the legend TASCIIOVANI being given at full length) that
we should find a divinity of the Roman Pantheon on both
obverse and reverse, rather than a mythical princess. If so,
however, the type was apparently derived from a Greek
rather than a Roman source, as Cybele on the family coins
is usually drawn in a chariot by lions, and does not appear
seated on a lion on any purely Roman coin of so early a date
as Augustus or Tiberius. The manner in which the NO on
the obverse is placed at a higher level than the CV, so as to
leave room for the lion, is worthy of notice.

PLATE X., Nos. 12 AND 13.

Obv.—CVNOBELINVS. Partially draped figure marching to
the right, holding in his right hand a short staff or

* Vol. ii. p. 271.

sword, and carrying a dead animal on his shoulders. The whole within a beaded circle.

Rev.—TASCIOVANI .. (?). Partially draped figure standing to the left; in the left hand a bow, the right pointing to the head of an animal standing behind. The whole within a beaded circle.

Æ. 17 grains, 16½ grains.

These are the only two coins at present known of this type, and both are engraved, so as to complete the devices as far as possible. The first is in the British Museum, and was published by me in the Num. Chron., vol. xviii., p. 44, No. 10; and the second, which was found at Cotton End, near Bedford, is, through Mr. Wyatt's kindness, in my own collection. Unfortunately neither is in fine preservation, and it is difficult to say whom the principal figures represent. That on the obverse appears to be Hercules carrying on his shoulders the fruits of one of his "labours." At one time I thought it was the Nemean lion or Erymanthean boar, but from my coin the animal appears to be a stag with its back downwards, and the hind-leg falling back above the arm of Hercules. It is therefore probably the stag of Cerynea with the golden horns and brazen feet. The figure on the reverse is probably that of Diana Venatrix with a dog at her feet, though it must be confessed that the chaste goddess is rather scantily clothed. There are coins of Augustus with much the same type on the reverse, struck between B.C. 12 and 10, of one of which a woodcut is here given. The type may also be compared with that of a coin of Rhegium, Hunter Coins, pl. xliv. 20. The purely mythological character of the devices on Nos. 9 to 13 on this Plate, is very remarkable. From the workmanship, it would appear that all the silver coins of Cunobeline with the name of Tasciovanus upon them were executed either by foreign artists, or by those who had had the benefit of Roman instruction. On a comparison with the coins which bear either the name of Cunobeline alone, or else associated with that of Camulodunum, it will be found that both these classes show far more of the purely British element, than that which we have just been considering.

PLATE X., No. 14.

Obv.—CVN. in the centre of a wreath, surrounded by a beaded circle.

Rev.—CAM. Dog or she-wolf standing on an exergual line, and placing one of its fore-feet upon a serpent.
Æ. 19 grains.

For an impression of this coin, which has, however, been slightly injured, I am indebted to Mr. C. Roach Smith. The original was formerly in the collection of the late Mr. John Trotter Brockett, of Newcastle-on-Tyne, but I do not know what became of it on the dispersion of his coins. The obverse bears a strong general resemblance to that of No. 7, though the name is not upon a tablet. The reverse is very remarkable, and must be regarded as in some manner connected with the early British mythology, though I must confess myself entirely at a loss to offer any satisfactory elucidation of the device. The attitude of the dog is very like that in which it is represented on the small brass coins of Campanian fabric bearing the name of Roma (Cohen, pl. lxxi. 11), but there is no serpent on those coins. The type is hitherto unpublished, and belongs to the third class of the coins of Cunobeline—those with the name of his capital, Camulodunum, upon them.

PLATE XI., No. 1.

Obv.—CVNO on a tablet within an olive (?) wreath. The whole surrounded by a beaded circle.

Rev.—CAMV on a tablet beneath a griffin seated to the right. The whole within a beaded circle. Æt. 17½ grains.

This coin, which was found at Ixworth, Suffolk, is engraved in the Archaeologia, vol. xxxiii. pl. ix.; Mon. Hist. Brit., pl. i. 40; and Akerman, pl. xxiii. 17; though in the latter case, from some inadvertence, it is not described in the text. The device of the obverse is much the same as that of the silver coins, Plate X., Nos. 7 and 14, and that in copper,

Plate XII., No. 13, though the wreath appears to be formed of olive instead of laurel. The reverse exhibits some analogy with that of the silver coin of Dubnovellaunus, Plate IV., No. 11. It may likewise be compared with the copper coins of Cunobeline, Plate XIII., Nos. 1 and 2, on which a sow and a lion occupy the position of the griffin on this coin, above a tablet similarly inscribed. Like the preceding coin, this and the succeeding silver coins belong to the class on which we find the name of the king combined with that of the town where the coins were struck. It shows, however, more of Roman art than the coins of the two succeeding types, though the devices may be regarded as almost purely British. The griffin occurs on the silver coin of Tasciovanus, Plate VI., No. 6, and on some of the copper coins of Cunobeline, as well as on that in silver of Dubnovellaunus already mentioned. The griffin in a similar posture is found on the coins of Abdera.

Plate XI., No. 2.

Obv.—CAMVL, in front of a bare beardless head to the left. The whole within a beaded circle.

Rev.—CVNO beneath Victory seated to the right, her right hand extended, and holding a garland; in front, a ring ornament. The whole within a beaded circle.

Æ. 18 1/2 grains.

Plate XI., No. 3.

Obv. and Rev.—In all respects as No. 2, but reading CAMV. Æ.

Specimens of each of these varieties are in the British Museum, and the type has been known ever since the days of Speed, who engraved one of those reading CAMV. This variety is also to be found in Gibson's Camden, pl. i. 21; Pegge, class ii. 3; Akerman, pl. xxiii. 9; Arch. Assoc. Journ., vol. v. 151; and Beale Poste, p. 151. That with CAMVL is engraved in White, No. 14; Stukeley, pl. v. 8; Gough's Camden, pl. i. 21; Ruding, pl. iv. 11; and Mon. Hist. Brit., pl. i. 39.

The head on the obverse is of rude workmanship, and

bears some resemblance to that on the copper coin No. 11, and on the coins of Tasciovanus, Plate VIII, Nos. 3 and 4. It has by some been thought to represent the head of Mars, to whom, under the name of Camulus, the city of Camulodunum is supposed to have been sacred; and the presence of a Victory on the reverse rather strengthens this view. Supposing this to be the case, the legend must, however, still be referred to the town, and not to the god of war. Though frequently bearded on Roman coins, Mars is in general represented with a youthful countenance and unbearded. There can be but very little doubt of the reverse of this coin having been copied from that of the denarii of the Porcia family, on which a Victory is seated in a similar attitude, and in a similar chair. There is, notwithstanding, considerable resemblance between this and the seated Victory on the Gaulish coin in brass, Rev. Num., vol. xx., pl. v. 2. The ring ornament in front, and the hat-like covering on the head, as well as the rudeness of the work, prove it, however, to have been engraved by a British artist. A similar seated Victory, but to the left, occurs on the copper coins of Cunobeline, Plate XI., Nos. 5, 7, and 8, and the figure on the uncertain coin, Plate XIII, No. 8, appears to be of the same character. Stukeley has referred the origin of the type to the gold quinarii of Augustus, with Victory seated on a globe; but the coin already cited is more probably the prototype.

Plate XI., No. 4.

Obv.—CA—MV. An object resembling a flower with two rolled leaflets at its base.

Rev.—CVNO in the exergue beneath a horse walking to the right, his head turned over his back; behind, a star (?). The whole within a beaded circle. Æ.

I have taken this coin, which is also engraved in Akerman, pl. xxiii. 21, from a cast kindly furnished to me by Mr. C. Roach Smith.

The device on the obverse is singular, but is evidently connected with the ear of corn upon the gold coins. The lower part bears some resemblance to the flower (?) above the horse on Plate IX., No. 3. The attitude of the horse on the reverse of this coin is very unusual, and taken altogether it is a most curious little coin. Its workmanship is remarkably good.

PLATE XI., No. 6.

Obr.—CVNO. Naked male figure, with mantle over his shoulders, his right hand extended, and holding a purse (?); his left resting on a *pedum*, or long caduceus. The whole within a beaded circle.

Rev.—SOLIDV in the centre of a circle, formed of two lines twisted into a guilloche pattern, with a pellet in each loop. The whole within a beaded circle.

Æ. 17, 16¾ grains.

Through inadvertence, I have engraved the obverse of this coin as the reverse, SOLIDV being on the convex side of the coin, and CVNO on the concave.

The type is engraved, but erroneously, as reading SOLIDO, in Taylor Combe, pl. i. 19; Ruding, App., pl. xxix. 6; Hawkins, pl. ii. 27; Akerman, pl. xxiii. 19; Lelewel, pl. viii. 52; Arch. Assoc. Journ., vol. ii. p. 18; and Beale Poste, p. 32.

The legend of this specimen, which is in the British Museum, is correctly given in the Mon. Hist. Brit., pl. i. 47. That here engraved is in my own cabinet, and was formerly in the Dimsdale and Huxtable collections.

The standing figure has been thought to be Bacchus,* copied from some Greek coin, or Hercules † with the lion's skin; and the object in his right hand has been regarded as a purse, a pair of scales, or a human head! The attitude of the figure is very much like that of Neptune on the common coins of Agrippa, but on these coins the object in the right hand is certainly not a dolphin, and that in the left has much more the appearance of a pedum or a long caduceus, than of a trident. It seems possible, therefore, that the figure may be

---
* Ruding, vol. ii. p. 290. † Beale Poste, p. 32.

Mercury, unless indeed the object in the right hand is a human head, in which case the figure must be that of Perseus, whom we find on the copper coin, Plate XII., No. 10; but we must wait for the discovery of a coin in perfect preservation before this question can be satisfactorily determined. The twisted circle around the SOLIDV is the same as that around SEGO, on Plate viii. 10, and this circumstance strengthens the probability of the legend having a local signification. As has been already remarked, the site of Solidunum, if such a town was designated by the coin, has still to be determined. Mr. Beale Poste[*] considers that this name is only another form of that of Aquæ Solis, or Bath, where the goddess Suli Minerva was worshipped, according to inscriptions found there. But these coins cannot have been struck at Bath, as there is no evidence of the western part of Britain ever having been under the rule of Cunobeline, and his coins do not range so far west as Bath. Ptolemy mentions Verulamium and Salinæ (Σαλῖναι, Σαλῆναι, or Σαλιναι), as the two principal towns of the Catyeuchlani, but whether Salinæ is to be identified with the Sallouiaron of the Itineraries, or, as seems more probable, with Sandy, in Bedfordshire, is matter of dispute. Dr. Thurnam[†] fixes it at Droitwich, in Worcestershire, with which the longitude, as given in many copies of Ptolemy, seems to agree. There are, however, various readings of the numerals, and it appears to me that Droitwich is considerably too far to the west, especially as it lies beyond the range of the coins of Tasciovanus and Cunobeline, who both appear to have been chiefs of the Catyeuchlani. But, wherever Salinæ was situate, there is just sufficient resemblance between its name and that upon these coins to make it possible that they were issued from a mint at that place. It will be remembered that the uncertain legend on the reverse of Plate X., No. 3, has some appearance of being a portion of the same word, SOLIDV.

We now come to the copper or bronze coinage of Cuno-

[*] Brit. Coins, p. 119; Celt. Inse., p. 70.   [†] Crania Brit., p. 110.

beline, which may be divided into the same three classes as his silver coins.

COPPER COINS OF CUNOBELINUS.

PLATE XI., No. 5.

Obv.—CVNOB (retrograde) ELINI in two compartments of a tablet; above and below, a ring ornament; the whole within a beaded circle.

Rev.—Naked (?) Victory seated to the left, her right hand extended and holding a wreath. Æ.

PLATE XI., No. 7.

Obv.—CVNOB-ELINI, as No. 5.
Rev.—As No. 5. Æ. 38 $\frac{1}{2}$, 35 $\frac{1}{2}$ grains.

PLATE XI., No. 8.

Obv.—CVNOBE-LINI, as on No. 7.
Rev.—As No. 7. Æ. 34 grains.

Of these coins No. 5 is in the Bodleian collection, at Oxford, and No. 8 in that of Mr. Joseph Warren, the latter was found near Ixworth, Suffolk. One of the same type, in my own collection, was found near Dorchester, Oxfordshire. No. 7, in the Hunter collection, is engraved in Ruding, pl. v. 20; Akerman, pl. xxiv. 14; and Mon. Hist. Brit., pl. i. 20. Coins of this type have been found at Chipping Warden (Arch. Assoc. Journ., vol. ii. p. 101), at Verulam (Num. Chron., vol. xx. p. 107), and at Oundle, Northamptonshire. The type of the obverse is the same as that of the silver coins, Plate X., Nos. 1 to 3, but with ring ornaments above and below the tablet, instead of stars. The inscription CAMVLODVNO is presented in a similar manner on the copper coin, Plate XII., No. 9.

The Victory on the reverse may be compared with that on the silver coins, Nos. 2 and 3 in the same Plate, though seated in the opposite direction. Although I have placed these coins in the first class, viz., those with the name of

Cunobeline only, I am very doubtful whether I am not wrong in so doing, as I believe it will eventually be found that the reverse has the legend CAMV in the exergue.

Plate XL, No. 9.

Obv.—Victory, partially draped, marching to the right, and holding a garland.

Rev.—CVN. Horseman galloping to the right. 49 grains.

This coin, found at Great Berkhamsted, Herts, is published in Akerman, p. 192, No. 34, and in the Num. Chron., vol. ii. p. 192, No. 7, from whence I have taken it. I have never seen the coin, but possibly there may here also be traces of CAMV on the obverse. The Victory appears to differ in the attitude and drapery from that on other coins of Cunobeline. The horseman is apparently unarmed; but judging from the engraving, the type must be rather indistinct upon the coin. A similar conjunction of the types of a Victory and horseman occurs on the gold coin of Eppillus, Plate III., No. 11, on which, too, the Victory presents much the same characters.

Plate XL, No. 10.

Obv.—Bearded full face, occupying the whole of the field, surrounded by a beaded circle.

Rev.—CVN. Wild boar standing to the left beneath a branch of a tree, his tail formed with a ring ornament.

Æ. 33 grains.

This most remarkable coin is in the British Museum, and was first published by Akerman, pl. xxiv. 16. The device on the obverse cannot be paralleled in the whole British series, though I have shown, at p. 108, the tendency of the reverse of the gold coins of the Sussex type to assume the form of a full face, as is exemplified by the coin of Tinc[ommius] with the head of Medusa, Plate II., No. 4. In the Gaulish series, however, we find, as has already been pointed out by Mr. Akerman, coins which correspond most closely in type with this. The small coins in billon, of which one is shown in the annexed woodcut, and of which a large number were found near Angers (Revue Num., vol. ii. pl. vii. 15; Lambert, pl. vii. 27; Lelewel, pl. vii. 65), though

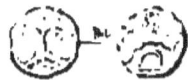

on a smaller scale, have the same full face on the obverse, and a boar on the reverse, though turned to the right. Though the workmanship of this coin of Cunobeline is good and very spirited, the types must be regarded as thoroughly British, without the slightest trace of Roman influence. The head on the obverse may indeed be the head of Hercules, such as is seen on the coins of Gades (Akerman, pl. iv. 4; Florez, pl. xxvii. 12), but in this case bearded; there appears, however, to have been a Hercules in the Celtic mythology, as testified by the Hercules of the Segontinci, before his worship was introduced by the Romans. The boar on the reverse is the favourite Celtic symbol, the *Sus Gallicus* of French numismatists, which is found on numerous other British coins. The branch above it occurs in much the same position upon the next coin. It has the appearance of an olive branch, but whether it is significant of Peace I will not attempt to decide. The introduction of the ring ornament, so as to form a constituent part of the boar's tail, is worthy of notice, and adds to the essentially native character of the coin, which seems to refer it to the early part of the reign of Cunobeline.

Plate XI., No. 11.

Obv.—CVNO retrograde, in front of a bare beardless head in profile to the left, the whole within a beaded circle.

Rev.—Boar standing to the left, above his head a branch; two stars (?) above his back; below, a ring ornament. The whole within a beaded circle. Æ. 18,³⁄₁₀ grains.

This coin, in the Hunter collection, is engraved in Ruding, pl. v. 22, and Akerman, pl. xxiv. 12. The head on the obverse appears to be the same as that on the silver coins, Plate XI., Nos. 2 and 3, and on some of the coins of Tasciovanus. The reverse is intimately connected with that of the last coin; but, in addition to the branch, shows two stars above the boar, the meaning of which it is hopeless to attempt to fathom.

If, as from the type we seem justified in doing, we are to refer this coin to the same period as the preceding coin, the difference in the weight and size may lead to the conclusion that it represented only one half of the value of the larger piece. We have seen that this was probably the case with some of the coins of Tasciovanus; but with those of Cunobeline there is so considerable a range in weight, even among coins of precisely the same type, that no satisfactory conclusion can be grounded on the evidence of two or three specimens only.

Plate XL, No. 12.

Obv.—Winged animal standing to the left, but with its head turned backwards to the right; the whole within a beaded circle.

Rev.—CVN. Victory standing to the left, completely draped; with her left hand holding a palm-branch downwards, and with what is possibly a scroll in her right; the whole within a beaded circle. Æ. 41, 34½, 31 grains.

This coin, in my own collection, was found near Canterbury. Another, of the same type, was found at the Slade, Boughton Monchelsea, Kent, where other British and several Roman coins have been found. It is engraved in C. Roach Smith's Coll. Ant., vol. i. pl. v. 1; and a third, from the collection of the late Mr. Bateman, is engraved in pl. lv. 13, of the same volume. The type is also given in White's plate, No. 14. Another specimen, in the collection of the Rev. J. H. Pollexfen, was found at Colchester. Unfortunately none of these coins are in good preservation; but as far as I have been able to observe, there is no legend on the obverse. Owing to the defective condition of the coins, the animal upon them was, by Mr. C. Roach Smith, considered to be an eagle.* It is, however, a winged four-footed creature, such as it has been found convenient to term a griffin, though in this case having more of the head of a deer. On the coin from the Slade—which, thanks to the kindness of Mr. C. Roach Smith, is now in my own cabinet—the head is, however, much more aquiline. In the better known coin of Cunobeline, Plate XII., No. 12, with a pegasus or griffin on the obverse to the left, and the legend CAMV, and with CVNO and a Victory holding a garland on the reverse, the Victory is nearly naked, and standing to the right, instead of being, as on these coins, draped and standing to the left. The position of the griffin, with its head turned back, resembles that of the horse on No. 4. The attitude of Victory holding the palm-branch downwards, and with what appears to be a scroll in her other hand, is singular, and no doubt significant, were the engraver now alive to interpret it. The dies from which the specimen engraved was struck, appear to have been remarkably large, and the letters of the legend are nearly twice the size of those on most of the coins of Cunobeline. The succeeding coin presents another variety of the same type.

PLATE XL, No. 13.

Obv.—As No. 12, but with a rosette of pellets beneath the animal.
Rev.—CVN. Victory, as on No. 12; behind, a ring ornament.
Æ. 28½ grains.

This coin, like most of those of the preceding variety, whose places of finding are known, was discovered in Kent, at Westgate Bay, near Margate. It differs from No. 12 in the points already mentioned, and in the legend running from above downwards, instead of from below upwards; the dies were also much smaller. It seems very improbable that there can have been any legend on the obverse; but this coin, like the others, is too imperfectly preserved for me to speak confidently upon this point.

* Num. Soc. Proc., April 25, 1844.

PLATE XI., No. 14.

Obv.—Lion (?) to the right, his head turned back, and tail erect. The whole within a beaded circle.

Rev.—Sphinx standing to the left, her wings expanded; below, a small triangle of pellets, one of them in front of the face. The whole within a beaded circle. Æ.

This coin is in the Hunter collection, at Glasgow, and is hitherto unpublished. Another specimen is in the Bodleian Library, at Oxford, from which I have in part compiled the description. A third, found at Oundle, is in the collection of Mr. Beal, of that town. On none of the specimens is there any inscription visible; but from the types, I think I am justified in assigning the coin to Cunobeline, the sphinx being of such frequent occurrence on his coins, and the "regardant" attitude of the animal being similar to that of the griffin on the two preceding coins.

PLATE XII., No. 1.

Obv.—CVNOBELINI. Laureate, beardless head in profile to the left. The whole within a beaded circle.

Rev.—TASCIOVANI. F. Centaur to the left, with a mantle over his shoulders, and blowing a horn. There is an exergual line, and the whole is within a beaded circle. Æ. 36, 34 $\frac{1}{2}$, 35, 35 $\frac{1}{2}$ grains.

This coin, which was found in the neighbourhood of Biggleswade, is in my own collection, and has been figured in the Num. Chron., vol. xviii. p. 36, No. 1. Another was found in the Black Grounds, near Chipping Warden, Northamptonshire (Arch. Assoc. Journ., vol. ii. p. 340). I have seen others that were found at Colchester and Harlow, Essex.

The type has been engraved with more or less accuracy by different authors, and will be found in Pettingal, No. 3, with TASCIOVANIT, which has been copied by Pegge, cl. iv. 4; Gough's Camden, pl. i. 14; and White, No. 4, who has inserted it among the silver coins. Stukeley (pl. xiv. 8) makes the legends CVNOBELINE and TASCIANOVANIT; and in pl. ix. 1, engraves an imperfect coin of the same type as being of gold. Ruding (pl. v. 17) omits the final F; but it is mentioned (vol. ii. p. 274) that Mr. Rebello's coin of this type reads TASCIO VAIF. Taylor Combe (p. 15, No. 27) reads TASCIOVANI. I. Pinkerton (vol. i. pl. ii. 0) shows the legend no farther than TASCIOVA. Mr. Birch was the first who established the true reading in the Num. Chron., vol. vii. pl. v. 4. It is also correctly given in Akerman, pl. xxiv. 9, but an imperfect coin appears to have been purposely selected for engraving in the Mon. Hist. Brit., pl. i. 20. Whitaker, in his History of Manchester, vol. i. p. 342, informs us that the head on the obverse wears a fillet ornament, with the "mussel pearls and sparry diamonds of the country."

The laureate head on the obverse, and the form of the legend CVNOBELINI, connect these coins with those in silver, Plate X., No. 8. Their fabric is such that there can be little doubt of their having been the work of Roman artists, and of the portrait being that of Cunobeline, represented after the manner of the Roman emperors. The centaur on the reverse, unlike that on the copper coin of Tasciovanus (Plate VII., No. 7), is blowing a single horn, instead of playing on the double flute. The short cloak which he wears seems adapted for protecting the human part of his skin; the equine part was no doubt in less need of such a defence.

The type appears to be original, and not derived from that of any Roman or Greek coin. The complete accordance of the legend TASCIOVANI. F, with that of DIVI. F, and DIVI. AVG. F, on the coins of Augustus and Tiberius, first pointed out by Mr. Birch, has already been mentioned. The face being represented beardless, like that of these emperors, is a circumstance worthy of notice; and on some of the coins the profile bears some resemblance to that of Tiberius, so much so as to remind one of the "restored coins" of the Roman series, on which the portrait of the emperor whose coin was restored has usually given to it a sort of family likeness to the reigning emperor under whom the restoration took place.

PLATE XII., No. 2.

Obv.—CVNOBELINVS. Beardless helmeted head, in profile, to the right. The whole within a beaded circle.

Rev.—TASCIIOVANII. in exergue F. Sow standing to the right on an ornamented exergual line; the whole within a beaded circle. Æ. 37½, 34 grains.

This coin, in my own collection, was found near Biggleswade, and is engraved in the Num. Chron., vol. xviii. p. 30, No. 2. Coins of this type usually give the legend of the reverse TASCIIOVANI F above the sow, as in Num. Chron., vol. vii. pl. v. 3; Akerman, pl. xxiv. 2; and Mon. Hist. Brit., pl. i. 18 and 22. It will be seen from the latter, that the coin in the Hunter collection is erroneously represented by Ruding, pl. v. 23, as reading CVNOBELINI and TASCIOVANIT. Taylor Combe has fallen into the same error as to the terminations of the legends, and the same was the case with Speed, who read CVNOBELINE—TASCHOVANIT. In this he was copied by Pegge, cl. iv. 2, and Gibson (Camden, pl. i. 22), who moreover calls it silver. Stukeley, pl. v. 4, makes the legend of the reverse TASC-NOVANII or IT.

Coins of this type have been found at Harlow, Essex (Gent's. Mag., 1821, p. 66), and Verulam (Num. Chron. vol. xx. 107).

It was suggested by Ruding (vol. ii. 274) that the head on the obverse is that of a Roman soldier, but this is out of the question. It appears far more likely that it is intended for Cunobeline himself. The animal on the reverse appears to be a sow rather than a boar; but there is a marked difference between its mane and that of the sow on Plate XIII., No. 1, so that possibly this is intended for the wild, and that for the domesticated animal. The ornamented exergual line is of frequent occurrence on the uninscribed gold coins, and is also found on some of those of the Iceni in silver. The form of the legend is well worthy of notice, as it proves beyond doubt, that the names Cunobelinus and Tasciovanus relate to two distinct personages, and that the latter cannot be a mere title, or it must have been in the nominative case, the same as Cunobelinus; and not in the genitive. The variety reading TASCIIOVANII shows that the British name Tasciovan—if that was really the native form—was Latinised both as Tasciovanus and Tasciovanius, unless indeed the double II be merely significant of a long I, as it would seem to be, in the middle of the name. We have already seen that this II usually represents an E. The next coin gives the name of Tasciovanus under yet another form.

PLATE XII., No. 3.

Obv.—CVNOB. Naked horseman galloping to the right, brandishing a dart in his right hand, and holding a large oval shield on his left arm. The whole within a beaded circle.

Rev.—TASCIIOVANTIS. An armed figure standing, with a plumed helmet on his head, his right hand resting on a spear, and with his left holding a circular buckler. There are greaves or boots upon the legs, and there is some appearance of a kilt round the loins, and possibly of a short sword. There is no exergual line, but the whole is surrounded by a beaded circle.

Æ. 40½, 26½, 34, 30 $\frac{7}{10}$, grains.

This splendid coin is in the British Museum, and was found at Sandy, Bedfordshire. I have specimens found near Biggleswade, in the same county (engraved in Num. Chron., vol. xviii. p. 36, No. 3), near Dorchester, Oxon., and near Abingdon, Berks. The latter was exhibited to the Numismatic Society, April 24, 1862, by Mr. Akerman, who kindly presented it to me. I have also seen a coin of this type found at Harlow, Essex.

The type is engraved, but as reading TASCNO ..., in Pegge, cl. iv. e, and other more or less imperfect specimens are engraved in Stukeley, pl. vii. 2; Ruding, pl. v. 20; Akerman, pl. xxiv. 9; and Mon. Hist. Brit., pl. i. 10.

The horseman on the obverse appears to be intended for a British warrior, who is armed in the same manner as the horseman on the coins of Tasciovanus, Plate VIII., Nos. 6, 7, and 8, though not wearing a cuirass. The shield is disproportionately large, even larger than that on the silver coin, Plate VI., No. 2. The military figure on the reverse must, I think, be regarded as a British foot soldier, accoutred to a great extent in the Roman fashion, and not, as Ruding suggests, a Roman soldier. The helmet represented on the preceding coin shows that at all events such defences were known in Britain in the days of Cunobeline, though they could never have been in general use. Tacitus expressly remarks on the absence of helmets and cuirasses among the Britons under Caractacus, with whom Ostorius engaged; but we have already seen that on some of the coins of Tasciovanus the horseman is represented wearing a cuirass, and here the foot soldier armed with the spear and target (the *scutum parvum* or *cetra brevis* of the Roman historians) has his head protected by a helmet. The greaves, for such they appear to be, on the legs, and not merely indications of *braccæ*, must have been derived from the Romans. It is, however, unfortunate that none of the coins hitherto discovered show the details sufficiently to determine the exact nature of the dress.

The legend is very remarkable, for though the name of Cunobeline is so much abbreviated, that of his father is given at full length, and in a form which, as far as is at present known, occurs only on this type. On the previous coins the name is Latinised as Tasciovanus, *genitice*—i, or Tasciovanius, *genitice*—ii, but here we have it under the form Tasciovans, *genitive*—antis. These seem to be the only three forms under which a British proper name ending in VAN could be Latinised, and judging from the coins on which the name of the father of Cunobeline appears alone, and which were struck before any Roman influences had been brought to bear upon the British mints, TASCIOVAN must have been the name by which he was known to the Catyeuchlani. The name Tenevan, given by Tysilio to the father of Cunobeline, has at all events the merit of having preserved the final syllable correctly.

Plate XII., No. 4.

Obv.—CVNOBIL. Helmeted beardless bust to the left; the shoulders draped; a laurel wreath around the helmet. The whole within a beaded circle.

Rev.—TASC . FIL (?). Boar to the left, seated on its haunches; in front, a branch. There is an exergual line, and the whole is within a beaded circle. Æ.

The coin here engraved is in the collection of Mr. Edward Wigan, and has been the subject of some controversy. It is engraved in the Num. Chron., vol. vii, pl. v. 2; and Akerman, pl. xxiv. 8, but as reading CVNODE, and the boar is there represented as biting a snake. In the woodcut given in the Arch. Assoc. Journ., vol. vii. p. 27, and Beale Poste, p. 214, the legend of the reverse is represented as TASC . FIR. In the collection formed by the late Lord Braybrooke, is another specimen found at Chesterford, and engraved in the Arch. Journ., vol. iv. p. 29. The legend of the obverse appears to be CVNOBEL, and the bust shows more of the shoulders and is more rudely executed. Above the boar on the reverse are three pellets arranged in a triangle. An account of this coin by Mr. C. Roach Smith is given in the Proca. Soc. Ant., vol. i. p. 170; and in the Archæol., vol. xxxii. p. 355. There is another coin of the same type, but very badly preserved, in the Bodleian Library, at Oxford.

With regard to the true reading of the legend on the reverse of these coins, I have already made some remarks in the eighteenth volume of the Numismatic Chronicle. It must be acknowledged that we have to wait for better specimens of this type, before the reading TASC . FIL. can be regarded as absolutely and indisputably settled, though at the same time there is every probability in favour of its being correct. In the meantime there is no doubt whatever that what Mr. Poste mistook for an R, is a straight stroke, most probably of an L honeycombed by corrosion. On many of the coins of Cunobeline the L's are so narrow that they cannot be distinguished from I's, and this appears to be the case upon Mr. Wigan's coin, on which the base of the letter touches the beaded circle. In Lord Braybrooke's coin the lower part of the letter on the die came beyond the margin of the coin, so that in the only two specimens showing the legend the most important letter is imperfect. The analogy of other coins, both Roman and British, is, however, sufficient to justify the reading TASC. FIL—Tasciovani Filius—until conclusive evidence can be adduced to the contrary. The helmeted bust on the obverse is probably that of Virtus, the same as on the denarii of the Aquillia family struck under Augustus. The boar on the reverse is a more purely British type. It is worth remarking that a branch or acorn is of frequent occurrence in front of the boar on the small silver coins of Abacænum, in Sicily. On Lord Braybrooke's coin the mouth of the animal is open, and it appears to be browsing on the branch.

PLATE XII., No. 5.

Obv.—CVNOBELINVS REX. Bare beardless bust in profile to the right; the whole within a beaded circle.

Rev.—TASC. Bull butting to the right; there is an exergual line, and the whole is surrounded by a beaded circle.

Æ. 36,⅛, 33,⅛, 33¼ grains.

This type has been frequently engraved, and will be found in Pettingal, No. 1; Pegge, cl. iii. 5; White, No. 11; Stukeley, pl. ix. 6,* and pl. xiv. 7; Gough's Camden, pl. i. 13; Ruding, pl. v. 19; Akerman, pl. xxiii. 18,† and pl. xxiv. 1; Lelewel, pl. viii. 57; and Mon. Hist. Brit., pl. i. 17 and 28. The head on the former appears to be laureate.

Specimens have been found at Chesterford (Archæol., vol. xxxii. p. 355; Procs. Soc. Ant., vol. i. p. 176), and at Colchester; as the coin in Morant's Essex, pl. i., also mentioned in the Archæol., vol. xvi. p. 147, with CVNOB .. REX ..., and on the reverse a horse feeding, below it .. MV .., was of this type, though misread. I have also had

* Erroneously reading CAMV. in exergue.
† Wrongly engraved as .B.

one in poor preservation which was found near Biggleswade. The engraving is from the Hunter coin, which is, however, in hardly such good condition as here shown.

The head to the obverse would appear to be that of Cunobeline. The device of the butting bull on the reverse, though turned in the other direction, occurs on the silver coins of Tasciovanus, Plate VI., No. 5, and is frequently seen both to the left and to the right on coins of Augustus. It is also common on the Gaulish coins in bronze, derived originally from those of Massilia.

With the exception of the coins of Verica and Eppillus, this affords the only example of the title "Rex" occurring on a coin of a British king. Cunobeline is indeed dignified with the title by both Suetonius and Dion Cassius, and from the coins being the work of Roman artists, and having Roman legends upon them, the wonder is that the Rex is not of more frequent occurrence.

Plate XII, No. 6.

Obv.—CVNOBELIN. Beardless head, with the Petasus, in profile, to the left; with either snakes or locks of hair appearing below the chin. The whole within a beaded circle.

Rev.—TASCIO. Seated figure, with a hammer in the right hand, at work upon a hemispherical vase. There is an exergual line, and the whole is surrounded by a beaded circle.

Æ. 39½, 37¾, 34½, 34, 31½, 30½, 26½ grains.

The coin here engraved is in my own cabinet, and was formerly in the Thomas and Huxtable collections. The type is well known, and the coins are among the commonest of those of Cunobeline, though it is difficult to get them in a good state. I have two specimens found near Biggleswade, Beds, and another from the neighbourhood of Cambridge. Others have been found at Harlow, Essex (Gent.'s Mag., 1821, p. 60).

The type was known to both Camden and Speed; but the former makes the legend on both obverse and reverse to run

in the opposite direction in the engraving, to what it does
upon the coins. It is, however, given more correctly in the
account of the Trinobantes. In Gough's edition, pl. i. 3,
the error in the legend is corrected, but the head is made
laureate, being copied from White, No. 9. The type is well
engraved in Gough's Camden, vol. ii. pl. iii.; in Pettingal,
No. 2, and Pegge, cl. iii. 0, but badly as cl. iii. 9; and in the
Pembroke Coins, pt. ii. pl. 64. Stukeley copies Camden in his
pl. v. 3, and gives a fancy sketch of the coin in pl. vi. 1. The
type is given also in Lagoy, No. 9; Ruding, pl. v. 18;
Akerman, pl. xxiv. 4; and Mon. Hist. Brit., pl. i. 21.

The devices on both obverse and reverse have been variously regarded. The head on the obverse was, by Camden,
thought to be the head of Cunobeline; but Pegge calls it
"the queen's head, for hers I take it to be, with the hair."
Whitaker, vol. i. p. 304, adduces it as showing the sort of
caps worn by the Britons, "apparently the same as are used
by our meaner Mancunians at present." Taylor Combe calls
it the winged head of Victory (p. 15, No. 28). Ruding considers it to be probably that of Mercury; and the editors of
the Mon. Hist. Brit. call it the head of Medusa. The latter
appears to me to be the correct view, as the head is probably
copied from the denarius of the Cossutia family (Cohen,

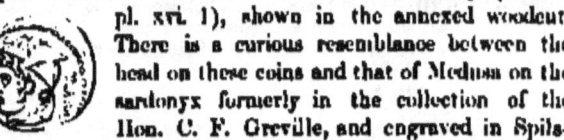

pl. xvi. 1), shown in the annexed woodcut.
There is a curious resemblance between the
head on these coins and that of Medusa on the
sardonyx formerly in the collection of the
Hon. C. F. Greville, and engraved in Spils-
bury's Antique Gems, No. 45. It will be remembered that
the full-faced head of Medusa occurs on the small gold coins
of Tinc[ommius], Plate II., No. 4, and Perseus is shown
on No. 10 in this Plate.

The seated figure on the reverse was thought by Camden
to be the coiner or mint-master of Cunobeline, and in his
engraving five coins are seen falling from a sort of anvil, on
which the moneyer is hammering. The five coins are, however, purely imaginary, and even Pegge suggests that the

original may have been misrepresented. The object which is being hammered or forged has, by Taylor Combe, Ruding, and others, been termed a helmet. If so, Vulcan must have been at work for some colossus of a god five or six times his own size. The shape of the object is, however, not that of a helmet, but of a large *crater*, though apparently without handles. On some of the coins of Lipara, Vulcan is seated, and holding his hammer in his right hand, while, with his left, he holds out a *diota*, and on coins of Magnesia he is forging a helmet; but I am not aware of any other coin on which he is represented in the same manner as on this. I believe, however, that he is thus drawn on certain antique gems. The hammer has usually the handle inserted at one end of the head, so as to give it the appearance of an axe, or make it like a file-cutter's hammer, of the present day.

PLATE XII., No. 7.

Obv.—CVNO. Pegasus springing to the right; the whole within a beaded circle.
Rev.—TASCI. Winged Victory to the right, sacrificing a bull. The whole within a beaded circle.
Æ. 35, 33, 21$\frac{7}{8}$, grains.

The coin here engraved is in the collection of Mr. J. B. Bergne. A specimen of this type was found near Saffron Walden (Arch. Journ., vol. viii. p. 91). I have others, found at Dorchester, Oxon, and Wigginton, near Tring, Herts; and have seen one that was found near Harlow, Essex, and another found at Thornborough, near Buckingham.

The type appears to have been first engraved by Stukeley, pl. viii. 10, who mistook the device of the reverse for a small winged figure squatting on the back of a horse. It is also engraved in Ruding, pl. v. 31; Akerman, pl. xxiv. 7; Lelewel, pl. viii. 58; and Mon. Hist. Brit., pl. i. 27.

The Pegasus on the obverse may be considered to have become, by the time of Cunobeline, a recognised British type; but our finding, on a British coin, the apparently Mithraic device of a figure sacrificing a bull, might well

excite surprise. The type, however, occurs on some coins of
Pyrrhus (Havercamp, pl. xxxix. 3), of Syracuse (Cat. d'
Ennery, p. 104, No. 306), and on coins of Augustus (Cohen,
No. 46), from which latter, probably, the device on these
coins of Cunobeline was derived.

The coin of Augustus appears to have been struck when
Tigranes was appointed by him to the kingdom of Armenia,
the legend being ARMENIA CAPTA, and the device has
been considered typical of the conquest of Armenia—Mount
Taurus, by a sort of rebus, being represented by the bull.
However that may have been, it appears improbable that
the device on a coin of Augustus, who was much opposed
to foreign superstitions, should have any affinity with the
worship of Mithras, which, moreover, was not established at
Rome until the time of Trajan. The figure sacrificing the
bull is, moreover, winged, and therefore most probably
Victory.

In the British Museum are two statues representing Victory sacrificing a bull, both found in the villa of Antoninus
Pius, near Lanuvium. The subject has been frequently
treated by Roman sculptors.

PLATE XII., No. 8.

Obv.—CAMV(?). Griffin walking to the right. There is an
    exergual line, and the whole is within a beaded circle.
Rev.—CVN[O](?). Horse galloping to the right; above a
    quatrefoil. The whole within a beaded circle.
    Æ.—16½ grains.

The coin here engraved was found at Colchester, and is
in the collection of the Rev. J. H. Pollexfen, of that town.
Another specimen, in the Hunter collection, is engraved in
Ruding, pl. v. 32; Akerman, pl. xxiv. 15; and Mon. Hist.
Brit., pl. i. 30. From a comparison of the two coins, I am
inclined to think that the legend CAMV runs round the head
of the griffin. There appears, also, to be a ring ornament
above the horse on the reverse of the Glasgow coin, which,
like the legend, has escaped the eyes of those who have

previously engraved the coin. I think, too, that there is
some other object above the tail of the horse. Both griffins
and horses are of not unfrequent occurrence on the coins of
Cunobeline; but the small cross or quatrefoil above the
horse is peculiar to this coin. A trefoil occupies much the
same position on many of the coins of Tasciovanus struck
at Verulam (see Plate VII.). With the possible exception of
Plate XI., Nos. 5 to 9, this coin is apparently the first of
those in copper, of the class on which the name of the
prince is conjoined with that of the place of mintage—a
name which appears at full length on the succeeding coin.

PLATE XII., No. 9.

Obv.—CAMVL-ODVNO in two compartments of a tablet; above
and below a scroll; the whole surrounded by a
beaded circle.

Rev.—CVNO in the exergue below a sphinx crouching to the
left, her wings expanded. Æ. 33 grains.

This type is engraved in the Num. Chron., vol. xx. p. 157,
No. 4. It was also published by Akerman, p. 199, No. 36,
but by inadvertence the sphinx is there described as to the
right. It has also been published by Beale Poste, in the
Arch. Assoc. Journ., vol. i. p. 233, and British Coins, p. 12,
but he has converted the sphinx into a pegasus. Both
authors, however, describe the same coin that is here engraved, viz., that which was formerly in the collection of
the late Mr. Huxtable, and is now in my own, and which
was found at Colchester. Another specimen was found in
1790,* in a field near the old Waterworks, Colchester, and
is now in the possession of Mr. W. D. Smith, of that place.
There is a woodcut of this coin in the Arch. Assoc. Journ.,
vol. ii. p. 40. A third specimen is in the possession of
Mr. Charles Gray Round, of Birch Hall, near Colchester,
and was no doubt found near that town.

The type is very remarkable, as being the only one on
which the name of Camulodunum appears at full length

---

* Cromwell's Colchester, p. 364. He calls the sphinx a winged horse.

z

upon a coin; and it is to be observed that it is given with the ablative or "locative" termination CAMVLODVNO, "At Camulodunum," in the same way that, on the only coins on which the name of Verulamium is found in an unabbreviated form, that word also presents the same inflexion, VERLAMIO.

I have already, p. 201, made some remarks as to the various readings of the name of Camulodunum which occur in ancient authors, and have also stated that there is a preponderance of numismatic evidence for fixing its site at Colchester and not at Maldon. It is certainly curious that two out of the three coins known with the name of Camulodunum at full length upon them, should be preserved at or close to Colchester, and that probably all three were found there. Some observations with regard to the sphinx on these coins will be found at p. 311, in which I have shown the probability of the seated sphinx on the silver coins having been reproduced by a Roman artist, from the coins of the Carisia family. It must, however, be borne in mind that there are instances where the existing devices upon British coins appear to have been adopted by these foreign artists, and reproduced under a classical form, in accordance with their own mythology rather than with British or Druidical traditions. The horse in this manner becomes converted into the pegasus or centaur; an almost shapeless figure reappears as the full-faced head of Medusa; and not improbably in the androcephalous horses of the Gaulish coins is to be found the germ of the crouching sphinx on the coins of Cunobeline. Horace, when penning his Epistola ad Pisones—

> "Humano capiti cervicem pictor equinam
> Jungere si velit, et varias inducere plumas
> Undique collatis membris—"

can hardly have had these coins in view, though there are certainly some to which the continuation applies—

> "Spectatum admissi risum teneatis, amici?"

Look for instance at those engraved in Lambert, pl. iii. 12, &c., where the horse has not only acquired the human head, but has wings also, and appears to be indisputably the connecting link between the *Equus caballus* and the *Sphinx Ægyptiaca*. It is not a little curious that about forty years ago* the figure of a winged sphinx, in stone, about two feet in height and the same in length, was discovered at Colchester, corresponding in all essential points with the figures upon the coins of Cunobeline.

PLATE XII., No. 10.

Obv.—CVNO. Sphinx crouching to the right. There is an exergual line, and the whole is surrounded by a beaded circle.

Rev.—CAM. Male figure standing to the left; over his right shoulder a mantle; with his right hand holding out a human head with long locks of hair represented by pellets, and in his left hand a staff, sceptre, or *harpe*; behind, an altar. There is an exergual line, and the whole is surrounded by a beaded circle.

Æ. 3½, 40 grains.

The coin here engraved is in the Hunter collection, at Glasgow, and has already been figured in Ruding, pl. v. 25; Mon. Hist. Brit., pl. i. 44; and Akerman, pl. xxiv. 18. I have a specimen which was found at Colchester, and of which a woodcut is given in Dr. P. M. Duncan's "Walls of Colchester," printed in the Transactions of the Essex Archæological Society. Another very fine specimen is engraved in Lagoy, No. 11, and Lelewel, pl. viii. 64, and a fourth in White, No. 6, and Gough's Camden, pl. i. 22. Morant, pl. i. 6, gives a coin of this type, but converts the sphinx into a pegasus on the obverse, and gives a naked figure holding a crook† on the reverse. The type of the obverse is so closely connected with that of the reverse of the preceding coin, as to require no farther comment. The figure on the reverse has, however, given rise to much discussion. Ruding doubtingly describes it as a British

* Cromwell's *Colchester*, p. 370.
† Can this have been the *harpe*, more clearly shown than on the other coin?

warrior with the head of an enemy in his right hand, but
the editor* of the third edition considers the type to have
been imitated from the brass coins of Maronea, in Thracia,
on which Bacchus is represented in a similar position
holding the *thyrsus* and a bunch of grapes. Akerman,
from the specimen of the coin in the British Museum, is of
the same opinion. The editors of the Mon. Hist. Brit.
describe the Hunter coin as bearing "a draped figure
standing between a vase and a building." Taylor Combe
(p. 15, No. 24) calls the object held in the hand of the
figure "quiddam ignotum, nisi sit caput humanum." Lagoy
terms it "une tête humaine (à ce qu'il paraît);" but any one
who will carefully examine the coin in the Hunter collection
will see that it is beyond all doubt a human head. Beale
Poste (p. 153) considers that if so, "the subject represented
may have been the head of an enemy, slain in battle, offered
at the altars of the Britons to their gods." I think, however, that judging from the number of subjects on the coins
of Cunobeline that were evidently derived from the Roman
mythology, we may safely refer this type to the same source.
We have already seen that the head of Medusa occurs as
the type of two British coins, and I make but little doubt
that we have here the representation of her destroyer—
Perseus, with the *harpe*. I am not, however, aware of his
being drawn in precisely the same manner on any Roman
or Greek coins, though the figure of Perseus holding the
harpe and the head of Medusa, with her dead body at his
feet, is of common occurrence on the coins of Pontus, and
especially of Amisus. On a large brass coin of Severus,†
struck at Argos, Perseus is represented "naked, adverse,
looking to left; in right hand, head of Medusa, in left,
harpe and chlamys." This, though of long subsequent
date, is much the same figure as that on the coins of Cunobeline, though the altar is absent. At the same time it
must be borne in mind that "*couped*" heads occur on

* Vol. ii. p. 274.
† Leake, Num. Hell.—Eur. Greece, p. 30.

several coins of the Gaulish series: such for instance as those of Dubnorix, on which there is a standing figure holding in the one hand a boar, and in the other a human head (see Revue Num., vol. v., N. S., pl. v. 5 and 6), and on several anepigraphous coins (see Revue Num., vol. xx. p. 101, and pl. iv.). It is, however, impossible to confound the figure on the coins of Dubnorix with that of Perseus, whereas on these coins the resemblance is obvious. In whatever manner, however, the device is to be interpreted, the coin is certainly one of the most remarkable in the British series.

Plate XII., No. 11.

Obv.—CVNO. Wingless griffin to the left; above, three pellets in triangle. The whole within a beaded circle.

Rev.—.. Horse to the left; around, a beaded circle. Æ.'

I have never seen this coin nor an impression of it, and have copied it from the woodcut given by Beale Poste, p. 52. He describes it as found near Colchester, and at the time he wrote, as in the possession of Mr. Samuel Shepherd, F.S.A., since deceased. The reverse is said to be indistinct, but to show M beneath the horse, "the remaining part of CAM, the legend which it formerly bore." I think that probably, on a well preserved coin, the griffin would be found to have wings, as on other coins. The griffin and horse are also conjoined as types on Plate XII., No. 8.

Plate XII., No. 12.

Obv.—CAMV. Pegasus (or griffin) springing to the left; the whole within a beaded circle.

Rev.—CVNO. Victory walking to the right, partially draped, and holding a garland. Æ. 46$\frac{7}{8}$, 43$\frac{1}{2}$, 34 grains.

Coins of this type have been engraved in Ruding, pl. v. 30; Akerman, pl. xxiv. 10; and Mon. Hist. Brit., pl. i. 41. One has also been engraved in White, No. 8, and Gough, pl. i. 33, as reading CVNOB. Another is given in the Pembroke Coins, pt. ii. pl. 94; Pogge, cl. ii. 6; and Lagoy,

No. 3, on which the wings of the Victory have been mistaken for a second standing figure. Pegge's* account of it is as follows:—" This brass coin has two figures standing upon the obv., with CVN. The foremost, which is naked all but about the loins, seems to be Cunobelin stretching out something which he holds in his hand; and the other, which seems to turn its back towards us out of modesty as it were, very probably is his Queen." A coin described as found at Colchester, in Cromwell's history of that town (p. 304)—*obv.*, a griffin sitting; *rev.*, a Victory, with CVNO. —was doubtless of this type. A specimen, found at Coddenham, Suffolk, has been communicated to me by Mr. C. Roach Smith, as well as another from Colchester. Beale Poste, p. 151, calls the animal on the obverse a griffin; but it is more probably a pegasus with a small head, like that of the horse on the gold coins, Plate IX., Nos. 7 and 10. There is a curved line in front of the neck, which may either represent the second wing or a rein.

Ruding thinks that both sides of the coin are imitations of coins of Augustus; but the pegasus is of such common occurrence on both Gaulish and British coins, that it had become, as it were, naturalised in Britain by the time of Cunobeline. The standing or marching Victory, holding out a wreath, also makes its appearance in the British series on coins of Eppillus (see Plate III., No. 11), and occurs on several other coins of Cunobeline.

The Victory on the coins of Augustus has its wings turned upwards, and usually carries a palm-branch as well as a wreath. On these coins the wings are downwards, and of great length, almost giving the notion that the Victory was provided with a feathered tail as well as with wings, unless some of the feathery strokes represent floating drapery, such as we see about the feet of Victory on so many Greek and Roman coins.

The coins of this type are considerably dished, and probably belong to the early part of the reign of Cunobeline.

* Page 67.

PLATE XII., No. 13.

Obv.—CVNO on a tablet in the centre of a wreath. The whole within a beaded circle.

Rev.—CAMV. Horse pacing to the right, full faced. There is an exergual line, and the whole is surrounded by a beaded circle. Æ. 41, 19 7/8 grains.

Coins of this type have been engraved in Stukeley, pl. xix. 4, and xx. 0; Ruding, pl. v. 27; Akerman, pl. xxiv. 6; Arch. Assoc. Journ., vol. i. p. 208; Beale Poste, p. 35; and Mon. Hist. Brit., pl. i. 42. The coin without the wreath on the obverse, and with CAM on the reverse, engraved in Ruding, pl. v. 28, and Akerman, pl. xxiv. 13, is probably a badly preserved specimen. In Stukeley, pl. viii. 8, the coin is erroneously called silver.

A specimen, found at Colchester, is engraved in Morant, pl. i. 3; and in Cromwell's Colchester, p. 373. Taylor Combe, p. 15, No. 21, describes the garland as composed of ears of corn, but I think it is more probably of leaves of laurel. As was the case with the other coins on which nearly the same device appears (Plate X., No. 7, and Plate XI., No. 1), the junction of the two branches of the wreath is at the end of the tablet, and not beneath it. The head of the horse on the reverse faces the spectator, instead of showing only the side view, as usual. In this respect it resembles the horse on the silver Icenian coin, Plate XV., No. 3. Though the workmanship is probably Roman, the types must be considered as British, rather than as immediately derived from any foreign source. The whole character of the coin is so like that of the one in silver, Plate X., No. 7, that it must be assigned to the same period, probably the latter half of Cunobeline's reign.

PLATE XII., No. 14.

Obv.—CVNOBELIN. Bearded head of Jupiter Ammon in profile to the left. The whole within a beaded circle.

Rev.—CAM. Horseman to the right; in his right hand a sword, with his left holding a large round shield. There is an exergual line, and the whole is surrounded by a beaded circle. Æ. 38, 25⅕, 34] grains.

The coin here engraved is in the collection of the Rev. J. H. Pollexfen, of Colchester, and was found at that place. I have another specimen, poorly preserved, from the same locality; it is mentioned in the Arch. Assoc. Journ., vol. iv. p. 144, but the horseman on the reverse was mistaken for a pegasus. Morant engraves a third specimen, found at Colchester, pl. i. 4. Another was found near Norwich (Num. Soc. Procs., May 25, 1848). A fifth was found at Hadstock, Essex, and is in the collection formed by the late Lord Braybrooke. The type is engraved from an imperfect specimen in Ruding, pl. v. 21; Akerman, pl. xxiv. 11; and Mon. Hist. Brit., pl. i. 45. Stukeley appears to have seen a much better preserved coin, which he has delineated, after his peculiar fashion, in his pl. vi. 10. Beale Poste has copied and reduced his drawing at p. 45.

There can be little doubt of the head upon the obverse being intended for Jupiter Ammon, as must also be that on Plate XIII., No. 2, though turned in the other direction. It is probably copied from the coins of the Cornuficia family (Cohen, pl. xv. 1), of which one is represented in the annexed woodcut.

The horseman on the reverse is armed in a different manner from that on No. 3, having a sword instead of a javelin, and a round instead of an oval shield, though still probably representing a British warrior. The combination of the two types—the one so thoroughly British, and the other derived, through Greece and Rome, from an Æthiopian or Libyan source—is sufficiently remarkable. The fabric of the coin is very good, and the design of the horseman on the reverse extremely spirited.

PLATE XIII. No. 1.

Obv.—CVNO on a tablet beneath the head of Janus. The whole within a beaded circle.

Rev.—CAMV on a tablet beneath a sow to the right, seated beneath a tree. Æ. 49, 40½, 36⅕ grains.

This coin, from the collection of the late Mr. Cuff, is now in my own cabinet. I am not aware of its place of finding, but the late Lord Braybrooke had one that was found at Colchester.

The type was known to Camden and Speed, who, however, make the animal on the reverse more like a tapir than a pig. It has also been engraved in the Pembroke Coins, pt. ii. pl. 94, but erroneously as reading CAMVL, which has been copied in Lagoy, No. 4; Revue Num., vol. v. pl. xix. 3; and by Pegge, cl. ii. 7, who, in class ii. 1, gives Camden's coin. Stukeley gives the type in pl. vii. 5, with the representation apparently of a donkey rubbing its back against an oak, on the reverse. In Ruding, pl. v. 24; Akerman, pl. xxiv. 17; Lelewel, pl. viii. 56; and Mon. Hist. Brit., pl. i. 40, the tree on the reverse is imperfectly shown. A marvellous article upon the head of Janus on these coins will be found in the Arch. Assoc. Journ., vol. vi. p. 30.

Camden suggests that the type of Janus was adopted "peradventure, because even at that time Britaine began to cast off and leave their barbarous rudenesse. For we reade how Janus was the first that changed barbarous manners into civill behaviour, and therefore was depainted with two foreheads, to signifie that he had of one shape made another." But Walker, in Gibson's edition of Camden (p. xci.), fears that it is not the head of Janus, for "this seems made for two young women's faces, whether Cunobeline's wives, sisters, or children," he knows not.

There can, however, be but little doubt that it is the head of Janus, who on many of the Roman or rather Campanian coins is represented as beardless. It is, notwithstanding, a question whether the type is derived directly from an Italian source, or from some of the Gaulish coins, such as those in Lelewel, pl. v. 15 and 16. There is indeed so close a resemblance between these latter and the coin of Cunobeline, that Duchalais (p. 305) has attributed them to Britain. In his opinion, the head, though derived from the Janus on Roman coins, represents some other divinity; but the workmanship

of this coin is so good that it was probably engraved by a
Roman artist, or by one educated in a foreign school; and we
have, moreover, on other coins, the heads of divinities much
less likely to appear on the British coinage than Janus.

The sow on the reverse has more the character of the
domesticated than of the wild animal, and the tree may
possibly be an idealised oak. The sow and the wild boar
occur on several other coins of Cunobeline, and I think the
device must be regarded as indigenous, and not derived from
a foreign prototype. The method of placing the legends in
tablets beneath the device may also be considered as a
British characteristic.

Plate XIII., No. 2.

Obv.—CVNOB. Head of Ammon in profile to the right. The whole within a beaded circle.

Rev.—CAM on a tablet beneath a lion couchant to the right; above, a tree. The whole within a beaded circle.
Æ. 36$\frac{4}{5}$ grains.

I have seen a specimen of this type which was found at
Harlow, Essex; and another was found at Farley Heath,[a]
near Guildford. Others are engraved in Morant's Colchester;
White, No. 13; Gough's Camden, pl. i. 34; Stukeley,
pl. vii. 1; Pegge, cl. ii. b; Ruding, pl. v. 20; Akerman,
pl. xxiv. 5; and Mon. Hist. Brit., pl. i. 43.

The type of the obverse is the same as that of Plate XII.,
No. 14, though the head of Ammon is turned in the opposite
direction. It is probably copied from the denarii of the
Pinaria family (Cohen, pl. xxii. 1), as here
shown. The lion is of so frequent occurrence
on the coins of Massilia, and on some other
Gaulish coins, that it is the less surprising
to meet with it here. The same animal,
apparently, occurs on the coin of Dubnovellaunus, Plate IV.,
No. 12. I do not, however, remember to have seen it in this
couchant posture on any other coin.

[a] Tupper's Farley Heath, 1850, p. 17.

Plate XIII., No. 3.

Obv.—CA—M[V]. Ear of bearded corn.
Rev.—CVN[O]. Horse galloping to the right.
Æ. 55, 60 grains.

I have copied this coin from the Num. Chron., vol. i. pl. ii. 13. This engraving has also been copied in Lelewel, pl. viii. 65; and in the Revue Num., vol. iv. pl. xiii. 15. The type is described in Akerman, p. 103, No. 42, and C. Roach Smith's Catalogue of London Antiquities, p. 99. The coin was found in the bed of the Thames near London Bridge.

Mr. Durden, of Blandford, has another specimen, found at Shapwick, near Blandford, which shows a star above the horse. I also have one similar to the gold coin, Plate IX., No. 6.

The types being precisely the same as those in gold require no farther comment. Indeed I have some hesitation as to engraving these among the copper coins, as I am convinced that they are merely ancient counterfeits of those in gold. Taylor Combe, p. 14, No. 6, mentions one as having been formerly gilt, and with the gold still adhering in places. I have mentioned a similar forgery of the gold coins of Dubnovellaunus (p. 203). The coin of Tinc[ommius], Plate II., No. 7, seems to afford another parallel instance.

Plate XIII., No. 4.

Obv.—CA—M[V]. Ear of bearded corn.
Rev.—CVNO. Horse to the left, upon an exergual line. The whole within a beaded circle. Æ.

I have copied this coin from C. Roach Smith's Coll. Ant., vol. i. pl. v. 9, but corrected the drawing from a cast. The original was found at Springhead, Kent, and like the former coin is probably an ancient forgery of one in gold—it would seem of the type Plate IX., No. 3.

Beside the coins which I have engraved, there are several types given by early writers, which are not at the present time known, and possibly may never be authenticated; such are—

1. *Obv.*—CVNOBELINI. Bare head to the right.
   Rev.—CAMV. Horse walking to the right. Æ.

—White, No. 5; Gough's Camden, vol. i. pl. i. 5; vol. ii. pl. iii. 13.

2. *Obv.*—CVNOBILINI (retrograde). Bare head to the right.
   Rev.—Horse galloping to the right; above, a ring ornament. Æ.

—Stukeley, pl. vi. 2.

3. *Obv.*—Naked figure standing with a lyre.
   Rev.—CVN. Pegasus to the right. Æ.

—Stukeley, pl. viii. 0.

The silver coin in Morant's Essex, pl. i. 2, and Stukeley, pl. viii. 7, has already been mentioned at page 309.

CHAPTER XIV.

UNCERTAIN COINS.

In addition to those coins on which the inscriptions can be read with sufficient certainty for them to be assigned to some one or other of the princes of whose coins I have been treating, there are several which, though evidently inscribed, have either been so imperfectly struck, or are in so bad a state of preservation, that their legends have hitherto remained undecipherable. As most of them undoubtedly belong to the same districts as the other inscribed coins which have been passed under review in the preceding pages, I have thought it best to insert them here, before proceeding to examine the coins which have been assigned to the Iceni and to the Brigantes.

It may be objected that it is useless to engrave from imperfectly preserved coins; but in a work professing to treat of the whole of the ancient British series, I should hardly be justified in ignoring any coins, however indistinct in their details; especially as, when they have once been put on record, it is possible that the possessors of other specimens may be enabled, by comparison, to remove some of the uncertainties as to type and legend which now exist. At all events, the representation of an imperfectly preserved coin, if faithfully given, and with the doubtful points still left doubtful, can do no harm; it is from the authoritative assumption of dubious points as being incontestably certain, that mischief has arisen.

Plate XIII., No. 5.

Obv.—Uncertain inscription on a tablet beneath a pig standing to the right.

Rev.—Eagle (?) with expanded wings standing to the right; beneath the tail, a ring ornament. Æ. 29 grains.

This coin, which was found, with other coins both British and Roman, at a place called "The Slade," in the parish of Boughton Montchelsea, Kent, was kindly presented to me by Mr. C. Roach Smith. It is engraved in the Coll. Ant., vol. i. pl. v. 3, but the legend, perhaps unintentionally, has too much of the appearance of being CVNO. The coin has in consequence been classed among those of Cunobeline, in Akerman, p. 103, No. 43. I have spent much time in examining the inscription, but have not attained any satisfactory result. I should not, however, be surprised if, when a more perfect specimen is found, it should turn out to be DVBNO, so as to prove the coin to be of Dubnovellaunus.

On the only coin of that prince known in copper the legend is placed on a tablet beneath the device, in the same manner as it is on several of the coins of Cunobeline. The pig is of common occurrence on the coins of this series, and the eagle is found on the coins of Eppillus, Tasciovanus, Epaticcus, and others. The treatment, however, of both pig and bird is different on this, from that on any of the other coins.

Plate XIII., No. 6.

Obv.—Uncertain legend in front of a laureate head to the left.

Rev.—Victory standing facing, but her head to the left, partially draped; in her right hand possibly a spear (?); in her left, a garland. The whole within a beaded circle. Æ. 27½ grains.

This coin was found at the same place as No. 5, and was also presented to me by Mr. C. Roach Smith. It is engraved in the Coll. Ant., vol. i. pl. v. 4; but by careful cleaning I have been able to make out considerably more of the devices than is there shown. The legend is so indistinct, that to the eye of an ordinary observer it is *invisible*. Notwithstanding, I think that it is EPPI, but we must await the discovery of better preserved specimens before this can be ascertained. The device and arrangement of the obverse appears to be much the same as on the brass coin of Eppillus, Plate IV., No. 4, while, in the treatment of the wings and general appearance, the Victory on the reverse bears considerable analogy to that on the gold coin of the same prince Plate III., No. 11. The place of finding accords well with the attribution of this coin to Eppillus, could such an attribution be sustained on sufficient grounds.

Plate XIII., No. 7.

Obv.—A, within a small circle in the centre of a wreath.
Rev.—AM. Hippocampus to the right. The whole within a beaded circle. Æ. 12 grains.

This coin is in the British Museum, and has unfortunately suffered much from oxidisation. It has been mis-described and mis-engraved more than once; first in the Mon. Hist. Brit., pl. i. 48, where the legend of the reverse is given as CVN; and, secondly, by myself, in the Num. Chron., vol. xvi. p. 80, No. 12, where I have mistaken a coil of the tail of the hippocampus for a C, and made the legend CAM, and the animal a capricorn, as it is also described to be in the Mon. Hist. Brit. Regarding the legends as A and AM (which I think I am now correct in doing), the attribution of this coin to AMMINVS follows as a matter of course. It was, indeed, my becoming acquainted with the copper coin which I have ascribed to that prince (Plate V., No. 2), which presents the same reverse as this coin, that led me to a conviction of my error. The type of the hippocampus occurs also on several of the coins of Tasciovanus, struck at Verulam, whose gold coins (Plate VI., No. 12) also present the same peculiarity as this, in having the initial of the king's name on the obverse, and the name in a more extended, but still abbreviated, form on the reverse.

Plate XIII., No. 8.

Obv.—Uncertain legend in front of a beardless head to the right.
Rev.—Uncertain legend beneath a seated figure, apparently holding a wreath. Æ. 14½ grains.

This coin, which was found at Verulam, is in my own collection. The legends are hopelessly illegible, but probably that on the reverse is VER, TASC, or CVNO. I have seen another specimen, found at Oundle, and in the collection of Mr. Beal, of that town; but on that also the legend is equally indistinct. The type of the obverse comes nearest to that of some of the coins of Tasciovanus, while the seated figure on the reverse is of common occurrence on the coins of Cunobeline. It is probably to one or other of these princes that the type will be assigned when better preserved specimens are discovered. The resemblance between the head and that on the silver coins of BODVOC, Plate I., No. 3, is worth notice.

Plate XIII., No. 9.

Obv.—Uncertain legend in front of a laureate (?) head to the right.
Rev.—Boar rushing to the right; in the field various ring ornaments and pellets. The whole surrounded by a beaded circle. Æ. 9½ grains.

This coin, in my own collection, was found near Biggleswade. A woodcut of another specimen of the same type, in the collection of Mr. Wigan, is given by Beale Poste, p. 51. On neither is the legend decipherable. Mr. Poste describes the head as helmed, but it is not so on my coin. From the general character of the coin, the place where it was found, and more especially the close resemblance of the reverse to that of the coin of Verulam, Plate VIII., No. 5, I think that it will eventually prove to be one of the coins of Tasciovanus struck at that town.

Plate XIII., No. 10.

Obv.—A·M on either side of an ear of corn.
Rev.—CAC beneath a horse to the left. Æ.

This coin was found at Springhead, near Southfleet, Kent, and is engraved in the Coll. Ant., vol. i. pl. Iv. 10, from whence, assisted by a cast of the coin kindly sent me by Mr. C. Roach Smith, I have copied it. It is described in the Arch. Journ., vol. i. p. 253, as reading CAM on the obverse, a legend which is considered to refer the coin to Camulodunum. The coin, however, the obverse of which is in very bad preservation, does not seem to show the C, and, from the workmanship of the reverse, I should not think that it came from the mint of Cunobeline, though the ear of corn certainly favours such an attribution. If the legend be merely AM, it may probably have been struck by Amminus, but nothing can be determined from this specimen alone. Under any circumstances, the legend CAC, on the reverse, would have still to be explained. At present it is equally mysterious with the DVN on the silver coin of Amminus, Plate V., No. 1. It will, however, be noticed that No. 12 in this Plate seems also to present nearly the same legend, AM and CA, which much strengthens the attribution to Amminus.

Plate XIII., No. 11.

Obv.—Beardless head in profile to the left, with a profusion of hair. A curved wreath falls down behind the ear from a ring ornament above the eye, and there are other ring ornaments in front of the face, and at the back of the head.

Rev.—Portion of a legend of which only an A is visible; a horse galloping to the left; above and below, a ring ornament. Æ 26½ grains.

This coin, formerly in the collection of Mr. Joseph Warren, of Ixworth, but now in mine, was found near Bury St. Edmunds. A similar coin, formerly in the collection of Mr. Dücke, and found near Colchester, has been communicated to me by Mr. C. Roach Smith, but the legend cannot be deciphered. The head upon it is unlike that on any other coin in the British series, though in some slight degree connected with that on the coins of Tasciovanus, and on the uninscribed coins, Plate G, No. 9.

The horse, on the reverse, is, however, very similar in character and workmanship to that on the gold coins of Dubnovellaunus, which I have supposed to have been struck in Essex. What little can be discerned of the legend would also agree with the name of that prince, to whom I expect this type will eventually be assigned.

PLATE XIII, No. 12.

Obv.—Boar to the left, within a beaded circle.
Rev.— . CA (?). Horse prancing to the left; above, a ring ornament. The whole within a beaded circle.
Æ. 27½, 30 grains.

This coin, in my own cabinet, was formerly in the collection of the late Mr. Rolfe, and was found in the Isle of Thanet. It is engraved in C. Roach Smith's Coll. Ant., vol. i. pl. Iv. 5. I have another specimen, found on the hill above Kit's Coty House, near Maidstone, on which I think I can trace the letters AM above the boar. If this be so, and the letters on the obverse of No. 10 are only AM, and not CAM, it would appear that the legends on these two coins correspond, that on the one being AM ⸱ CAC; and that on the other, AM ⸱ CA. Unfortunately the coins are not sufficiently well preserved for me to speak confidently as to the inscriptions upon them, but for the present I think they may be classed among those of Amminus; in which case the CA and CAC of the reverse may possibly bear relation to the Cantii, among whom he is supposed to have reigned. The horse on the reverse is much the same in character as that on the gold coins of Vose[nos], which also appear to have been struck in Kent.

PLATE XIII., No. 13.

Obv.—Cruciform ornament formed of wreaths, with two crescents in the centre; in three of the angles thin crescents with pellets at their points and encircling ring ornaments. In the fourth the remains of the clothing of the neck of the original laureate bust.

Rev.—MOD (?). Horse to the right, with ring ornaments on his shoulder and hind-quarters; above, a ring ornament connected by a band with the shoulder; in the field several ring ornaments and annulets. *N.*

This coin was found at Ravensdale, near Grimsby, Lincolnshire, and was kindly communicated to me by the Hon. J. Leicester Warren. I had already engraved the same type among the uninscribed coins, Plate B, No. 11, from a specimen in the Bodleian Library, which does not show the letters with equal distinctness. But though the coin is evidently inscribed, it is impossible to say whether there were not upon the die some other letters before the MOD, so that at present it is premature to speculate upon the meaning of the legend, or the part of the country to which this type is to be assigned. It is, however, not improbable that it will prove to belong to the Midland counties.

Plate XIII., No. 14.

Obv.—Plain and convex, with a raised band across it.

Rev.—Uncertain legend. Horse to the right, with a ring ornament on his shoulder; in front, two ring ornaments; below, a wheel; above, a figure like the astronomical ♌; in the field, various annulets and pellets. The whole surrounded by a ring of pellets set at some distance apart. *N.* 83 grains.

This coin is in the Hunter Collection, and is engraved in Ruding, pl. i. 5. It is also engraved in White, No. 7. A coin of the same type is engraved in Stukeley, pl. xiv. 3; but the figure above the horse is there converted into a snake, with a head at each end, of the genus called *Amphisbæna* by Pliny. I have another specimen, found near Colchester, with the legend also imperfect, only the lower portions of the letters being visible. As far as I can make it out, I fancy it to be DIBORIG, but it is not sufficiently clear to authorise our adding the name of Diborigus to the roll of British princes. The general analogy of the type with that of the gold coins of Dubnovellaunus and Vose[nos], Plate IV.

Nos. 10 and 13, shows that the prince who struck this coin was probably one of their contemporaries, but the place of finding and the character of the workmanship are more in accordance with the presumption that the dominions of Diborigus (if that was his name) were in Essex or Suffolk, rather than in Kent.

For other coins which may eventually prove to be inscribed, the reader is referred to Plate G, Nos. 7 to 14.

CHAPTER XV.

COINS OF THE EASTERN DISTRICT.

The tribe of the Iceni, which appears to have inhabited that part of England now comprised by the counties of Norfolk and Suffolk, and probably portions of adjacent counties, is mentioned by more than one ancient writer, though under a variety of names. That of "Iceni" is the form under which it appears in most copies of Tacitus, and that which is generally adopted. By Ptolemy, they are called the Simeni (Σιμενοί, or, as some copies give it, Ἰκενοί), and their chief town is said to be Venta. (Οὐέντα). The ninth Iter of Antoninus is from Venta Icenorum (or Icierum) to Londinium; and the geographer of Ravenna makes mention of the same town, but under the form Venta Cenomum. It is agreed on all hands that the site of this Venta was at Caistor, near Norwich; and the reason of the name of the tribe being so constantly mentioned in association with it, is, that there were at least two other Ventas in Britain, which were, in like manner, known as Venta Belgarum (*Winchester*), and Venta Silurum (*Caer Went, Monmouth*). In addition to this knowledge of the position of the capital town of the tribe, we learn from the narrative of Tacitus[*] that the territory of the Iceni cannot have been far distant from Camalodunum, and must have abutted on that of the Trinobantes. There is, moreover, a class of coins which are principally found in the counties of Norfolk and Suffolk, and which possess sufficient peculiarities of type to distinguish them as the currency of an

[*] See Smith's Dict. of Geography, s. v. Iceni.

independent tribe. On some of these coins the inscription ECEN occurs, which has been thought to refer to the name of the tribe, and seems to justify the reading ICENI in preference to SIMENI, or any of the other forms. A tribe called Cenimagni is specified among those who, after the surrender of the Trinobantes, sent ambassadors, and submitted themselves to Julius, and it has been suggested by Camden, and accepted by some other writers, that in the first portion of this name we are to recognise that of the Iceni. The principal facts which are known in connection with this tribe are those related by Tacitus.* In A.D. 50, the Iceni are spoken of as a powerful nation, and unbroken by war, because they had voluntarily entered into alliance with the Romans. At that time, however, they came into collision with the invaders, and were defeated by Ostorius; after which it would appear that they retained a kingly form of government, only by sufferance of the Romans. This may be gathered from the testamentary dispositions of one of their kings, who, in A.D. 61, when next the Iceni are mentioned, it would seem was but recently dead. This king, Prasutagus by name, renowned for his immense wealth, made the Roman emperor and his own two daughters his joint-heirs, thinking by this expedient to place both his kingdom and family beyond the reach of injury. How this arrangement succeeded is well known; the tyranny of the Romans having brought about the sanguinary revolt under Boadicea, or Bunduica, the widow of Prasutagus, in which the Iceni, in conjunction with the Trinobantes, and other tribes not accustomed as yet to the Roman yoke, destroyed the Roman garrison town of Camulodunum, the *municipium* Verulamium, and Londinium, which, though a great commercial mart, had not then been raised to the dignity of a *Colonia*. No less than 70,000 of the Romans and their allies are said to have been slaughtered, before Suetonius Paullinus, the Roman governor and general, was in a position to engage with the insurgents. In the engagement, however, which ensued, the defeat of the

* Ann., lib. xii. cap. 31, et seqq.

Britons was complete, their army having been nearly annihilated, and Boadicea driven to end her life by poison. From this time forward there is no mention of the Iceni in the pages of Roman history.

In speaking of the coins inscribed DODVOC, I have shown the extreme improbability of any coins having been struck in the name of Boadicea, and have also mentioned that no coins are known which can with safety be assigned to her husband, Prasutagus. The Iceni are said to have embraced the alliance of the Romans before A.D. 50, and whether Prasutagus was their king before that date appears to me very doubtful. Their entire defeat in that year by the Romans would lead to the conclusion that on their being again allowed to have a king of their own, he was not the same person who had formerly headed them in their hostile movement, but was, in accordance with the Roman policy, a nominee of the Roman emperor; appointed, like Cogidunus, " vetere ac jam pridem receptâ populi Romani consuetudine, ut haberet instrumenta servitutis et reges." The disposal of his property by his will, and the wealth he had been allowed to accumulate, both strengthen the supposition that Prasutagus was a mere creature of the Romans, and this leads to the inference that his coins, had any been struck by him, would, even more than those of Cunobeline, have shown marks of Roman influences. There are, however, not only no coins known which bear any portion of his name, but none of the coins which can with any probability be attributed to the Iceni, bear any other devices than those which must be regarded as purely British. The conclusion to be drawn from this circumstance, is, that the native coinage of the Iceni must have ceased in A.D. 50, if not before, and that we must not expect to find upon their coins either of the names mentioned by Tacitus.

There is, indeed, but one legend upon any of them that can with any degree of certainty be referred to one of their princes, and even in that case the evidence which connects the prince with the district of the Iceni, though strong, may be regarded as not absolutely conclusive. I think, however, that I am justified in placing the coins ascribed to Addedomaros at the head of those of the Eastern district, though they are probably earlier in date than the other coins. As, however, the proofs of his existence are entirely numismatic, it will be well to postpone what few remarks there are to be made upon his name, and the period at which he probably lived, until I come to the description of his coins.

The attribution to the district formerly inhabited by the Iceni, of the other coins both in gold and silver which follow in Plates XIV., XV., and XVI., rests partly on their types and partly upon the places of their discovery. As in several of the hoards which have been found, the inscribed and uninscribed coins have occurred together, and as there is little doubt as to the district to which the uninscribed coins are to be assigned, I have departed from the practice which I adopted in other cases, and have brought both classes of coins together. The only gold coins on which any legend is found are those of Addedomaros above mentioned; the inscriptions on the silver coins, as far as at present known, are ECEN, ECE, SAEMV, AESV, ANTED or ANTED, and CAV(?) DVRO, some remarks on each of which are appended to the descriptions of the coins. The uninscribed types present a considerable number of varieties, but with a general bond of union running through nearly all of them.

The first person who, as far as I know, suggested the attribution of coins of this class to the Iceni, was Sir Thomas Browne, the author of Pseudodoxia Epidemica. In his Hydriotaphia (p. 7, ed. 1669), he relates that at the two Caistors, by Norwich and Yarmouth "some British coyns of Gold have been dispersedly found; and no small number of Silver-pieces near Norwich, with a rude Head upon the Obverse, and with an ill-formed Horse on the Reverse, with Inscriptions *IC*, *Duro*, *T.*, whether implying *Iceni*, *Durotriges*, *Tascia*, or *Trinobantes*, we leave to higher conjecture." Gale, in his Itinerary of Antoninus (4to, 1709, p. 100), seems to refer to the same coins, and is, indeed, probably quoting Sir Thomas Browne. White, in the description of his Plate of British Coins (1773), also refers a coin of the type, Plate XV., No. 3, to the Iceni; and Akerman, Num. Chron., vol. i. p. 83, expresses his opinion that this class of coins is peculiar to Norfolk and Cambridgeshire. To Mr. Beale Poste, however, belongs the credit of having been the first to engrave a series of these coins in one plate, as coins of the Iceni (Arch. Assoc. Journ., vol. iv. p. 107; British Coins, p. 95), and this attribation was corroborated by Mr. C. Roach Smith, in his account of the find of coins of this class at Weston, near Attlebridge, Norfolk, printed in the Num. Chron., vol. xv. p. 98.

This celebrated hoard is supposed to have comprised from two to three hundred coins, which had been buried in a small urn. Among them were the following Roman family denarii:—

   Antonia—Legionary; much worn.
   Cassia—(Cohen, pl. xi. 4).
   Claudia—(Cohen, pl. xii. 6).

Though none of these coins appear to have been struck later than about 30 B.C., yet the state of wear of the coin of the Antonia family shows that the British coins interred with it, many of which were quite fresh and unworn, must have been struck many years subsequently, and probably some considerable time after the Christian era. In this hoard the inscribed and uninscribed coins were associated in something like equal proportions, and the same was the case in a hoard of about forty which were dug up in a small earthen vessel at March, in Cambridgeshire. It was the same in a find which took place at Battle, Sussex. Both these hoards are noticed in the Num. Chron., vol. i. p. 89. That a deposit of them should have been found in Sussex is very remarkable, as it so rarely occurs that British coins are found, at least in any number, at a distance from the district in which they were struck.

The types of most of these coins also afford testimony of

their belonging to a late period in the British series. On all
the gold coins the original laureate bust has degenerated to
such an extent as to be beyond all chance of recognition by
a casual observer, the principal features which are left being
usually but two crescents placed back to back. On some,
however, as Plate XIV., No. 11, these crescents form the
centre of a cruciform ornament, allied to, but more simple
than, that which we find on the coins of Tasciovanus and Andoco[mius], and the descent of which from the laureate bust
of the Macedonian stater has already been demonstrated. On
others the cruciform ornament has a kind of rosette in the
centre, instead of the two crescents. Now, taking the obverse
of the common gold coins of Tasciovanus as representing the
degree of degeneration of the original prototype at that
period, it is evident that (assuming the conditions under
which the alteration of the types took place to have
remained constant) these coins belong to a later stage in the
British series. Their usual weight, from 81½ to 83½ grains,
is also significant of the same thing. The difficulty in the
case is the absence of some of the types intermediate between
these very rude forms and the more complicated cruciform
ornaments, but probably future discoveries will supply some
of the missing links in the gold series. Among the silver
coins no such gap exists, as we have, in Plate XVI, Nos. 1
and 2, the cruciform ornament, in a stage but little removed
from that in which it occurs on the coins of Tasciovanus;
while on all the inscribed coins, the device of the obverse
preserves one of the wreaths, with the two crescents dividing
it in the centre, the place of the transverse wreath being
supplied by clusters of leaves, the whole device still preserving its general cruciform character. The constant occurrence
of the horse on the reverses of these coins, is what might be
expected from the obverse types. Many of the horses, however, show a peculiarity in the pellets on the shoulder, and
the hairy or branched character of their tails, which is, I
think, confined to this district. I have, however, noticed
this peculiar formation of the tail on some Gaulish coins;

see, for instance, those attributed to the Morini, Revue Num., vol. xii. pl. xiii. 2, and pl. xiv. 4. That so extensive a series of silver coins should have been struck with types derived from the gold coinage is another peculiarity. The second series of silver coins, with a head upon the obverse, which first assumes the form of a nondescript swine-like animal, and then becomes a perfect boar, is apparently derived from some other prototype. The various steps of this strange transmutation are pointed out in the description of Plate XVI., No. 11. The average weight of twenty-three of these silver coins in my own collection is fully 18 grains, which approximates very closely to the weight of the silver coins of Antedrigus, &c., found at Nunney (see page 145). What relation they bore to the Roman denarii found with them, it is impossible to say, as they are of much baser metal. If weight alone were the criterion, it would appear that three of them went to the denarius. Their relation to the gold coins is also of course unknown.

Of copper coins which can with any degree of certainty be attributed to the Iceni, there are none. It is, however, probable that those engraved in Plate G, Nos. 11 and 12, belong to this district.

ADDEDOMAROS.

I was the first to assign coins to this prince* in the year 1850, since which time some two or three more of his coins have been found, which have, however, thrown but little new light upon his history. It was only by the comparison of several coins that I was enabled to complete the name of ADDEDOMAROS; but I have little doubt that the form in which I have given it is correct. The termination MAROS or MARVS is the same as that of several Gaulish names, such, for instance, as Indutiomarus and Virdomarus the well-known chieftains. That the A of the penultimate is short, and not long, as from its possible derivation from

* Num. Chron., vol. xviii. p. 155.

"Mawr," *great*, I should otherwise have been inclined to pronounce it, must be conceded from the passage of Propertius, lib. iv. c. 11, v. 41:

"Virdomari genus hic Rheno jactabat ab ipso."

Unless, indeed, this was a poetical license taken with a word which otherwise "verum dicere non est." The resemblance of the name of Addedomaros to that of the traditional Aedd-mawr, or Ædd the Great, of the Welsh chronicles, is well worthy of notice; but though we may trace this similarity of name, the same as we do that of Caractacus and Caradog, and Dyfnwal or Dunwallo and Dubnovellaunus, yet, even were we to accept these chronicles as true, there appears to be nothing recorded of Aedd-mawr, except that he was one of the progenitors of a long line of British kings who are assumed to have reigned in this island for ages before the art of coining was introduced, and even before it had been invented.

For the history of the Addedomaros of the coins we must therefore refer to the coins themselves, though the information to be gathered from them is but scanty. And first, as to the territory over which he reigned. The places where his coins are recorded to have been found are—Barrington, near Cambridge; the neighbourhood of Norwich; Ipswich; Colchester, Mark's Tey, and Halstead, in Essex; and Reculver, in Kent. From this it would appear that his dominions were certainly in the Eastern counties, but whether he ruled over the Iceni is not so certain, though the probabilities are greatly in favour of such an assumption. The types of his coins, with the exception of those with the regular cruciform ornament, have but little in common with those of the Trinobantes, and even the coins with the cruciform type have their distinctive peculiarities. And, moreover, the type of the obverse of Nos. 1 to 4, and the branch-like tails of the horses on the reverses, show a strong affinity to the coinage of the Iceni. Indeed, Mr. Beale Poste (p. 100), before the name of Addedomaros had been read on these coins, expressed his opinion from the types alone, that Plate XIV., Nos. 1 and 4 (Ruding, pl. ii. 40 and 41) were to be referred to the Iceni. It is probable that, as appears to have been the case with many of the British tribes, the boundary of the territory possessed by the Iceni was not always the same; and it is possible that before the days of Cunobeline, under whom Camulodunum became for the first time the principal city of Britain, the Iceni occupied some portion of the country which was afterwards held by the Trinobantes.

With regard to the period at which Addedomaros lived, conjectures on this point can only be founded on the weight of the coins, and the analogies of their types with those of coins whose dates we have some means of ascertaining. Now the weight of the coins ranges from $84\frac{1}{2}$ to 87 grains, the average weight of seven of them in my own collection being $85\frac{5}{7}$ grains; while the usual weight of the gold coins of Cunobeline is about 84 grains, and of those of Tasciovanus with the cruciform ornament, about 85 grains. The inference to be drawn from the weight is, therefore, that they are at least as early in date as the time of Tasciovanus, assuming the rate of diminution in weight from that of a common prototype to have been the same in each case. The types, which are three in number, are, in two cases, peculiar to the coins of Addedomaros, but are all derivatives of the type of the Macedonian stater. On the obverse of those of the first class, Plate XIV., Nos. 1 to 4, the crescents and clothing of the neck seem to have been combined to form an ornament closely allied to that on the silver coins of the Iceni, Plate XV., Nos. 1 to 13. On the second is a star composed of six wreaths with three crescents in the centre, and on the third a regular cruciform ornament of two wreaths at right angles to each other, with two crescents in the centre. The workmanship of the coins of the third class is superior to that of those of the second, and these in turn excel those of the first. Whether all three were the contemporaneous issues of three distinct mints, or whether they were the successive productions of one and the same mint, is of course uncertain. I am, however, inclined to the latter opinion; and if so, the types appear to have succeeded each other in the order in which I have arranged them. Now, on this hypothesis, the coins Nos. 7 to 9 must have been struck towards the close of the reign of Addedomaros, and though in general character they more closely resemble the uninscribed coins, Plate D, Nos. 6, 7, and 8, yet there is sufficient correspondence between them and the coins of Tasciovanus, Plate V., Nos. 7 to 9, to show that they belong to much the same period. The horse on the reverse of the coins of the second class is of much the same character as that on the coins of the third, but has above it the singular ornament, like that on the coin of Commius, Plate I., No. 10. On the coins of the first class the horse is of much ruder work, but is connected with that on the coins of the Iceni by its branched or bushy tail, and with those of Dubnovellaunus, in having a palm-branch beneath it. Of this type there are coins in two modules, the smaller being the fourth part of the larger. I do not know that this latter circumstance is of any real assistance in fixing the date of the coinage, nor is the absence of silver coins any sure guide, as such may possibly hereafter be found. Still this absence of silver coins, and the presence of small gold coins, is one of the features of the coins of Tinc[ommius], and altogether the impression left upon my mind, after a careful examination of the coins of Addedomaros, is, that they are to be assigned to a period commencing not very long after the accession of Tasciovanus, and extending over a considerable portion of his reign.

The form of the name, terminating as it does in OS,[*] instead of in VS, is another argument for assigning this degree of antiquity to the coins. The other princes whose names are thus terminated on their coins, Commius (?), Dubnovellaunus and Vos[onos], are all, as far as we have

---

[*] For interesting articles on the termination OS, on British and Gaulish coins, see papers by Mr. E. Oldfield in the Num. Chron., vol. xv, p. 107, and M. A. de Longpérier, in the Revue Num., N.S., vol. viii. p. 160.

the means of judging, of a date anterior to Cunobeline, whose name on his coins when written in full is Cunobelinus, and the legends on whose coins adopt Latin forms. It is true that the termination OS occurs also on the coins of the Brigantes, which are of a later period. They were, however, struck in a district remote from Roman influences, while the dominions of Addedomaros must have abutted on those of Cunobeline had they been contemporaries, and he would, therefore, probably have been brought in contact with Roman influences. It is, after all, by no means certain that some portion of these dominions of Addedomaros were not also comprised within those of Cunobeline, who, in that case, certainly was a successor, and not a predecessor, of Addedomaros.

The only argument in favour of assigning a later date to them, is afforded by the great baseness of their metal; but this, though of some weight, is by no means conclusive.

It will, however, be thought that enough time has been spent upon what is, after all, more conjecture; and I will, therefore, proceed to the consideration of the coins.

Plate XIV., No. 1.

Obv.—Ornament, consisting of two narrow solid crescents back to back, the cusps retorted and terminating in pellets; in the interior of each crescent a chevron-shaped compartment, enclosing five pellets; a pellet in each angle, between the crescents.

Rev.—ADDEDOMAROS. Horse prancing to the right, with a ring ornament on his hind-quarters, his tail branched; above, a rosette and a ring ornament; beneath, a branch and a ring ornament; in front and behind, two similar ornaments connected in the form of an 8.

Æ. 80, 85½, 84 grains.

This coin, in my own collection, has already been engraved in the Num. Chron., vol. xviii. p. 155, No. 1. I do not know where it was found. Another engraved in Ruding, pl. ii. 40, Hawkins, pl. i. 3, and Lelewel, pl. viii. 37, shows a string of three more ring ornaments behind the horse. A coin of this type, found at Mark's Tey, in Essex, was exhibited to the Num. Soc., April 25, 1844; and it is stated in Ruding* that a large parcel of them was found within five miles of Colchester in the year 1807, the metal of which was so base, that intrinsically the coins were worth only five shillings and sixpence each. An ancient forgery of a coin of this type, plated with gold, was found near Oxford, and is in the collection of the Rev. Richard Gordon, of Elsfield. There is some difference in the formation and in the number of leaves of the rosette, on different specimens of this type, as well as in the arrangement of the ring ornaments.

The type of the obverse differs from that of any other British coin known, but the crescents in the centre prove its derivation from the wide-spread laureate bust. The chevron-shaped portions of the ornament may either be reminiscences of the clothing of the neck, or even abbreviated forms of the wreath. Were the sides of the wreath on the coins of Dubnovellaunus, Plate IV., Nos. 6 to 9, made to converge to a point, instead of remaining parallel, a nearly similar ornament would result.

The legend on the reverse commences at the bottom, and runs from left to right beneath and in front of the horse, but owing to the die having been much larger than the coin, only the tops of the letters are visible. The S is apparently reversed, Ƨ. The rosette above the horse appears to be connected with the figure in the same position on the coins found near Guildford, Plate D, Nos. 6, 7, and 8; and on some specimens the linked ring ornaments are close together, like those on the coin found near Maidstone, Plate B, No. 12. The branched tail of the horse connects it with the Icenian coins, though the branches are on the inner side, as in Plate XVI., No. 6. The branch beneath the horse occurs in the same position on the gold coins of Dubnovellaunus.

The metal, a dark red gold, appears to be very base, and the coin is considerably dished.

* Vol. ii. p. 272.

Plate XIV., No. 2.

Obv.—Nearly similar to that of No. 1.

Rev.—ADDEDOMAROS. Horse with branched tail standing to the right; above, a branch of three leaves; below, a square with diagonal lines across; in front, a ring ornament between three pellets. *N.* 21½ grains.

This coin, which is of reddish gold, was formerly in the collection of the late Mr. Cuff, but is now in the British Museum. It is engraved in the Num. Chron., vol. xviii. p. 153, No. 2. It is difficult to say what plant the branch above the horse is intended to represent; the leaves, however, are of much the same shape as that above the horse on the coin of Cunobeline, Plate IX., No. 1. The square object beneath the horse occurs on no other coin of the British series. It is, however, found on several Gaulish coins, and on the gold coins and denarii of the Arria family, Cohen, pl. vii. 1 and 2. The Count Borghesi was the first to recognise in this latticed square on the Roman coins the *phalera* bestowed as the reward of valour on the Roman soldiers, and M. Deville,[*] of Rouen, and M. A. de Longpérier,[†] identified the object held so frequently by the charioteer on the Gaulish coins, with the same *phalera*. An article on the subject from the pen of Mr. Akerman will be found in the Num. Chron., vol. xi. p. 147, with a plate of the coins. On one of these the figure upon the horse is holding a branch in the one hand and the *phalera* in the other, while on this coin of Addedomarus we have the branch above the horse, and the *phalera* beneath. On the Gaulish coins the presence of these military decorations has been supposed to typify a conquest over the Romans; but this can hardly have been the case in this instance, though possibly the type may have been adopted as significant of independence of the Roman power.

The weight of this coin shows that, like the other small

[*] Mém. de la Soc. des Antiquaires de Normandie, 2nd serm, vol. iv.
[†] Revue Num., vol. xiii. p. 83.

British coins, it was intended to be current for the fourth part of the larger coins.

Plate XIV., No. 3.

Obv.—Similar to No. 1, but the chevrons ending in ring ornaments.

Rev.—ADDEDO.... As No. 1, but a wheel instead of the rosette above the horse, and with a pellet on its body, and no ring ornament on its haunches. *N*. 85 grains.

This coin, of pale yellow gold, was found near Norwich, and is in my own collection. The difference in type from No. 1 is but slight; the workmanship is a trifle better. It is engraved in the Num. Chron., vol. xviii. p. 155, No. 3.

Plate XIV., No. 4.

Obv.—As No. 3.

Rev.—[AD]DED[OM]ARO[S]. As No. 2, but with a wheel below the horse, and no pellets in front. *N*. 19 grains.

This coin, which is in the British Museum, is engraved, though not quite accurately, in Ruding, pl. ii. 41, and Lelewel, pl. viii. 39. From the wheel upon it, it would appear to have belonged to the same coinage as the preceding piece, of which it is the quarter.

Plate XIV., No. 5.

Obv.—Convex. Star-shaped ornament, formed of six curved wreaths or torses with pointed ends, enclosed by lines on either side, and diverging from three open crescents in the centre. The inner part of the crescents is ribbed, and there is a pellet and ring ornament in each of the spaces between the wreaths. The whole is surrounded by a beaded circle.

Rev.—AOOIIDO[M]. Long-tailed horse prancing to the right, with a beaded line forming a sort of dew-lap; above, an ornament somewhat like a bucranium, but in fact composed of three figures like the nose and mouth of the horse, combined into a star with three pellets; beneath the tail a ring ornament, and below the horse what may be called a cornu-copia, with three pellets above. *N*. 84¼ grains.

PLATE XIV., No. 6.

Obv.—As No. 5.

Rev.—AD[DII]DOM. As No. 5, but showing a pellet or small cross between two ring ornaments in front of the horse. *N.* 86¼ grains.
Other specimens, 81½, 83, 87 grains.

Of these two coins, the first, which is of red gold, is in my own collection, and the second in that of Mr. Bergne. I have another specimen, weighing 87 grains, which gives the perfect type of the obverse, and shows the whole of the cornucopiæ-like figure beneath the horse, with pellets on either side at its base; it has also two ring ornaments beneath the tail of the horse. Both the coins here engraved have already been published in the Num. Chron., vol. xviii. p. 155, Nos. 4 and 5. Other specimens are engraved in the Num. Journ., vol. i. pl. ii. 3 and 4, which are repeated in Ruding, pl. A, 89 and 90; Beale Poste, pl. iii. 1 and 2; Arch. Assoc. Journ., vol. iii. pl. iv. 1 and 2. The first of these two coins is also given in the Revue Num., vol. iv. pl. xiii. 7; Arch. Assoc. Journ., vol. ii. p. 22; and Beale Poste, p. 30; but in all these cases the device on the obverse is wrongly drawn, and the object above the horse made to look like a bucranium. Other coins, not showing the inscription, are engraved in Ruding, pl. ii. 35 and 36; and Lelewel, pl. viii. 43.

Coins of this type have been found at Mark's Tey (Num. Soc. Procs., May 25, 1843), and at Reculver (Battely, pl. vi. 1). Mr. Joseph Warren, of Ixworth, has one, found at Halstead, Essex. Mr. R. Almack, of Long Melford, Suffolk, has another found at that place.

The type of the obverse differs from that of any other British coins, and though, like many of them, composed of wreaths with crescents in the centre, yet the ornament is a star instead of a cross, and the number of wreaths and crescents are six and three, instead of four and two.

How this variety originated is a question which has still to be solved; for I must confess that I am not quite satisfied with the derivation I suggested in the Num. Chron., vol. xii. p. 127, though there appears a great tendency on some of the coins of the Channel Islands for the locks of hair to resolve themselves into some such figure. The furrowing of the inside of the crescents is very remarkable, and occurs also on the coins of the next type.

The principal characteristics of the reverse are the adjuncts above and below the horse, which itself much resembles in character those on the coins of the subsequent type, and the long-tailed horses on some of the gold coins of Dubnovellaunus and Tasciovanus. The object above the horse is precisely the same as that on the gold coin of Commius (?) Plate I., No. 10, being composed of three figures, each like the nose and mouth of the horse, though turned in the opposite direction. I am at a loss to know what it is intended to represent. The object below the horse has been called "a case of sacrificial knives," on what grounds I cannot say. The same object occurs on some of the Gaulish coins, as for instance those of the Belindi, Revue Num., vol. xvi. pl. xv. 1, and is, by M. de la Saussaye, called a cornu-copiæ, and such it appears to be on these coins, though whence derived it is no easy matter to say.* It may, however, possibly be a modification of the lyre-like figure on the gold coins, Plate D, Nos. 2, 3, and 4, and on some of those of the Channel Islands.

It is needless to remark upon the errors that have resulted from reading the legend on these coins as AΘOHI,† as that reading is now universally abandoned. As far as I have been able to observe, the final AROS of the name is never given on the coins of this type, nor on those of the next, the legend being in all cases ADDIIDOM, with the D's barred, and often Θ-like, and the double II for the E. I have made some remarks on this form of the letter at p. 258. On the coins of the preceding type the E is, as far as I have seen, always of the usual form.

* There are cornua-copiæ on the coins of Verica, Plate III., Nos. 5 and 6.
† See for instance Shakspere's Puck, by W. Bell, vol. ii. p. 140, where this coin is adduced as proof positive of the god Thor's appreciation in England in the pre-Romanic period!

It will have been observed that coins of both this and the preceding type were found at Mark's Tey, and as there is no record of any of the coins of the next type having been found there, this circumstance rather strengthens my hypothesis, that the coins with the cruciform ornament were the latest of the three varieties issued by Addedomarus. Could it be clearly shown that in a large hoard the coins of the two types were abundantly represented, and those of the third entirely absent, there would be little doubt upon this point.

Plate XIV., No. 7.

Obv.—Cruciform ornament formed of two wreaths at right angles, with two open crescents back to back in the centre. The wreaths formed of five lines, the outer and central lines plain and terminating in pellets, the others corded; the outer lines joined at the angles of the cross, and one of the centre lines carried through between the crescents, the inner portions of which are furrowed. The die with which this coin was struck was cracked and flawed.

Rev.—ADDIID[OM]. Horse prancing to the right; above, a ring ornament; below, a wheel and pellet; in front and behind, a pellet and ring ornament. *N*. 87 grains.

Plate XIV., No. 8.

Obv.—As No. 7.
Rev. [ADD]IIDOM. As No. 7. *N*. 85½ grains.

Plate XIV., No. 9.

Obv.—As No. 7.
Rev.—AOOIID[OM]. As No. 7. *N*. 85 grains.

In order more fully to exemplify this type, I have engraved these three coins, all of which are in my own collection. I do not know where Nos. 8 and 9 were found, but No. 7 was discovered at Barrington, near Cambridge, in 1851, and has been engraved in the Num. Chron., vol. xviii. p. 155, No. 6, and in a mistaken form, as regards the legend, in the Arch. Assoc. Journ., vol. vii. p. 122, though corrected at p. 308. It is also in Beale Poste, pp. 204 and 228. Mr. Warren has a coin of this type, found near Ipswich (weight, 82 grains), and one, supposed to have been found in Essex, is mentioned in the Arch. Assoc. Journ., vol. xvii. p. 69. Another, in the British Museum, weighing 86¼ grains, is engraved in the Num. Chron., vol. xiv. p. 71, No. 1.

The obverse type of these coins comes nearest to those of Andoco[mius] and Tasciovanus among the inscribed, and the Wonersh coins, Plate D, Nos. 6, 7, and 8, among the uninscribed, and is a legitimate descendant of the original laureate bust. The horse on the reverse, with the wheel beneath and the head formed with a ring ornament, is also of much the same character as that on these Surrey coins. The legend is the same as on the preceding coins, though I am not so sure that the final AROS may not eventually be found upon some specimen which shows the field in front of the horse. As it is, we have the legend ADDIIDOM, with the D's ranging in form from the Roman D, through the Saxon Ð to the Greek Θ. The silver Icenian coins, with ANTED, or ANTED, in monogram, afford another instance of the same variation, and a like peculiarity is found on the coins of Antedrigus. I have already remarked that it affords a commentary on the passage in Cæsar, as to the use of Greek letters by the Druids. The mixture of Greek and Roman letters, on the Gaulish coins, can of course be accounted for by the civilisation derived from the Greek colonies in the south of France, and these Θ-like D's occurring in Britain, may have come originally from the same source. It is to be observed, that among the Welsh the double D has still the sound of the Greek Θ.

In workmanship, the coins of this type are superior to those of the preceding, and far excel those of the first type described. As has already been observed, they are probably the latest of those of Addedomaros.

GOLD COINS ATTRIBUTED TO THE ICENI.

The attribution of the following coins to the Iceni rests entirely upon their types and the localities where they have been found, there being no inscription whatever upon them by which to determine it. Still the fact of their being, I believe, exclusively found within the territory of that tribe, and the analogies they present with the silver coins of much more certain attribution to the Iceni, are so conclusive, that I have arranged them with the coins of this district rather than among the other uninscribed coins. With regard to their date, we have nothing certain to guide us, as all the coins appear to have been found singly. The uninscribed silver coins were, however, current at the same time as the inscribed, and there is nothing in the type or weight of these gold coins, to render it improbable that they belong to the same period; there is, on the contrary, much to strengthen such a supposition, especially in the types of the three first coins.

PLATE XIV., No. 10.

Obv.—Two solid crescents back to back, their cusps forked; in each of them two pellets; between them, above, a star of five points; below, a triangle of pellets. A line runs below the crescents, beyond which the field is sunk to a lower level, and on this is another star.

Rev.—Rudely-formed horse galloping to the right; above, a peculiar looped figure combined with pellets, and bearing some general resemblance to a bucranium; below, a sort of flower of seven leaves and a pellet; behind, two pellets; beneath the horse's head a V-shaped figure. *N*. 82 grains.

This coin, which is in the British Museum, was found at Oxnead, Norfolk, in 1831, and is engraved in the Num. Journ., vol. i. pl. ii. 1; Hawkins, pl. i. 2; Ruding, pl. A, 87; Lelewel, pl. viii. 44; Revue Num., vol. iv. pl. xiii. 3; and Beale Poste, p. 100.

Mr. Akerman remarks upon it in the Num. Journ., vol. i. p. 224, that its type and place of finding are " in favour of an opinion entertained by some of our best numismatists, that the ancient British coins may some day not only be shown to belong to England, but also to particular districts." Mr. Beale Poste, however, was the first to assign this coin and No. 12 with any degree of confidence to the Iceni.

The type of the obverse is one of the most degenerate of the descendants of the Philippus, nothing being left even of the cruciform development, except the central crescents and a row of pellets. The combination of the crescents and the stars on the obverse is peculiar to this coin, as is also the figure above the horse on the reverse. The horse is most barbarously drawn, the neck terminating in almost a point behind the ear, and the nose being formed by a mere loop. The V-shaped figure is probably a bridle of some kind.

PLATE XIV., No. 11.

Obv.—Two solid crescents back to back in the centre of a cross formed by single lines of three pellets each, and with four ring ornaments in the spaces between the limbs.

Rev.—Horse to the right, ambling on an ornamented exergual line, its tail divided into branches; above, below, and in front, stars of pellets; in the field, two ring ornaments, one plain, the other beaded. N. 83½ grains.

This coin was found near Norwich, in 1853, and is now in the British Museum. I have already published it in the Num. Chron., vol. xix. p. 65, No. 1. The type of the obverse shows the cruciform ornament reduced to its simplest form, simpler even than that on Plate XVI., No. 1. Though so distinctly cruciform, the design is evidently closely connected with that on the preceding and subsequent coin. The horse bears some resemblance to that on No. 10, and the pendant beneath its eye is possibly a bridle. The branching of the tail is the same as on so many other Icenian coins, both in gold and silver, and differs from that on the coins of the first type of Addedomaros only in the branches being turned outwards instead of inwards. The ornamented exergual line may be compared with that of Plate XVI., Nos. 13 and 14.

Plate XIV., No. 12.

Obv.—Similar to No. 10, but without the stars, and with the triangle of pellets on the sunk part of the field.

Rev.—Horse prancing to the right; above, a beaded ring enclosing a triangle of pellets, and with others on each side; below, a star of five points. *N.* 81½, 81 grains.

This coin was found near Norwich, and is now in the British Museum. Another, showing triangles of pellets on each side of the crescent, and a ring ornament in front of the horse, was found at Colchester, and is engraved in Morant, pl. i. 5. A third, in the Hunter collection, is engraved in Ruding, pl. ii. 42, and in Lelewel, pl. viii. 38. This is like the coin in Morant, but shows that the shoulder of the horse is formed by a ring enclosing three pellets. The analogy of the type of the obverse, with that of the coin above it, No. 10, is obvious. There is, however, a considerable difference on the reverses, both in the character of the horse and the adjuncts on the field. The beaded circles, the triangle of pellets, and the star beneath the horse, all connect the reverse of this coin with that of the silver coins, Plate XVI., Nos. 10, 11, and 12. The comparatively light weight would seem to show that these coins were struck at a late period of the British coinage.

Plate XIV., No. 13.

Obv.—A voided cross, formed by arched lines with rows of pellets between; in the centre, a ring enclosing three crescents, clustered round a ring ornament.

Rev.—Horse to the right, its tail branched, with a pellet beneath it; above, a thin solid crescent, enclosing a star of pellets; below, a wheel of four spokes.
N. 83 grains.

This coin was found, in 1800, at Acle, Norfolk, and is in my own collection. A coin of the same type, in the British Museum, engraved in the Num. Journ., vol. i. pl. i. 6; Ruding, pl. A, 78; and the Rev. Num., vol. iv. pl. xiii. 5, shows an ornamented exergual line beneath the horse, very like that on No. 11. The type of the obverse is nearly, but

not quite, the same as that of the next coin, and presents a
curious phase of the cruciform ornament. The single lines of
pellets connect it with No. 11, and the three crescents in the
centre have something in common with the coins of Addedomaros, Nos. 5 and 6. The whole device, as it appeared on
the die, must have had more than usual of the shield-like
character so often apparent on the obverses with cruciform
devices, and must, in general design, have closely resembled
the coins of Verulam, Plate VIII., No. 1. Mr. Akerman
(Num. Journ., vol. i. p. 223) has suggested that the type
may possibly have been imitated from some Jewish or Macedonian coin with the shield; but it seems to me to be only
another instance of the natural process by which the laureate
head, when once reduced to an unintelligible shape, was
converted into a symmetrical figure, formed by the repetition
of a few simple crescents, pellets, lines, and circles.

The head of the horse on the reverse is of the peculiar
open form of that on the next coin, and on some of the
Icenian coins in silver; its tail is, as usual, branched, and the
hair of the mane is represented in the same manner by
straight strokes instead of by pellets. The narrow crescent
ending in pellets above it, is like that in front of the horse
on the coin found at Mark's Tey, Plate D, No. 1.

PLATE XIV., No. 14.

Obv.—Cross, as upon the last coin, but in the centre a circle with
three crescent-shaped indentations around a ring ornament.

Rev.—Horse galloping to the right, its tail branched; from the
root proceeds a crescent-shaped figure divided by a
zig-zag line into compartments with pellets in each;
beneath this is a triangle of pellets; behind the
horse a star of pellets and a ring ornament; beneath its tail a pellet; below, a ring ornament.
N. 80½ grains.

This coin, in my own collection, was found in Norfolk,
and is engraved in the Num. Chron., vol. xix. p. 64, No. 2.
Its chief characteristic is the peculiar crescent-shaped figure

above the horse, which is ornamented in the same manner as the exergue of many of the uninscribed gold coins. This figure does not occur in this position on any other British coin; but the tail of a horse on a Gaulish gold coin of the same class as those inscribed LVCOTTINA (?), engraved in Lambert, pl. vii. 17, is of precisely the same character, crescent-shaped and latticed. The horse has the long, open mouth, as on the preceding coin, and its tail has even more of the branched character. Its feet are flat, much like those of the animal on Plate C, Nos. 2 and 3, and the fore-legs are formed with two lines, near the shoulder, as if the artist had thought that both the *ulna* and *radius* ought to be shown with equal distinctness. This peculiarity is common on the silver coins of the Iceni. The weight of this coin is probably exceptionally high. It may, however, be of rather earlier date than the preceding coin. The length from the central ring ornament to the extremity of the only limb of the cross which is shown, will give a good idea of the great disproportion of size there was between the dies and the coins struck from them.

SILVER COINS ATTRIBUTED TO THE ICENI.

It will be seen that I have arranged the inscribed and uninscribed coins attributed to the Iceni, in two distinct series, and have allotted a Plate to each. It must, however, be borne in mind that the two series must have been contemporary, as was proved by the large hoards at Weston having consisted of coins of both classes in something like equal proportions, and showing an equal amount of wear. This co-existence of an inscribed and an uninscribed coinage in silver has been remarked in another part of the kingdom, the coins of Antedrigus, and SVFI, having been associated with a large number of anepigraphous coins of a similar type, in the hoard found at Nunney, near Frome. Among the Icenian coins there is, however, in nearly all cases, a difference in type between the two classes; the coins with

the obverse like that of Plate XV., Nos. 1 to 13, having
apparently always been inscribed, though, from the manner
in which the coins were struck, not always showing the
inscription, while none of the undoubtedly uninscribed coins
present that obverse. The only exception to this general
rule is Plate XV., No. 14, which it will hereafter be shown
has the same types, or nearly so, as Plate XVI., No. 9.
Among the inscribed coins the principal differences consist
in the legends, and the minor varieties in the character of
the horses or the number of pellets on their shoulders.

The uninscribed coins may be subdivided into four
classes:—

1. Those with a cruciform device on the obverse.
2. Those with a horse or other animal on both sides, but retaining portions of a wreath.
3. Those with a head on the obverse, and a horse on the reverse.
4. Those with a boar on the obverse, and a horse on the reverse.

There is, however, a sort of family likeness running
through the whole series; and the metamorphosis of the
human head into the boar, which has been before alluded
to, shows how one of the classes may be said to blend with
another. There are, besides, a few exceptional types which
occur on coins of great rarity, and as these have usually
been found by themselves, and not, as was the case at
Weston, associated with a number of coins of different
types, it is difficult to say whether they belong to an earlier
or later period than that of the Weston coins.

The weight of one piece (Plate XVI., No. 3) would seem
to indicate that it was the half of the larger coins. That in
the Hunter collection, of which a woodcut is given at p. 385,
seems to have been of the same denomination. I have also
a small coin, of which a woodcut is given at p. 402, and
which weighs but 8¼ grains.

PLATE XV., No. 1.

Obv.—Two open crescents back to back, with two pellets between
them; on their concave sides two curved lines meeting
and forming a foliation at their junction; above and

below the crescents, a transverse line with foliated ends; and beyond these a five-fold wreath, the outer and centre lines corded, the others plain.

Rev.—ECEN. Horse galloping to the right; above, a beaded ring ornament and pellets, and a sort of laurel branch instead of mane; below, three pellets; beneath the tail two pellets; beneath the head an S-shaped figure. The E connected to the horse's hind-leg.

Æ. 11¾ grains.

This coin, in my own collection, was found at Weston, but some of the details of the description are supplied from other specimens. Its weight is so small that I think it must be a plated coin. Another from the same find, with pellets above the horse, is engraved in the Num. Chron., vol. xv. p. 98, No. 5. Others with the letters indistinct are engraved in Wise, pl. xvi. 9; and in Gibson's Camden, pl. ii. 5, where Walker remarks on the type of the obverse, that if it " be not a pavilion or seat of state, he knows not what it is." Stukeley gives three coins of this type at pl. xv. 6, xvi. 10, and xvii. 5, but in all cases as reading CEN only. See also his pl. iii. 3 and 6, where one is given as reading ICE for the Iceni, and the other ELI for " Eli Maur Rex."

PLATE XV., No. 2.

Obv.—As No. 1.

Rev.—ECEN. As No. 2, but with three pellets or ovals on the shoulder of the horse. Æ. 19½ grains.

The difference between this coin and the last is but slight, and it is possible that the trefoil or triangle of pellets is absent on the coins of the first type, only in consequence of the wear, either of the dies or of the coins. Specimens were in the hoard found at Weston, and also in those at Battle and March. Examples from the two latter places are engraved in the Num. Chron., vol. i. pl. ii. 17 and 19. They weighed 19 and 18 grains respectively. One of them is copied by Lelewel, pl. viii. 45; in the Revue Num., vol iv. pl. xiii. 12; and Beale Poste, p. 33. Another coin is engraved in Beale Poste, p. 102, No. 2; and the Arch. Assoc.

Journ. vol. iv., pl. ii. 2. Another, found at Threxton, Norfolk, was exhibited to the Num. Soc., May 23, 1850.

PLATE XV., No. 3.

Obv.—As No. 1.
Rev.—ECE. Horse standing pawing with one fore-leg, the head full faced, a trefoil on the shoulder, the mane as on No. 1; above, a star of pellets; beneath the head an S.
Æ. 20 grains.

The coin here engraved is in my own collection. Others are engraved after Stukeley's peculiar manner in his pl. xiv. 2, xvii. 6, and xxiii. 3. Another in White's pl. No. 8, and Gough, No. 10, is made to read ICE. The type is correctly given in Taylor Combe, pl. i. 9; Lelewel, pl. viii. 46; Beale Poste, p. 102, No. 1; and the Arch. Assoc. Journ., vol. iv. pl. ii. 1. Mr. Warren of Ixworth has a specimen found at Icklingham, Suffolk.

The art displayed on these coins is usually rather superior to that of the generality of the Icenian coins, especially as regards the drawing of the horse, which has somewhat of the character of that on the coin of Cunobeline, Plate XII., No. 13. There are locks of hair at each fetlock, the same as on Nos. 7 and 8 in this Plate. The S-shaped figure beneath the head of the horse has much the appearance of being really the letter S, and has usually been considered to make the legend ECES. We find, however, a figure of nearly the same shape beneath the horse's head on most of these coins, varying in form from a complete S to a nearly straight line, as on No. 10, or an S reversed as on No. 11. It varies also very much in size. I am, therefore, rather inclined to the opinion that it is a form of bridle or halter, rather than a letter, though the point cannot be decided with certainty.

PLATE XV., No. 4.

Obv.—As No. 1.
Rev.—ECE. Horse prancing to the left, its fore-legs bifurcated upwards from the knee, a trefoil on the shoulder, the nose and mouth represented by a sort of trefoil; above, a star of pellets; below the head a small S-shaped figure.
Æ. 18½, 17½ grains.

Coins of this type were found at Weston (Num. Chron., vol. xv. p. 98, No. 4). One was found also at Sherborne, Dorsetshire, in 1843, and is engraved in the Num. Chron., vol. vi. p. 200; and Akerman, p. 182. That in Stukeley, pl. xxiii. 4, appears to be also of this type.

Plate XV., No. 5.

Obv.—As No. 1.
Rev.—ECE. As No. 4, but with six pellets on the shoulder of the horse. Æ. 17 grains.

This coin was also from the Weston hoard, and was presented to me by the late Mr. Goddard Johnson. I think it is a variety which has not before been engraved.

Plate XV., No. 6.

Obv.—As No. 1.
Rev.—As No. 5, but reversed, and without the S-shaped object beneath the head of the horse. Æ. 19½ grains.

I purchased this coin at the sale of the coins of the late Lord Northwick, and have already published it in the Num. Chron., vol. xx. p. 157, No. 12. I have another specimen which does not show the legend, but has the S-shaped figure beneath the horse's head.

This type is the last of those which I have engraved with the legend ECEN, or ECE, so that a few remarks on the types and legend will not be out of place. The obverse, beyond all doubt, is a reminiscence of the type of the gold coins derived originally from the Macedonian stater. The five-fold wreath with the crescents in the centre is a sufficient evidence of this fact. The crescents are, however, at right angles to the wreath, instead of being, like those on the gold coins of Dubnovellaunus, in the same line with it. The types most useful for comparison are, perhaps, those of Plate E, No. 5; Plate V., No. 14; Plate VIII., No. 6; Plate IX., No. 1; and Plate XIV., Nos. 10 and 12; though none present exactly the same conformation. The horses on the reverse testify to the same derivation, and some of them also show a connection with the gold coins attributed to the Iceni, in the open formation of the head, and the triangular rendering of the fore-arm. The principal characteristic of those coins is, however, the tendency which each portion of the device has to bud out into leaves. The ends of the crescents, the curved lines placed within their concave sides, the shoulders, and even the noses of the horses, are all more or less liable to sprout into leaves and trefoils, while the mane of the horse in many cases ceases to be the mane, and becomes metamorphosed into the leaves of one side of a branch, which arches over the neck of the horse. Another feature which some of the coins possess, in common with those reading ANTED, is the utilisation of parts of the legs of the horse to aid in forming the letters of the legend. The same appears to have been the case with some of the coins of the Brigantes, Plate XVII., No. 1.

With regard to the meaning of the legend ECEN, I think we cannot be far wrong in accepting for the present, the conclusion at which most of those who have treated of this subject have arrived, that it bears reference to the tribe of the Iceni, assuming that to have been really the name of the tribe. The difference in the spelling between ECEN and ICEN is so slight as not to be of any moment. The difficulties which attend this interpretation are of another character. The principal one is this, that if we attach a local meaning to the legend ECEN, analogy would compel us to attach local meanings also to the other legends which we find on kindred coins; such, for instance, as SAEMV, AESV, ANTED, and CAV(?). DVRO. With the exception of ANTED these legends are, however, of very rare occurrence, so that it is possible that they may relate to towns within the territory of the Iceni, the names of which, like that of Verulamium in some instances, formed the sole inscription on the coins struck there. But if so, why do we not find the name of Venta among them? Another difficulty is that it is contrary to the analogy of all the other classes of British coins to find merely the name of the tribe on the coins, and not that of the prince. This may, however, be met by the consideration that the coins of one district do not of necessity follow the same rules as those of another, especially when, as is the case here, one portion of the island was much more subject than another to Roman influences. Or again it may be supposed that we have in ANTED the name of the prince, and in ECEN and the other legends the names of the tribe over which he reigned, and of various towns within their territory. But of this more hereafter. Besides the coins of the larger modulo engraved in the Plates, there appear to be a few coins of small size which were probably representatives of half of their value. The woodcut shows one of these from the Hunter collection, which

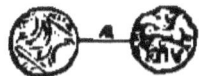

is, however, in poor condition; the legend, which has the appearance of being ECIV, was probably originally ECEN. See also Wise, pl. xvi. 10.

Plate XV., No. 7.

Obv.—As No. 1.

Rev.—SAEMV or SAFMV. Horse, as on No. 4, but with six pellets on the shoulder; above, a star of pellets. R. 18½ grains.

This coin, in the Bodleian collection at Oxford, is engraved in Wise, pl. xvi. 11, but so imperfectly, that the inscription cannot be made out. I have already engraved it in the Num. Chron., vol. xvi. p. 80, No. 7. I have another specimen of the same type, which was formerly in the collection of the late Mr. Huxtable, and is engraved in the Num. Chron., vol. xv. p. 98, No. 12. It is also given in the Arch. Assoc. Journ., vol. iv. pl. ii. 7; and in Beale Poste, p. 102, No. 7, as reading SITMV, and is there referred to Sitomagus, a city of the Iceni. The legend is, however, the same as on the Bodleian coin, though the A has been partially obliterated. Such being the case, the attribution to Sitomagus must be abandoned, unless possibly the name of that town has come down to us in a corrupt form, and originally commenced in a manner more like the inscription on these coins. The name of the tribe as given by Ptolemy is, it will be remembered, Σιμενοί, with which SAEMV may appear to have some affinity. It is, however, very doubtful whether the passage in Ptolemy is not corrupt. A coin of this type, but showing only the three first letters of the legend, was found at Brancaster, Norfolk, and has been communicated to me by Mr. C. Roach Smith. The legend on the next coin has more resemblance to the name of a British town, but the correspondence between the two coins is such, that they would almost appear to have been engraved by the same hand.

Plate XV., No. 8.

Obv.—As No. 1.
Rev.—AESV. Horse, &c., in all respects as on No. 7.
Æ. 18½ grains.

This coin, in my own collection, has been engraved in the Num. Chron., vol. xvi. p. 80, No. 8, and formed part of the Weston find. Camden (p. lxxxix., Gibson's Ed.) makes mention of a coin with a horse, but ill shaped, and EISV, and on the reverse an ear of corn, which was possibly of this type. Although no town of the name AESV is known within the province of the Iceni, the similarity of this legend to the name of Isu-brigantum, or Isurium, is worth notice, and the fact that the name of the Brigantes was appended to the Yorkshire ISV may indicate that there was another town of much the same name from which it required to be distinguished. At all events this similarity gives some colour to the supposition that the inscriptions AESV and SAEMV may designate the names of some towns of the Iceni.

Plate XV., No. 9.

Obv.—As No. 1.
Rev.—ANTED in monogram, part of the A being formed of the hind-leg of a horse going to the right. Above the horse a beaded ring ornament and triangles of pellets;

below, a triangle of pellets; beneath the tail two pellets; the mane converted into a branch, as on No. 1; the tail branched at the end; beneath the head, which is large and open at the mouth, an S-shaped figure. On some coins there are three pellets on the shoulder. Æ.

PLATE XV., No. 10.

Obv.—As No. 1.

Rev.—As No. 9, but reading ANTD. The three first letters in monogram. Æ.

PLATE XV., No. 11.

Obv.—As No. 1.

Rev.—As Nos. 9 and 10, but reading ANTD. Æ.

The usual weight of these coins is from 15 to 20 grains, the average being about 18 grains. There were many of them in the Weston find, and also in that of March, Cambridgeshire. Specimens are engraved in the Num. Journ., vol. i. pl. ii. 2; Num. Chron., vol. i. pl. ii. 20; and vol. xv. p. 98, Nos. 7 and 8; Ruding, pl. A, No. 88; Arch. Assoc. Journ., vol. iv. pl. ii.; and Beale Poste, p. 102, Nos. 4, 5, and 6. Compare also Stukeley, pl. iii. 1, and pl. xvii. 8. Mr. Warren of Ixworth has a coin like No. 11, found at Icklingham, Suffolk.

The type of the obverse is precisely the same as that of the coins reading ECEN, with which these coins appear to have been contemporary. The horse also has the same large head, and differs in this respect from those on the coins with ECE only, these latter having the peculiar head with the foliated nose. The legend is no doubt ANTED or ANTED, but it is barely possible that there may be another letter or more in front of the horse. The utilisation of the leg of the horse to form part of a letter is one of the characteristics of this class of coins, and may be observed also on the coins reading ECEN, as well as on Nos. 12 and 14 in this Plate.

With regard to the meaning of the legend ANTED or ANTED, I have already observed that if that of ECEN or ECE may be referred to the name of the tribe of the Iceni, this may be considered to represent the name of some prince

who ruled over that tribe. The question is, how far we are
justified in assuming such a view to be correct, and if so, in
what manner to complete the name of the prince. I am much
inclined to think that his name was ANTEDRIGVS, and
that he was in fact the same prince, of whose coins I have
already treated among those of the Western District, at
p. 144. The correspondence in the name as far as it appears
on these silver coins is perfect, for on the silver coins found
at Nunney (Plate I., No. 8, &c.,) the name of Antedrigus is
in like manner given as ANTED or ANTED. As far as the
date of the two classes of coins is concerned, they appear to
have been nearly, though not quite, contemporary. We
have already seen that in both the Weston and Nunney
finds, the British coins were associated with several Roman
coins—in the Weston case, with family coins showing considerable wear, and in the Nunney case, with both family
and Imperial coins;—so that the Nunney hoard would appear
to be of rather later date than that of Weston. The approximate date which I have assigned to the Nunney deposit is
from A.D. 50 to 55, while I have shown the probability of
the Icenian coinage having ceased at all events in A.D. 50,
after their defeat by Ostorius. It does not appear from
history who was their chieftain at that time, but I think it
very improbable that it was Prasutagus, who was far more
probably a mere creature of the Romans, appointed by them
as the regulus of the tribe, on their submission to the
Imperial power. I would therefore suggest that it was
Antedrigus who was their ruler at the time of their attempt
to liberate Britain from the Roman yoke, and that after the
defeat of the Iceni by Ostorius, he retreated into the west,
either with some remnant of his people, or else as having
been elected to the sovereignty over some other British
tribe or league of tribes. If the latter were the case, his
career would be, to some extent, similar to that of Caractacus, who, though a son of Cunobeline, the king of the
Trinobantes, appears eventually to have become a chief of
the Silures. Under any circumstances, the occurrence of

the name ANTED on coins belonging, the one class to the East and the other to the West of Britain, is a fact worthy of attentive consideration. That coins of the Iceni should have been found near Portsmouth, and at Sherborne, Dorsetshire, affords some corroboration of the ANTED on the two classes of coins referring to the same individual. There were not, however, so far as I am aware, any Icenian coins in the Nunney hoard.

I may here mention that one of the silver coins of Antedrigus, of the type Plate I., No. 8, was found in March, 1858, in a barrow in Whichwood Forest, Bucks, or about midway between Norfolk and Somersetshire. Some Roman coins of Augustus, Nero, and Vespasian were found in the same barrow, but apparently not in association with the British coin. A notice of the discovery was communicated to the Num. Chron., N.S., vol. iii. p. 145, by Mr. A. W. Franks.

PLATE XV., No. 12.

Obv.—As No. 1.
Rev.—ED. Horse to the right, as on No. 9. Æ.

This coin, in the British Museum, was found near Portsmouth, and has been engraved by Beale Poste, p. 102, No. 3. The complete legend is probably ANTED, as on the preceding coins, though the E is joined on to the horse's leg instead of the A. It affords another instance of a British coin being found at a distance from the district to which it belongs; but, as already observed, it rather confirms the view of there having been some close connection between the tribes of the West and of the East, under Antedrigus.

PLATE XV., No. 13.

Obv.—As No. 1.
Rev.—T. Horse to the right, as on No. 9, but with claw-like feet. Æ.

This coin, which is in the British Museum, formed part of the Weston hoard, and is engraved in the Num. Chron., vol. xv. p. 98, No. 6. It seems probable that though showing merely the T, the legend may have been originally ANT on the die; or again, both this and the preceding coin may have been contemporary forgeries with blundered legends.

Sir Thomas Browne (see p. 360) cites a coin inscribed T as having been found in Norfolk.

PLATE XV., No. 14.

Obv.—Portions of a pig-like animal to the right; beneath, a figure like an A with a ring above it. The whole within a double circle, the outer one beaded.

Rev.—CAV(?) .. DVRO. Horse to the right, the mane formed by a double line of pellets, the tail slightly branched, a pellet beneath it, and another beneath the body. The D of the legend partly formed of the hind-leg of the horse. Æ.

This coin, from the Weston find, is in the British Museum, and is engraved in the Num. Chron., vol. xv. p. 98, No. 2, but the obverse is drawn the wrong way upwards, on account of the device not having been understood. A woodcut of it is given by Beale Poste, p. 258, who goes so far as to read the legs of the animal and the figure beneath it as IIVG, which he completes as Jugantes, and regards as another name of the Iceni. The annexed woodcut, from a coin in

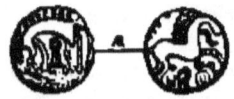

the Hunter collection at Glasgow, will, however, show the true character of the obverse, and prove that it is of precisely the same class as Nos. 9, 10, and 11, in Plate XVI, some of which were found in the same hoard. A specimen of the same type was engraved by Gibson, pl. ii. 8; but he also has drawn the animal with its feet in the air, which made Walker take it to be "a ship or galley with oars." He says it was coined by a Christian prince or city, as the ship is adorned with a cross. The DVRO on the reverse, he "questions not was *Durobernia*, or Canterbury, now the chief seat of the great Archbishop and Primate of the Nation." Stukeley seems to have understood the nature of the animal better, as he has, in pl. iii. 2, given a coin with DVRO on the reverse, and no doubt, of this type, with a well-formed pig on the obverse.

I have already mentioned that Sir Thomas Browne in his Hydriotaphia (p. 7, ed. 1669) cites coins with the inscriptions *Ic: Duro: T*, as found in Norfolk; a statement which Gale, in his Itinerary of Antoninus (ed. 1709, p. 109) repeats. There seems little doubt that Browne must have referred to three distinct classes of coins, which may safely be identified as the three principal classes in this Plate, those with ECE; the coin now under consideration; and those reading ANTED (and even T).

Some remarks upon the derivation of the type of the obverse will be found at p. 400, where the coins in Plate XVI., bearing the same device, are described. The only differences in the type consist in the A-shaped figure beneath the animal, which corresponds to the triangle of pellets on Nos. 10 and 11, and in there being a double circle surrounding the whole.

The legend on the reverse shows the usual peculiarity of the Icenian coins, in having one of the letters linked to the hind-leg of the horse; there is also the S-shaped figure beneath the head. There is some uncertainty attaching to the first portion of the legend, as it may be either CAV (the last two letters linked), CAN, or CAM. The probability is in favour of the latter. Both CAM and DVRO enter frequently into the composition of the names of British towns, and there were, as Mr. C. Roach Smith has already pointed out (Num. Chron., vol. xv. p. 101), places called Camboricum, Durolipons, and Durobrivæ, within the territory of the Iceni; still, as he further remarks, the two inscriptions upon one coin can hardly be supposed to indicate two places. Beale Posto completes the legend, CAMVLOS DVROTRIGON, implying the god Camulus of the Iceni Durotriges. It is, however, out of the question to suppose that the name of a divinity forms the only

legend on a coin of this class, and it is a violation of all
probability to bring upon an Icenian coin the name of the
Durotriges, a tribe placed by Ptolemy south and west of
the Belgæ; though Mr. Poste assumes that Durotriges and
Coritani are synonymous, in order to get over this difficulty.
I have nothing to offer that will afford any satisfactory solution of the enigma presented by this inscription. I think,
however, that in all probability it is of local signification,
and for want of a better interpretation, would suggest that
like Cornovium or Corinium in Britain, and Catalaunum in
Gaul, Camboricum or Camboritum may possibly have had
the prefix of Duro attached to it, in which case the inscription would be read DVRO-CAM [BORICVM].

We now come to the uninscribed silver coins, which from
their types or places of finding are supposed to have been
struck by the Iceni.

PLATE XVI., No. 1.

Obv.—Cruciform ornament formed of four branches diverging
from two open crescents and two ring ornaments in
the centre; in each angle of the cross, a triangle of
pellets.

Rev.—Horse prancing to the left, the nose foliated, the ears
curved forwards like horns, the fore-arm divided as on
Plate XV., No. 4; six pellets on the shoulder; above,
a wheel and various pellets; below, a ring ornament.
Æ. 19¼ grains.

This coin formed part of the Weston hoard, and is in the
British Museum. I have another from the same find, which
shows a triangle of pellets above the horse's head, the lower
one connected to a curved line coming from above the wheel.
There are traces of a wheel or ring ornament in front
of the horse; and the same is the case on another coin
from the same place, engraved in the Num. Chron., vol. xv.
p. 98, No. 1.

Until the discovery of the hoard at Weston, this type
appears to have been unknown. It is of great interest, as
affording so decided a connecting link between these Icenian

silver coins and those in gold, Plate XIV., No. 11, as well as with so many other British coins, on which the laureate head of the prototype has assumed the cruciform condition. The horse on the reverse, with the six pellets on the shoulder and with the divided fore-arm, is the same as that on many of the inscribed coins of the Iceni. The ears, which are hardly shown on the coin here engraved, resemble those of the horse on Plate B, No. 4, but both appear, instead of only one. Though rather longer and more curved, they resemble also those of the horse on No. 13, on which, too, the wheel occurs in the same position.

Plate XVI., No. 2.

Obv.—Cruciform ornament formed of wreaths, with open crescents in the centre, and with ring ornaments and pellets in the angles; the outer lines of the wreaths are plain, and the inner ones (in one case two and in the other three) are corded.

Rev.—Uncertain animal running to the right, looking backwards, with its tail erect, its head and shoulder formed with ring ornaments; above, an annulet and pellets; below, two annulets or lyre-shaped objects and a pellet; behind, an annulet. Æ. $14\frac{7}{8}$ grains.

This coin, which is in the British Museum, was found in Suffolk. I have already published it in the Num. Chron., vol. xix. p. 64, No. 6. The type of the obverse bears a considerable resemblance to that of the gold coins of Addedomaros, Plate XIV., Nos. 7, 8, and 9, and the crescents in the centre present the same peculiarity of being furrowed or ribbed inside. It is hard to say what animal the artist intended to represent on the reverse, but it bears much analogy with that on the coin of Cunobeline, Plate XI., No. 14. In general character there is considerable resemblance between this coin and that in gold inscribed MOD (?) Plate XIII., No. 13, but it seems entitled to a place among the coins of the Iceni until cause can be shown to the contrary. A coin of apparently much the same type is engraved in Stukeley, pl. xiv. 5.

PLATE XVI., No. 3.

Obv.—Horse to the left; above, a wreath springing from an open crescent; in the field a ring ornament and a decorated ring ornament with plain ring ornaments above and below, and another below the horse, rudiated.

Rev.—Bird-headed animal to the right, with long ears and a tail ending in a ring, apparently pecking at a snake; in front; behind, a beaded wheel; in the field, ring ornaments. Æ. $7\frac{1}{5}$ grains.

This coin, which is in the Museum collection, is engraved in the Num. Chron., vol. xix. p. 64, No. 7. It is not known where it was found, but its general character seems to justify its being assigned to the Iceni. It is hard to say which side of such a coin should be called the obverse; strictly speaking, that with the ornithocephalous animal, being the convex side, should be so termed. I have, however, taken the other side on account of the crescent and wreath, the quarter of the well-known cruciform ornament, being above the horse upon it. On the next coin, which in type is closely connected with this, there are traces of a wreath in front of the animal, which there appears on the obverse. The reverse of No. 3 must therefore be compared with the obverse of No. 4, and *vice versa*. The occurrence of the wreath and crescent in conjunction with the horse, shows how completely the original derivation of the cruciform ornament had been forgotten. It will be observed that on No. 5 a wreath makes its appearance beneath the horse on the reverse. From the diminutive weight of the coin now under consideration, it would seem, like some other specimens, to have been current as the half of the larger coins.

PLATE XVI., No. 4.

Obv.—Animal with but one fore and one hind-leg, standing on a beaded exergual line; its head formed of a ring ornament, with long ears and open mouth; above, a ring ornament with three corded lines springing from it; behind and below, ring ornaments;

in front, a horizontal wreath or double row of pellets, with small solid crescents above and below.

Rev.—Horse to the left; above, a star formed of solid crescents (?); below, a ring ornament. Æ.

This coin, in the collection of the late Lord Braybrooke, was found at Chesterford, and has not, I believe, before been published. Its analogy with the preceding coin is obvious; though, as before observed, the obverse of the one must be compared with the reverse of the other. It would appear as if the artist, in engraving the obverse of this coin, must have had as a pattern some coin with the remains of the laureate head upon it, but on which he most excusably failed to recognise anything of the kind, and accordingly converted the device into a nondescript animal, though retaining a portion of a wreath running between locks of hair in front of it. Or again, the device may have originated from a head in profile, of somewhat the same character as that on No. 5, on which, if viewed sideways, the forehead, cheek, and chin readily assume a zoomorphic character. Compare also such coins as Plate F, No. 9. The place of finding of this coin rather strengthens its attribution to the Iceni.

Plate XVI., No. 5.

Obv.—Head in profile to the right, with long flowing locks of hair, prominent cheek-bones, projecting lips, and a pellet for the eye.

Rev.—Horse to the left, its fore-arms slightly forked, and with an S-shaped object connecting its mouth to a small ring-ornament; above, a large ornamented pellet; below, a wreath and a conical line attached to one hind-leg; in front, some s-shaped objects; behind, two small ring-ornaments. Æ. 14 grains.

This coin, which was found at Icklingham, Suffolk, is, through the kindness of Mr. Joseph Warren, of Ixworth, now in my own collection. Its edge has unfortunately been broken, so that the profile of the face is lost. Though turned in the opposite direction, there is some resemblance, especially in the arrangement of the hair, between the head on this coin and that on Plate G, No. 2, which was found near Bury St. Edmund's. The x-shaped objects on the reverse are also probably portions of the same figures as appear in front of the face on the Bury coin, though also turned in the opposite direction. The horse on the reverse exhibits the usual tendency of the Icenian horses to show their *ulna* and *radius* as distinct. The wreath beneath the horse is a very curious feature in the coin, especially as it differs in character from the usual wreaths, in the two rows of leaves being close together.

The corded line between the hind-leg and the body may possibly be an accidental elongation of the mane. The S-shaped object attached to the mouth appears to be much the same as what is found upon the inscribed coins, and bears out the supposition that it is merely the bridle, and not a letter S.

PLATE XVI., No. 6.

Obv.—Head in profile to the left, the principal features being the eye and ear; the hair formed by a crescent of three beaded lines enclosed by plain lines on either side.

Rev.—Horse to the right, with one fore-arm divided; the tail branched; beneath it a triangle of pellets; above, an open crescent (?); below, a ring ornament; below the mouth an S-shaped figure. Æ. 14½ grains.

This coin, which is apparently unique, was found at March, Cambridgeshire, and is now in my own collection. It has already been engraved in the Num. Chron., vol. ii. p. 74, No. 8. The hoard out of which it came seems to have consisted entirely of Icenian coins; and the branched tail and general character of the horse on the reverse, prove this coin to belong to that class. The head on the obverse, which is beautiful in its simplicity, shows some slight analogy with that on the preceding coin, but otherwise stands by itself. It is difficult to conceive what might have been the next phase of such a head, had this coin served a native artist as a prototype from which to engrave dies.

Plate XVI., No. 7.

Obv.—Barbarous head in profile to the right, cusped below the chin, the hair standing up beyond the outline of the head; behind, a branch; in front, two triangles of leaves; below, a triangle of pellets. The whole apparently within a beaded circle.

Rev.—Horse to the right, its nose foliated and its tail branched, both its fore-legs continued in relief across its shoulder; above, a compartment formed by three beaded or corded lines (each a portion of a circle with the convex side downwards), enclosing a triangle with its sides curved inwards; below, a diamond with its sides curved inwards, and a pellet at each angle, and sometimes in the centre; above and below the tail a pellet. Æ, 19½ grains, 18 grains.

Plate XVI., No. 8.

Obv.—As No. 7, but the head still more barbarous, the features being rendered by raised lines, and the outlines of the neck and cheek forming a sort of triangle, with a curved end projecting, to form the eyebrow or forehead.

Rev.—As No. 7. Æ, 19½ grains, 17½ grains.

Both the coins here engraved are mine, and came from the Weston hoard, where a considerable number of them were found. Some of the particulars of the description of the types are taken from other specimens. A coin from the find at Battle, much like No. 7, is engraved in the Num. Chron., vol. i. pl. ii. 15. Those in Stukeley, pl. xxiii. 6, 7, 8, 9, appear also to have been of this type. A coin from March, Cambridgeshire, like No. 8, is engraved in the Num. Chron., vol. i. pl. ii. 16; another from Weston, in vol. xv. p. 98, No. 3. Mr. Warren of Ixworth has a coin like No. 7, which was found at that place; and another like it from Mildenhall, but with the mane of the horse the same as on No. 11. He has also specimens like No. 8, found at Pakenham and Ixworth, Suffolk. Other specimens of these types are given in Gibson's Camden, pl. ii. 6; Wise, pl. xvi. 16 and 18; Stukeley, pl. xvi. 2, and xviii. 9; Num. Journ., vol. i. pl. i. 6; Ruding, pl. A, 70; Revue Num., vol. iv. pl. xiii. 11, and Lambert, pl. xi. *bis* 15.

The head on these coins has a character of its own, and it is hard to say whence it was originally derived. That on No. 8 is, however, evidently a degeneration from that on No. 7, and has a much more truculent expression, besides having the hair bristling upon it like a hog's mane. The branch behind and the trefoils in front are very characteristic of the Icenian coinage. On the reverse, the canopy-like figure above the horse and the diamond below are peculiar to these types. A form very similar to the latter occurs on the small copper coins of Verulam, Plate VIII., No. 1, and those in silver of Verica (?), p. 185, No. 3.

Plate XVI., No. 9.

Obv.—Pig-like animal, with long bristling mane, to the right; the hind-legs crossed, and one of the fore-legs detached and coming down in front of the head; pellets beneath the body and tail. The whole surrounded by a beaded circle (?).

Rev.—Horse to the right, with open mouth and ears curved forwards; above, a wheel between two pellets; below, a curved figure, like the astronomical sign ♌ with a pellet in the centre, and a triangle of pellets on either side; beneath the tail two pellets, others in front. Æ. 14½, 17½ grains.

Several coins of this type were found at Weston, from some of which I have added details in the description, not shown on the coin, from my own collection, here engraved. I have another coin of the same type found at Wangford, Suffolk, and Mr. Warren has one found at Ixworth.

As the obverse so closely resembles some of the succeeding coins, I will defer any remarks upon it for the present. The horse is much like that on the coins reading ANTED, but the Ω-shaped figure beneath it is peculiar to this type among the silver coins. I cannot say what it was intended to represent, but a nearly similar figure occurs above the horse on the gold coin, Plate XIII., No. 14.

PLATE XVI., No. 10.

Obv.—Boar-like animal to the right, its mane erect, one of its fore-legs connected to its snout and joined to the other below, so as to form a triangle with the head; above, a portion of a triangle between two ring ornaments (?); below, a triangle of pellets; behind, a ring ornament.

Rev.—Horse to the right, on an exergual line, the mane represented by a curved line connected by spokes to the neck; the tail bifurcated, and curved both upwards and downwards; above, a triangle of pellets; below, a star of six points. Æ. 17$_{\frac{7}{8}}$ grains.

This coin is also from the Weston find, and is in the British Museum. Another specimen found in Suffolk is engraved in Hawkins, pl. i. 16, but the ring ornament and tail of the animal are made to look as if they were the head. Above the pig there appear to be two, if not three, ring ornaments. The mane of the horse on the reverse of these coins is represented in the same manner as it is on some of the coins of Cunobeline (Plate IX., Nos. 8 and 14), but the most remarkable feature of the coins is their correspondence in type with those in brass ascribed to the Aulerci Eburovices (Lambert, pl. viii. 21; Lelewel, pl. ix. 46), which have for types a boar to the right on the obverse, and a horse to the right with a star beneath, on the reverse. The bifurcation of the tail of the horse is something like that on the gold coin, Plate XIV., No. 14.

I have a plated coin of this type, an ancient forgery, which was found at Icklingham, Suffolk, and kindly presented to me by Mr. Joseph Warren. It shows that the animal on the obverse stands on an ornamented exergual line, consisting of two straight lines with a row of pellets between them, and that the head of the horse on the reverse is most disproportionately large, and formed with a ring ornament like that on Plate XIV., No. 11, which it also resembles in having the pendant beneath.

PLATE XVL, No. 11.

Obv.—Animal like that on No. 10, but showing a sort of tusk at the snout; at the end of the snout a pellet with an open crescent above; in front, an annulet (?) and a triangle of pellets; above, two beaded rings; below, a triangle of pellets; beneath the tail, another pellet.

Rev.—Horse to the right, the mane as on No. 10, the tail branched; above, a ring of pellets enclosing three others, and a triangle of pellets. There is an exergual line, beneath which is a row of pellets.

Æ. 15½ grains.

This coin, which was found at March, Cambridgeshire, is in my own collection. It is engraved in the Num. Chron., vol. ii. p. 74, No. 7, and in the Revue Num., vol. v. pl. xix. 2. A coin of the same type from the Weston hoard is engraved in the Num. Chron., vol. xv. p. 98, No. 10, and shows that the beaded rings above the boar enclose triangle of pellets, and that there is a kind of wreath between them of three lines, that in the centre beaded.

The animal on the obverse of this and the two preceding coins is evidently intended for a boar, as will at once be seen by comparing it with that on the next coin, No. 12. There is, however, something very peculiar in the triangular outline presented by the upper part of the fore-legs, as well as in the enormous development of mane so apparent on Nos. 9 and 10.

It may appear fanciful, but I think that these peculiarities are to be accounted for by regarding the animal as presenting an intermediate phase between the human head on No. 9 and the perfect boar on No. 12. If the reader will look at the head on No. 9 with the face *downwards*, he will at once understand my meaning, and perceive how an engraver copying such a coin on to a die, might engrave this pig-like animal from it—the triangular neck and chin forming the head and fore-legs, the continuation of this triangle round the face being converted into the body, and the hair into the mane. The animal in this case would, however, be turned to the left; but assuming it to have been copied on to the dic, the coins would show it as we have it, to the right. Such a metamorphosis as this is insignificant when compared with others which can be traced in the British series; and, moreover, this theory of the derivation of the type derives great support from the conformation of the fore-legs of the animal, which is so thoroughly unnatural, that it seems impossible for the type to have been original.

PLATE XVI, No. 12.

Obv.—Boar to the right, its fore-legs bifurcated from the knee to the shoulder; above, a rosette and a ring ornament, others beneath and behind (?).

Rev.—Horse to the left, its fore-legs bifurcated from the knee to the shoulder; above, a rosette; in front and below, ring ornaments. There is a beaded exergual line.
Æ. 21½ grains.

This coin is in my own collection, and is engraved in the Num. Chron., vol. xv. p. 98, No. 11, and Beale Poste, p. 102, No. 10. The type is given by Camden, pl. i. 8; Stukeley, pl. x. 7, xvi. 5 and 6, and xxi. 10; and by Lelewel, pl. iv. 28. In some of these, the ring ornaments have triangles of pellets in the centre. A coin of this type was found at Castor, near Peterborough (Arch. Assoc. Journ., vol. ii. p. 102).

The boar on this coin is much better drawn than those on the previous coins, but still preserves some of their peculiarities. Both it and the horse have the Y-shaped fore-legs so common on the coins of this district. Mr. Walker's remarks upon the horse are worth transcribing. He says:—
" It seems fastened by one fore and the opposite hinder foot to some weight; as if it signified the invention of one of their Princes to teach them some pace or motion. The wheel under him, amongst the Romans, intimated the making of a Highway for Carts, so many of which being in the Romans time made in this country well deserved such a memorial." (Gibson's Camden, p. xcii.)

Plate XVI., No. 13.

Obv.—Boar to the right, as on No. 12, standing on an exergual line composed of two rows of pellets connected by vertical strokes; in front and behind a wheel.

Rev.—Horse to the right, the fore-legs bifurcated; above, a wheel between two triangles of pellets; in front, a ring; below the tail, a pellet. Æ. 20 grains.

This coin is in my own collection, but I do not know where it was found. I am inclined to think it is the same coin that is engraved in Stukeley's peculiar manner in his pl. xxi. 9. It is evidently closely connected in type with the preceding coin, though there are wheels instead of the ring ornaments and rosettes. The ornamented exergue may be compared with that of Plate C, No. 1, and of the next coin.

I have another small coin somewhat allied to this, of which a woodcut is here given. The obverse shows a tail-less

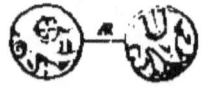

boar to the right; above, a wheel with four spokes and a crescent (?), behind, a ring ornament. On the reverse is a horse of the same character as on No. 13; above, the semicircular termination of a triple wreath (?), and below, a star. The wreath may be compared with that on No. 3, and the star occurs in the same position on No. 10. Like No. 3, this coin appears to have been current as the half of the larger coins, as its weight is only 8½ grains. I am not aware of the place of its discovery.

Plate XVI., No. 14.

Obv.—Boar to the right, as on No. 12, with a rosette (?) and ring ornament above, and another at the tail. The whole surrounded by a beaded circle.

Rev.—Horse to the left, as on No. 12; above, a rosette; below, a ring ornament; there is a beaded exergual line fringed by vertical strokes beneath. Æ. 21½ grains.

This coin is in the British Museum, and is of much the same type as that in Stukeley, pl. v. 2. The mane of the boar is much less coarse than on No. 12, and altogether the workmanship is tamer and more finished. The ring ornament behind is placed in such a manner as to form a sort of curl in the tail. The same is the case with the coin, like No. 10, engraved in Hawkins, pl. i. 16. The propensity for ornamental exergues exhibited by the artists who designed these coins is just what might be expected from their limited amount of skill. The same tendency to multiply simple forms, so as to produce a certain amount of richness of effect, may be observed on many of the gold coins both of the Britons and Gauls.

With this coin ends the series of uninscribed Icenian coins; I must, however, caution the reader against supposing that there is the slightest attempt at chronological arrangement in the Plate just described. There are not at present any facts known on which to base such an arrangement, and all that can be said is, that coins of the types Nos. 1, 6, 7, 8, 9, 10, and 11, have been found in hoards which also contained inscribed coins, such as are comprised in the preceding Plate, with which, therefore, these anepigraphous coins probably synchronise.

CHAPTER XVI.

COINS OF THE YORKSHIRE DISTRICT.

The dominions of the Brigantes, to whom the coins of this district have been usually attributed, appear to have comprised Yorkshire, Lancashire, and other Northern counties, and are described by Ptolemy as extending from sea to sea. By Tacitus, the most populous state in Britain is said to be that of the Brigantes. The former writer enumerates eight of their towns, among which Caturactonium (*Cattrick Bridge*), Isurium (*Aldborough*), Olicana (*Ilkley*), and Eboracum (*York*), are those whose sites are best authenticated. Being situated so far north, it is not until *A.D. 50 or 51 that we find any mention of the Brigantes or their rulers in Roman history; but in the former year we learn that Ostorius quelled an insurrection among them, and in the latter year we are told that Caractacus, having sought refuge with Cartismandua, their queen, was by her treacherously given up to the Romans. By so doing, however, she gained their goodwill, and increased in power, wealth, and prosperity. Her husband, Venusius, a distinguished warrior, but of the tribe of the Jugantes (who by Baxter and others are supposed to be the same as the Iceni, though the name is possibly, after all, only a misreading for Brigantes), appears to have held a subordinate position to the queen his wife. After continual quarrels,† Cartismandua, having at length openly espoused Vellocatus, her husband's armour-bearer, nearly the whole state rose against her, and though she called in the aid of

* Tac. Ann., xii. 32, 36.   † Tac. Hist., iii. 45.

the Romans, all that they could do was to effect her rescue, and leave Venusius in possession of the kingdom. This happened in A.D. 69; and shortly afterwards the greater part of the territory of the Brigantes was reduced by Petilius Cerealis into submission to the Roman power.

Such is a brief sketch of the principal historical facts that are recorded concerning the Brigantes, and but little or nothing can be added from numismatic evidence, though we have some four or five types of inscribed coins, which can, with considerable certainty, be referred to this tribe.

Although Mr. Akerman* had pointed out the fact that the gold coins of large module and peculiar type found in Yorkshire are unlike all others of the series, and evidently belong to a part of Britain remote from the Southern counties, yet the credit of first classifying these coins as those of the Brigantes, and bringing a selection of them together on a single plate, is due to Mr. Beale Poste.† I have indeed but very few types, and those unimportant, to add to those which he has already published.

But though, from the district in which these coins seem to be almost exclusively found, there is little doubt of their having been struck by the Brigantes, yet the legends which appear upon them have not hitherto proved susceptible of any interpretation that would connect them either with the name of the tribe, or of any of its known cities or princes. The principal of these legends are as follows: VOLISIOS — DVMNO CO VEROS; DVMN — TIGIP - SENO (?); IISVP (?)-SV; and VEP-CORF.

It seems possible that the DVMN on No. 3 in the Plate may refer to the same name as the DVMNO on Nos. 1 and 2; and barely possible that the VEP CORF of No. 5 may be connected with the CO VEROS of No. 1, but beyond this at present there is no clue to guide us.

I cannot agree with Mr. Birch‡ in reading No. 1 as VOSIMOS (or rather VOSILIOS) DVMNOCO [N]EPOS,

* Num. Chron., vol. i. p. 83.   † Arch. Assoc. Journ., vol. vi. pl. III.
‡ Num. Chron., vol. xviii. p. 170.

the grandson of Dumnoco. Neither can I, with another author, translate the words as, "I flee from the war chariots." For the present, at all events, I regard these legends as hopelessly obscure.

With regard to the date of these coins we have rather more to guide us. Their type—which is, perhaps, the rudest of all the derivations from their common prototype, itself the barbarous imitation of the Philippus—places them among the latest of the British coins. The baseness of the metal of which they are composed is also significant of a comparatively late date; but, beyond this, they have in several instances been found associated with Roman coins. Some sixteen or eighteen of them were found in the year 1829, at Almondbury,* in Yorkshire (the Cambodunum of the Itinerary?), together with two hundred Roman family coins, a few of which were in tolerable preservation, but the greater part worn nearly smooth by circulation. Unfortunately, no accurate record appears to have been kept of these Roman coins, so that nothing can now be determined, from the date and degree of wear of the different coins, as to the period when the hoard was deposited, but many of the British coins appear to have been sharp and unworn. In the case of another hoard discovered at Lightcliffe,† near Halifax, in 1827, not only were family coins associated with the British, but a few Imperial coins, including one of Caligula and Agrippina I., probably struck about A.D. 40. This hoard, which comprised four British coins and nearly thirty Roman, could not, therefore, have been deposited until after that year, and the large proportion of Roman coins in both hoards would seem to prove that the Romans had already established an extensive footing in some part of Britain, before either of them was deposited. We have already seen that in the Western district the native coinage survived until after the accession of Claudius, and it seems probable that the same was the case in the Northern parts of Britain. As, however, we do not find any names upon

* Num. Chron., vol. I. p. 82.   † Num. Chron., N.S., vol. I. p. 79.

these coins which can in any way be identified with those of Cartismandua or Venusius, and as the Roman coins found with the British are, as far as we know, of no later date than A.D. 40, it seems probable that the coinage of the Brigantes had ceased before A.D. 50, in which year Ostorius put down an insurrection among them. When the coinage commenced cannot of course be determined with any degree of accuracy; but from the great similarity of type among the coins, the period over which they extend cannot well be long.

As far as I know, the coins are confined to the south-eastern portion of the territory of the Brigantes, and have not been found in Lancashire or the counties further north than Yorkshire; and it seems probable that some of the uninscribed coins—which, from their similarity of type, I have classed with the inscribed—are the connecting links between the proper coins of the Brigantes and those of the more Southern parts of Britain. They certainly do not appear to have derived their coinage from the Iceni, the type of the gold coins being so different, and a silver currency, except of Roman coins, having been apparently unknown, though the native coins of the Iceni are so abundant in that metal. It seems more probable that the acquaintance with the art of coining spread to the Brigantes through the Coritani (or Coritavi), of whose coinage little or nothing is at present known. As has been already remarked, the gold of which the coins of the Brigantes is struck is very base, so much so that in some cases they hardly deserve the name of gold; and as the coins which are apparently of brass are of the same module and types as those of gold, it is difficult to draw the line between them, and I am inclined to think that of whatever metal they were composed, they were all originally intended to rank as gold. In fabric these coins are extremely rude, and are also generally much dished.

PLATE XVII, No. 1.

Obv.—VO-LI SI-OS in two lines in a sort of compartment across a wreath of rectangular leaves running in opposite directions from the centre of the coin; in two of the angles a beaded ring surrounding a pellet; in the other two, wheels with curved spokes (?).

Rev.—DVM NOCO VEROS, the VE in monogram with the foreleg of a disjointed horse to the left, with long ears and an open mouth; beneath the head a triangle of pellets, and a pellet beneath the tail.

N. 82½, 83, 84 grains.

Coins of this, which is the most common of the Yorkshire types, were in both the Almondbury and Lightcliffe hoards; others have been found in Lincolnshire. Specimens are engraved in White, No. 13; Gough's Camden, pl. i. 27; Num. Journ., vol. i. pl. i. 10; Ruding, pl. A, 63; Hawkins, pl. i. 8; Rev. Num., vol. iv. pl xiii. 6; Lelewel, pl. viii. 41; Arch. Assoc. Journ., vol. vi. pl. iii. 1, 2; and Beale Poste, pl. vi. 1, 2, and pp. 34, 62, &c.

The legend on the obverse has by some been read as VOSIMOS or VOSILIOS, but I think VOLISIOS is the preferable reading. It would seem from its position on the coin and the termination OS, that this was the name of some chief of the Brigantes, who can, however, hardly be identified with Vennsius. The legend of the reverse has also been read as EPOS DVMNOCO; DVMNO CO VEPOS (and even [N]EPOS); but the supposed P is, by the coin engraved as No. 2, shown to be an R, and the VE in monogram is there distinct from the horse's legs, so that the reverse legend of the present coin must be regarded as DVMNO CO VEROS, though its meaning is enveloped in mystery. Dr. Pegge* read the legend on White's coin NO COIVER, or *Nova Colonia Verolamium!*

It is worth notice that the word DVBNOCOV† occurs on the obverse of some of the coins of Dumnorix the Æduan, and the form DVBNOCOVE is preserved on an inscribed

---

* Gough's Camden, p. cxiv.
† Rev. Num., N.S., vol. viii. p. 61; vol. xix. p. 145.

stone in the wall of a house near the cathedral of Puy. Mr. Poste, p. 36, cites an inscribed stone found near Amiens, as bearing the word VERIVGVDVMNO.

The type of the obverse, with the leaves of the wreath converted into rectangular billet-shaped figures, is not unlike that of Plate C, No. 1. The wheels with curved spokes are possibly derivatives of the open crescents which originally represented the front hair of the laureate bust. The ring ornaments, with pellets at intervals on the ring, appear to be peculiar to the coins of this district. The horse on the reverse, so far as the component pieces of its body and limbs are concerned, is the same as that on the reverse of the coin already cited; it differs, however, in the head, in which it comes nearer to the Icenian coins, Plate XIV., Nos. 13 and 14. The triangle of pellets is also of frequent occurrence on the coins of that district, but the horse and the obverse type are quite distinct from those on the coins of the Iceni.

There is a modern forgery of this type, which may usually be distinguished by the paleness of the metal and the excessive weight, in some cases being as much as 120 grains.

Plate XVII., No. 2.

Obv.—Portions of an unintelligible legend across a wreath, as on No. 1.

Rev.—DVMNOVERO[S]. Horse, &c., as on No. 1.

N. 75 grains.

I have already published this coin, which is in my own collection, in the Num. Chron., vol. xvi. p. 80, No. 5. The legend on the obverse is possibly VOLISIOS, as on the preceding coin; but the O looks very like a D. The legend on the reverse is remarkable as omitting the CO, and seems to prove that the formula on No. 1 should be divided into three words, DVMNO CO VEROS, of which only the first and last occur on the present coin. It will be observed that the V and E are here also linked into a monogram, and that the fore-leg of the horse, not being so applicable to form part of an R as of a V, is on this coin set free from the legend. Its weight is remarkably small, though the coin has suffered but little by wear. The metal of which it is composed is very base.

PLATE XVII, No. 3.

Obv.—DVMN (?) between two lines across a wreath; the type in other respects as No. 1.
Rev.—TIGIP-SENO (?). Horse, &c., as on No. 1.
  N. 83,¹⁄₁₀ grains.

This coin, which is in the British Museum, has been engraved in Hawkins, pl. i. 9; Num. Chron., vol. xiv. p. 71, No. 8; Arch. Assoc. Journ., vol. vi. pl. iii. 5; and Beale Poste, pl. vi. 5.

I think there can be little doubt of the legend on the obverse being DVMN, so that it is probably connected with the DVMNO CO VEROS of No. 1. The legend on the reverse has been variously read. Mr. Hawkins merely gives TIGII; Mr. Birch, in the Num. Chron., reads it TIGII or TIGIL N. .S, and Mr. Beale Poste makes it TIGIION. On an examination of the coin, one of the letters below the horse appears to be an E, while the letter in front seems to be an S. Each of these would, however, be reversed, were the legend to be read continuously as on the preceding coins; and I therefore conclude that the lower portion of the legend follows the same rule as the CORF on No. 5, and is to be read as SENO. From a specimen found at Wisbeach, communicated to me by Mr. C. Roach Smith, the last letter of the upper portion appears to be certainly a P, making it TIGIP. Both Mr. Hawkins and Mr. Poste have called attention to the partial resemblance of this part of the legend to TIGVOCOBAVC, which, by Asser, is said to have been the British name of Nottingham, but there can hardly be any connection between the two words. I cannot suggest any interpretation for it. The other portion of the legend, SENO (if I have read it correctly), occasionally enters into the composition of Gaulish names of places and tribes, such for instance as SENOMAGUS and the SENONES, but I do not know of any British names of the kind, though Sitomagus is given as SINOMAGI on the Tabula Peutingeriana.

PLATE XVII, No. 4.

Obv.—Uninscribed; a wreath, as on No. 1, crossed by a line with a thin crescent at each end clasping a ring beaded at intervals and with a pellet in the centre. There are pellets in the spaces between the billets forming the wreath.

Rev.—IISVP SV (?). Horse even ruder than that on No. 1; a star beneath its tail. *N*. 83 grains.

This coin, in the Museum of the Yorkshire Philosophical Society, has been published by Beale Poste, pl. vi. 3, and Arch. Assoc. Journ., vol. vi. pl. iii. 3. He reads the legend as ASVP AS, but I am doubtful whether the first letter is an A, as the two straight strokes seem parallel. The lower portion of the legend should, I think, be read like the CORF on the next coin from left to right, giving SV in exactly the same position as it occurs on the coins reading SVEI, Plate I., No. 9.

On a coin of this type found in Lincolnshire, and communicated to me by Mr. C. Roach Smith, there are traces of other letters in front of the horse, the tail of which is converted into a wheel like that on No. 6.

PLATE XVII., No. 5.

Obv.—As No. 4, but with dolphin-shaped figures on each side of the wreath.
Rev.—VEP CORF. Extremely rude horse; a pellet beneath the head, and a triangle of pellets beneath the tail. *N*. 82$\frac{1}{2}$, 85, 80 grains.

This coin, which is also in the York Museum, has been engraved by Beale Poste, pl. vi. 4, and Arch. Assoc. Journ., vol. vi. pl. iii. 4. Two other coins are engraved in the Num. Chron., vol. i. pl. ii. 11, and vol. xiv. p. 71, No. 7. The former of these was from the Almondbury hoard, and is now in my own collection. Both of them have ring ornaments beneath the tail instead of the triangle of pellets. A woodcut of a coin with CORF beneath a horse, given by Beale Poste, at p. 91, would seem to have been taken from a very rough sketch, and not from an actual coin. Like those on all the other coins of this district, the legend appears to be inexplicable. The V and E are linked together in monogram in the same manner as the VE of VEROS on Nos. 1 and 2. The legend, however, on this coin is VEP, and not VER, as the R could not occur under two distinct forms in the VER and CORF on the same coin. The horse on this and most of the other coins with the uninscribed obverse has its neck split up in the most singular manner, while those on the coins with the inscribed obverse generally have solid necks.

I have another specimen of this type, found at Cirencester, of such base metal as to have been much corroded and covered with green rust. It has, in fact, all the appearance of being a brass coin, and its weight is only 61 grains.

PLATE XVII., No. 6.

Obv.—As No. 5, but with pointed crosses in the wreath.

Rev.—VEP (VE in monogram) retrograde, [CO]RF. Rude horse with a star beneath the tail, as on No. 4, giving it the appearance of a wheel. *R.*

This coin was found with three of the type of No. 1 at Lightcliffe, near Halifax, in 1827. They were buried in an urn with about twenty-five or thirty Roman denarii, mostly family coins, but three of them Imperial, viz., two of Augustus, and one of Caligula with the reverse of Agrippina I. I have given an account of the discovery in the Num. Chron., N.S., vol. i. p. 79. The cruciform objects in the wreath are remarkable, as similar though smaller crosses are of frequent occurrence on the coins of Antedrigus and others of the West of England which belong to nearly the same period as these. The legend on this coin is the same as that on the preceding, but partly retrograde, though in type it seems to correspond more closely with No. 4; all six of the types last described are however so closely connected together, that they must be nearly, if not quite, contemporary.

Plate XVII., No. 7.

Obv.—Plain and convex.

Rev.—VEP. Rude horse to the left, the head formed by a triangle with a pellet at the apex, the ears curved forwards; in front of the head a star of pellets, below it two other pellets. Æ.

This coin was formerly in the collection of Dr. Duncan, of Colchester, and was found at that place. A woodcut of it is given in the Arch. Assoc. Journ., vol. ii. p. 100, but the coin is there assigned to Verulamium. There can, however, be no doubt, from the character of the horse, the module, and the inscription, that it belongs to the same class as the preceding coins, notwithstanding its having been found so far south as Colchester. I find also, from a note I made when I examined Dr. Duncan's collection, in 1850, that I considered the metal to be base gold rather than brass. Though I have little doubt that the inscription would, if complete, have proved to be VEP CORF, yet there are several rather important particulars in which the details of this type differ from those of the preceding coins. The plain obverse, the square nose of the horse, and the pellets in front, all form points of difference; but it is rather singular that in these very points this coin agrees with the uninscribed variety No. 11, from which, indeed, it appears to have derived its type, while the other coins with VEP CORF are more nearly connected with Nos. 9, 10, and 12.

Plate XVII., No. 8.

Obv.—As No. 5.

Rev.—AVN · T · and other uncertain letters. Rude horse as on No. 5, but with two pellets in and above the back, another beneath the tail, and a trefoil below the body. Æ. 60 grains.

This coin, which has not before been published, is in my own collection, but I do not know where it was found. It has all the appearance of being of brass, but probably, when fresh from the die, was intended to pass as gold. It is indeed possible that the metal would be correctly described as copper slightly alloyed with tin and gold. The type of both obverse and reverse is much the same as that of Nos. 4, 5, and 6, but the legend is entirely different, though as usual, unintelligible. The only letters that can be made out with any approach to certainty are AVN above, and T below the horse, and it is a curious circumstance that these same letters occur on a small coin in the Hunter collection at Glasgow, with the difference only that the T is beneath the neck and not under the body of the horse. The metal of which this small coin is composed is apparently silver, though it is possibly very base and pale gold. It has a plain obverse, as will be seen by the annexed woodcut,

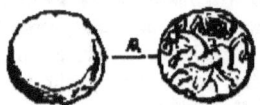

and the horse is also far less rude than on the larger coins. What the object beneath it may be, I cannot say. This same coin is engraved by Stukeley, pl. xvi. 7, in his first *Tabula argentea Musseliana*. I think the coin must be regarded as the quarter of the larger piece, but I can offer no suggestion as to the meaning of the legend on either of them.

The remaining four coins of this plate are uninscribed, but from the character of the types, Mr. Beale Poste has attributed the majority of them to the Brigantes, and, I think, with reason.

Nos. 9 and 10 are so much alike that they may be described together.

PLATE XVII, Nos. 9 and 10.

Obv.—Portions of the degenerate laureate bust consisting of the wreath with billet-shaped leaves, between locks of hair, and an open crescent and ring ornament.

Rev.—Extremely rude disjointed horse to the left, a straight line joined on T-wise to the crescent forming the back, with a pellet on either side; another pellet beneath the tail, and beneath the horse a star.

N. 82 $\frac{7}{8}$, 83 grains.

Of these coins, No. 9 is in the British Museum, and No. 10 in that of Mr. J. B. Bergne. The latter was found near Lincoln. The type is engraved in Ruding, pl. i. 8, and Beale Poste, pl. vi. 7. It is also given, though very inaccurately, in Gibson's Camden, pl. ii. 22, apparently from a coin in Thoresby's collection. The correspondence in type between these coins and the inscribed varieties Nos. 1 to 6, is such that there can be but little doubt that they belong to much the same district, though whether to the Coritani or to the Brigantes may be an open question. Looking back to the uninscribed coins, the type most nearly allied appears to be Plate C, No. 1, a type which unfortunately I am not able to assign to any particular district, though it probably belongs to the Midland Counties. The finding of No. 10 near Lincoln would seem to favour the opinion that these uninscribed coins were struck among the Coritani.

Plate XVII., No. 11.

Obv.—Plain and convex.

Rev.—Horse, &c., as on Nos. 9 and 10, but with the head as on No. 7, and with a star of pellets in front.

N. 81½ grains.

This coin is in my own collection, but I cannot say where it was found. It is engraved in the Num. Chron., vol. xix. p. 64, No. 3. The obverse is not perfectly smooth, but has protuberances on it, as if the engraver had a vague notion that it was customary to have a device of some kind upon the die. As has already been pointed out, this type seems to be that from which No. 7 was immediately derived. The reverse agrees closely in general character with that of the two preceding coins. The occurrence of coins with the same reverse, but with obverses both plain, and bearing some portions of the laureate bust upon them, has been already commented upon at pp. 64 and 67.

PLATE XVII., No. 12.

Obv.—Much like No. 10, but the wreath diverging in opposite directions from a cross line ending in a sort of crescent, which connects two open crescents at the side of the wreath.

Rev.—Extremely barbarous horse, as on No. 11, but with a large pellet in front, and the star beneath formed with a large pellet in the centre. Æ. (?).

This coin, with another of the same type, was found at Pickering, Yorkshire, in 1853, and was communicated to me by the late Mr. Bateman, of Youlgrave. He described the metal as "a kind of white bronze, or billon, though it may possibly contain a trace of gold." Another of much the same type, but with two ring ornaments above the horse, has been communicated to me by Mr. C. Roach Smith. It is of a mixed metal, somewhat like brass or bell-metal, and weighing 66 grains. A nearly similar coin of gold is engraved in the Arch. Assoc. Journ., vol. vi. pl. iii. 8, and in Deale Poste, pl. vi. 8, from a specimen in the British Museum. The divergence of the wreath from a central line is of very frequent occurrence on the uninscribed coins, but these form the connecting link between the coins on which the two open crescents typical of the front hair are preserved, and those, such as No. 6, where they are merged altogether. Taken as a whole, it is difficult to imagine more barbarous art than is found on this coin; nor can we well conceive a type in which the noble laureate head and the spirited bigu on the Macedonian prototype are more completely degenerated, and indeed entirely forgotten, than in this, with which the series I have attempted to describe, appropriately concludes.

FINIS.

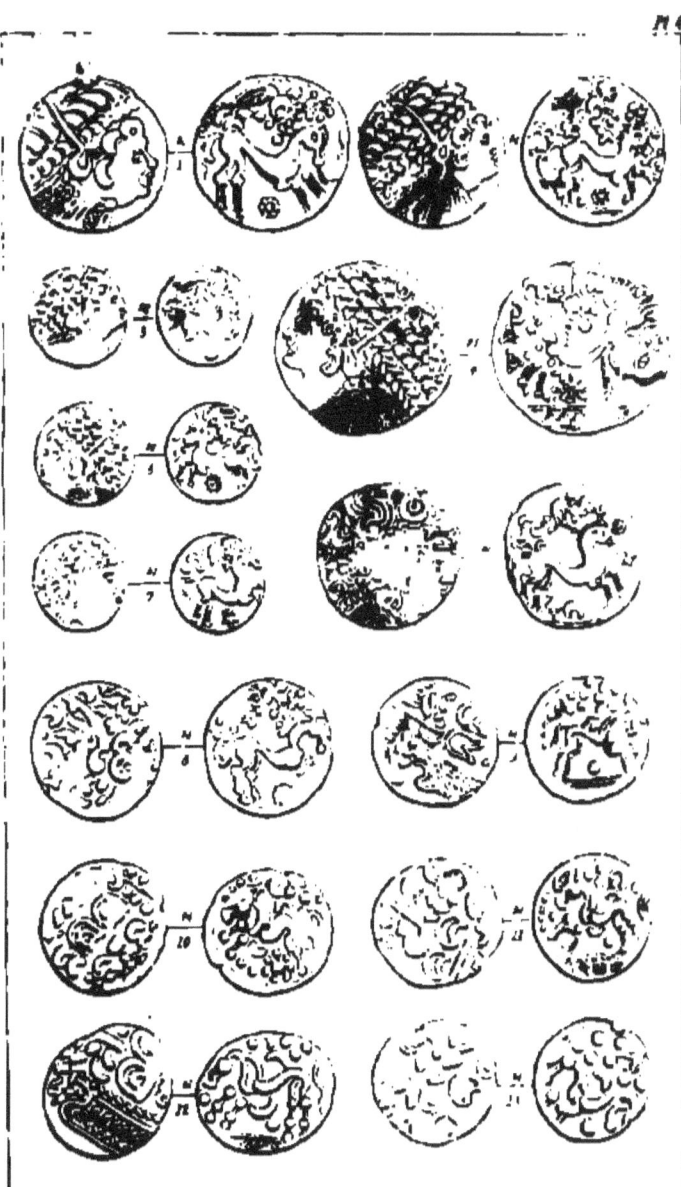

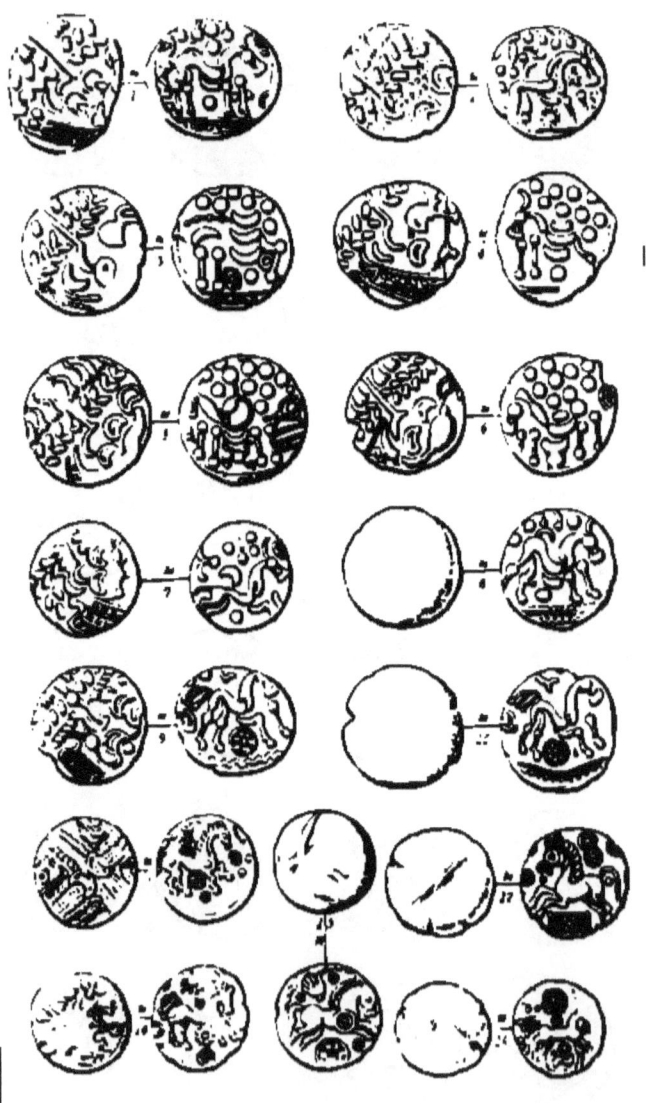

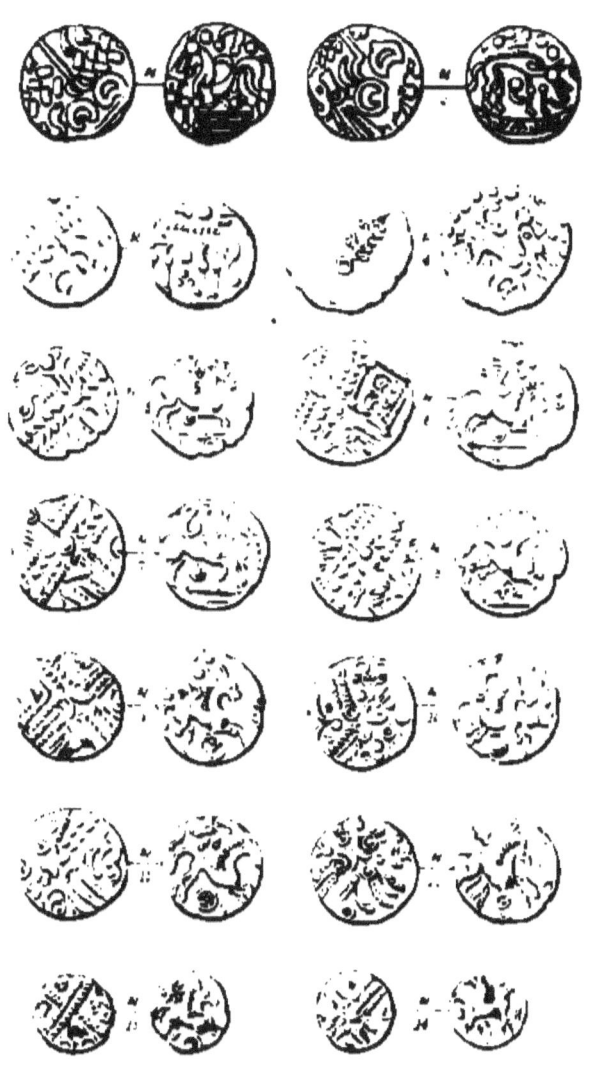

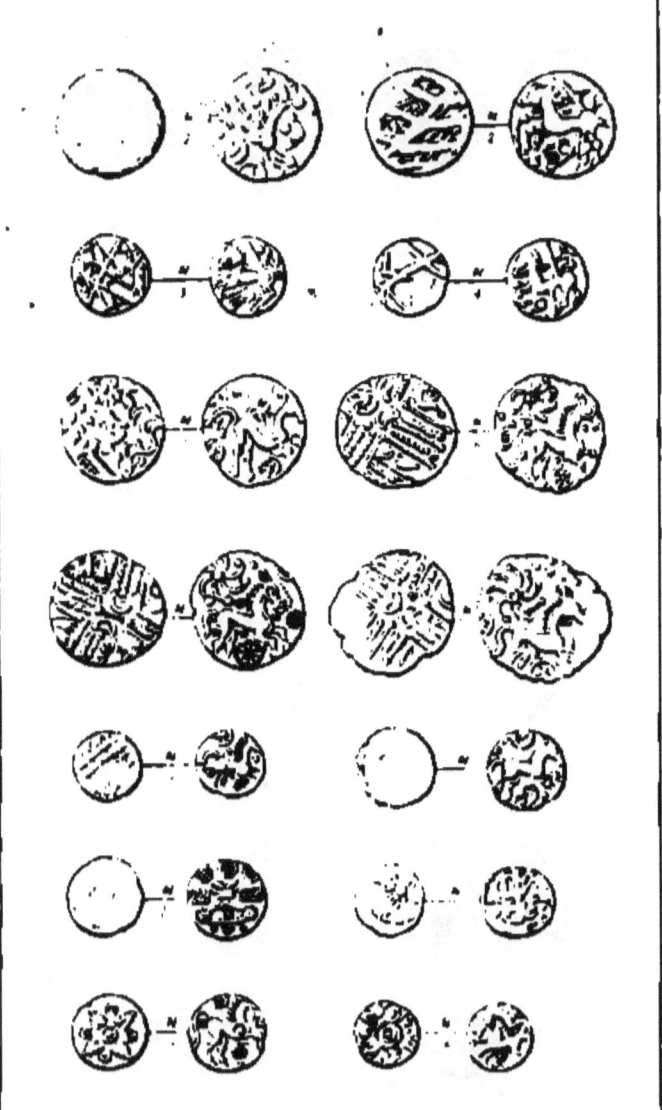

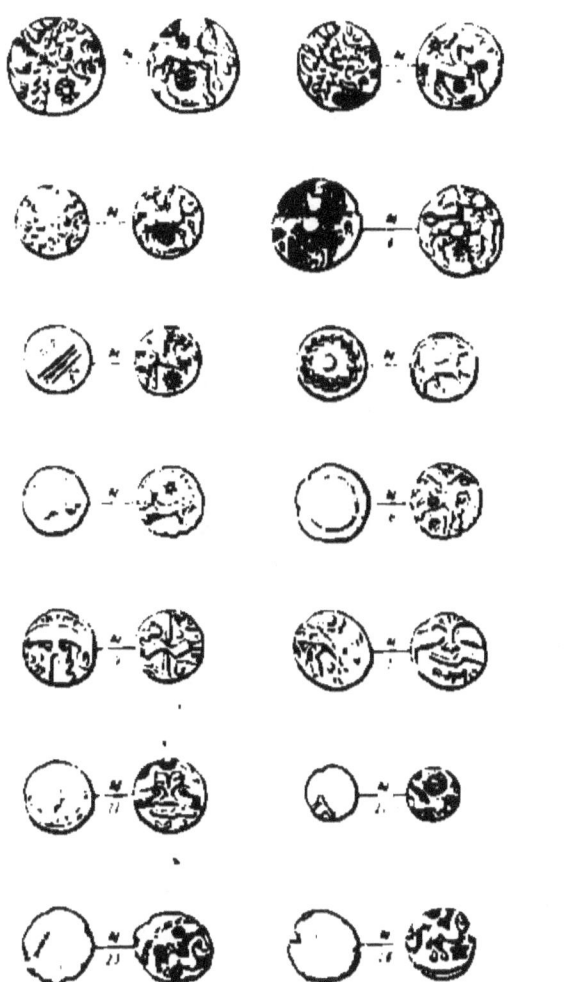

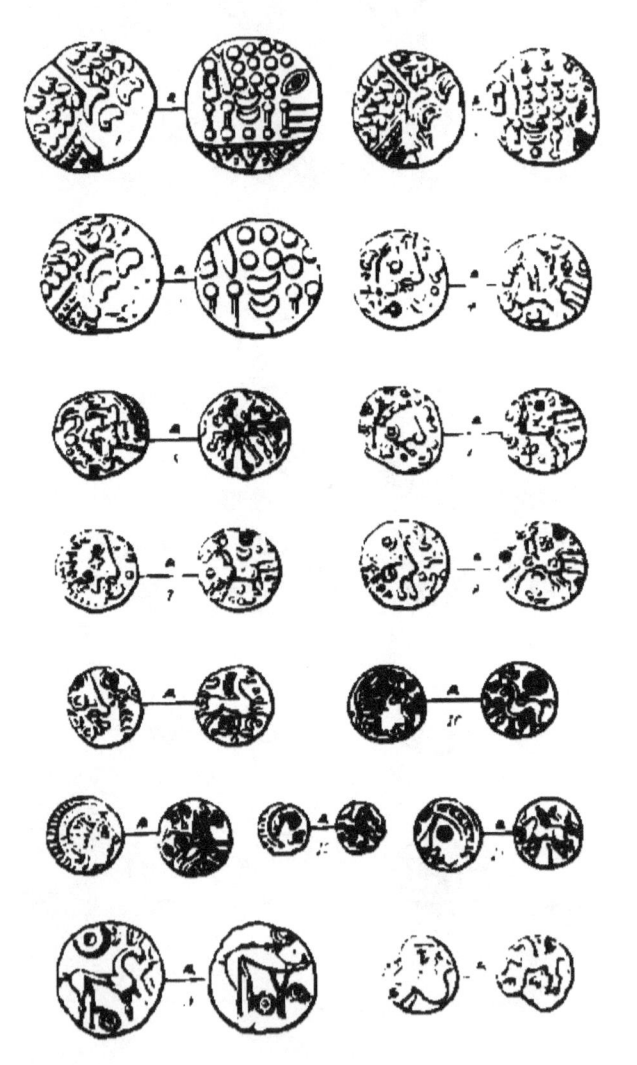

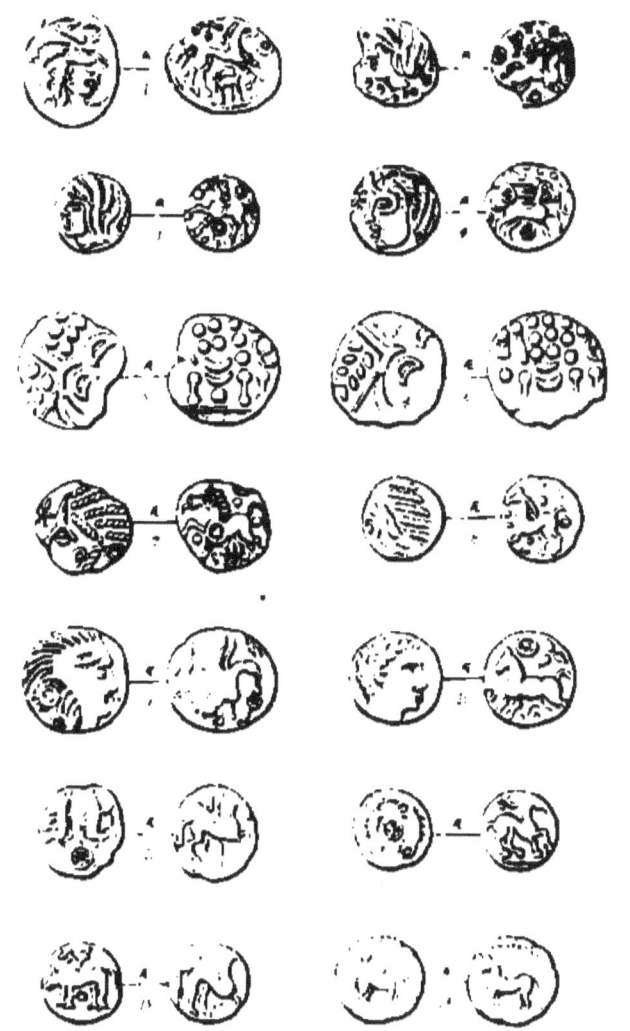

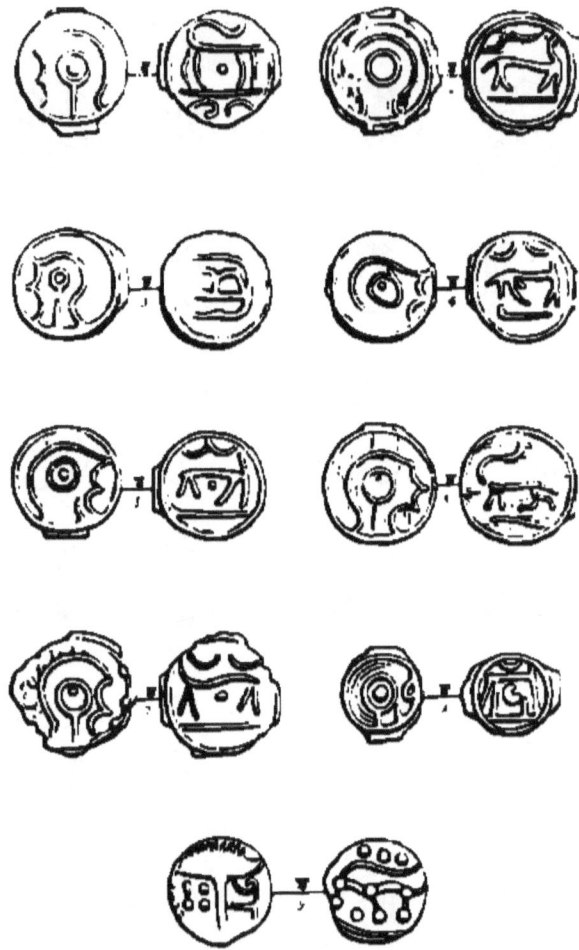

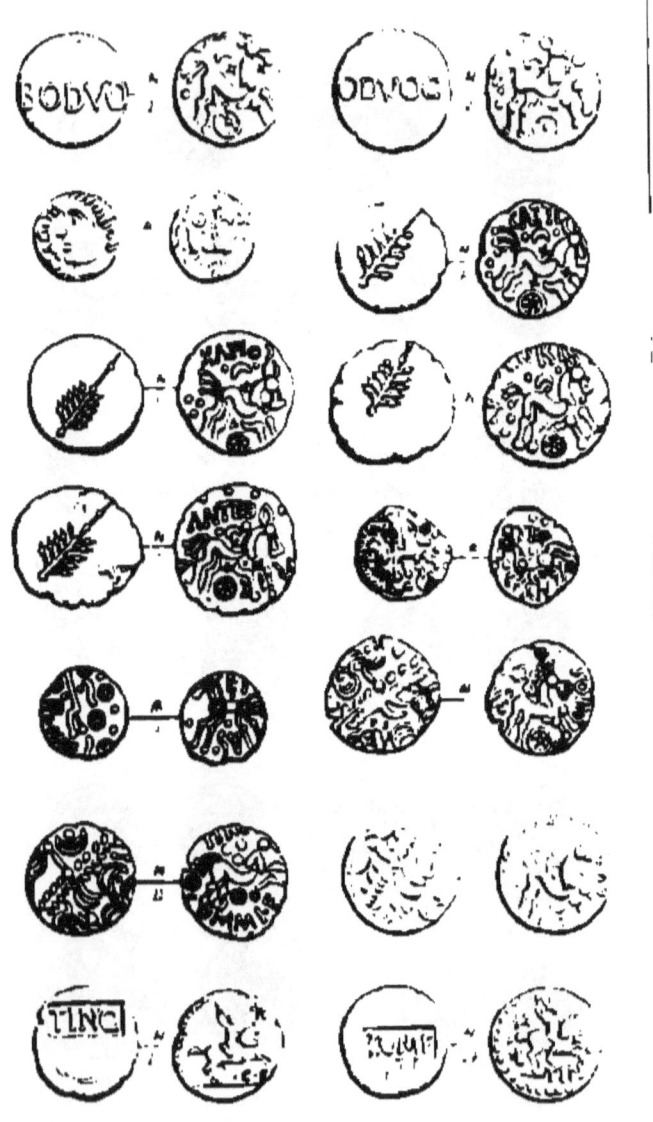

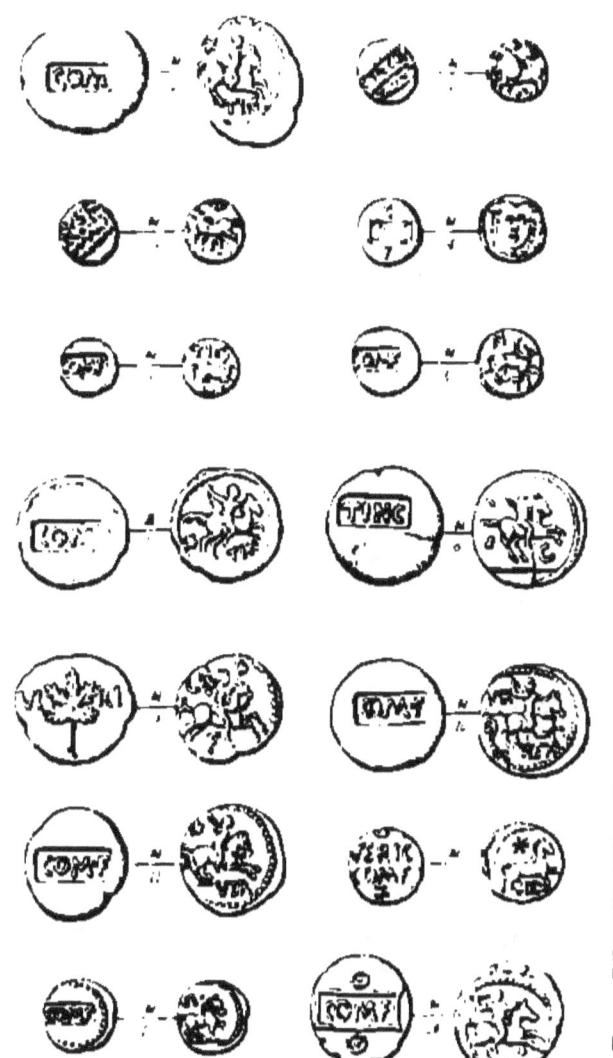

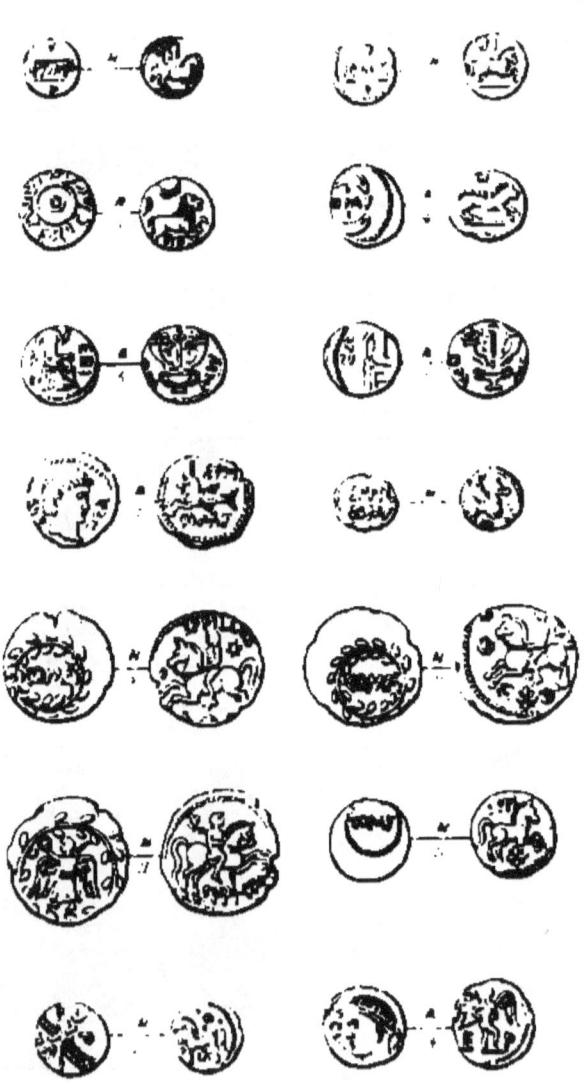

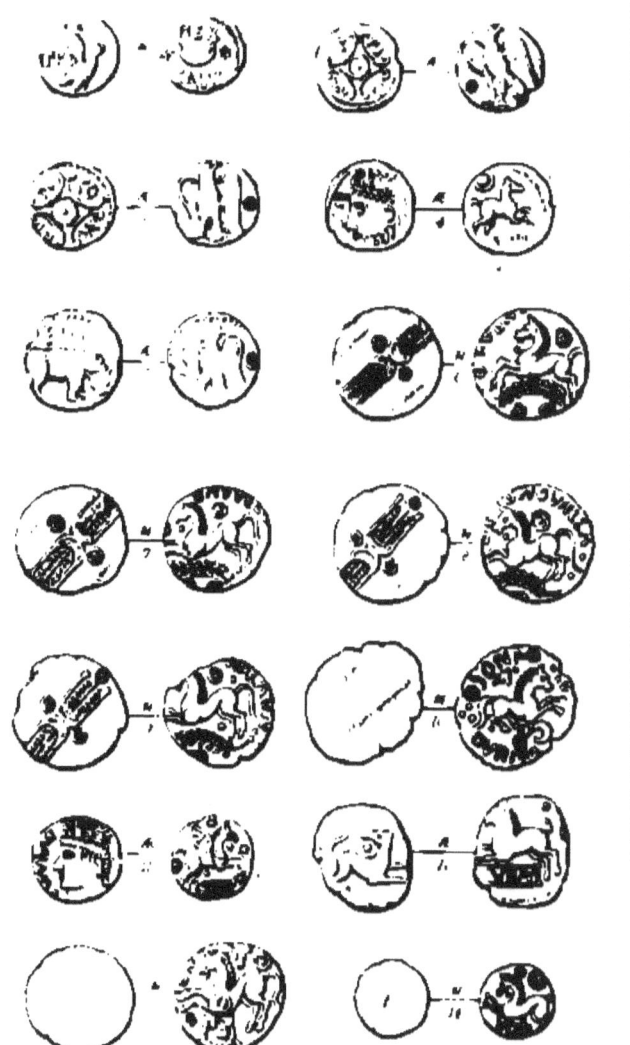

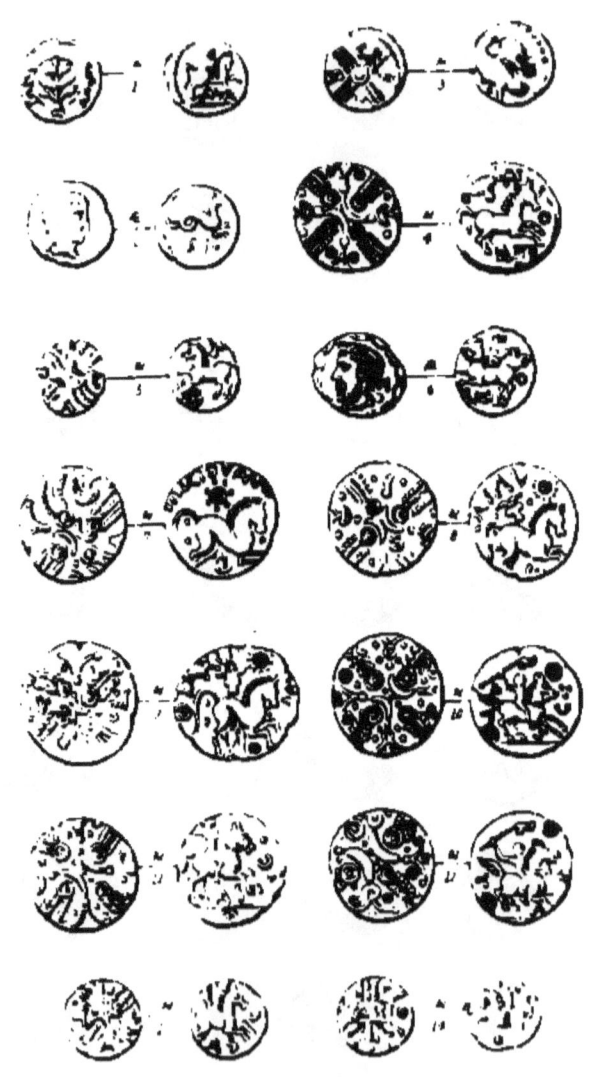

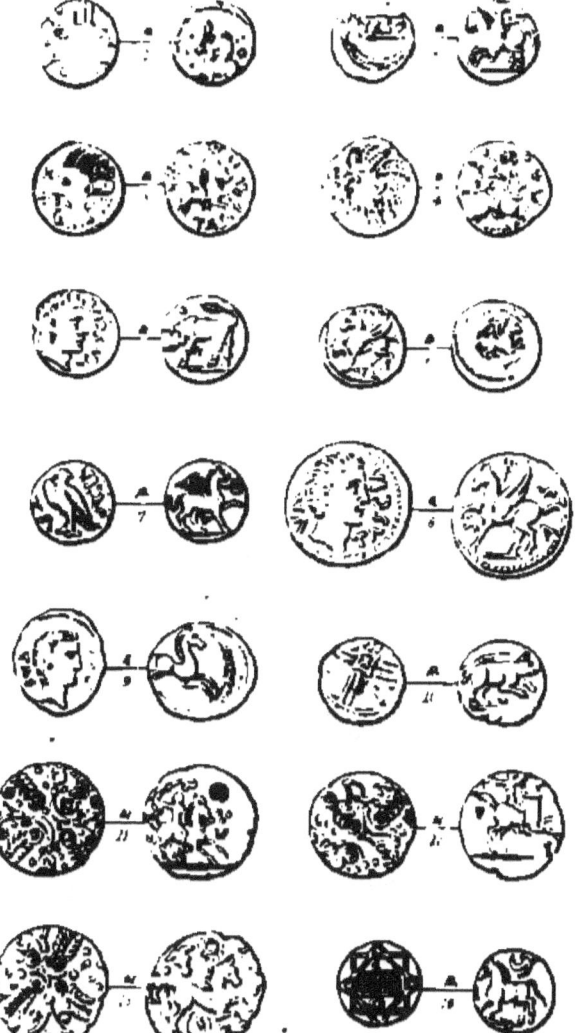

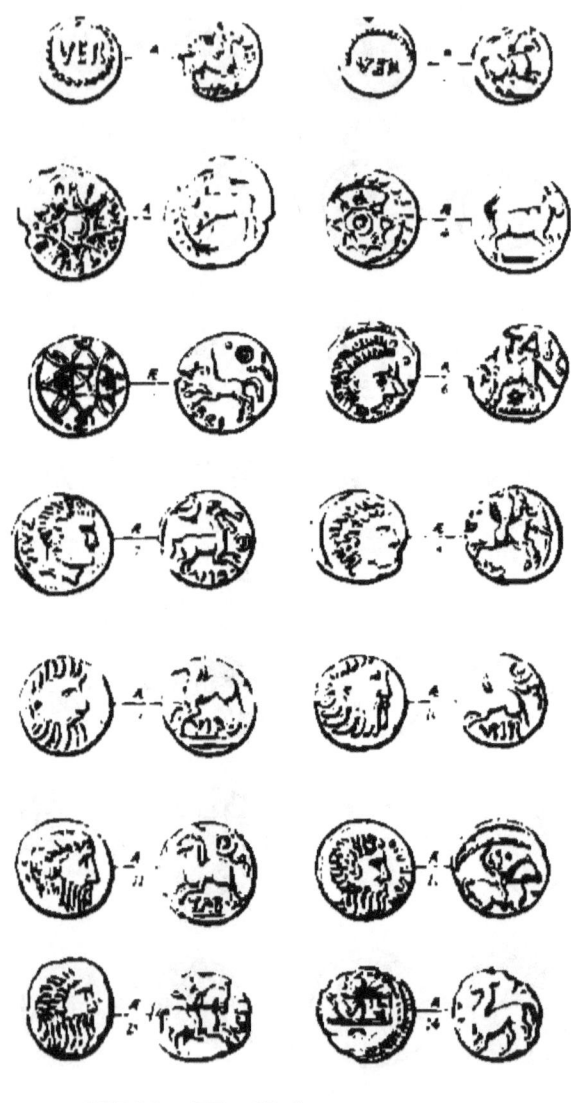

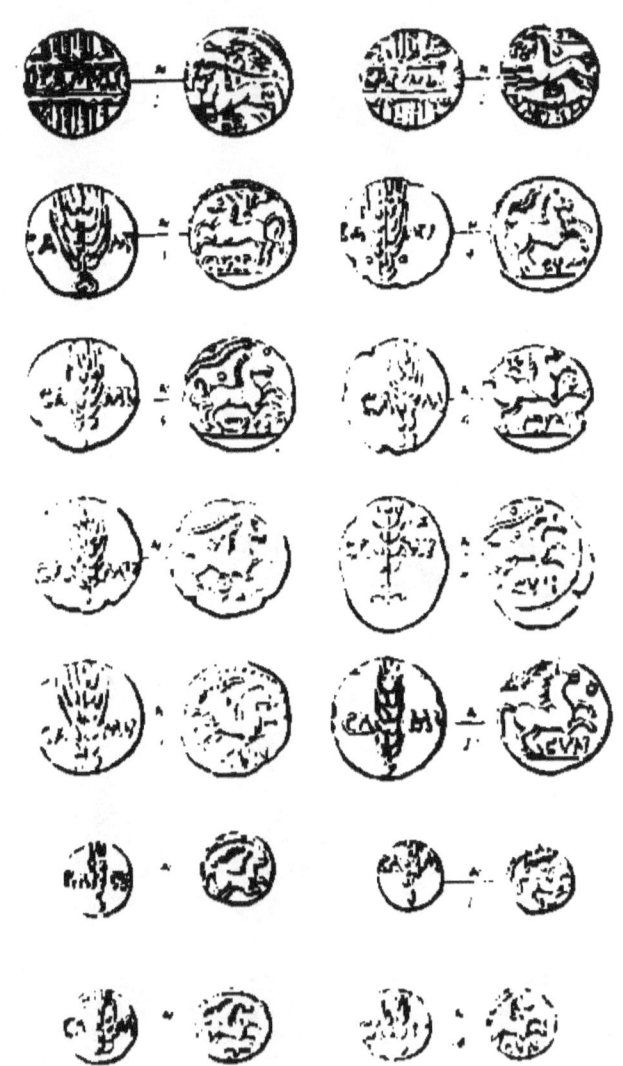

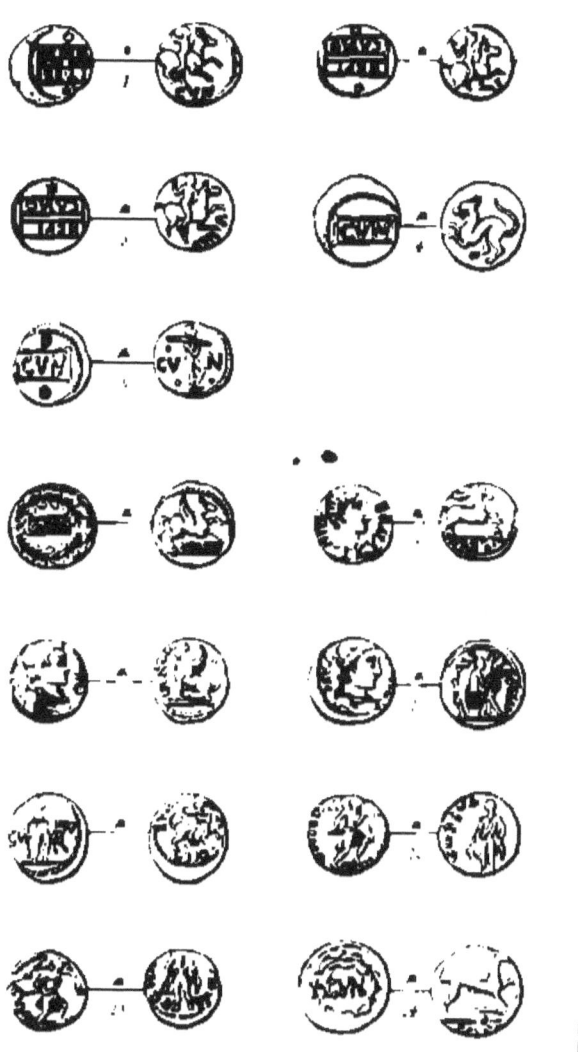

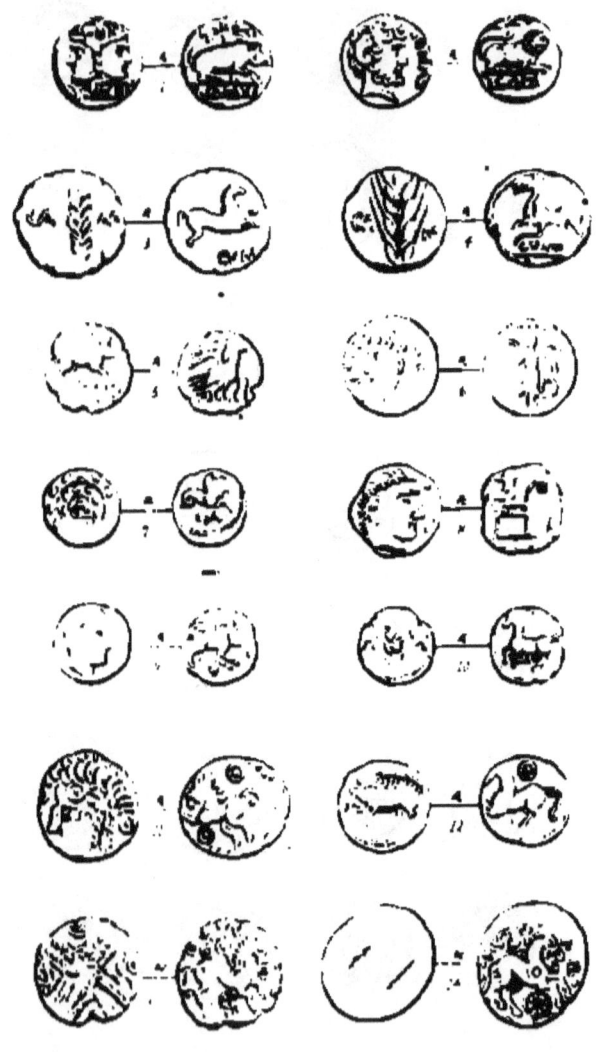

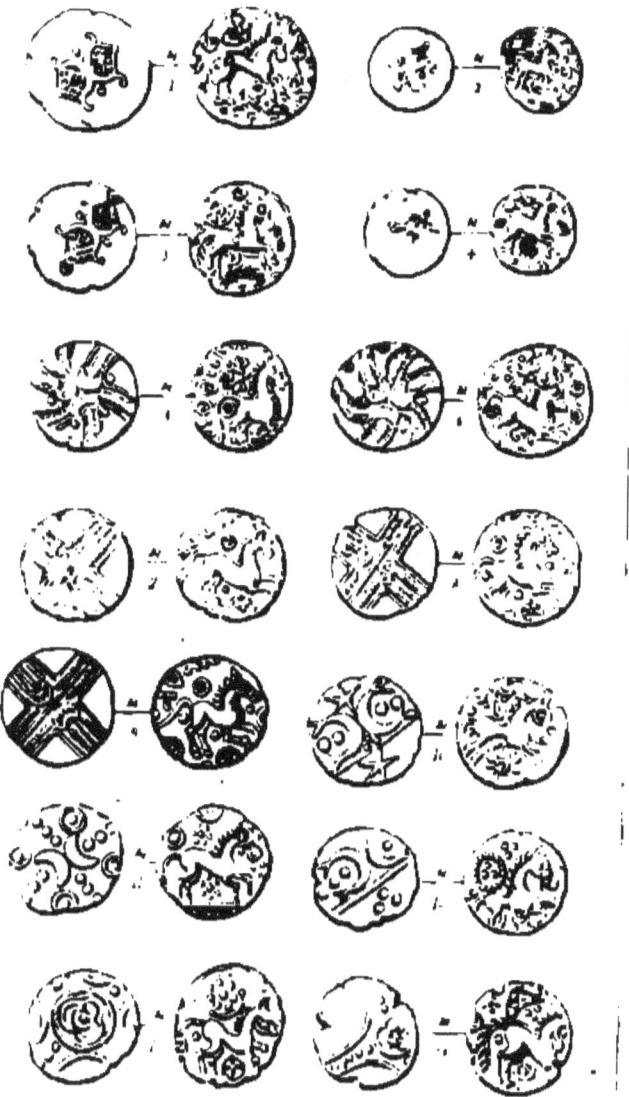

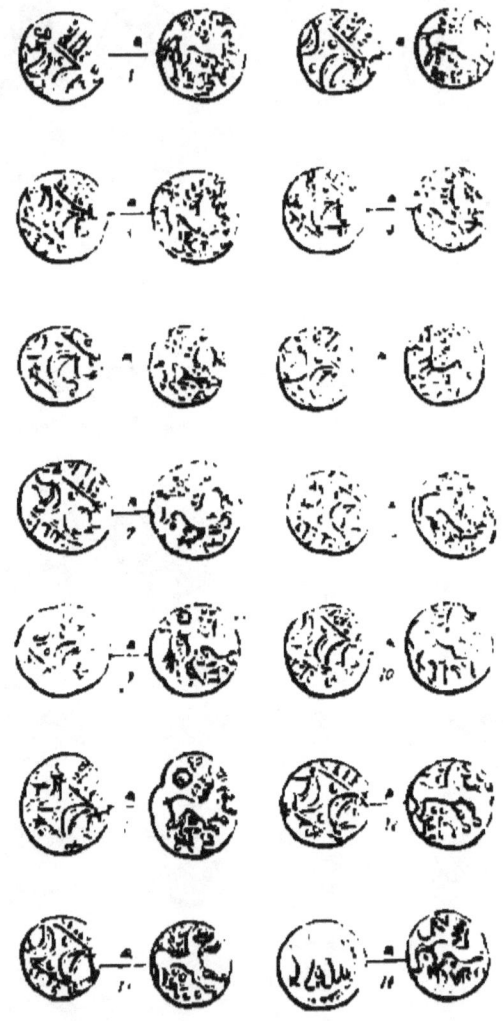

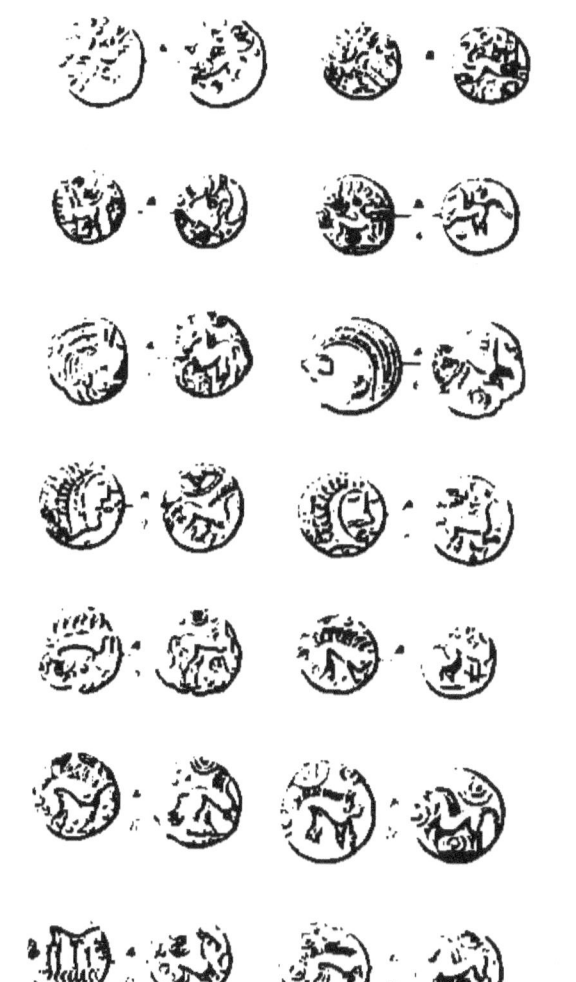

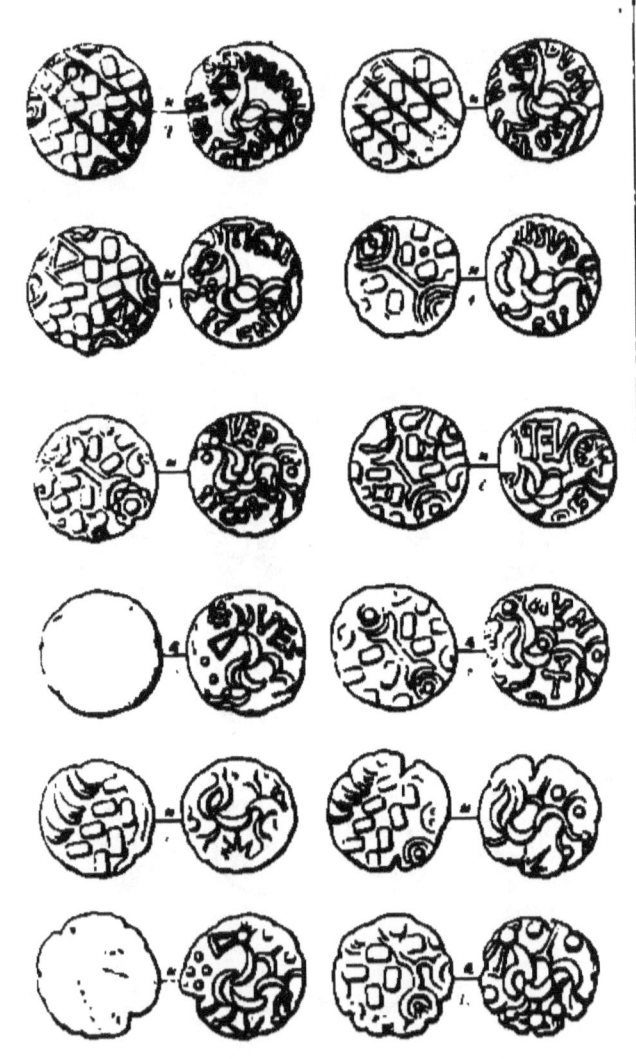

INDEX.

Addedomaros, 303.
Adminius, 208, 285.
Acidd-mawr, 364.
AESV, 386.
Akerman (Mr. J. Y.) his works, 12.
Amiens, British coin, found at, 260.
Amminus, 208, 351, 353, 354.
Ammon, Jupiter, on coins, 309, 344, 346.
Amphisbæna, 355.
Ancalites, the, 131, 216.
Ancyra, inscription at, 150, 159, 193.
Andoco[mius], 218.
ANTED, 387, et seqq.
Antedrigus, 141, 388.
Apollo, Belinus, head of, 48.
Apollo on coins, 312.
ASVP AS, the supposed legend, 410.
AGORI, the supposed legend, 372.
Atrebates, the, 41, 151.
Augustus, his seal, 311.
AVN T, 413.
Avranches, coins found at, 120.

Bacchus (?) on coins, 319, 340.
Belgæ, the, 38.
Berkshire, coins of, 41.
Bibroci, the, 131.
Birch (Mr. S.), 221, 302.
Boadicea, mistaken opinions with regard to her coins, 137, 359.
Boar on coins, 120, 126, 215, 206, 322, 323, 331, 352, 354, 401.
Bodvad, the, 41, 137.
BODVOC, 131.
Borlase (Rev. W.), 5, 82.

Bridle, 234.
Brigantes, the, 404.
Britain, tribute paid by, 19.
——— metals produced in, 20, 43.
——— connection with Gaul, 21.
British coins, earliest type of, 25, 47.
——— development of type, 27.
——— progressive degradation, 29.
——— weight of, 29.
——— approximate date, 31.
——— range of prototype, 35.
Browne (Sir Thomas), 3.
Buckinghamshire, coins of, 41.
Bucranium on coins, 207, 218, 219, 230, 234.
Bull on coins, 198, 241, 253, 254, 332.

CAC, the legend, 353.
Cæsar, passages in, 18, 145, 234.
CALLE, 195.
CAM, the supposed legend, 210, 351.
Camden, his opinions, 1, 220, 231, 277, 345.
Camulodunum, 291, 338.
Camulus (Mars), 318.
Cangi, the, 148.
Capricorn on coins, 211.
Caractacus, supposed coins of, 277, 294.
Carnyx, or war trumpet, 192, 232.
Cartismandua, 404.
CAS, the supposed legend, 211.
Cassi, the, 215.

Cassivellaunus, 220.
CATTI, 119.
Catyeuchlani, the, 41, 138, 141, 215.
CAM (?) DVRO, the legend, 390.
Celt found with British silver coin, 102.
Centaur on coins, 256, 326.
Central District, 215.
Channel Islands, coins of, 127.
CIMONMVA, the supposed legend, 165.
Cock on coins, 113.
Combe (Taylor), 10.
COME, the supposed legend, 101.
COMMIOS, 157.
Commius, his history, 152.
COMVX, 111.
Corinium, 144.
Coritani, the, 407, 415.
Cornu-copiæ on coins, 181, 370, 372.
Cotton (Sir Robert), 2.
CRAB, 211.
Cross on coins, 72, 134, 337.
Cuirass on coins, 233, 241, 272.
Cunetio, supposed mint at, 305, 308.
CVNO, the altered legend, 204.
Cunobelinus, 281.
CVNOBIIL, the supposed legend, 206.
Cybele on coins, 314.

D merges into Θ, 145, 259, 374.
Damnonii, the, 40.
Davies (Rev. E.), 11.
Denominations of coins, numerous, 186, 263.
Diana on coins, 313, 315.
DIAS, 249.
Dilorigas (?), 353.
Dies, nature of, 43, 230.
Divitiacus, 151.
Dion Cassius, 137, 171, 286.
Districts, arrangement under, 130.
Dog (?) on coins, 316.
Donnop (Baron de), 129.
Dorsetshire, coins of, 38, 92.
Duchalais (M.), 16, 345.

Dubnovellaunus, 198, 350, 351.
Durden (Mr. H.), 101, 148, 213.
Durotriges, the, 38, 351.
DV, 160.
DVMNO COVEROS, the legend, 408.
DVMNO VEROS, the legend, 409.
DVMN, the legend, 410.
DVN, 208.

E and I interchanged, 171.
Eagle on coins, 119, 197, 198, 213, 243, 262, 281, 350.
Ear of Corn, 297, et seqq., 347, 352.
Eastern District, 357.
ECEN, the legend, 381, et seqq.
Eckhel, his opinion, 9.
EISV, the supposed legend, 386.
Epaticcus, 276.
Eppillus, 188, 351.
Europa (?) on coins, 314.

F, form of the letter, 262.
Flints, coins found in, 85, 228.

G, form of the letter, 145.
Gaul, coins, possibly British, found in, 51, 63, 65, 68, 83, 90, 94, 96, 103.
Gaulish coins, 123, 322, 379.
———— in Ruding's plates, 10.
Gaulish coinage, origin of, 23.
Genius, winged, on coins, 194.
Gibson's Camden, 3.
Gloucestershire, coins of, 41, 133.
Goat on coins, 114, 261.
Gough's Camden, 6.
Greek letters, the use of, 145, 296, 374.
Griffin on coins, 205, 242, 243, 316, 324, 336, 341, 352.

Haigh (Mr.), 273.
Hampshire, coins of, 37, 158.
Hawkins (Mr. E.), his opinions, 13.
Hercules on coins, 281, 307, 313, 315, 323.

Hippocampus on coins, 211, 258, 259, 351.
Hoards of coins:—
  Almondbury, 108.
  Ashdown Forest, 92.
  Battle, 361.
  Bognor, 90, 108.
  Dorsetshire, 101.
  Haverhill, 63.
  High Wycombe, 227.
  Karn Bré, 40.
  Lancing Downs, 110, 183.
  Lightcliffe, near Halifax, 406, 412.
  March, 361.
  Mount Batten, 72, 106, 128.
  Nunney, 104, 140, 146.
  Quex Park, near Birchington, 125.
  Weston, 361.
  Whaddon Chase, 73.
  Wonersh, 84.
Huiccii, the, 303.

I and E interchanged, 174.
ICE, the supposed legend, 382.
Iceni, the, 357, et seqq.
II for E, 203, 206, 258, 372.
IISVP-SV, 411.
Immanuentius, supposed coins of, 47, 149.
INARA or INMA, 149.
Inscribed and uninscribed coins current together, 106, 148, 301, 379.
Inscriptions, 138, 292, 294, 400.
———— found at Silchester, 274, 308.
———— " Ancyra, 150, 159, 199.
IP, the supposed legend, 193.
Laurium, 386.

Janus on coins, 344.
Jugantes, the, 380, 404.
Jupiter Ammon on coins, 309, 344, 316.

Kair Segont, its situation, 271.

Karn Bré coins, 40.
Kent, coins of, 37, 62, 100, 187.
Kent, Kings of, 187.
KERATI, the supposed legend, 195, 278.
Knives, supposed, 96, 372.

L, the shape of, 331.
Lagoy (Marquis de), 11, 192, 208, 232.
Lelewel cited, 51, 53, 83, 95, 221.
Lloyd (Edward), 6.
Lion, 178, 180, 206, 326, 346.
Londinium, 215, 358.
Longpérier (M. A. de), 113, 262, 369.

Mandubratius, 216.
Massilia, commerce with Britain, 22.
Medusa, head of, 166, 331.
NEPATI, the supposed legend, 282.
Middlesex, coins of, 37.
Mistletoe and knife, 96.
Mithraic device, supposed, 335.
MOD, the legend, 355.
Monumenta Historica Britannica, 15.
———— false coins in, 247.
Morant (Rev. P.), 5.

Nicolson (Bishop), 4.
Norfolk, coins of, 357.

OS, the termination, 368.
OMI, or OMB, the supposed legend, 178.

Pegasus on coins, 189, 210, 219, 235, 236, 242, 244, 257, 308, 335, 311.
Pegge (Samuel), 7, 342.
Peiresc (N. Fabri de), 2, 174, 272.
Pentalpha, 68.
Perseus on coins, 332.
Pettingal (Rev. Dr.), 6.
Phalerae on coins, 360.
Philippus, 21.

420   INDEX.

Pig on coins, 266, 328, 350.
Pinkerton's Medals, 2.
Plant on coins, 210, 318.
Plot (Dr.), 3.
——— finds faces of Boadicea and Prasutagus on a coin, 66.
Pol whele (Mr.), finds the plan of Damnonium on a coin, 82.
Poste (Rev. Beale), his opinions, 14, 142, 155, 195, 211, 271, 278, 303, 361, 391, 405.
Prasutagus, 137, 358, 388.

QVANTES, the supposed legend, 144.

Ram on coins, 255.
Regni, the, 37.
REX, the title, 171, 178, 195, 332.
RICONI, &c., 225, 267.
Roman coins found with British, 106, 117, 282, 361, 406.
Roman coins used as Prototypes, 163, 182, 183, 212, 283, 311, 313, 318, 331, 344, 348.
Roman historians, 18, 19, 152, 238, 285, 358, 401.
Rome, Brit. coin bought at, 270.
Rouen Museum, coin in the, 270.
Ruding (Rev. Rogers), 10.
RVFI, RVFS, or RVLI, 360.

Sacrificial knives, supposed, 372.
SAEMV, the legend, 385.
Salinæ, 293, 320.
Sankey (N. F. dr.), 16, 51, 63, 83, 113, 200, 265.
Seated figure, 181, 317, 321, 352.
SEGO, 272.
Segontiaci, the, 200, 223, 272, 280.
Serpent on coins, 204, 207.
Shields on coins, 173, 179, 238, 329.
Silures, the, 36, 295.
SITMV, the supposed legend, 385.
Sleipnir, 49.
Smith (C. Roach), his Coll. Ant., 14, 162, et passim.
Soldier, British, 322.

SOLIDV, 292, 306, 319.
Somersetshire, coins of, 39, 100, 153.
South-eastern District, 181.
Sow on coins, 328, 344.
Sphinx on coins, 319, 328, 337, 339.
Speed, his opinions, 2, 195, 231, 278.
Stukeley (Rev. Dr.), 7, 217, 273, 311, 313, 318.
SVEI, 149.
Suffolk, coins of, 357.
Surrey, coins of, 40, 100, 171.
Sussex, coins of, 37, 100, 131, 171.

TASC-F, the legend, 308.
TASC FIL, 331.
TASCIA, supposed meanings of, 220.
TASCIOVANTIS, 329.
TASCIOVANI-F, 221, 290, 326.
Tasciovanus, 220.
TASCIO-RICON, 225, 267.
Terms used, 45.
Thoresby (Ralph), 3.
TI. VI. FP., the legend, 194.
TIGIP SEXO, 110.
Tin coins cast in wooden moulds, 124.
TIN, the supposed countermark, 163.
Tine[ommius], 158.
Togodumnus, 286, 294.
Tribute paid by Britain, 19.
Trinobantes, the, 41, 215, 225, 282.

Uncertain coins, 349.
Uriconium, supposed coins of, 267.

Vellocatus, 404.
Veneti, intercourse with Britain, 20, 151.
Venusius, 404.
VEP CORF, 411.
VERDOD, false coins reading, 217.
Verica, or Virica, 170.
VERO, altered coin with, 247.
Verulamium, 120, 246, 352.

Victory on coins, 181, 101, 194, 317, 321, 324, 325, 335, 341, 350.
Victory killing a bull, 335.
Vine-leaf, 172.
VO-CORIO-AD, 113.
VOLISIOS, the legend, 408.
Vow [nos], 200.
Vulcan on coins, 333.

Walker (Obadiah), 3, 66, 320.
Western District, 152.
Whitaker (Rev. Mr.), 8, 327, 344.
White (John), 8, 278.

WICV, the supposed legend, 303.
Wilts, coins of, 38, 101.
Wise (Rev. Francis), 5, 220, 251.
Wolf (?) on coins, 71, 122, 206, 307, 316.
Wreath, circular, 92, 190, 191, 308, 316, 343.

X, the letter, 231.

Yorkshire coins, 404.

Zoology unsettled on British coins, 307.

PLACES AT WHICH BRITISH COINS HAVE BEEN FOUND.

BEDFORDSHIRE.
Biggleswade, 79, 118, 119, 218, 237, 255, 258, 263, 271, 299, 326, 328, 329, 332, 333, 352.
Cotton End, near Bedford, 315.
Leighton Buzzard, 50.
Lilly Hoo, Luton (Gaulish), 121.
Potton, 300.
Sandy, 229, 309, 310, 329.
Upper Stondon, 261.
Wootton, 61.

BERKSHIRE, 244.
Abingdon, 329.
Hampstead Norris, 60.
Letcombe Regis, 104.
Maidenhead, 65, 67.
Newbury, 304.
Ruscombe, 65, 67.
Weycock, 125.

BUCKINGHAMSHIRE.
Buckingham, 58.
Chesham, 218.
Creslow, 260.
Cublington, 299.
Ellesborough, 218.

High Wycombe, 78, 227, 229, 231, 247, 248.
Quainton, 300.
Thornborough, near Buckingham, 335.
Wendover, 52.
Whaddon Chase, 57, 61, 65, 67, 70, 73, 74, 75.
Whichwood Forest, 339.

CAMBRIDGESHIRE.
Burrington, 373.
Cambridge, 244, 296, 333.
Childerley Gate, 300.
Fleam Dyke, 261.
March, 361, 381, 387, 396, 400.
Over, 63.
Swaffham, 304.
Wisbech, 410.

CORNWALL.
Karn Brê, 6, 50, 51, 52, 62, 81, 94.

DEVONSHIRE, 128.
Mount Batten, 72, 106, 122.

DORSETSHIRE.
Bere Regis, 102.
Blandford, 101.

DORSETSHIRE (continued).
Cann, 102.
Conygore Hill, near Dorchester, 117.
Dorchester, 61.
Farnham, near Thickthorne, 101.
Hod Hill, 101, 102, 117, 125, 146, 213.
Iwerne Minster, 101.
Jordan Hill, nr. Weymouth, 102.
Langton, 101, 117.
Moore Critchell, 101.
Oakford Fitzpaine Hill, 101.
Poole, 61.
Shapwick, 101, 347.
Sherborne, 383.
Shroton, 101.
Sturminster Newton, 61.
Tarrant Crawford, 102.
Tarrant Gunville, 61, 101.
Wareham, 61.
Worbarrow Bay, 102.

ESSEX.
Ardley, 47.
Brentwood, 230.
Castle Hedingham, 271.
Chesterford, 253, 264, 266, 391, 392, 395.
Chingford, 304.
Colchester, 64, 78, 107, 203, 296, 299, 301, 302, 311, 324, 326, 332, 336, 337, 339, 341, 342, 343, 344, 345, 346, 353, 355, 368, 377, 416.
Colne, near Halstead, 296.
Debden, 304.
Epping, 271.
Hadstock, 65, 344.
Halstead, 271.
Harlow, 119, 253, 254, 201, 326, 328, 329, 333, 335, 348.
Haverhill, 65.
Layer de la Haye, 51.
Meunden, 76.
Mark's Tey, 77, 80, 203, 367, 371.
Saffron Walden, 335.
Walton-on-the-Naze, 202.
Wenden, near Saffron Walden, 263.

GLOUCESTERSHIRE.
Beckford, 136.
Birdlip, 135.
Bisley, near Stroud, 142.
Cirencester, 104, 136, 412.
Rodmarton, 135.
Stow, 135.
Tewkesbury, 104.

HAMPSHIRE.
Andover, 80.
Basingstoke, 81, 84, 157.
Danebury Hill, 101.
Odiham, 84, 157.
Portsmouth, 94, 101, 129, 213, 389.
Romsey, 95, 172.
Sandown, Isle of Wight, 84.
Silchester, 102.
Titchfield Downs, 162.
Winchester, 169.

HERTFORDSHIRE, 254.
Baldock, 302.
Barnet, 61.
Great Berkhamsted, 329.
St. Alban's, 234.
Stanston, 75.
Tring, 304.
Verulam, 119, 251, 253, 257, 258, 321, 328, 352.
Wigginton, near Tring, 325.
Wildhall, 50.

HUNTINGDONSHIRE, 258.
St. Ive's, 270.

KENT, 50, 64, 114, 104, 196, 201, 203.
Bapchild, 197.
Barden, near Tunbridge Wells, 50.
Birchington, Thanet, 51, 104.
Boxley, near Maidstone, 51.
Broadstairs, 65.
Canterbury, 122, 203, 204.
Chittenden, 65.
Elham, 52, 63, 64.
Erith, 51.
Folkstone, 64.
Goshall, near Ash, 207.
Gravesend, 50, 63, 204.
Harrietsham, 52.

PLACES AT WHICH BRITISH COINS HAVE BEEN FOUND.   423

KENT (continued).
  Hollingbourne, 67.
  Kit's Coty House, near Maidstone, 122, 197, 344.
  Lenham Heath, 125.
  Maidstone, 62, 68, 95.
  Margate, 192.
  Moldash, 207.
  Mount Ephraim, near Ash, 80.
  Northbrook, 54.
  Northfleet, 51.
  Quex Park, near Birchington, 125.
  Reculver, 87, 98, 234, 304, 371.
  Richborough, 112, 181.
  Ryarsh, 62, 64.
  Sevenoaks, 232.
  Sevenscore, near Ramsgate, 204.
  Shorne, near Gravesend, 229.
  Sittingbourne, 190.
  Slade, the, Boughton Monchelsea, 111, 211, 324, 350.
  Springhead, 122, 243, 347, 352.
  Staple, near Ash, 191.
  Sutton Valence, 51.
  Swanscombe, near Gravesend, 51.
  Thanet, Isle of, 52, 111, 354.
  Walmer, 52.
  Westgate Bay, near Margate, 86, 95, 325.
LANCASHIRE.
  Liverpool, 120.
LEICESTERSHIRE.
  Hallaton, 76.
  Loughborough, 44.
LINCOLNSHIRE, 146, 408, 411.
  Lincoln, 413.
  Ravendale, near Grimsby, 355.
  Sleaford, 65.
MIDDLESEX.
  Enfield Chase, 80.
  Harlington, 67.
  London, 83, 97, 122.
  St. James's Park, 125.
  St. John's Wood, 70.
  Thames, the, 347.
  Victoria Park, 232.

MONMOUTHSHIRE.
  Chepstow, 140.
  Llanthony Abbey, 113.
NORFOLK, 50, 378.
  Acle, 377.
  Brancaster, 386.
  Brettenham, 120.
  Norwich, 72, 270, 344, 370, 376, 377.
  Oxnead, 375.
  Sherringham, 65.
  Thrcxton, 382.
  Weston, 361, 381, 382, 386, 387, 389, 390, 391, 397, 398, 399, 400.
NORTHAMPTONSHIRE.
  Castor, 401.
  Chipping Warden, 253, 321, 328.
  Earl's Barton, 79.
  Eaton, 218.
  Furthinghoe, 76.
  Gayton, near Blisworth, 210.
  Oundle, 235, 258, 304, 321, 326.
  Thrapstone, 235.
  Weedon, near Loys Weedon, 298.
NORTHUMBERLAND.
  Hexham, 120.
NOTTINGHAMSHIRE.
  Nottingham, 298.
OXFORDSHIRE.
  Aston Rowant, 300.
  Bourton, near Banbury, 144.
  Chipping Norton, 67.
  Churchill, 142.
  Cowley, 67.
  Dorchester, 65, 88, 203, 229, 291, 298, 321, 329, 355.
  Garlington, 304.
  Little Milton, 68.
  Oxford, 104, 303, 304, 368.
  Stanlake, 135.
  Swacliffe, 61, 102.
  Whitman Hills, 81.
  Wood Eaton, 95, 301.
SOMERSETSHIRE.
  Freshford, 148.
  Frome, 140, 141.

424   PLACES AT WHICH BRITISH COINS HAVE BEEN FOUND.

SOMERSETSHIRE (*continued*).
   Nunney, near Frome, 104, 105,
      140, 144, 146, 150.
   Radstock, 145.
   North Petherton, 102.
SUFFOLK, 392, 392.
   Bury St. Edmund's, 113, 115,
      353.
   Coldenham, 312.
   Icklingham, 118, 382, 387, 305,
      399.
   Ipswich, 374.
   Ixworth, 310, 321, 397, 398.
   Lawshall, 298.
   Mildenhall, 397.
   Pakenham, 397.
   Stoke, 50.
   Waldingfield, 60.
   Wangford, 398.
SURREY.
   Albury, 181.
   Farley Heath, 81, 85, 90, 108,
      110, 117, 157, 176, 179, 181,
      282, 348.
   Godalming, 50, 64, 83.
   Guildford, 280.
   Horley, 69.
   Horne, 61.
   Kingston, 83, 169.
   Leatherhead, 50.
   Oxted, 50.
   Reigate, 85.
   Woneresh, 60, 84, 86.
SUSSEX.
   Alfriston, 64, 161, 164.
   Ashdown Forest, 92, 93, 108,
      110.
   Battle, 361, 381, 397.
   Bognor, 90, 92, 94, 95, 97, 166,
      177, 178.
   Bracklesham, 80, 95.

Bramber Castle, 161.
Brighton, 208.
Chichester, 90.
Eastbourne, 95.
East Wittering, 162, 178.
Goodwood, 62.
Lancing Downs, 110, 169, 181.
Pagham, 65, 95, 172.
Pevensey, 160.
Selsey, 66, 90.
Shoreham, 173.
Steyning, 161, 174.
Tarring, 61, 67.
Wiston, 65.
Worthing, 67.
WESTMORELAND.
   Brough (?), 165.
WILTSHIRE.
   Mere, 101.
   Old Sarum, 217.
   Savernake Forest, 80, 282.
   Swindon, 164.
   Tisbury, 101.
   Tollard Royal, 101.
WORCESTERSHIRE.
   Evesham, 219.
   Worcester, 143, 150.
YORKSHIRE.
   Almonbury, 400, 408, 411.
   Lightcliffe, near Halifax, 406,
      408, 412.
   Pickering, 418.
SCOTLAND.
   Birkhill, near Dumfries, 135.
   Lesmahago, Lanarkshire, 199.
FRANCE.
   Amiens, 268.
   Rouen, 270.
ITALY.
   Rome, 270.

www.ingramcontent.com/pod-product-compliance
Lightning Source LLC
Chambersburg PA
CBHW032004300426
44117CB00008B/900